OPENING ARGUMENTS

A Brief Rhetoric with Readings

OPENING ARGUMENTS

A BRIEF RHETORIC WITH READINGS

ERIK MULLER
Lane Community College

HARCOURT BRACE COLLEGE PUBLISHERS
Fort Worth   Philadelphia   San Diego   New York
Orlando   Austin   San Antonio
Toronto   Montreal   London   Sydney   Tokyo

Publisher: Ted Buchholz
Acquisitions Editor: Stephen T. Jordan
Developmental Editor: Helen Triller
Production Manager: Debra A. Jenkin
Cover Designer: John Ritland
Editorial & Production Services: Michael Bass & Associates
Cover Image: *Pastel on Paper* © John Abrams
Text Designer: Linda M. Robertson

Printed in the United States of America

3 4 5 6 7 8 9 0 1 2   066   9 8 7 6 5 4 3 2 1

Library of Congress Catalog Card Number: 93-22960

ISBN: 0-15-501189-8

CONTENTS

CHAPTER FIVE
STYLE AND ARGUMENT   190

THEMATIC CONTENTS OF READINGS

Arts
    Baraka (music)
    Huxtable (architecture)

Education, Communication
    Bacon (uses of study)
    McKibben (sources of information)
    Boulding (information structures)
    Gibbons and Schlossman (scientific method)
    Rogers (empathic listening)
    Johnson (education reform)

Environment
    Carson (pesticides)
    Berry (appropriate technology)
    Leopold (ecological principles)
    Dinesen (appropriating nature)
    Peterson (eating wild game)
    Lifton (nuclear weapons and disruption of nature)
    Woolum (mercantilism and materialism)
    Meininger (garbage)
    Crombie (noise)
    Kocian (animal rights)

Food
    Brody (carbohydrate diet)
    Peterson (eating wild game)
    Howell (food aid for Americans)

Issues Concerning Women
    Rich (motherhood)
    Faludi (anti-feminist trends)
    Woolf (defying conventions)
    Glencoe (abortion)
    Harper-Clausen (harassment)
    Pritchett (homemaking)

Other Political Issues and Occasions
    Paine (American independence)
    Lincoln (emancipation)
    Zinn (unjust courts and prisons)
    Howell (food aid for Americans)
    Whitelaw (economic change)
    Kennedy (inaugural)
    Bush (inaugural)

PREFACE

The early 1990s is a time for assessing values and approaches, not a time of upheaval but of sorting out what works from what does not work. The end of Cold War confrontations and the acknowledgment of cultural diversity in American society call for more understanding and tolerance and less unexamined thought and posturing. In addition, the huge backlog of unsolved, pressing problems indicates the coming of deliberations and debates on many issues.

At every point, *Opening Arguments: A Brief Rhetoric with Readings* presents students with choices about their writing of arguments: What issue? What stand? What audience? What support? What order? What language? Such choices are strategic. To write clearly and convincingly, students must be aware of choices and understand them. They must make their own choices and then explain and defend them.

CONTENT AND FEATURES

Opening Arguments, by its compactness, by its practical and encouraging words, offers to be a guide to writing argument, to the kind of writing that enables students to know their issues and their audiences, to know where they stand and with what authority and certainty. *Opening Arguments* guides students as they work to clarify their views and to express them convincingly to readers. These distinctive features characterize *Opening Arguments:*

Motivates students by showing them the uses of argument and the several means for discovering issues important to them

Provides a clear process to use in writing arguments and a well-stocked toolbox for building support

Explains in practical terms the theories of audience change proposed by Aristotle, Kenneth Boulding, Stephen Toulmin, and Carl Rogers

Assigns a variety of simple and complex tasks for response and writing and provides thoroughly integrated readings by professionals and students

Presents style—from tone to word selection—as choices contributing to the argument's aim

ORGANIZATION

Five chapters compose a brief rhetoric of argument. Chapters 1 and 2 introduce definitions, theories, and activities that help prepare students for writing arguments. Chapters 3 and 4 demonstrate techniques and tools for finding and using support. Chapter 5 presents a broad range of style choices essential to effective argument.

Within each chapter, professional essays illustrate main points, and numerous exercises give students practice in applying concepts and using tools. Argument activities at the end of each chapter offer additional opportunities for student involvement. Readings, exercises, and activities connect closely to the points discussed in the rhetoric chapters.

The section Argument Assignments describes six essay assignments in detail and includes successful student examples and advice about the process steps of planning, drafting, and revising.

WAYS TO USE THIS BOOK

Instructors can use this book a number of ways. The book is structured, yet versatile. Although the five rhetoric chapters progress from basic elements to greater elaboration and refinement, instructors may want to teach the style elements of Chapter 5 throughout the course. Even though the argument assignments progress toward greater concern for audience and greater demands for varied support, instructors may prefer using another order. They may want students to repeat assignments, using a different audience or a different issue. Instructors may prefer giving some of their own assignments in conjunction with the six presented here.

Because each assignment is designed to be a complete unit, students are able to write these assignments very independently. No assignment prescribes the argument issue, but instructors may easily modify an assignment in terms of subject, length, or any other component. Indeed, the book's layout of the assignment components invites tinkering.

Students using this text need to write frequently. They are asked to begin a notebook and to write in response to most exercises. Students will be able to draw from these responses as they draft their arguments. Both exercises and assignments help students understand that writing essays is a process of planning and rewriting. Instructors may choose to expand some of the exercises or argument activities into longer essay assignments.

The readings, like the exercises and the assignments, form a progression that instructors may or may not choose to follow. Each reading has a particular place and function, although instructors can find many other uses for the readings. The introductory note to each reading selection identifies the author and context of the reading and directs students to the rhetorical elements discussed in the particular section of the book. Grouping the readings thematically—see the Thematic Contents of Readings listing following the table of contents—suggests some alternatives.

ACKNOWLEDGMENTS

Pascal warns authors not to speak of their books as "my book," because there is in them "more of other people's work than their own." Authors, Pascal chides, should call their work "our book."

This book's author must admit that his 30 years of using other people's books, his reading of journals and attending conferences, and his talking to colleagues have made him indebted to a long, involved conversation. What he writes, therefore, has roots in the exciting discussions of rhetoric of the last three decades. He has been lucky to study with Roger Garrison, to attend Janet Laurer's rhetoric seminar, and to teach from the groundbreaking *Rhetoric: Discovery and Change* by Young, Becker, and Pike. He has had challenging and helpful co-teachers and co-philosophers of teaching writing, including Clara Radcliffe, Ted Berg, and Dan Armstrong. He has benefitted in writing *Opening Arguments* from the help of friends and colleagues—Ann Staley, Elaine Weiss, Bill Woolum—and from the staff at Harcourt Brace College Publishers, especially Stephen T. Jordan and Helen Triller. He also owes a debt of gratitude to the following reviewers, whose comments and suggestions helped refine the book: T. W. Crusius, Southern Methodist University; Michael Marx, Skidmore College; Patricia Morgan, Louisiana State University; Arthur Quinn, University of California, Berkeley; William E. Smith, Western Washington University; and Victor Vitanza, University of Texas, Arlington.

Taking Pascal's cue, the author passes "our book" to instructors and students. May they make it their own!

Erik Muller

OPENING ARGUMENTS

A Brief Rhetoric with Readings

CHAPTER ONE
ARGUMENT: AN OVERVIEW

YOU ALREADY KNOW A LOT

At many colleges and universities, the English composition sequence includes a course that deals with the writing strategy known as argument. After completing one course of composition, you already know a lot applicable to the study of argument. You know several important things about writing essays.

First, you know that college compositions are focused on a major point or points. In writing courses, the thesis identifies the clearest, most concise statement of the essay's main idea. The thesis is often compressed to a sentence. It is a central statement to which all sections of the essay relate. It is important enough to repeat and restate. Occasionally the thesis is not stated, only implied, but its influence is felt nevertheless.

Second, you know that the thesis, although it is a complete sentence, is not a complete presentation of what you want to say about a subject. Alfred North Whitehead wrote, "There is not a sentence which adequately states its own meaning." A thesis grows into or unfolds a discussion. Or sometimes a discussion finally focuses on a thesis. Either way, this combination of thesis and discussion is basic to college writing. Naming the essentials and developing them, previewing a subject and then viewing it, stating a purpose and following through—these two elements are as essential as positive and negative in electricity, right and left in marching. Such combinations are implied by the word *composition*, which means positioning things together.

Third, you know how to construct or craft an essay. You know that writers start, draft, and finish an essay in stages, by means of a process. This process gives the writer opportunities to accomplish tasks more or less one at a time and more or less in order. You can appreciate the breadth of the writing process by considering the necessarily clipped version of it used during an essay exam. Exam writing allows only brief planning and checking steps, and the first draft must usually stand as the only draft. For most essays, fortunately for the writer and reader, the first draft is not the final one. The writing process includes all the steps taken to produce a first draft and all the steps taken to advance that draft to its most considered form.

You may imagine the writing process as a linear set of operations, an assembly line, yet you have probably experienced some repeated steps and dead ends, as well as some remarkable discoveries that you would not have allowed for if you had not fired up the process and followed its course. If you are not yet habitually a process writer, you can review the writing process sections of any up-to-date handbook. There you will find a quick overview of how to start, draft, revise, and edit a composition.

Fourth, you know you write to be read; you write for readers. The writing process aims to produce a readable essay. In every English class thus far, audience has been a concern—and, perhaps, a worry of yours. What will my teacher think of this? Will she like it? Will he make me rewrite it? For every essay you write in college, a teacher is your audience, although not necessarily the sole audience. Often you will write to classmates, whose commentary may help you revise your writing. Also, you may select audiences outside the classroom, either a more general academic audience or specific audiences you need to address, perhaps in your community. Thus, you bring to your work the sense that you are writing for somebody. You have already experienced your essay's being sent *from* you to some reader, real or imagined. Your essay was not merely *by* you.

Academic audiences, as you know, expect and reward well-focused, well-developed, organized writing that you have revised and edited. Samuel Johnson, English critic and lexicographer, quipped, "What is written without effort is in general read without pleasure." Or as my Uncle Wilbur likes to say, "Easy writing makes damn hard reading!" You may say good writing is what a teacher assigns an A to, but most likely your teacher is reading with the same expectations that Donald Murray believes all readers have as they get ready to read an essay. Murray, a successful writer and teacher, lists those expectations in *A Writer Teaches Writing*:

> *Voice and Honesty:* Readers listen to an individual writer speaking to an individual reader in an individual way. Readers appreciate the genuine and suspect the false.
>
> *Focus:* Readers appreciate writing that says one dominant thing and develops it.
>
> *Development:* Readers appreciate moving to understanding.
>
> *Information:* Readers appreciate abundant information because it helps them think about and master a subject. Readers need evidence, not just assertions, to believe the writer.
>
> *Closure:* Readers appreciate a feeling of completeness, of arriving at a destination.

A course in argument builds on what you already know about written communication. Many of the tasks of argument will be familiar to you because they are special applications of writing skills you have already mastered.

EXERCISE 1.1 Apply Donald Murray's expectations to Jane Brody's essay, "Dietary Lessons from Human Evolution." In your notebook, list the features of Brody's essay that fulfill those expectations. State your opinion of how well the essay meets those expectations.

 ## DIETARY LESSONS FROM HUMAN EVOLUTION

Jane Brody

Jane Brody (b. 1941) writes a personal health column for *The New York Times*. She has written cookbooks and guides to nutrition and health. This selection is from *Jane Brody's Good Food Cook Book: Living the High-Carbohydrate Way* (1985). Based on her understanding of human food gathering and human physiology, Brody argues for a return to a low-meat diet. Note how Brody catches your attention and focuses it and then develops informative and compelling discussion that leads to the closing statement of her thesis.

Most of us have an impression of early man as a successful hunter who, dressed in a loin cloth, went out each day with a club over his shoulder to catch something for supper. Usually, however, early man came back empty-handed because most animals were simply too swift for a man armed with only a club. The real hero of the survival of the human species was not early man but early woman. She spent her days near the base camp gathering fruits, nuts, seeds, tubers, roots, berries, beans, and grains and made meals for the early human family out of complex carbohydrates—starchy foods—and fresh fruits and vegetables, with occasional feasts of meat when her mate was lucky enough to bag a mole or lizard.   1

Until recently, archaeological evidence had greatly exaggerated the role of meat in the diets of prehumans and prehistoric humans because animal bones are far better preserved in the rocky fossil record than are softer plant materials. Even recently abandoned sites of modern aboriginal tribes show no plant remains, although these tribes are known to eat mostly vegetable foods. However, in the last decade or so, anthropologists and archaeologists have devised some ingenious techniques that clearly reveal the vegetarian emphasis of our progenitors.   2

For example, microscopic studies of fossilized teeth from early human ancestors who roamed the earth some 4 million years ago indicate that they were primarily fruit eaters, according to Dr. Alan Walker, a Johns Hopkins   3

University anthropologist. The wear patterns on the fossil teeth of the fore-bears of *Homo sapiens* look exactly like those on the teeth of modern fruit eaters, and there are almost no marks that result from eating meat and bones. Not until the evolution about 1.5 million years ago of *Homo erectus*, the immediate ancestor of our species, was there evidence of a mixed diet of plant and animal foods. But even then, there is reason to believe that ani-mal foods were not the primary fare until quite recently in our evolutionary history. Analyses of fossils of human feces deposited by North American peoples from 300,000 years ago to a few hundred years ago reveal that our human ancestors subsisted primarily on a vegetable diet, consuming over 100 different varieties of plant foods. In rock-shelter sites in southwestern Texas that are less than 3,000 years old, evidence indicates that except for grasshoppers, a limited amount of animal protein was eaten by those who dwelled there. The Human Nutrition Program at the University of Michigan has been examining the diets of Stone Age people who inhabited the lower Illinois Valley 5,000 years ago. Studies of their remains show that they con-sumed seeds, nuts, berries, and roots from hundreds of plant species, many of which still grow in the area and most of which ironically are now consid-ered weeds.

4   The hunting and eating of mammoths, those now-extinct elephantlike creatures pushed southward by the advancing glaciers of the Ice Age, date back only about 300,000 years. And even then, meat was not the central item in the diet. Plants were. Dairy products did not become a significant part of the diet until the domestication of cattle, about 10,000 years ago. Eggs, too, were a rare luxury, obtained only by robbing birds' nests before fowl were domesticated. In short, if the human species had had to depend on large supplies of animal protein for its survival, it would have died out 2 million years ago.

Modern Tribes Eat Mostly Plant Foods

5   The hunter-gatherer tribes that today live like our prehistoric human ances-tors consume primarily a vegetable diet supplemented with animal foods. An analysis of 58 societies of modern hunter-gatherers, including the !Kung of southern Africa, revealed that one-half emphasize gathering of plant foods, one-third concentrate on fishing, and only one-sixth are primarily hunters. Overall, two-thirds or more of the hunter-gatherer's calories come from plants. Detailed studies of the !Kung by A. S. Truswell, food scientist at the University of London, showed that gathering is a more productive source of food than is hunting. An hour of hunting yields on average about 100 edible calories, whereas an hour of gathering produces 240. Plant foods provide 60 percent to 80 percent of the !Kung diet, and no one goes hungry when the hunt fails. Interestingly, if they escape fatal infections or acci-dents, these contemporary aborigines live to old ages despite the absence of

medical care. They experience no obesity, no middle-aged spread, little dental decay, no high blood pressure, no coronary heart disease, and their blood cholesterol levels are very low (about half that of the average American adult). While no one is suggesting that we return to an aboriginal life style, we certainly could use their eating habits as a model for a healthier diet.

Even among less primitive cultures that have not yet achieved the affluence of twentieth-century America, dietary patterns more closely resemble human evolutionary destiny. In the meals of Mexico, India, Japan, the Middle East, China, Turkey, Greece, and Italy, emphasis is on the starchy foods, using animal protein more as a condiment and as a complement to the protein in plant foods than as the centerpiece of the menu. To be sure, as affluence increases in these and similar countries, so does the consumption of animal foods, especially red meat. And along with it goes an increase in the chronic health problems that now afflict Americans.   6

A look at our digestive apparatus is also revealing. Our teeth are structured more for grinding, like those of herbivorous cattle, than for tearing meat, like the teeth of carnivorous cats and dogs. And our long and convoluted intestinal tracts are better designed for the slow digestion of fibrous plant foods, rather than the short, straight, fast tract needed by carnivores to process meat and quickly dispose of the resulting toxic wastes. Noted anthropologist Dr. F. Clark Howell of the University of California, Berkeley, points out that our gastrointestinal tract, liver, metabolic enzymes, and kidneys evolved long before our big brains did some 3 million years ago. "We are little different in these respects from modern subhuman primates," he says.   7

Our Diet Is Out of Balance

But while our digestive and metabolic systems have not changed in any substantive way in the last 2 million years, our diet has changed drastically. Compared with our evolutionary ancestors, most people in industrialized countries today are voracious meat eaters. Throughout the world, diets rich in animal foods like red meat, fish, poultry, and eggs have become symbols of affluence.   8

This is especially so in the United States, where per-capita consumption of animal foods has been rising steadily throughout this century. Even as recently as 1900, Americans were far less dependent on animals to flesh out their diets. In 1900, two-thirds of our protein came not from animals, but from plant foods. Today that statistic is turned completely around: 70 percent of the protein we consume is derived from animals, and only 30 percent comes from plants. The problem with animal-derived protein is the baggage it usually comes with. The most popular animal protein foods are nearly all more fat than protein. About 80 percent of the calories in steak or hamburger   9 are fat calories, not protein; 75 percent of the calories in most hard cheeses come from fat; and even chicken (when eaten with the skin) is 50 percent to 60 percent fat calories.

10   Most plant proteins, on the other hand, derive the bulk of their calories from complex carbohydrates—starches—which are not linked to any serious health risks. (Exceptions are nuts and seeds, which contain large amounts of fat, though not the artery-clogging saturated fats found in most animal foods.) Although diet is not the only important factor, there is ample evidence that the shift away from a diet rich in complex carbohydrates has seriously undermined our health and limited our longevity. If we're truly interested in improving the quality of life as well as its length, it's time to return to a healthier diet that more closely resembles our biological destiny.

WHAT IS ARGUMENT?

Let's consider argument from several perspectives. After the preceding review of what you already know about the kinds of writing you do in college, you may find this statement useful: In argument the writer asserts something and builds a case for it. Implicit here are the familiar concepts of thesis and development. You can think of an argument thesis as a position statement and the development as your attempt to build support for your position. Examine how the following thesis statements differ:

> Uncle Wilbur's philosophy has influenced me.
>
> Let's have a moratorium on nuclear-powered generation of electricity until we can safely dispose of the waste.

Both statements call for further development. However, the first, more personal thesis does not provoke opposition. You might say in response, "If you think your uncle influenced you, you ought to know!" Still, you might be interested to learn about specific influences. Those who disagree with the energy thesis might exclaim, "You ought to know better!" Like the more personal thesis, the argument thesis benefits from development; indeed, it needs a discussion especially suited to the skeptical or dissenting audience. The writer of the first thesis can help you understand an uncle's influence. The writer of the second thesis can explain policy so you can understand it. But the argument also urges you to consider the thesis seriously and possibly to accept it. The discussion in an argument certainly explains clearly; it tries to be convincing as well. The discussion tries to make the writer's position your position.

      Another way to consider argument is to range it alongside other writing types. Examine this model:

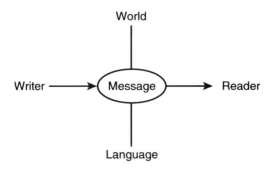

This simple communication model presents the writer sending a message about the world to a reader by means of a language code. Imagine a writing situation in which one or another of these elements had primary emphasis. For example, imagine the writer is most interested in expressing self. Or imagine the writer is most interested in depicting aspects of the world. Or imagine the writer is most interested in affecting the reader. Or, finally, imagine the writer is most interested in working with the medium itself, the written language. With each different emphasis, you can expect a different written product.

The writer's emphasis on self could produce autobiography, journals, or letting off steam. The emphasis on the world could produce reportage, operation manuals, or detailed observation and presentation of facts. The emphasis on reader change could produce argument, propaganda, advertising, or sermons. The emphasis on language could produce literary crafting, even art.

You probably realize that an essay may include all of these elements to one degree or another. Yet for this book, consider argument as one of the kinds of writing that emphasizes impact on reader, especially the impact that changes the reader's mind, the reader's view of or stand on an issue. Remember, an argument about safe disposal of nuclear waste aims at changing readers. The argument thesis states how you want readers to change. The development of support provides good reasons to convince readers to change. You may preface the argument thesis, at least in your mind and your drafts, with the words, "I want the reader to believe that" or "I want the reader to consider seriously that." You might say such wishes underlie all writing. Perhaps they do. In argument, though, a writer deliberately chooses to change readers. The argument thesis is a change order, and the writer often chooses an audience that is resistant to that very thesis.

Maybe you are uncomfortable with this emphasis on changing a reader rather than on the student writer showing the teacher what he or she knows. The writer of argument often brings to readers what they do *not* want to hear and what they probably do *not* agree with. If writer and readers agreed, there would be no need to argue. They might write each other, but they would be celebrating their likeness as they do when they pledge allegiance to the flag or speak their creed aloud in common worship or ceremony. It would be an unusual moment during the pledge of allegiance if somebody shouted, "What do you mean 'one nation indivisible'?" People usually understand when argument is appropriate. If oaths and pledges and credos express people's similarities, argument expresses their disagreements, their differences of opinion. Argument, as you will see, is one way to respond to disagreement. As Lance Sparks, my colleague, observes, argument lies somewhere between silence and warfare. I propose that argument is a reasonable, expected response to a world where people often honestly disagree.

EXERCISE 1.2   After reading the two selections from Rachel Carson, write your responses to these questions: What is the message of each selection? Is it a message that primarily expresses the writer's self? Depicts aspects of her world? Affects readers? Discuss which selection exemplifies this chapter's discussion of argument: The writer of argument often brings to readers what they do not want to hear and what they probably do not agree with.

 THE MARGINAL WORLD
Rachel Carson

Rachel Carson (1907–1964) is best known for *Silent Spring* (1962), a pioneering study of the ecological damage caused by pesticides. The book created a worldwide awareness of environmental pollution. Her career as a marine biologist for the federal government provided Carson with subjects for her books: *Under the Sea Wind, The Sea Around Us*, which received a National Book Award, and *The Edge of the Sea*. "The Marginal World" is from *The Edge of the Sea* (1955). The selection bears the title of the chapter from which it is drawn.

1   And so in that enchanted place on the threshold of the sea the realities that possessed my mind were far from those of the land world I had left an hour before. In a different way the same sense of remoteness and of a world apart came to me in a twilight hour on a great beach on the coast of Georgia. I had come down after sunset and walked far out over sands that lay wet and gleaming, to the very edge of the retreating sea. Looking back across that immense flat, crossed by winding, water-filled gullies and here and there holding shallow pools left by the tide, I was filled with awareness that this intertidal area, although abandoned briefly and rhythmically by the sea, is always reclaimed by the rising tide. There at the edge of low water the beach with its reminders of the land seemed far away. The only sounds were those of the wind and the sea and the birds. There was one sound of wind moving over water, and another of water sliding over the sand and tumbling down the faces of its own wave forms. The flats were astir with birds, and the voice of the willet rang

insistently. One of them stood at the edge of the water and gave its loud, urgent cry; an answer came from far up the beach and the two birds flew to join each other.

The flats took on a mysterious quality as dusk approached and the last   2
evening light was reflected from the scattered pools and creeks. Then birds became only dark shadows, with no color discernible. Sanderlings scurried across the beach like little ghosts, and here and there the darker forms of the willets stood out. Often I could come very close to them before they would start up in alarm—the sanderlings running, the willets flying up, crying. Black skimmers flew along the ocean's edge silhouetted against the dull, metallic gleam, or they went flitting above the sand like large, dimly seen moths. Sometimes they "skimmed" the winding creeks of tidal water, where little spreading surface ripples marked the presence of small fish.

The shore at night is a different world, in which the very darkness that   3
hides the distractions of daylight brings into sharper focus the elemental realities. Once, exploring the night beach, I surprised a small ghost crab in the searching beam of my torch. He was lying in a pit he had dug just above the surf, as though watching the sea and waiting. The blackness of the night possessed water, air, and beach. It was the darkness of an older world, before Man. There was no sound but the all-enveloping, primeval sounds of wind blowing over water and sand, and of waves crashing on the beach. There was no other visible life—just one small crab near the sea. I have seen hundreds of ghost crabs in other settings, but suddenly I was filled with the odd sensation that for the first time I knew the creature in its own world—that I understood, as never before, the essence of its being. In that moment time was suspended; the world to which I belonged did not exist and I might have been an onlooker from outer space. The little crab alone with the sea became a symbol that stood for life itself—for the delicate, destructible, yet incredibly vital force that somehow holds its place amid the harsh realities of the inorganic world.

The sense of creation comes with memories of a southern coast, where   4
the sea and the mangroves, working together, are building a wilderness of thousands of small islands off the southwestern coast of Florida, separated from each other by a tortuous pattern of bays, lagoons, and narrow waterways. I remember a winter day when the sky was blue and drenched with sunlight; though there was no wind one was conscious of flowing air like cold clear crystal. I had landed on the surf-washed tip of one of those islands, and then worked my way around to the sheltered bay side. There I found the tide far out, exposing the broad mud flat of a cove bordered by the mangroves with their twisted branches, their glossy leaves, and their long prop roots reaching down, grasping and holding the mud, building the land out a little more, then again a little more.

The mud flats were strewn with the shells of that small, exquisitely colored mollusk, the rose tellin, looking like scattered petals of pink roses.   5

There must have been a colony nearby, living buried just under the surface of the mud. At first the only creature visible was a small heron in gray and rusty plumage—a reddish egret that waded across the flat with the stealthy, hesitant movements of its kind. But other land creatures had been there, for a line of fresh tracks wound in and out among the mangrove roots, marking the path of a raccoon feeding on the oysters that gripped the supporting roots with projections from their shells. Soon I found the tracks of a shore bird, probably a sanderling, and followed them a little; then they turned toward the water and were lost, for the tide had erased them and made them as though they had never been.

6   Looking out over the cove I felt a strong sense of the interchangeability of land and sea in this marginal world of the shore, and of the links between the life of the two. There was also an awareness of the past and of the continuing flow of time, obliterating much that had gone before, as the sea had that morning washed away the tracks of the bird.

7   The sequence and meaning of the drift of time were quietly summarized in the existence of hundreds of small snails—the mangrove periwinkles— browsing on the branches and roots of the trees. Once their ancestors had been sea dwellers, bound to the salt waters by every tie of their life processes. Little by little over the thousands and millions of years the ties had been broken, the snails had adjusted themselves to life out of water, and now today they were living many feet above the tide to which they only occasionally returned. And perhaps, who could say how many ages hence, there would be in their descendants not even this gesture of remembrance for the sea.

8   The spiral shells of other snails—these quite minute—left winding tracks on the mud as they moved about in search of food. They were horn shells, and when I saw them I had a nostalgic moment when I wished I might see what Audubon saw, a century and more ago. For such little horn shells were the food of the flamingo, once so numerous on this coast, and when I half closed my eyes I could almost imagine a flock of these magnificent flame birds feeding in that cove, filling it with their color. It was a mere yesterday in the life of the earth that they were there; in nature, time and space are relative matters, perhaps most truly perceived subjectively in occasional flashes of insight, sparked by such a magical hour and place.

9   There is a common thread that links these scenes and memories—the spectacle of life in all its varied manifestations as it has appeared, evolved, and sometimes died out. Underlying the beauty of the spectacle there is meaning and significance. It is the elusiveness of that meaning that haunts us, that sends us again and again into the natural world where the key to the riddle is hidden. It sends us back to the edge of the sea, where the drama of life played its first scene on earth and perhaps even its prelude; where the forces of evolution are at work today, as they have been since the appearance of what we know as life; and where the spectacle of living creatures faced by the cosmic realities of their world is crystal clear.

❖ RIVERS OF DEATH

"Rivers of Death" is from *Silent Spring* (1962). This selection illustrates Carson's need to move beyond observing nature to advocate protecting nature. Again, the selection bears the title of the chapter from which it is drawn.

Nowhere has the effect of pesticides on the life of salt marshes, estuaries, and all quiet inlets from the sea been more graphically demonstrated than on the eastern coast of Florida, in the Indian River country. There, in the spring of 1955, some 2000 acres of salt marsh in St. Lucie County were treated with dieldrin in an attempt to eliminate the larvae of the sandfly. The concentration used was one pound of active ingredient to the acre. The effect on the life of the waters was catastrophic. Scientists from the Entomology Research Center of the State Board of Health surveyed the carnage after the spraying and reported that the fish kill was "substantially complete." Everywhere dead fishes littered the shores. From the air sharks could be seen moving in, attracted by the helpless and dying fishes in the water. No species was spared. Among the dead were mullets, snook, mojarras, gambusia.

1

The minimum immediate over-all kill throughout the marshes, exclusive of the Indian River shoreline, was 20–30 tons of fishes, or about 1,175,000 fishes, of at least 30 species [reported R. W. Harrington, Jr., and W. L. Bidlingmayer of the survey team].

2

Mollusks seemed to be unharmed by dieldrin. Crustaceans were virtually exterminated throughout the area. The entire aquatic crab population was apparently destroyed and the fiddler crabs, all but annihilated, survived temporarily only in patches of marsh evidently missed by the pellets.

3

The larger game and food fishes succumbed most rapidly . . . Crabs set upon and destroyed the moribund fishes, but the next day were dead themselves. Snails continued to devour fish carcasses. After two weeks, no trace remained of the litter of dead fishes.

4

The same melancholy picture was painted by the late Dr. Herbert R. Mills from his observations in Tampa Bay on the opposite coast of Florida, where the National Audubon Society operates a sanctuary for seabirds in the area including Whiskey Stump Key. The sanctuary ironically became a poor refuge after the local health authorities undertook a campaign to wipe out the salt-marsh mosquitoes. Again fishes and crabs were the principal victims. The fiddler crab, that small and picturesque crustacean whose hordes move over mud flats or sand flats like grazing cattle, has no defense against the sprayers. After successive sprayings during the summer and fall months (some areas were sprayed as many as 16 times), the state of the fiddler crabs was summed up by Dr. Mills: "A progressive scarcity of fiddlers had by this

5

time become apparent. Where there should have been in the neighborhood of 100,000 fiddlers under the tide and weather conditions of the day [October 12] there were not over 100 which could be seen anywhere on the beach, and these were all dead or sick, quivering, twitching, stumbling, scarcely able to crawl; although in neighboring unsprayed areas fiddlers were plentiful."

6   The place of the fiddler crab in the ecology of the world it inhabits is a necessary one, not easily filled. It is an important source of food for many animals. Coastal raccoons feed on them. So do marsh-inhabiting birds like the clapper rail, shorebirds, and even visiting seabirds. In one New Jersey salt marsh sprayed with DDT, the normal population of laughing gulls was decreased by 85 per cent for several weeks, presumably because the birds could not find sufficient food after the spraying. The marsh fiddlers are important in other ways as well, being useful scavengers and aerating the mud of the marshes by their extensive burrowings. They also furnish quantities of bait for fishermen.

7   The fiddler crab is not the only creature of tidal marsh and estuary to be threatened by pesticides; others of more obvious importance to man are endangered. The famous blue crab of the Chesapeake Bay and other Atlantic Coast areas is an example. These crabs are so highly susceptible to insecticides that every spraying of creeks, ditches, and ponds in tidal marshes kills most of the crabs living there. Not only do the local crabs die, but others moving into a sprayed area from the sea succumb to the lingering poison. And sometimes poisoning may be indirect, as in the marshes near Indian River, where scavenger crabs attacked the dying fishes, but soon themselves succumbed to the poison. Less is known about the hazard to the lobster. However, it belongs to the same group of arthropods as the blue crab, has essentially the same physiology, and would presumably suffer the same effects. This would be true also of the stone crab and other crustaceans which have direct economic importance as human food.

8   The inshore waters—the bays, the sounds, the river estuaries, the tidal marshes—form an ecological unit of the utmost importance. They are linked so intimately and indispensably with the lives of many fishes, mollusks, and crustaceans that were they no longer habitable these seafoods would disappear from our tables.

9   Even among fishes that range widely in coastal waters, many depend upon protected inshore areas to serve as nursery and feeding grounds for their young. Baby tarpon are abundant in all that labyrinth of mangrove-lined streams and canals bordering the lower third of the western coast of Florida. On the Atlantic Coast the sea trout, croaker, spot, and drum spawn on sandy shoals off the inlets between the islands or "banks" that lie like a protective chain off much of the coast south of New York. The young fish hatch and are carried through the inlets by the tides. In the bays and sounds—Currituck, Pamlico, Bogue, and many others—they find abundant food and grow rapidly. Without these nursery areas of warm, protected, food-rich waters the

populations of these and many other species could not be maintained. Yet we are allowing pesticides to enter them via the rivers and by direct spraying over bordering marshlands. And the early stages of these fishes, even more than the adults, are especially susceptible to direct chemical poisoning.

THREE AXIOMS BASIC TO ARGUMENT

One: Human lives are full of differences.

Two: Human differences have contexts.

Three: Argument is one response to these differences.

I have stated my assumptions about argument in a formal way so that I can present some ideas and challenge others. At this point, you need to be able to distinguish between this book's use of the word *argument* and the more common use of the word illustrated in the photograph on the following page.

Now here is an argument! Someone clearly wins, and someone takes a walk to the shower; the voices are loud, the words unprintable. For umpire and manager, argument can be an angry discussion, a quarrel. Although argument is often defined this way—and often occurs this way—the word also refers to a different use of language. As this book uses the term, and as the term is used in debate in the presentation and defense of ideas, argument is characterized by reason. Surely people's ideas contend and compete, yet people need not quarrel. Argument, the result of thinking and reasoning, presents evidence to support a point. People argue, in this sense, when they present reasons for or against a position, even when they present them in their normal voices and in words fit to print. Later, you will see how this definition, even though it places parties in opposition, need not require a winning and a losing side. If it is helpful, think of the word *argument* as academic argument.

Let's look at the first axiom: Human lives are full of differences. The Book of Genesis tells us of a time when "all the world spoke a single language and used the same words." Then people agreed to build a tower that would reach the heavens and thus bring them fame. The Lord was astounded: "Here they are, one people with a single language, and now they have started to do this." Wondering about what they might next try, the Lord confused their speech so they could no longer understand each other. The tower remained unfinished; the people dispersed, spreading over the earth "a babble of the language of all the world." The Tower of Babel may illustrate why people cannot cooperate with one another or even understand one another. To paraphrase philosopher Kenneth Burke, argument is concerned with the state of Babel after the fall.

Thearon Henderson/Focus on Sports

Daily newspapers report on lives full of differences. A glance at the headlines reminds us of people's struggles. Their disagreements are news. Headlines from a recent newspaper included:

Soviet Georgians celebrate being free of Moscow

Anti-abortion measure vetoed

City could outlaw lighting up in pubs

County may cut 25 jobs

In the same paper, there were these details from the articles:

The proposed reductions appear certain to generate debate.

The discussion drew sharp dissent from Justice Antonin Scalia.

Iraqi Kurdish rebels, pressed hard by relentless attacks from government forces, retreated into the mountains. . . . their leader . . . urged the United States, Britain and France to stop genocide and torture against his people.

Fuming pub owners said, "The proposed law is dangerous to the health of business."

Indeed, human lives are full of differences. These differences, states the second axiom, have contexts. These differences do not stand in isolation; they are shaped by and, in turn, shape their circumstances. For example, a county administrator, in the article about cutting jobs, has been directed by a budget committee to trim $3 million from a projected $34 million budget. The county expects a drop in proceeds from the sale of timber on federal lands in the county. The outcome of the debate about cutting county employees—some sheriff's deputies and some clerical staff—depends on timber sales, which connect to the ongoing debates about ancient forest and spotted owl habitat, as well as to debates about how to revive a depressed building industry.

The issue of abortion also has a complicated context. Hardly an American is unaware of this debate or has no position on the issue. People's disagreements on the issue have a history, public or private. People are aware of court cases and have some firsthand or secondhand experience with abortion issues. Notice how many issues intersect in this debate. The woman has a right to control decisions affecting her body; the fetus has a right to live. Pro and con arguments draw on the subjects of sex education, sexual mores, safe medical practices, confidentiality, and the spending of public monies. People have different opinions about the future they would like to see and how to achieve it.

You can appreciate the rich contexts of people's differences on any issue by asking yourself some questions:

ISSUE CONTEXT QUESTIONS

What is the range of positions on this issue?

What is my experience with this issue?

What is my position on this issue?

What is the history of all such positions, mine included?

How does my position relate to my personal values? To my positions on related issues?

What do I and others want to have happen in regard to this issue? What future do we envision? What means do we recommend to reach that future?

Such questions may complicate an issue and slow progress toward a resolution, yet they also help writers and readers to be thoughtful and considerate about differences that concern them.

The third axiom states that argument is one response to human differences. What are some other responses? Once the Tower of Babel toppled, people dispersed, spoiling for a fight. The news media report war between nations, civil war, and violence between races, classes, and individuals. In a response that moves parties with divergent views toward harmony, the Supreme Court reaches a decision; groups or individuals who cannot resolve their differences at least agree to submit to law or counsel. In sports, vigorous contests lead to a clear win and a clear loss and a handshake.

There are many ways to respond to differences. Predictably, people disagree about which response is best in a given situation. Should the United States and its allies in the Gulf War intervene to help the Iraqi Kurds? Should they send arms? Or only humanitarian aid? Or should they let the neighboring countries, Turkey and Iran, deal with the huge exodus of refugees? Is talk needed? Or firepower? Or blankets and food? Or all of these? And to what degree?

In academic argument, a writer chooses to use words in ways that explain his or her viewpoint and build a case for it. Note that this in itself is a choice from among many other options of language use: threatening, belittling, flattering, stonewalling, bluffing, and so on.

EXERCISE 1.3 Return to the Jane Brody article you read for Exercise 1.1. Consider it now in terms of the three axioms. Write your responses to these questions: What differences divide writer and reader? What is the context of these differences? How is the article an attempt to deal with these differences? Is the attempt successful? How might it be more successful?

EXERCISE 1.4 Look at today's newspaper. List specific differences people have and the ways they deal with them. Note if argument, as defined in this chapter, is being used. Could it be helpful in situations where it is not being used?

MOTIVES FOR ARGUMENT

Why might students want to learn to write arguments? Several motives are described in this section and supplemented later by activities that invite your response. One recurring question in this text is "Why should I argue?"

An academic community especially values knowledge. This knowledge includes knowledge of the issue and of your audience and yourself. First of all, argument is an opportunity to learn where you stand, where others stand, and what information and judgments form the ongoing debate about the issue. Argument, then, helps you clarify, learn, and express, even if your exchanges result in no converts, only the mutual respect of "We agree to disagree."

Like many academic tasks, argument asks you to use your perspective in an informed manner. It asks you to take time to consider and evaluate your own point of view as part of the exchange of many views. What supports your stand? What questions it? How, in the light of new understanding, must you re-see your stand? Must you change it? What more do you need to know? How do you deal with opposing views and contrary evidence?

In argument, you may also wish to use your viewpoint to influence others; thus, you have to know where they stand on the issue. Often argument draws you into an ongoing debate. You are unlikely the first to address the issue and unlikely the last. When you consider intellectual history or culture or tradition, you are considering the great debates that have characterized history, debates about the sources of political authority, about the value and autonomy of local customs, about the use and abuse of natural resources. So, as you argue, you will learn about your values, you will gather information, and you will discover your place in the debate. Also, you will discover who your audience is and begin addressing them directly, perhaps even changing them. To the advice "Know Thyself," please add "Know the Issue" and "Know the Audience."

THE FAR SIDE   By GARY LARSON

"Wait! Wait! Listen to me! . . . We don't HAVE to be just sheep!"

Although there are many debates that at first glance do not concern you, there are some that do. Some debates, after you have examined them, clearly touch you and may even compel your participation. Thus, in addition to using argument to explore knowledge and traditional debates, you argue to indicate where you stand, usually in opposition to what you disagree with. To argue, then, is to take the risk of differing with others. To argue presumes that you can possibly change other people's views. You do not argue solely to learn; you argue to weigh in on the side you believe to be the right side. As the Larson cartoon suggests, people do not always need to be in the herd, passive about the issues. Sometimes they take a stand for what they believe is good.

EXERCISE 1.5 The essays by Bill McKibben and Francis Bacon, although separated by almost four centuries, discuss the uses of information. Write your responses to these questions: What information sources do McKibben and Bacon discuss? What advice do they give about using these sources effectively? According to McKibben and Bacon, what motivates people to misuse information? What do their essays imply about why people argue issues and how they can be prepared to do so effectively?

 From THE AGE OF MISSING INFORMATION
Bill McKibben

Bill McKibben (b. 1960) has been a staff writer for *The New Yorker*. In his book *The End of Nature* (1989), he argued that unless the industrialized nations changed their production habits the greenhouse effect would end nature as we know it. This selection from *The Age of Missing Information* (1992) presents McKibben's experience of two different days and what he learned about using different sources of information. McKibben urges readers to be critical and active in an age that claims to supply all we need to know.

1   We believe that we live in the "age of information," that there has been an information "explosion," an information "revolution." While in a certain narrow sense this is the case, in many important ways just the opposite is true. We also live at a moment of deep ignorance, when vital knowledge that humans have always possessed about who we are and where we live seems beyond our reach. An Unenlightenment. An age of missing information.

2   This account of that age takes the form of an experiment—a contrast between two days. One day, May 3, 1990, lasted well more than a thousand hours—I collected on videotape nearly every minute of television that came across the enormous Fairfax cable system from one morning to the next, and then I watched it all. The other day, later that summer, lasted the conven-

tional twenty-four hours. A mile from my house, camped on a mountaintop by a small pond, I awoke, took a day hike up a neighboring peak, returned to the pond for a swim, made supper, and watched the stars till I fell asleep. This book is about the results of that experiment—about the information that each day imparted.

These are, of course, straw days. No one spends twenty-four hours a day   3 watching television (though an impressive percentage of the population gives it their best shot). And almost no one spends much time alone outdoors—the hermit tradition, never strong in America, has all but died away. (Thoreau came up twice on television during May 3. Once, he was an answer on *Tic Tac Dough* in the category "Bearded Men," and later that evening, in the back of a limousine, a man toasted his fiancée with champagne and said, "You know how we've always talked about finding our Walden Pond, our own little utopia? Well, here it is. This is Falconcrest.") I'm not interested in deciding which of these ways of spending time is "better." Both are caricatures, and neither strikes me as a model for a full and happy life. But caricatures have their uses—they draw attention to what is important about the familiar. Our society is moving steadily from natural sources of information toward electronic ones, from the mountain and the field toward the television; this great transition is very nearly complete. And so we need to understand the two extremes. One is the target of our drift. The other an anchor that might tug us gently back, a source of information that once spoke clearly to us and now hardly even whispers.

◆   ◆   ◆

The relentless flood of information we receive, then, does not necessarily   4 equal an understanding of our situation. The principal boast of electronic communication is speed, and speed doesn't help much in grasping these situations—it doesn't matter if you learn about the greenhouse effect this week or next week or next month. What matters is that when you do hear about it you understand it so deeply and thoroughly that you begin to question the way you live. It doesn't matter if you hear constantly, night after night, about poor children or abused elders. It matters that you hear about them in some way both deep enough and complicated enough that you'll go out and do something useful. Sometimes speed does count, of course—if you learn about starvation in Africa soon enough, you can stage a massive rock concert in time to spend the profits on milk powder. But even here the immediacy of television takes its toll. The famine in Africa in 1985, all the experts said, was as much a structural famine as a matter of crop failures; once the food aid arrived, the political infighting, development patterns, and environmental mismanagement of the region needed serious and prolonged attention. But when the starvation subsided, the cameras left, and with them the pressures from outside to do something. When starvation resumed in 1991, most of the cameras were elsewhere—in Kurdistan, or in Bangladesh. It's important that we see the effects of a cyclone in Bangladesh, but the real story is that a cyclone of poverty and overpopulation batters Bangladesh each and every day, and until it is somehow solved people will continue to build villages on floodplains.

5   Here's one way of asking the question—if instead of watching the news each night on television, or devouring the newspaper each morning, say you heard only one newscast a week, or read every third or fourth issue of *Newsweek.* If you reflected carefully on what you did read, I think in some ways you'd understand more about the planet. You'd still be more familiar with what was going on than almost any human being in history—you'd know about the gap between rich and poor, about ecological threats, about styles and trends, about political shifts and disasters. You'd know from repetition what really counted. And anything you didn't find out about—anything that flared up for just a day or two and then died out—couldn't matter much. I'm not seriously suggesting that anyone do this, of course—it takes a monumental act of will for most of us to remain in the dark even for a day or two. My wife and I live deep enough in the country that our paper comes a day late in the mail, which means we can skip whole stories, confident that whatever battle they describe has been superseded. But most evenings we tune in *All Things Considered* on the radio, and just its familiar theme music helps order the day.

6   Many of us tell ourselves that we need such constant updating so that we'll be able to cope with the "rapidly changing future." But it's not as if, by watching every moment of television, or reading every newspaper, you can really glimpse what the future holds. This May day came only three months before Saddam's invasion of Kuwait, the biggest news event in years, and no one even mentioned Iraq. Well, almost no one. A thin old man in a vested suit named Dr. Charles Taylor did appear on a program called *Bible Prophecy Today,* and he said that Iraq was trying to get a "nuclear trigger," and that it had a chemical capability, and that it would soon attack Israel— "in the fall is the most likely time." Dr. Taylor wasn't entirely right—he had Egypt on the wrong side, and he didn't know about Kuwait, and he said George Washington had had visions of nuclear attacks on America. But watching the tape of his confident analysis—"President Hussein has long harbored ambitions to dominate the region"—during the following winter as Scuds were slamming into Tel Aviv certainly added some zip to his tag line: "I'll see you next week—or I'll see you in glory!" I don't mean that Dan Rather *should* have known that Saddam Hussein was going to invade Kuwait—*The New York Times* didn't know, and the State Department hadn't a clue, nor did the CIA. And Dr. Charles Taylor clearly had well-placed sources. I mean only that watching the news on the theory that you'll find out what's going to happen is like buying a truckload of Coke because one of the cans might be the million-dollar prize winner. It's remotely possible, but you'd be so sugar-bloated and caffeine-jangled by the time you got to it you'd likely not even notice. By the way, the only mention all day of

the Stealth aircraft we'd soon come to know so well was in an ad for Thunderjets fruit snacks, which also come in the shape of F16s, F14 Tomcats, and MiG 27s.

It's undeniable that if you spent a lot of time on a mountain, or any- 7 where else distant from a tube, you might miss something. The even tone of the Emergency Broadcast System, which all children of the TV age intuitively know will be the last sound they hear before they die—you might miss that. But on a mountain, or anyplace well away from the noise of the world, there is room for reflection on what you *do* know. Who better understood the war in the Persian Gulf—the person who watched every nerve-jangling second of CNN's wraparound wall-to-wall coverage or some mythical person who heard only the most important points of the debate and had time to ponder? Some Denver researchers attempted to answer part of this question, and their findings, reported by Alexander Cockburn in the *San Francisco Examiner,* are suggestive. Knowledge of the facts of the conflict varied inversely with the amount of time spent watching the coverage—that is, only 16 percent of light viewers mistakenly believed Kuwait was a democracy, a fraction that increased to 32 percent among heavy viewers.

Even on a mountain you can't escape the news. Escaping the news is 8 an ignoble goal—in a nuclear, damaged, suffering world what happens elsewhere is all of our business and all of our shame. Access to news of distant events is one of modernity's true miracles—in the last few years it has shaken tyrants and brought them down. But the people of Eastern Europe or China didn't rise up out of an intricate and detailed knowledge of daily events in our system—they knew that people elsewhere lived more freely, and much more easily, and those broad understandings helped encourage them in their revolt. And it's not as if *we* need to know every jot and tittle in order to act— cranky old Thoreau is a useful witness in this matter. He scorned those who kept fanatically up-do-date ("Hardly a man takes his half hour's nap after dinner but when he wakes he holds up his head and asks 'What's the news?'"). He ridiculed attempts to speed communication between continents ("Perchance the first news that will leak through into the broad, flapping American ear will be that the Princess Adelaide has the whooping cough"). And yet he knew enough about the world to act. He knew that the Mexican war was wrong, and on reflection knew it was wrong enough to require that he go to jail. His protest was not based on extensive reporting from Mexico—"Civil Disobedience" includes no list of atrocities from the front. His protest was based on small amounts of information fed, in long hours of wilderness reflection, through the mill of principle. True, he went to jail only for a night. And his calm stand went unreported, save in his essay. And yet it has come down to us through the generations, a model for much that followed. We say "information" reverently, as if it meant "understanding" or "wisdom," but it doesn't. Sometimes it even gets in the way.

OF STUDIES

Francis Bacon

Francis Bacon (1561–1626) was an English statesman, scientist, and essayist. Practical and secular in his interests, Bacon tried organizing human knowledge, separating science from religion, and establishing a scientific community that might add material benefits to society. His *Essayes or Counsels, Civil and Morall* contains fifty-eight essays on a wide range of topics. "Of Studies" is Bacon's attempt to tell his readers about the proper uses of study and books. Even though Bacon addressed the literate elite of his time, the advice—whether you accept it or not—challenges you to consider your own use of reading, especially in relation to your life in society. As you read, evaluate what Bacon advises about the use of reading in argument.

1   Studies serve for delight, for ornament, and for ability. Their chief use for delight is in privateness and retiring; for ornament, is in discourse; and for ability, is in the judgement and disposition of business. For expert men can execute and perhaps judge of particulars, one by one, but the general counsels and the plots and marshalling of affairs come best from those that are learned. To spend too much time in studies is sloth; to use them too much for ornament is affectation; to make judgement wholly by their rules is the *humour*° of a scholar. They perfect nature, and are perfected by experience, for natural abilities are like natural plants, that need *proyning*° by study; and studies themselves do give forth directions too much at large, except they be bounded in by experience. Crafty men contemn studies, simple men admire them, and wise men use them, for they teach not their own use; but that is a wisdom without them and above them, won by observation. Read not to contradict and confute; nor to believe and take for granted; nor to find talk and discourse; but to weigh and consider. Some books are to be tasted, others to be swallowed, and some few to be chewed and digested; that is, some books are to be read only in parts; others to be read, but not *curiously;*° and some few to be ready wholly and with diligence and attention. Some books also may be read by deputy, and extracts made of them by others, but that would be only in the less important arguments and the meaner sort of books; else distilled books are like common distilled waters, *flashy*° things. Reading maketh a full man; conference a ready man; and writing an exact man. And therefore, if a man write little, he had need have a great memory; if he confer little, he had need have a present wit: and if he read little, he had need have much cunning, to seem to know that he doth not.

°*humour:* peculiar behavior.   *proyning:* pruning.   *curiously:* carefully.   *flashy:* momentarily sparkling.

Histories make men wise, poets witty, the mathematics subtile, natural philosophy deep, moral grave, logic and rhetoric able to contend. *Abeunt studia in mores.*° Nay there is no *stond*° or impediment in the wit, but may be wrought out by fit studies, like as diseases of the body may have appropriate exercises. Bowling is good for the *stone and reins;*° shooting for the lungs and breast; gentle walking for the stomach; riding for the head; and the like. So if a man's wit be wandering, let him study the mathematics, for in demonstrations, if his wit be called away never so little, he must begin again. If his wit be not apt to distinguish or find differences, let him study the schoolmen, for they are *cumini sectores.*° If he be not apt *to beat over*° matters, and to call up one thing to prove and illustrate another, let him study the lawyers' cases. So every defect of the mind may have a special *receipt.*°

"Who can define what is good?" you might wonder. I wonder, too, yet I believe there are circumstances that motivate me to speak out, to be no longer the comfortable grazer. Aristotle believed that people of good will need to learn argument because too much is at stake in our debates to let the opportunists have all the influence. His *Rhetoric* is an early how-to guide for public speakers. Aristotle observed that arguments can assert the good or the bad and make either one acceptable and believable. He concluded that people must argue for the good effectively: they cannot afford to be silent or, when not silent, inept. Good ideas do not automatically prevail or even make themselves evident.

Aristotle divided arguments into types that include most of the issues you are called to address. People argue, according to Aristotle, for the just, the useful, and the beautiful. Your arguments involve, again and again, competing views about what law or action is just, what plan or process is useful, and what artwork or human trait is beautiful. To think of it, argument embraces any subject matter about which people energetically disagree. Certainly, here are motives enough to develop your argument skills and enter the debates of your time and place.

EXERCISE 1.6 Examine the stands taken by Wendell Berry and Aldo Leopold in their essays. Use Aristotle's terms to write a description of their positions: What kind of good do these writers stand up for? the just? the useful? the beautiful? What elements of the essays reveal what is good for these writers?

°*Abeunt studia in mores:* "Studies become manners."   *stond:* obstacle.   *stone and reins:* kidney stones and kidneys.   *cumini sectores:* "hair splitters."   *to beat over:* to study.   *receipt:* prescription, Rx.

WHY I'M NOT GOING TO BUY A COMPUTER

Wendell Berry

Wendell Berry (b. 1934) is a fiction writer, poet, and essayist. An English professor at the University of Kentucky, Berry writes about culture and agriculture, revealing a connection between how we live and how we cultivate the soil. A traditionalist or a radical, depending on how you view him, Berry is a strong voice in debates about farming and its influence on American life. Berry's "Why I'm Not Going to Buy a Computer" is from the essay collection *What Are People For?* (1990). His stand for what he believes to be good seems unshakeable. His voice is clear and certain. You may find his voice bracing or irritating. In any case, you will have no question about what his position is.

1 Like almost everybody else, I am hooked to the energy corporations, which I do not admire. I hope to become less hooked to them. In my work, I try to be as little hooked to them as possible. As a farmer, I do almost all of my work with horses. As a writer, I work with a pencil or a pen and a piece of paper.

2 My wife types my work on a Royal standard typewriter bought new in 1956, and as good now as it was then. As she types, she sees things that are wrong, and marks them with small checks in the margins. She is my best critic because she is the one most familiar with my habitual errors and weaknesses. She also understands, sometimes better than I do, what *ought* to be said. We have, I think, a literary cottage industry that works well and pleasantly. I do not see anything wrong with it.

3 A number of people, by now, have told me that I could greatly improve things by buying a computer. My answer is that I am not going to do it. I have several reasons, and they are good ones.

4 The first is the one I mentioned at the beginning. I would hate to think that my work as a writer could not be done without a direct dependence on strip-mined coal. How could I write conscientiously against the rape of nature if I were, in the act of writing, implicated in the rape? For the same reason, it matters to me that my writing is done in the daytime, without electric light.

5 I do not admire the computer manufacturers a great deal more than I admire the energy industries. I have seen their advertisements, attempting to seduce struggling or failing farmers into the belief that they can solve their problems by buying yet another piece of expensive equipment. I am familiar with their propaganda campaigns that have put computers into public schools that are in need of books. That computers are expected to become as common as TV sets in "the future" does not impress me or matter to me. I do not own a TV set. I do not see that computers are bringing us one step nearer

to anything that does matter to me: peace, economic justice, ecological health, political honesty, family and community stability, good work.

What would a computer cost me? More money, for one thing, than I can afford, and more than I wish to pay to people whom I do not admire. But the cost would not be just monetary. It is well understood that technological innovation always requires the discarding of the "old model"—the "old model" in this case being not just our old Royal standard, but my wife, my critic, my closest reader, my fellow worker. Thus (and I think this is typical of present-day technological innovation), what would be superseded would be not only some thing, but some body. In order to be technologically up-to-date as a writer, I would have to sacrifice an association that I am dependent upon and that I treasure.

My final and perhaps my best reason for not owning a computer is that I do not wish to fool myself. I disbelieve, and therefore strongly resent, the assertion that I or anybody else could write better or more easily with a computer than with a pencil. I do not see why I should not be as scientific about this as the next fellow: When somebody has used a computer to write work that is demonstrably better than Dante's, and when this better is demonstrably attributable to the use of a computer, then I will speak of computers with a more respectful tone of voice, though I still will not buy one.

To make myself as plain as I can, I should give my standards for technological innovation in my own work. They are as follows:

1. The new tool should be cheaper than the one it replaces.
2. It should be at least as small in scale as the one it replaces.
3. It should do work that is clearly and demonstrably better than the one it replaces.
4. It should use less energy than the one it replaces.
5. If possible, it should use some form of solar energy, such as that of the body.
6. It should be repairable by a person of ordinary intelligence, provided that he or she has the necessary tools.
7. It should be purchasable and repairable as near to home as possible.
8. It should come from a small, privately owned shop or store that will take it back for maintenance and repair.
9. It should not replace or disrupt anything good that already exists, and this includes family and community relationships.

Editor's Note: This selection prompted many letters of rebuttal when first published. Additional commentary on this essay may be found in Wendell Berry's volume *What Are People For?*

❖ THINKING LIKE A MOUNTAIN

Aldo Leopold

Aldo Leopold (1886–1948) was a naturalist and conservationist who founded the discipline of wildlife management by applying the principles of ecology to the study of wildlife. He worked for the U.S. Forest Service and taught at the University of Wisconsin. "Thinking Like a Mountain" is collected with Leopold's other personal essays in *Sand County Almanac* (1949), a classic of American nature writing. The essay is unusual because it portrays Leopold changing his mind. There is something deeply mysterious about the experience that changes him. Leopold is a good enough writer to create for us a sense of thinking at a superhuman level.

1   A deep chesty bawl echoes from rimrock to rimrock, rolls down the mountain, and fades into the far blackness of the night. It is an outburst of wild defiant sorrow, and of contempt for all the adversities of the world.

2   Every living thing (and perhaps many a dead one as well) pays heed to that call. To the deer it is a reminder of the way of all flesh, to the pine a forecast of midnight scuffles and of blood upon the snow, to the coyote a promise of gleanings to come, to the cowman a threat of red ink at the bank, to the hunter a challenge of fang against bullet. Yet behind these obvious and immediate hopes and fears there lies a deeper meaning, known only to the mountain itself. Only the mountain has lived long enough to listen objectively to the howl of a wolf.

3   Those unable to decipher the hidden meaning know nevertheless that it is there, for it is felt in all wolf country, and distinguishes that country from all other land. It tingles in the spine of all who hear wolves by night, or who scan their tracks by day. Even without sight or sound of wolf, it is implicit in a hundred small events: the midnight whinny of a pack horse, the rattle of rolling rocks, the bound of a fleeing deer, the way shadows lie under the spruces. Only the ineducable tyro can fail to sense the presence or absence of wolves, or the fact that mountains have a secret opinion about them.

4   My own conviction on this score dates from the day I saw a wolf die. We were eating lunch on a high rimrock, at the foot of which a turbulent river elbowed its way. We saw what we thought was a doe fording the torrent, her breast awash in white water. When she climbed the bank toward us and shook out her tail, we realized our error: it was a wolf. A half-dozen others, evidently grown pups, sprang from the willows and all joined in a welcoming mêlée of wagging tails and playful maulings. What was literally a pile of wolves writhed and tumbled in the center of an open flat at the foot of our rimrock.

5   In those days we had never heard of passing up a chance to kill a wolf. In a second we were pumping lead into the pack, but with more excitement

than accuracy: how to aim a steep downhill shot is always confusing. When our rifles were empty, the old wolf was down, and a pup was dragging a leg into impassable slide-rocks.

We reached the old wolf in time to watch a fierce green fire dying in her   6
eyes. I realized then, and have known ever since, that there was something new to me in those eyes—something known only to her and to the mountain. I was young then, and full of trigger-itch; I thought that because fewer wolves meant more deer, that no wolves would mean hunters' paradise. But after seeing the green fire die, I sensed that neither the wolf nor the mountain agreed with such a view.

◆   ◆   ◆

Since then I have lived to see state after state extirpate its wolves. I have   7
watched the face of many a newly wolfless mountain, and seen the south-facing slopes wrinkle with a maze of new deer trails. I have seen every edible bush and seedling browsed, first to anaemic desuetude, and then to death. I have seen every edible tree defoliated to the height of a saddlehorn. Such a mountain looks as if someone had given God a new pruning shears, and forbidden Him all other exercise. In the end the starved bones of the hoped-for deer herd, dead of its own too-much, bleach with the bones of the dead sage, or molder under the high-lined junipers.

I now suspect that just as a deer herd lives in mortal fear of its wolves,   8
so does a mountain live in mortal fear of its deer. And perhaps with better cause, for while a buck pulled down by wolves can be replaced in two or three years, a range pulled down by too many deer may fail of replacement in as many decades.

So also with cows. The cowman who cleans his range of wolves does not   9
realize that he is taking over the wolf's job of trimming the herd to fit the range. He has not learned to think like a mountain. Hence we have dust-bowls, and rivers washing the future into the sea.

◆   ◆   ◆

We all strive for safety, prosperity, comfort, long life, and dullness. The deer   10
strives with his supple legs, the cowman with trap and poison, the statesman with pen, the most of us with machines, votes, and dollars, but it all comes to the same thing: peace in our time. A measure of success in this is all well enough, and perhaps is a requisite to objective thinking, but too much safety seems to yield only danger in the long run. Perhaps this is behind Thoreau's dictum: In wildness is the salvation of the world. Perhaps this is the hidden meaning in the howl of the wolf, long known among mountains, but seldom perceived among men.

EXERCISE 1.7 Virginia Woolf's portrait of Mary Wollstonecraft is an admiring one. List the reasons, stated or implied, that Woolf gives to you to admire her subject. Write a page in response to the statement: Mary Wollstonecraft took impassioned stands on issues; informed by principles, she succeeded or failed in a life that was an ongoing argument against all forms of tyranny.

❖ MARY WOLLSTONECRAFT
Virginia Woolf

Virginia Woolf (1882–1941) was an English novelist, short story writer, and essayist. Her experimental fiction contributed to the development of the novel. Recently, her social criticism has been rediscovered, her plea for a woman's workspace in *A Room of One's Own* (1929) and her anti-war tract *Three Guineas* (1939). The essay "Mary Wollstonecraft" is one of the portraits in "Four Figures" from *The Second Common Reader* (1932). While the portrait is not polemical, it does have elements of argument. Woolf writes an essay praising her subject and providing you with materials supporting her view. Woolf also presents Mary Wollstonecraft as a person dedicated to taking positions on issues and to redefining those positions as she matured. She exemplifies a life shaped by argument.

1   Great wars are strangely intermittent in their effects. The French Revolution took some people and tore them asunder; others it passed over without disturbing a hair of their heads. Jane Austen, it is said, never mentioned it; Charles Lamb ignored it; Beau Brummell never gave the matter a thought. But to Wordsworth and to Godwin it was the dawn; unmistakably they saw

> France standing on the top of golden hours,
> And human nature seeming born again.

Thus it would be easy for a picturesque historian to lay side by side the most glaring contrasts—here in Chesterfield Street was Beau Brummell letting his chin fall carefully upon his cravat and discussing in a tone studiously free from vulgar emphasis the proper cut of the lapel of a coat; and here in Somers Town was a party of ill-dressed, excited young men, one with a head too big for his body and a nose too long for his face, holding forth day by day over the tea-cups upon human perfectibility, ideal unity, and the rights of man. There was also a woman present with very bright eyes and a very eager tongue, and the young men, who had middle-class names, like Barlow and Holcroft and Godwin, called her simply 'Wollstonecraft', as if it did not matter whether she were married or unmarried, as if she were a young man like themselves.

2   Such glaring discords among intelligent people—for Charles Lamb and Godwin, Jane Austen and Mary Wollstonecraft were all highly intelligent— suggest how much influence circumstances have upon opinions. If Godwin had been brought up in the precincts of the Temple and had drunk deep of

antiquity and old letters at Christ's Hospital, he might never have cared a straw for the future of man and his rights in general. If Jane Austen had lain as a child on the landing to prevent her father from thrashing her mother, her soul might have burnt with such a passion against tyranny that all her novels might have been consumed in one cry for justice.

Such had been Mary Wollstonecraft's first experience of the joys of married life. And then her sister Everina had been married miserably and had bitten her wedding ring to pieces in the coach. Her brother had been a burden on her; her father's farm had failed, and in order to start that disreputable man with the red face and the violent temper and the dirty hair in life again she had gone into bondage among the aristocracy as a governess—in short, she had never known what happiness was, and, in its default, had fabricated a creed fitted to meet the sordid misery of real human life. The staple of her doctrine was that nothing mattered save independence.'Every obligation we receive from our fellow-creatures is a new shackle, takes from our native freedom, and debases the mind.' Independence was the first necessity for a woman; not grace or charm, but energy and courage and the power to put her will into effect, were her necessary qualities. It was her highest boast to be able to say, 'I never yet resolved to do anything of consequence that I did not adhere readily to it'. Certainly Mary could say this with truth. When she was a little more than thirty she could look back upon a series of actions which she had carried out in the teeth of opposition. She had taken a house by prodigious efforts for her friend Fanny, only to find that Fanny's mind was changed and she did not want a house after all. She had started a school. She had persuaded Fanny into marrying Mr Skeys. She had thrown up her school and gone to Lisbon alone to nurse Fanny when she died. On the voyage back she had forced the captain of the ship to rescue a wrecked French vessel by threatening to expose him if he refused. And when, overcome by a passion for Fuseli, she declared her wish to live with him and been refused flatly by his wife, she had put her principle of decisive action instantly into effect, and had gone to Paris determined to make her living by her pen.

The Revolution thus was not merely an event that had happened outside her; it was an active agent in her own blood. She had been in revolt all her life—against tyranny, against law, against convention. The reformer's love of humanity, which has so much of hatred in it as well as love, fermented within her. The outbreak of revolution in France expressed some of her deepest theories and convictions, and she dashed off in the heat of that extraordinary moment those two eloquent and daring books—the *Reply to Burke* and the *Vindication of the Rights of Woman,* which are so true that they seem now to contain nothing new in them—their originality has become our commonplace. But when she was in Paris lodging by herself in a great house, and saw with her own eyes the King whom she despised driving past surrounded by National Guards and holding himself with greater dignity than she expected, then, 'I can scarcely tell you why', the tears came to her eyes. 'I am going to bed,' the letter ended, 'and, for the first time in my life, I cannot put out the candle.' Things were not so simple after all. She could not understand even her own feelings. She saw the most cherished of her convictions put into practice—and her eyes filled with tears. She had won fame and independence and the right to live her own life—and she wanted something different. 'I do not want to be loved like a goddess,' she wrote, 'but I wish to be necessary to you.' For Imlay, the fascinating American to whom her letter was addressed, had been very good to her. Indeed, she had fallen passionately in love with him. But it was one of her theories that love should be free—'that mutual affection was marriage and that the marriage tie should not bind after the death of love, if love should die'. And yet at the same time that she wanted freedom she wanted certainty. 'I like the word affection,' she wrote, 'because it signifies something habitual.'

5   The conflict of all these contradictions shows itself in her face, at once so resolute and so dreamy, so sensual and so intelligent, and beautiful into the bargain with its great coils of hair and the large bright eyes that Southey thought the most expressive he had ever seen. The life of such a woman was bound to be tempestuous. Every day she made theories by which life should be lived; and every day she came smack against the rock of other people's prejudices. Every day too—for she was no pedant, no cold-blooded theorist—something was born in her that thrust aside her theories and forced her to model them afresh. She acted upon her theory that she had no legal claim upon Imlay; she refused to marry him; but when he left her alone week after week with the child she had borne him her agony was unendurable.

6   Thus distracted, thus puzzling even to herself, the plausible and treacherous Imlay cannot be altogether blamed for failing to follow the rapidity of her changes and the alternate reason and unreason of her moods. Even friends whose liking was impartial were disturbed by her discrepancies. Mary had a passionate, an exuberant, love of Nature, and yet one night when the colours in the sky were so exquisite that Madeleine Schweizer could not help saying to her, 'Come, Mary—come, nature-lover—and enjoy this wonderful spectacle—this constant transition from colour to colour', Mary never took her eyes off the Baron de Wolzogen. 'I must confess,' wrote Madame Schweizer, 'that this erotic absorption made such a disagreeable impression on me, that all my pleasure vanished.' But if the sentimental Swiss was disconcerted by Mary's sensuality, Imlay, the shrewd man of business, was exasperated by her intelligence. Whenever he saw her he yielded to her charm, but then her quickness, her penetration, her uncompromising idealism harassed him. She saw through his excuses; she met all his reasons; she was even capable of managing his business. There was no peace with her— he must be off again. And then her letters followed him, torturing him with their sincerity and their insight. They were so outspoken; they pleaded so passionately to be told the truth; they showed such a contempt for soap and alum and wealth and comfort; they repeated, as he suspected, so truthfully

that he had only to say the word, 'and you shall never hear of me more', that he could not endure it. Tickling minnows he had hooked a dolphin, and the creature rushed him through the waters till he was dizzy and only wanted to escape. After all, though he had played at theory-making too, he was a business man, he depended upon soap and alum; 'the secondary pleasures of life', he had to admit, 'are very necessary to my comfort'. And among them was one that for ever evaded Mary's jealous scrutiny. Was it business, was it politics, was it a woman, that perpetually took him away from her? He shillied and shallied; he was very charming when they met; then he disappeared again. Exasperated at last, and half insane with suspicion, she forced the truth from the cook. A little actress in a strolling company was his mistress, she learnt. True to her own creed of decisive action, Mary at once soaked her skirts so that she might sink unfailingly, and threw herself from Putney Bridge. But she was rescued; after unspeakable agony she recovered, and then her 'unconquerable greatness of mind', her girlish creed of independence, asserted itself again, and she determined to make another bid for happiness and to earn her living without taking a penny from Imlay for herself or their child.

It was in this crisis that she again saw Godwin, the little man with the big head, whom she had met when the French Revolution was making the young men in Somers Town think that a new world was being born. She met him—but that is a euphemism, for in fact Mary Wollstonecraft actually visited him in his own house. Was it the effect of the French Revolution? Was it the blood she had seen spilt on the pavement and the cries of the furious crowd that had rung in her ears that made it seem a matter of no importance whether she put on her cloak and went to visit Godwin in Somers Town, or waited in Judd Street West for Godwin to come to her? And what strange upheaval of human life was it that inspired that curious man, who was so queer a mixture of meanness and magnanimity, of coldness and deep feeling—for the memoir of his wife could not have been written without unusual depth of heart—to hold the view that she did right—that he respected Mary for trampling upon the idiotic convention by which women's lives were tied down? He held the most extraordinary views on many subjects, and upon the relations of the sexes in particular. He thought that reason should influence even the love between men and women. He thought that there was something spiritual in their relationship. He had written that 'marriage is a law, and the worst of all laws . . . marriage is an affair of property, and the worst of all properties'. He held the belief that if two people of the opposite sex like each other, they should live together without any ceremony, or, for living together is apt to blunt love, twenty doors off, say, in the same street. And he went further; he said that if another man liked your wife 'this will create no difficulty. We may all enjoy her conversation, and we shall all be wise enough to consider the sensual intercourse a very trivial object.' True, when he wrote those words he had never been in love; now for the first time he was to experience that sensation. It came very quietly and naturally, growing 'with equal advances in the mind of each' from those talks in Somers Town, from those discussions upon everything under the sun which they had held so improperly alone in his rooms. 'It was friendship melting into love . . . ', he wrote. 'When, in the course of things, the disclosure came, there was nothing in the manner for either party to disclose to the other.' Certainly they were in agreement upon the most essential points; they were both of opinion, for instance, that marriage was unnecessary. They would continue to live apart. Only when Nature again intervened, and Mary found herself with child, was it worth while to lose valued friends, she asked, for the sake of a theory? She thought not, and they were married. And then that other theory—that it is best for husband and wife to live apart—was not that also incompatible with other feelings that were coming to birth in her? 'A husband is a convenient part of the furniture of the house', she wrote. Indeed, she discovered that she was passionately domestic. Why not, then, revise that theory too, and share the same roof. Godwin should have a room some doors off to work in; and they should dine out separately if they liked—their work, their friends, should be separate. Thus they settled it, and the plan worked admirably. The arrangement combined 'the novelty and lively sensation of a visit with the more delicious and heart-felt pleasures of domestic life'. Mary admitted that she was happy; Godwin confessed that, after all one's philosophy, it was 'extremely gratifying' to find that 'there is someone who takes an interest in one's happiness'. All sorts of powers and emotions were liberated in Mary by her new satisfaction. Trifles gave her an exquisite pleasure—the sight of Godwin and Imlay's child playing together; the thought of their own child who was to be born; a day's jaunt into the country. One day, meeting Imlay in the New Road, she greeted him without bitterness. But, as Godwin wrote, 'Ours is not an idle happiness, a paradise of selfish and transitory pleasures'. No, it too was an experiment, as Mary's life had been an experiment from the start, an attempt to make human conventions conform more closely to human needs. And their marriage was only a beginning; all sorts of things were to follow after. Mary was going to have a child. She was going to write a book to be called *The Wrongs of Women*. She was going to reform education. She was going to come down to dinner the day after her child was born. She was going to employ a midwife and not a doctor at her confinement—but that experiment was her last. She died in child-birth. She whose sense of her own existence was so intense, who had cried out even in her misery, 'I cannot bear to think of being no more—of losing myself—nay, it appears to me impossible that I should cease to exist', died at the age of thirty-six. But she has her revenge. Many millions have died and been forgotten in the hundred and thirty years that have passed since she was buried; and yet as we read her letters and listen to her arguments and consider her experiments, above all, that most fruitful experiment, her relation with Godwin, and realise the high-handed and hot-blooded manner in which she cut her way to the quick of life, one form of immortality is hers undoubtedly: she is alive and active, she argues and experiments, we hear her voice and trace her influence even now among the living.

ARGUMENT ACTIVITIES

1. "There is not a sentence which adequately states its own meaning."— Alfred North Whitehead. Can you think of single sentences that have authority? Consider the slogans of bumper stickers or the maxims of culture: Just Do It; Live Simply So That Others May Simply Live; When Guns Are Outlawed, Only Outlaws Will Have Guns; Live and Let Live; If It Ain't Broke, Don't Fix It. Do such thesis statements actually need further development?

2. Write briefly about your personal views concerning argument. Do you like to argue? What methods do you use? Do your arguments ever conclude? What feelings do your arguments arouse? Do these opinions expressed by other students reflect your attitudes?

   a. If I am around people where decision making is going on, it's a sure bet that I will voice my opinion.

   b. There comes a point where you put both feet down and stand up for what you believe. When you put both feet down you must be clever and tactful so as not to arouse a violent response that can make things worse.

   c. If you do not state your case and let it be known how you feel about an issue, then you should not complain about the effects.

   d. You both might find out new information about the topic you're arguing about.

   e. I don't believe anyone should push their views on someone else. This is part of being a free society, and I don't want to tell someone else how to live or what decisions to make.

   f. People need to know that they are acknowledged as human beings here on this earth; then shovel some information at them.

   g. People may be ill-informed about a topic and need accurate, well-detailed information so that they may weigh each side of an issue with great care.

   h. Most people can make up their own minds without my influence.

   i. Sometimes I feel like I need to take a stand and defend my case, but most of the time I should probably keep my mouth shut. I am worried that I'll hurt others.

   j. It builds character to take a stand and build a case.

   k. Once two have taken time to argue, they have also taken time to listen to each other . . . usually bringing the people with the disagreement closer because now they understand each other.

3. Lady Bracknell is an aristocrat in Oscar Wilde's comedy *The Importance of Being Earnest.* She has decided opinions about everything, including argument. Does her statement below reflect your views?

   I dislike arguments of any kind. They are always vulgar and often convincing.

4. We sometimes get caught in that unpleasant exchange called "blind argument." Can you illustrate? What about being caught in "blind agreement"? Can you illustrate this situation?

5. Consider a situation where you have changed someone's opinion or where someone has changed yours. What was at issue? How strongly did you feel about the issue? What caused the change? How did each of you feel about the outcome?

6. You may begin work on Assignment One or Assignment Two in the part of the book titled Argument Assignments. These assignments ask you to write whole essays about issues of your choice. Complete instructions and successful student examples are included with each assignment.

CHAPTER TWO
PREPARATION FOR ARGUMENT

Chapter 1 provided an overview of argument, explaining what argument is and why you might use it. This chapter and the next two chapters advance from the questions "What is argument?" and "Why argue?" to "How do you argue?" This chapter outlines activities that prepare you to write an argument. Preparation includes reading other people's arguments, examining their thesis statements and support, and defining the issues they discuss. You will come to appreciate the wide range of issues available for argument and their complexity and uncertainty as well as the variety of stands people take on them. In preparing to write arguments, you will examine the debate about the issue you choose and determine where you stand. You will consider your audience, identifying who they are, what they believe or disbelieve about your thesis, and what other likenesses and differences exist between you and them. Chapters 3 and 4 will discuss organizing and supporting an argument.

EXAMINING ISSUES

Read the following short selection that will help you focus on defining issues and identifying a writer's thesis or position on an issue.

 THE IGUANA

Isak Dinesen

Isak Dinesen (1885–1962), a Danish writer of short stories, owned a coffee plantation in Kenya. *Out of Africa* (1937) is her memoir of her years in Africa and of the disappearance of an Africa she admired. "The Iguana," from the memoir, concentrates in a short essay Dinesen's struggle to capture, yet not kill, the natural beauty of the continent. Dinesen skillfully presents her own experiences, from which she draws a thesis pertinent to readers everywhere.

1   In the Reserve I have sometimes come upon the Iguana, the big lizards, as they were sunning themselves upon a flat stone in a riverbed. They are not pretty in shape, but nothing can be imagined more beautiful than their coloring. They shine like a heap of precious stones or like a pane cut out of an old church window. When, as you approach, they swish away, there is a flash of azure, green and purple over the stones, the color seems to be standing behind them in the air, like a comet's luminous tail.

2   Once I shot an Iguana. I thought that I should be able to make some pretty things from his skin. A strange thing happened then, that I have never afterwards forgotten. As I went up to him, where he was lying dead upon his stone, and actually while I was walking the few steps, he faded and grew pale, all color died out of him as in one long sigh, and by the time that I touched him he was grey and dull like a lump of concrete. It was the live impetuous blood pulsating within the animal, which had radiated out all that glow and splendor. Now that the flame was put out, and the soul had flown, the Iguana was as dead as a sandbag.

3   Often since I have, in some sort, shot an Iguana, and I have remembered the one of the Reserve. Up at Meru I saw a young Native girl with a bracelet on, a leather strap two inches wide, and embroidered all over with very small turquoise-colored beads which varied a little in color and played in green, light blue and ultramarine. It was an extraordinarily live thing; it seemed to draw breath on her arm, so that I wanted it for myself, and made Farah buy it from her. No sooner had it come upon my own arm than it gave up the ghost. It was nothing now, a small, cheap, purchased article of finery. It had been the play of colors, the duet between the turquoise and the "nègre"—that quick, sweet, brownish black, like peat and black pottery, of the Native's skin—that had created the life of the bracelet.

4   In the Zoological Museum of Pietermaritzburg, I have seen, in a stuffed deep-water fish in a showcase, the same combination of coloring, which there had survived death; it made me wonder what life can well be like, on the bottom of the sea, to send up something so live and airy. I stood in Meru and looked at my pale hand and at the dead bracelet, it was as if an injustice had been done to a noble thing, as if truth had been suppressed. So sad did it seem that I remembered the saying of the hero in a book that I had read as a child: "I have conquered them all, but I am standing amongst graves."

5   In a foreign country and with foreign species of life one should take measures to find out whether things will be keeping their value when dead. To the settlers of East Africa I give the advice: "For the sake of your own eyes and heart, shoot not the Iguana."

At first glance, Dinesen's essay seems to be an account of personal experience; Dinesen does not initially seem intent on presenting a thesis or argument. At a certain point, however, she does signal her intention to "make something" of the iguana experience. Can you find that place in the essay? What finally is Dinesen's main point or thesis? Where is it stated? What is the effect of understanding the selection's aim later on instead of at the outset? How do the three examples Dinesen uses fit together? Such questions may help you review Dinesen's essay. To put this review in the terms of argument, you can ask questions from the following list.

ARGUMENT ANALYSIS QUESTIONS

What is the argument about?

How can you state this essay's subject as an issue?

What is the writer's position on the issue?

What kind of support does the writer present to help you understand his or her position—and, perhaps, even accept it?

These questions help you see the argument. Clearly, people argue about something. At first, you might suspect Dinesen's argument is about lizards or about killing animals, yet other parts of the piece force you to reassess what the argument is really about. When a subject is argued about, you should be able to define the argument as an issue. When you define the issue, you have a clearer view of the positions or sides you and others take.

An issue can be stated as a question using the verb helper *should*. *Should* people shoot iguanas in order to possess their beauty? *Should* people try capturing beauty? The answers to such questions are position statements. Yes, people should try to capture beauty. No, people should not. *Yes* and *no* establish a dramatic difference, the core of the argument. Other possible answers range between these poles. Yes, in some cases, people should try. No, seldom is it wise to remove a creature or artifact from its place of origin. Position statements are not questions, although they can use the word *should* or the same implication of should as the issue questions.

When you can state a position, you are able to consider support. As a thoughtful person, you want to know for yourself what you think and on what you base your opinions. Also, when you take a position on an issue, you often need to explain yourself to others. You need to make your views clear to readers. You try to convince them of your views.

As you read the Dinesen article, you can see her using personal experience as a main source of support. She presents three episodes. Yet, note that she uses the remembered quote from "the hero in a book" and, thus, points to the open-ended search for materials pertinent to a writer's stand on an issue. Notice as well how the physical detail that Dinesen presents helps support her claim that the iguana and bracelet indeed changed.

Now read another hunting essay, "Growing Up Game" by Brenda Peterson.

❖ GROWING UP GAME

Brenda Peterson

Brenda Peterson (b. 1950), a Seattle-based novelist and essayist, collected her essays in *Nature and Other Mothers* (1992) and *Living By Water* (1990), which included "Growing Up Game." This essay shows the writer herself challenged by all she knows. Peterson knows two cultures, two traditions, and she needs to come to terms with both. In resolving her conflict, she answers those of her readers who would disapprove of her actions and values. Peterson's essay illustrates an internal argument that clearly has consequences for others.

1   When I went off to college my father gave me, as part of my tuition, 50 pounds of moose meat. In 1969, eating moose meat at the University of California was a contradiction in terms. Hippies didn't hunt. I lived in a rambling Victorian house which boasted sweeping circular staircases, built-in lofts, and a landlady who dreamed of opening her own health food restaurant. I told my housemates that my moose meat in its nondescript white butcher paper was from a side of beef my father had bought. The carnivores in the house helped me finish off such suppers as sweet and sour moose meatballs, mooseburgers (garnished with the obligatory avocado and sprouts), and mooseghetti. The same dinner guests who remarked upon the lean sweetness of the meat would have recoiled if I'd told them the not-so-simple truth: that I grew up on game, and the moose they were eating had been brought down, with one shot through his magnificent heart, by my father—a man who had hunted all his life and all of mine.

2   One of my earliest memories is of crawling across the vast continent of crinkled linoleum in our Forest Service cabin kitchen, down splintered back steps, through wildflowers growing wheat-high. I was eye-level with grasshoppers who scolded me on my first solo trip outside. I made it to the shed, a cool and comfortingly square shelter that held phantasmagoric metal parts; they smelled good, like dirt and grease. I had played a long time in this shed before some maternal shriek made me lift up on my haunches to listen to those urgent, possessive sounds that were my name. Rearing up, my head bumped into something hanging in the dark; gleaming white, it felt sleek and cold against my cheek. Its smell was dense and musty and not unlike the slabs of my grandmother's great arms after her cool, evening sponge baths. In that shed I looked up and saw the flensed body of a doe; it swung gently, slapping my face. I felt then as I do even now when eating game: horror and awe and hunger.

3   Growing up those first years on a forest station high in the Sierra was somewhat like belonging to a white tribe. The men hiked off every day into their forest and the women stayed behind in the circle of official cabins, breeding. So far away from a store, we ate venison and squirrel, rattlesnake

and duck. My brother's first rattle, in fact, was from a King Rattler my father killed as we watched, by snatching it up with a stick and winding it, whip-like, around a redwood sapling. Rattlesnake tastes just like chicken, but has many fragile bones to slither one's way through; we also ate salmon, rabbit, and geese galore. The game was accompanied by such daily garden dainties as fried okra, mustard greens, corn fritters, wilted lettuce (our favorite be-cause of that rare, blackened bacon), new potatoes and peas, stewed toma-toes, barbecued butter beans.

I was 4 before I ever had a beef hamburger and I remember being dis-   4
appointed by its fatty, nothing taste and the way it fell apart at the seams whenever my teeth sank into it. Smoked pork shoulder came much later in the South; and I was 21, living in New York City, before I ever tasted leg of lamb. I approached that glazed rack of meat with a certain guilty self-consciousness, as if I unfairly stalked those sweet-tempered white creatures myself. But how would I explain my squeamishness to those urban sophisti-cates? How explain that I was shy with mutton when I had been bred on wild things?

Part of it, I suspect, had to do with the belief I'd also been bred on—   5
we become the spirit and body of animals we eat. As a child eating venison I liked to think of myself as lean and lovely just like the deer. I would never be caught dead just grazing while some man who wasn't even a skillful hunter crept up and konked me over the head. If someone wanted to hunt me, he must be wily and outwitting. He must earn me.

My father had also taught us as children that animals were our broth-   6
ers and sisters under their skin. They died so that we might live. And of this sacrifice we must be mindful. "God make us grateful for what we are about to receive," took on a new meaning when one knew the animal's struggle pitted against our own appetite. We also used *all* the animal so that an elk became elk steaks, stew, salami, and sausage. His head and horns went on the wall to watch us more earnestly than any babysitter, and every Christmas Eve we had a ceremony of making our own moccasins for the new year out of whatever Father had tanned. "Nothing wasted," my father would always say, or, as we munched on sausage cookies made from moosemeat or venison, "Think about who you're eating." We thought of ourselves as intri-cately linked to the food chain. We knew, for example, that a forest fire meant, at the end of the line, we'd suffer too. We'd have buck stew instead of venison steak and the meat would be stringy, withered-tasting because in the animal kingdom, as it seemed with humans, only the meanest and lean-est and orneriest survived.

Once when I was in my early teens, I went along on a hunting trip as   7
the "main cook and bottle-washer," though I don't remember any bottles; none of these hunters drank alcohol. There was something else coursing through their veins as they rose long before dawn and disappeared, return-ing to my little camp most often dragging a doe or pheasant or rabbit. We ate

innumerable cornmeal-fried catfish, had rabbit stew seasoned only with blood and black pepper.

8   This hunting trip was the first time I remember eating game as a conscious act. My father and Buddy Earl shot a big doe and she lay with me in the back of the tarp-draped station wagon all the way home. It was not the smell I minded, it was the glazed great, dark eyes and the way that head flopped around crazily on what I knew was once a graceful neck. I found myself petting this doe, murmuring all those graces we'd been taught long ago as children. *Thank you for the sacrifice, thank you for letting us be like you so that we can grow up strong as game.* But there was an uneasiness in me that night as I bounced along in the back of the car with the deer.

9   What was uneasy is still uneasy—perhaps it always will be. It's not easy when one really starts thinking about all this: the eating game, the food chain, the sacrifice of one for the other. It's never easy when one begins to think about one's most basic actions, like eating. Like becoming what one eats: lean and lovely and mortal.

10   Why should it be that the purchase of meat at a butcher shop is somehow more righteous than eating something wild? Perhaps it has to do with our collective unconscious that sees the animal bred for slaughter as doomed. But that wild doe or moose might make it without the hunter. Perhaps on this primitive level of archetype and unconscious knowing we even believe that what's wild lives forever.

11   My father once told this story around a hunting campfire. His own father, who raised cattle during the Depression on a dirt farm in the Ozarks, once fell on such hard times that he had to butcher the pet lamb for supper. My father, bred on game or their own hogs all his life, took one look at the family pet on that meat platter and pushed his plate away from him. His siblings followed suit. To hear my grandfather tell it, it was the funniest thing he'd ever seen. "They just couldn't eat Bo-Peep," Grandfather said. And to hear my father tell it years later around that campfire, it was funny, but I saw for the first time his sadness. And I realized that eating had become a conscious act for him that day at the dinner table when Bo-Peep offered herself up.

12   Now when someone offers me game I will eat it with all the qualms and memories and reverence with which I grew up eating it. And I think it will always be this feeling of horror and awe and hunger. And something else— full knowledge of what I do, what I become.

Brenda Peterson's rich essay develops from her mixed feelings about eating meat. Note that Peterson, far from being sure of herself and her opinions, writes to explore an issue, to gain insight and articulateness. She cannot "explain her squeamishness to those urban sophisticates," partly because the social differences are intimidating and partly because she has not yet fathomed the paradox of being "shy with mutton," although "bred on wild things." Peterson's father is the thesis sayer in the essay's first half, with his "Nothing wasted" and "Think about who you're eating." *Who*, not what! The uneasiness of her first hunt is present in the essay: "It's never easy when one begins to think about one's most basic actions, like eating. Like becoming what one eats: lean and lovely and mortal."

Her essay allows her to express a mixture of feelings and to defend that complexity against those whose eating may seem "somehow more righteous," probably because they have thought and experienced less about the matter. Strong arguments do not depend on a writer's being finished with his or her thinking—or absolutely clear about it. Rachel Carson's writings in Chapter 1 show her development from appreciation to advocacy. Aldo Leopold and Isak Dinesen must rethink the killing of an animal. In these cases, arguments develop when writers recognize, "I thought that way once, but now I'm up to something else, which you, reader, might consider."

EXERCISE 2.1 Return to the Brenda Peterson essay. Use the Argument Analysis Questions presented earlier in this chapter to examine the essay's argument elements. Bring your written responses to class for use in discussion.

When I identified the Peterson essay as another hunting essay, I was aware of how experiences of many kinds present different, yet related, voices and constitute a debate or dialogue. Every religion, every political system, every profession or hobby or scholarly discipline has ongoing debates about key issues. Such debates involve energetic contributors—some last decades, even centuries. In the United States, for example, debates occur within the political system: the tug between state and federal power, the tug between individual rights and group welfare. Americans debate to what degree and in what manner a powerful nation ought to be a factor in world affairs. They debate the morality of abortion, euthanasia, and capital punishment. They continue to debate the causes of crime and its remedies. They have difficulty fitting punishment to the crime because they have contested views of what crime is. However, not all points of argument are central and enduring. You may think trivial what some people have argued and died for or struggled to attain so as to be stylish or modish. After all, TV commercials debate which is better, Coke or Pepsi!

The study of argument helps you consider what is worth arguing about. You may find in argument the opportunity to be human in various ways. You can weigh in on long-standing debates; you can expend energy on short-term issues with values that are sometimes hard to determine. You can choose apathy and nonparticipation.

Recently, an argument developed about what sort of cups a college cafeteria should use, styrofoam or paper. Who cares? What difference does it make? Yet, in the context of the debate, clearly it matters to personnel responsible for the cafeteria's budget—paper cups cost more—and to environmentalists—paper biodegrades more readily. Often a trivial issue, if it generates heated controversy, is revealed to be part of larger debates and of cherished values. Maybe people can get to know other people, really know them, not by finding out what they do for a living or what movies they like, but by finding what they argue about.

EXERCISE 2.2 Consider the essays by Dinesen and Peterson as parts of a debate. In preparation for class discussion, list in your notebook the key terms of the debated issue or issues. Identify what is proposed, defended, and condemned. Add personal experience and your values that apply to the debate. In class, compare your construction of the debated issue with those of classmates. In what ways are their constructions of the issue like yours?

TAKING A STAND

You may be daunted by having to take a stand. In many stories and episodes of history, speaking one's mind is preliminary to ridicule or martyrdom. Why should you go out on a limb? Why should you stick your neck out? You are no Joan of Arc or Martin Luther. You are good enough and bright enough, but, perhaps, have little or nothing to say to others about your values or the conduct of their lives. America is a free country, right? Doesn't that mean you are free from other people's uninvited influence, free from having to sit through their arguments or from having to present your own?

You may be daunted, as well, by the hard work needed to determine your stand on an issue. Most issues allow for opposing views. If you listen and read with an open mind—and keeping an open mind requires effort, too—you may not be confirmed in the view that you brought to the debate originally. Instead, you may be encouraged, even pushed, to change your view. Depending on the issue, this could require a lot of energy, a lot of excruciating rethinking. Abraham Lincoln was approached by abolitionists during the Civil War and asked to free the slaves. Lincoln hesitated at first and then complied after a thorough consideration of moral, military, and political impacts.

Who You Are and What You Know

Are you like everyone else? What do you know? If you answer, "Yes, I am like everyone else" and "I know nothing or very little" your project in argument begins with inertia. A heavy wheel is hard to turn. Inertia is not an unusual starting point, considering the fact that the mind has its seasons of torpor, of labor-saving standstill. If you are a lot like your readers, then you may not be impelled to say much to them, certainly not to argue with them or to try to influence them. If you know nothing or very little, you have no motive to bring news to other people—you have no news to bring. Perhaps you can overcome this inertia by reconsidering who you are and what you know.

EXERCISE 2.3 Trace a circle wide enough to fill most of a notebook page. Begin to section the circle with your various identities. Label each one and include as many as you can. No one else has the same components. Be ready to discuss your circle with classmates. Although you and they share some identities, your identity is a unique blend with some distinctive traits. Examine such a circle:

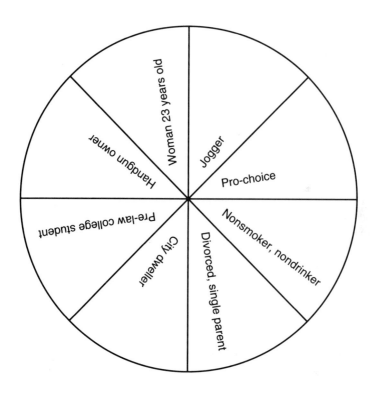

By accepting your expanded self, you can begin to recognize not only your individuality but your knowledge as well. In my circle, for example, I can see that some of my identities—composition instructor, for one—allow me to address others as an author, authoritatively. Also, in those identities I share with others—parent, for example—I might begin to appreciate that my experience in parenting is in some manner unlike that of other parents. I am looking for how I am unlike others so that I can discover what I have to offer them and what I might argue about.

EXERCISE 2.4 Examine the identity of two writers in their arguments. Take notes on what use Adrienne Rich makes of being female and feminist writing to the broad readership of *The New York Times*. Note what use Thomas Paine makes of being an American addressing fellow Americans.

❖ MOTHERHOOD IN BONDAGE
Adrienne Rich

Adrienne Rich (b. 1929) is a poet, essayist, and influential feminist. Since her first poetry volume in 1951, Rich has built a major body of work. Rich teaches English and feminist studies at Stanford University. Her book *Of Woman Born: Motherhood as Experience and Institution* (1976) examined the ideology of motherhood. In "Motherhood in Bondage," published in *The New York Times*, Rich acknowledges to general readers the difficulty of accepting new political movements. The piece is noteworthy for Rich's attempt to recognize discomfort, even fear, among those who do not share her political agenda.

1   Every great new movement in human consciousness arouses both hope and terror. The understanding that male-female relationships have been founded on the status of the female as the property of the male, or of male-dominated institutions, continues to be difficult for both women and men. It is painful to acknowledge that our identity has been dictated and diminished by others, or that we have let our identity depend on the diminishment and exploitation of other humans. This idea still meets with the resistance that has always risen when unsanctioned, long-stifled realities begin to stir and assert themselves.

2   Resistance may take many forms. Protective deafness—the inability to hear what is actually being said—is one. Trivialization is another: the reduction of a troubling new complexity to a caricature, or a clinical phenomenon. A literary critic, reviewing two recent anthologies of women's poetry, declares that "the notion that the world has been put together exclusively by men, and solely for their own benefit, and that they have conspired together for generations to discriminate against their mothers and sisters, wives and daughters, lovers and friends, is a neurosis for which we do not yet have a name." It is striking that, even in his denial, this writer can describe women only as appendages to men.

3   In her history of birth control in America, the Marxist historian Linda Gordon writes, "For women . . . heterosexual relations are always intense, frightening, high-risk situations which ought, if a woman has any sense of self-preservation, to be carefully calculated."[1] The power politics of the relations

---

[1]Linda Gordon, *Woman's Body, Woman's Right: A Social History of Birth Control in America* (New York: Viking Grossman, 1976).

between the sexes, long unexplored, is still a charged issue. To raise it is to cut to the core of power relations throughout society, to break down irreparably the screens of mystification between "private life" and "public affairs."

But even more central a nerve is exposed when motherhood is analyzed as a political institution. This institution—which affects each woman's personal experience—is visible in the male dispensation of birth control and abortion; the guardianship of men over children in the courts and the educational system; the subservience, through most of history, of women and children to the patriarchal father; the economic dominance of the father over the family; the usurpation of the birth process by a male medical establishment. The subjectivity of the fathers (who are also sons) has prescribed how, when, and even where women should conceive, bear, nourish, and indoctrinate their children. The experience of motherhood by women—both mothers and daughters—is only beginning to be described by women themselves.

Until very recently, the choice to be or not to be a mother was virtually unavailable to most women; even today, the possibility of choice remains everywhere in jeopardy. This elemental loss of control over her body affects every woman's right to shape the imagery and insights of her own being. We speak of women as "nonmothers" or "childless"; we do not speak of "nonfathers" or "childless men." Motherhood is admirable, however, only so long as mother and child are attached to a legal father: Motherhood out of wedlock, or under the welfare system, or lesbian motherhood, are harassed, humiliated, or neglected. In the 1970s in the United States, with 26 million children of wage-earning mothers, 8 million in female-headed households, the late nineteenth-century stereotype of the "mother at home" is still assumed as the norm—a "norm" that has, outside of a small middle-class minority, never existed.

In trying to distinguish the two strands: motherhood as *experience*, one possible and profound experience for women, and motherhood as enforced identity and as political *institution*, I myself only slowly began to grasp the centrality of the institution, and how it connects with the dread of difference that infects all societies. Under that institution, all women are seen primarily as mothers; all mothers are expected to experience motherhood unambivalently and in accordance with patriarchal values; and the "nonmothering" woman is seen as deviant.

Since the "deviant" is outside the law, and "abnormal," the pressure on all women to assent to the "mothering" role is intense. To speak of maternal ambivalence; to examine the passionate conflicts and ambiguities of the mother-daughter relationship, and the role of the mother in indoctrinating her daughters to subservience and her sons to dominance; to identify the guilt mothers are made to feel for societal failures beyond their control; to acknowledge that a lesbian can be a mother and a mother a lesbian, contrary to popular stereotypes; to question the dictating by powerful men as to how

women, especially the poor and nonwhite, shall use their bodies, or the in-
doctrination of women toward a one-sided emotional nurturing of men, is to
challenge deeply embedded phobias and prejudices.

8   Such themes anger and terrify, precisely because they touch us at the
quick of human existence. But to flee them, or trivialize them, to leave
the emotions they arouse in us unexamined, is to flee both ourselves and the
dawning hope that women *and* men may one day experience forms of love
and parenthood, identity and community that will not be drenched in lies,
secrets, and silence.

❖ THOUGHTS ON THE PRESENT STATE OF AMERICAN AFFAIRS

Thomas Paine

Thomas Paine (1737–1809) was an English-American writer whose *Common Sense*
(1776) was the most widely read pamphlet in America up to that time. George
Washington ordered sections of Paine's essays to be read to his soldiers during the
winter at Valley Forge. Paine was a fiery propagandist against monarchy. He wrote
to defend the French Revolution and the separation of religion from the state. Also
an inventor, he tried developing a smokeless candle and an iron bridge without piers.
The following selection from *Common Sense* shows Paine's combative, blunt manner as he wrestles with opposing views and forces his readers to consider armed
struggle against England.

1   In the following pages I offer nothing more than simple facts, plain arguments, and common sense; and have no other preliminaries to settle with the
reader, than that he will divest himself of prejudice and prepossession, and
suffer his reason and his feelings to determine for themselves; that he will
put *on*, or rather that he will not put *off*, the true character of a man, and gen-
erously enlarge his views beyond the present day.

2   Volumes have been written on the subject of the struggle between
England and America. Men of all ranks have embarked in the controversy,
from different motives, and with various designs; but all have been ineffec-
tual, and the period of debate is closed. Arms, as the last resource, decide
the contest; the appeal was the choice of the king, and the continent hath accepted the challenge.

3   It hath been reported of the late Mr Pelham (who tho' an able minister
was not without his faults) that on his being attacked in the house of commons, on the score, that his measures were only of a temporary kind, replied,
'*they will last my time.*' Should a thought so fatal and unmanly possess the
colonies in the present contest, the name of ancestors will be remembered by
future generations with detestation.

The sun never shined on a cause of greater worth. 'Tis not the affair of   4
a city, a country, a province, or a kingdom, but of a continent—of at least
one eighth part of the habitable globe. 'Tis not the concern of a day, a year,
or an age; posterity are virtually involved in the contest, and will be more or
less affected, even to the end of time, by the proceedings now. Now is the
seed time of continental union, faith and honor. The least fracture now will
be like a name engraved with the point of a pin on the tender rind of a
young oak; the wound will enlarge with the tree, and posterity read it in full
grown characters.

By referring the matter from argument to arms, a new æra for politics is   5
struck; a new method of thinking hath arisen. All plans, proposals, &c. prior
to the nineteenth of April, *i.e.* to the commencement of hostilities, are like the
almanacks of the last year; which, though proper then, are superceded and
useless now. Whatever was advanced by the advocates on either side of the
question then, terminated in one and the same point, viz. a union with Great
Britain; the only difference between the parties was the method of effecting
it; the one proposing force, the other friendship; but it hath so far happened
that the first hath failed, and the second hath withdrawn her influence.

As much hath been said of the advantages of reconciliation, which, like   6
an agreeable dream, hath passed away and left us as we were, it is but right,
that we should examine the contrary side of the argument, and inquire into
some of the many material injuries which these colonies sustain, and always
will sustain, by being connected with, and dependant on Great Britain. To
examine that connexion and dependance, on the principles of nature and
common sense, to see what we have to trust to, if separated, and what we are
to expect, if dependant.

I have heard it asserted by some, that as America hath flourished un-   7
der her former connexion with Great-Britain, that the same connexion is necessary towards her future happiness, and will always have the same effect.
Nothing can be more fallacious than this kind of argument. We may as well
assert, that because a child has thrived upon milk, that it is never to have
meat; or that the first twenty years of our lives is to become a precedent for
the next twenty. But even this is admitting more than is true, for I answer
roundly, that America would have flourished as much, and probably much
more, had no European power had any thing to do with her. The commerce
by which she hath enriched herself are the necessaries of life, and will always have a market while eating is the custom of Europe.

But she has protected us, say some. That she hath engrossed us is true,   8
and defended the continent at our expence as well as her own is admitted,
and she would have defended Turkey from the same motive, viz. the sake of
trade and dominion.

Alas, we have been long led away by ancient prejudices, and made   9
large sacrifices to superstition. We have boasted the protection of Great-
Britain, without considering, that her motive was *interest* not *attachment;*

that she did not protect us from *our enemies* on *our account,* but from *her enemies* on *her own account,* from those who had no quarrel with us on any *other account,* and who will always be our enemies on the *same account.* Let Britain wave her pretensions to the continent, or the continent throw off the dependance, and we should be at peace with France and Spain were they at war with Britain. The miseries of Hanover last war ought to warn us against connexions.

10   It hath lately been asserted in parliament, that the colonies have no relation to each other but through the parent country, *i.e.* that Pensylvania and the Jerseys, and so on for the rest, are sister colonies by the way of England; this is certainly a very round-about way of proving relationship, but it is the nearest and only true way of proving enemyship, if I may so call it. France and Spain never were, nor perhaps ever will be our enemies as *Americans,* but as our being the *subjects of Great Britain.*

11   But Britain is the parent country, say some. Then the more shame upon her conduct. Even brutes do not devour their young, nor savages make war upon their families; wherefore the assertion, if true, turns to her reproach; but it happens not to be true, or only partly so, and the phrase *parent* or *mother country* hath been jesuitically adopted by the — and his parasites, with a low papistical design of gaining an unfair bias on the credulous weakness of our minds. Europe, and not England, is the parent country of America. This new world hath been the asylum for the persecuted lovers of civil and religious liberty from *every part* of Europe. Hither have they fled, not from the tender embraces of the mother, but from the cruelty of the monster; and it is so far true of England, that the same tyranny which drove the first emigrants from home, pursues their descendants still.

12   In this extensive quarter of the globe, we forget the narrow limits of three hundred and sixty miles (the extent of England) and carry our friendship on a larger scale; we claim brotherhood with eve-European christian, and triumph in the generosity of the sentiment.

13   It is pleasant to observe by what regular gradations we surmount the force of local prejudice, as we enlarge our acquaintance with the world. A man born in any town in England divided into parishes, will naturally associate most with his fellow parishioners (because their interests in many cases will be common) and distinguish him by the name of *neighbour;* if he meet him but a few miles from home, he drops the narrow idea of a street, and salutes him by the name of *townsman;* if he travels out of the county, and meet him in any other, he forgets the minor divisions of street and town, and calls him *countryman,* i.e. *countyman;* but if in their foreign excursions they should associate in France or any other part of *Europe,* their local remembrance would be enlarged into that of *Englishmen.* And by a just parity of reasoning, all Europeans meeting in America, or any other quarter of the globe, are *countrymen;* for England, Holland, Germany, or Sweden, when compared with the whole, stand in the same places on the larger scale,

which the divisions of street, town, and county do on the smaller ones; distinctions too limited for continental minds. Not one third of the inhabitants, even of this province, are of English descent. Wherefore I reprobate the phrase of parent or mother country applied to England only, as being false, selfish, narrow and ungenerous.

But admitting that we were all of English descent, what does it amount to? Nothing. Britain, being now an open enemy, extinguishes every other name and title: And to say that reconciliation is our duty, is truly farcical. The first king of England, of the present line (William the Conqueror) was a Frenchman, and half the peers of England are descendants from the same country; wherefore by the same method of reasoning, England ought to be governed by France. 14

Much hath been said of the united strength of Britain and the colonies, that in conjunction they might bid defiance to the world. But this is mere presumption; the fate of war is uncertain, neither do the expressions mean any thing; for this continent would never suffer itself to be drained of inhabitants to support the British arms in either Asia, Africa, or Europe. 15

Besides, what have we to do with setting the world at defiance? Our plan is commerce, and that, well attended to, will secure us the peace and friendship of all Europe; because it is the interest of all Europe to have America a *free port*. Her trade will always be a protection, and her barrenness of gold and silver secure her from invaders. 16

I challenge the warmest advocate for reconciliation, to shew, a single advantage that this continent can reap, by being connected with Great Britain. I repeat the challenge, not a single advantage is derived. Our corn will fetch its price in any market in Europe, and our imported goods must be paid for buy them where we will. 17

But the injuries and disadvantages we sustain by that connection, are without number; and our duty to mankind at large, as well as to ourselves, instruct us to renounce the alliance: Because, any submission to, or dependance on Great Britain, tends directly to involve this continent in European wars and quarrels; and sets us at variance with nations, who would otherwise seek our friendship, and against whom, we have neither anger nor complaint. As Europe is our market for trade, we ought to form no partial connection with any part of it. It is the true interest of America to steer clear of European contentions, which she never can do, while by her dependance on Britain, she is made the make-weight in the scale of British politics. 18

Europe is too thickly planted with kingdoms to be long at peace, and whenever a war breaks out between England and any foreign power, the trade of America goes to ruin, *because of her connection with Britain.* The next war may not turn out like the last, and should it not, the advocates for reconciliation now will be wishing for separation then, because, neutrality in that case, would be a safer convoy than a man of war. Every thing that is right or natural pleads for separation. The blood of the slain, the weeping 19 voice of nature cries, 'TIS TIME TO PART. Even the distance at which the Almighty hath placed England and America, is a strong and natural proof, that the authority of the one, over the other, was never the design of Heaven. The time likewise at which the continent was discovered, adds weight to the argument, and the manner in which it was peopled encreases the force of it. The reformation was preceded by the discovery of America, as if the Almighty graciously meant to open a sanctuary to the persecuted in future years, when home should afford neither friendship nor safety.

20   The authority of Great-Britain over this continent, is a form of government, which sooner or later must have an end: And a serious mind can draw no true pleasure by looking forward, under the painful and positive conviction, that what he calls 'the present constitution' is merely temporary. As parents, we can have no joy, knowing that *this government* is not sufficiently lasting to ensure any thing which we may bequeath to posterity: And by a plain method of argument, as we are running the next generation into debt, we ought to do the work of it, otherwise we use them meanly and pitifully. In order to discover the line of our duty rightly, we should take our children in our hand, and fix our station a few years farther into life; that eminence will present a prospect, which a few present fears and prejudices conceal from our sight.

21   Though I would carefully avoid giving unnecessary offence, yet I am inclined to believe, that all those who espouse the doctrine of reconciliation, may be included within the following descriptions. Interested men, who are not to be trusted; weak men who *cannot* see; prejudiced men who *will not* see; and a certain set of moderate men, who think better of the European world than it deserves; and this last class by an ill-judged deliberation, will be the cause of more calamities to this continent than all the other three.

22   It is the good fortune of many to live distant from the scene of sorrow; the evil is not sufficiently brought to *their* doors to make *them* feel the precariousness with which all American property is possessed. But let our imaginations transport us for a few moments to Boston, that seat of wretchedness will teach us wisdom, and instruct us for ever to renounce a power in whom we can have no trust. The inhabitants of that unfortunate city, who but a few months ago were in ease and affluence, have now no other alternative than to stay and starve, or turn out to beg. Endangered by the fire of their friends if they continue within the city, and plundered by the soldiery if they leave it. In their present condition they are prisoners without the hope of redemption, and in a general attack for their relief, they would be exposed to the fury of both armies.

23   Men of passive tempers look somewhat lightly over the offences of Britain, and, still hoping for the best, are apt to call out, '*Come we shall be friends again for all this.*' But examine the passions and feelings of mankind. Bring the doctrine of reconciliation to the touchstone of nature, and then tell me, whether you can hereafter love, honour, and faithfully serve the power

that hath carried fire and sword into your land? If you cannot do all these, then are you only deceiving yourselves, and by your delay bringing ruin upon posterity. Your future connection with Britain, whom you can neither love nor honour, will be forced and unnatural, and being formed only on the plan of present convenience, will in a little time fall into a relapse more wretched than the first. But if you say, you can still pass the violations over, then I ask, Hath your house been burnt? Hath your property been destroyed before your face? Are your wife and children destitute of a bed to lie on, or bread to live on? Have you lost a parent or a child by their hands, and yourself the ruined and wretched survivor? If you have not, then are you not a judge of those who have. But if you have, and can still shake hands with the murderers, then are you unworthy the name of husband, father, friend, or lover, and whatever may be your rank or title in life, you have the heart of a coward, and the spirit of a sycophant.

This is not inflaming or exaggerating matters, but trying them by those 24 feelings and affections which nature justifies, and without which, we should be incapable of discharging the social duties of life, or enjoying the felicities of it. I mean not to exhibit horror for the purpose of provoking revenge, but to awaken us from fatal and unmanly slumbers, that we may pursue determinately some fixed object. It is not in the power of Britain or of Europe to conquer America, if she do not conquer herself by *delay* and *timidity*. The present winter is worth an age if rightly employed, but if lost or neglected, the whole continent will partake of the misfortune; and there is no punishment which that man will not deserve, be he who, or what, or where he will, that may be the means of sacrificing a season so precious and useful.

The French nobleman Michel de Montaigne (1533–1592) gave the name *essays* to his excursions in personal writing. His motto was "What do I know?" He considered his essays—from the verb *essayer, to try*—tests or trials of his judgment. He arrived at a position about any subject by composing, or bringing together, observations he derived from his considerable public service and his reading of history, literature, and philosophy. He used the question "What do I know?" to challenge inertia and to get the mind's wheel turning. Admittedly, Montaigne was not a specialist, so he claimed no authority as priest, governor, or scholar. But as an observant, experienced person, Montaigne saw the potential energy of exploring the richness of his own mind. There was no whining or making excuses in the question about what he might know; rather, there was confidence that the mind would respond if challenged. Incidentally, Shakespeare (1564–1616) read the essays of Montaigne, most likely in translation, and, perhaps, drew from them for his portrait of one of the liveliest minds in literature: Hamlet. Hamlet's stirring vision of human potential is in the spirit of Montaigne:

What a piece of work is man! how noble in reason! how infinite in faculties! in form and moving how express and admirable! in action how like an angel! in apprehension how like a god! the beauty of the world! the paragon of animals!

Use your self-portrait circle to select two or three identities in which you have special knowledge or special experience or perspectives. In preparation for argument, also think of which identities involve strong beliefs and vivid differences with others.

EXERCISE 2.5 The following exercise is another task to help energize your preparation for argument. Use a notebook page to record your responses to these probes. List as many responses as you can.

TWO STEPS TO ARGUMENT SUBJECTS

Step 1: Look to yourself to find subjects for argument.
    What interests you?
    What concerns you?
    What do you know about?

Step 2: Use the liveliest subjects from Step 1 and ask the following, again jotting down responses:
    Concerning this subject, what makes you angry? What makes you hopeful or depressed?
    What controversies or issues exist with this subject?
    How is this subject changing? Are the changes good or bad? What needs changing?
    What are some "should" statements that reflect your opinions about the subject?

Universal and Local Issues

In the discussion about subjects for argument a range of issues was presented—some timely, some enduring, some trivial, and some grave. The mass media exert great influence on what you attend to, including what you argue about. National issues are articulated often and in detail. Repeated exposure may not trivialize these issues, but people can become numb to them and find it difficult to say something fresh about them or to master the volume of what others have already said. You are aware of the issues that make up a kind of national agenda, with some issues coming to the foreground and others receding, with new issues being added and others dropped. Recent subjects of concern include capital punishment, gun control, drug use and abuse, medical care costs, abortion, euthanasia, violence, and pornography, as well as international concerns such as trade and disarmament.

Not every issue that is vital to you is a national issue discussed widely by the media. Here are some other issues, local or even personal, listed as "should" questions:

- Should the community spend more to maintain its covered bridges?
- Should parents use cloth diapers for babies, not plastic or paper ones?
- Should writing courses be required for a two- or four-year degree?
- Should male students be more careful to avoid sexist language in the classroom?
- Should colleges and local bus systems do more to encourage students to ride the bus?
- Should fishermen, before getting a license, learn how to release fish correctly?

These issues illustrate how you can develop arguments from perspectives outside of the national agenda.

One way to measure the importance of an issue is to look at how frequently and heatedly a society discusses it. Another way, Montaigne-like, is to consider the issue's importance to you. Indeed, if you are going to prepare an argument, you must feel the issue is worth your effort. And, as you will see later, an issue is important if it engages an audience's interest. Sometimes you need to convince the audience that the issue is important. Often, even when arguing, both parties do share this sense of importance—for them, the issue is involving, even essential.

EXERCISE 2.6   Look back at your list of lively subjects. Respond to the following questions by writing in your notebook. Which subjects are drawn from the public agenda? For these subjects will it be possible to say anything new? Is it possible for you to take a heartfelt stand on the issue? Can you find subissues, aspects of the debate compact enough to deal with in a short argument assignment? Now determine which subjects are local or personal. Will it be possible to discuss them, to find support? Are these issues important to anybody else?

Simple and Complex Issues

Thus far, you have examined some steps to help direct you toward choosing a workable argument subject. Reading the work of other writers is essential, as is knowing your own mind and heart. You also may generate topics from local and personal experience, not solely from the well-used public agenda.

Sometimes you might hesitate to speak and write if you feel you know too little about a subject. Sometimes, when you feel you know everything, you might hesitate and reconsider. What if your knowledge is illusory? Incomplete? Uncertain? Before you launch into an argument, you should appreciate its complexity. Yet, you should appreciate, too, that even if you never know enough, you may still present your views, signaling to your audience your awareness of how complex the issue is and how incomplete your arguments may be.

After ordering soldiers to fire on demonstrators in Beijing in 1989, the Chinese Communist leadership blamed foreigners for introducing liberal, decadent books to China. Hence, a simple response to a problem: the government seized the offending literature from bookstores. Yet, to see matters more complexly, maybe the Chinese aspirations were fueled in part by economic failure and a decade or more of slow political reform? And what is to be made of the leadership's continued welcoming of foreign investors and tourists? One wonders about solving the problem of dissent by using censorship.

Roger Heyns, a former teacher and university chancellor, now a foundation president, cautions against answering complex questions too simply. The unpredictability and uncertainty of the future, Heyns believes, produces anxiety, and "zealotry is often, it seems to me . . . an escape from anxiety. If you're really scared, the simple answer is going to be better than the complicated answer. And so our tolerance for complexity is going down." Yet, oversimplifications may not work—people should make things as simple as possible, but not simpler.

Issues are complicated by several factors. You know already that most arguments include two or more sides. Many questions central to an argument elicit a diversity of responses. No one, for example, seems to understand why Oregon led the nation in bank robberies per capita in 1988. Only New York, California, and Florida reported more such holdups overall. Portland, with a population of 388,000, reported two hundred more bank robberies than Chicago, with a population of 3 million! In order to reduce Oregon bank robberies, many people began asking what caused them. The explanations, you can imagine, were varied. Some pointed to the state's overcrowded prisons. Some pointed to drug addiction. Some pointed to "user-friendly" banks which are "open, airy, and inviting." Perhaps, a simple effect can have more than one cause, and, perhaps, to some degree, each explanation can have merit.

Often, an issue that looks simple on the surface becomes complex when one breaks out the issue's components. Consider the issue of using the death penalty. A 1989 survey in New York State found that the death penalty was favored by 72 percent of all respondents and opposed by 22 percent; the rest of those surveyed were undecided. These results appear to support capital punishment. Yet, when pollsters asked additional questions, the issue became subtler, less starkly pro and con. Whereas 80 percent favored the death penalty for a serial killer, only 39 percent favored death for someone who had killed in a moment of passion, and only 10 percent favored it for the mentally retarded criminal. Further complications arose when the pollsters asked, "Do you prefer the death penalty or an alternative which would put a convicted murderer in prison for life, without any possibility of parole, and which would force him to work in a prison industry where earnings would go to the victim's family?" To that, 62 percent preferred the life sentence, 32 percent the death penalty.

Such outcomes of polling point out difficulties in statements characterizing how a group feels or thinks. Indeed, the poll raises questions about what we think of as facts. The word itself, *fact*, has a reassuring ring to it. Yet, views clash when "my facts" oppose "your facts." Cesar Chavez, former president of the United Farm Workers, organized a 1989 boycott of table grapes to pressure growers to stop using dangerous pesticides. The California Table Grape Commission, representing growers, claimed Chavez launched the boycott to bolster union membership. As for the pesticide dangers, the Commission cited a state of California pesticide monitor report indicating 75 percent of the harvest had no pesticide residues and 25 percent had residues significantly below tolerances. Chavez responded by claiming that some residues cannot be detected by the inadequate testing and that tolerance levels were set twenty to forty years ago, some without scientific study. Clearly, this was a complex disagreement demanding sharper definitions and further research.

When issues and answers are complicated, you do not have to throw your hands up in dismay. It is better if you factor into your discussions all you know. It is better if you expect the complex and suspect the simple. It is better if you recognize people may change slowly. When in 1989 in El Salvador, a nation in a protracted civil war, the government and the rebels sat down to talk, one observer said, "The mere fact that they didn't break off the talks is a great success." Concerning the need to adjust hopes to realities, he added, "Any other hopes for greater achievement from the meeting were wishful thinking. . . . But if you look at the problems underneath, it is unreal and naive to have expected immediate results." This observer spoke with a wise appreciation of deep-seated, complicated problems.

Certainty and Uncertainty

Writers have a common need to appear certain in arguments. When you assert "such and such is so," the English language pushes you toward trouble. First, the verb *to be* conceals that *you* think such and such is so, that what *you* say is a perspective and is often arguable. When you understand that an assertion ought to be prefaced by *I think, I believe,* or *I conclude,* then you understand that your opinion originates with and may be limited to you. Then you recognize you may need to convince others. Aware of this hazard of the verb *to be,* you are alert to the limits of your assertion and yet you are relieved from having to speak for everyone as group leader or spokesperson.

Also, a statement using *is* may obscure what was or will be. This verb can freeze its subject in time. The statement "Oregon is the leader in bank robberies" has to be limited to 1988, changed to *was,* or possibly rewritten to reflect the state's current ranking. This ability of *is* to freeze subjects may misrepresent them. For example, to think of people as radical or conservative or as "my little cousin" may falsely characterize them and not allow for their changing views and size.

If argument can be defined as the rational use of language to change people, you can see that argument thrives in situations that are uncertain. You do not argue when the answer is certain and generally accepted. You do not present your views to others who are certain that their different views are correct. However, you might decide to enter an argument in a situation that will allow you to take your viewpoint—one that is less than certain—and refine, correct, and develop it.

In most arguments, participants generally do not claim to know everything, to have a corner on the facts, an armlock on truth. While president, Lyndon Johnson responded to critics of his Vietnam policy by saying they would see things his way if they only had access to his facts. Of course, many such facts were classified at that time, and President Johnson declined to disclose what he knew. War protesters could not wait for all the cows to come home, for a more complete record of the times. They had to act on what they did know, although it was incomplete. The question, when the record is incomplete, should not be who is certain. Any zealot can claim certainty. The question, based on what you do know, should be "How probable is this conclusion?" or "How sound is this belief or action?" Specialists in science and social science, although appreciative of what is known, express how much is uncertain, yet to be known, or possibly unknowable. Remember, Socrates was told by the oracle that he was the wisest man. "Why?" he wondered. Then, after interviewing other philosophers and leaders of Athens, he came to understand that even though he did not know everything, others did not either. Socrates was the only one of them with the insight to recognize this shortcoming.

EXERCISE 2.7 Examine how uncertainty and complexity are acknowledged in the essay by Robert Jay Lifton and in the Lincoln selection. List the words by which Lifton signals the tentativeness of his approach, for example, "I shall suggest" and "it is quite possible." For the Lincoln selection, list the difficulties Lincoln has in signing an emancipation decree. What makes this a hard decision?

After reading both selections, return to Berry (Chapter 1) and Rich (Chapter 2) and list the advantages and disadvantages of arguments whose writers do not present themselves as certain or their issues as simple or easy. Consider for an argument you are writing the wisdom of acknowledging uncertainty and complexity. Finally, write a one-page summary of what you have discovered about uncertainty and complexity in arguments. Include details from the lists you have made for this exercise.

❖ DEATH AND LIFE
Robert Jay Lifton

Robert Jay Lifton (b. 1926) is a psychiatrist who studies groups of people caught in extreme situations. His studies of Hiroshima survivors, Vietnam veterans, and Nazi doctors are considered to be psychohistory, studies of human behavior interacting with historical forces of a given age. *Death in Life: Survivors of Hiroshima* (1969) received the National Book Award in science. Lifton believes that people react to profound historical disturbance with "psychic numbing." The essay "Death and Life" is part of *Boundaries: Psychological Man in Revolution* (1970). The essay is crisply organized, yet Lifton frequently signals his uncertainty about his position on the subject.

One cannot really think seriously about Hiroshima without raising questions   1
about nuclear weapons in general, and their influence upon that ultimate boundary between death and life.

Once more, I wish to approach the problem not in terms of the specific   2
physical destructive power of these weapons, but of our psychological—in the broadest sense, symbolic—responses to them. For man's mental processes are such that he never notes or records a fact, a thing, or an event in a totally passive way. Rather he inwardly recreates, gives inner form to, every fact, thing, or event that impresses itself upon him. This inner recreation, his bringing something to whatever he observes or feels, is what makes man a symbolizing creature, and a formative one as well. So when I speak of his symbolic and formative responses to nuclear weapons, I am really speaking of the kind of imprint these weapons make upon his mind. And with weapons whose capacity to kill is so great as to approach infinity, only the naïve and the deluded could claim that this imprint does not, in some important way, alter the general boundaries of death and life. Unfortunately, the impact of the weapons themselves can also foster precisely such naïveté and delusion in the most dangerous ways, as I shall in a moment suggest.

But I want first to say something about man's general approach to the   3
fact of his own death, and about a theory of symbolic immortality I have attempted to develop. For I would claim that man requires a *sense* of immortality in the face of inevitable biological death. This sense of immortality need not be merely a denial of the fact of his death, though man is certainly prone to such a denial. It also represents a compelling, universal urge to

maintain an inner sense of continuity, over time and space, with the various elements of life. This sense of immortality is man's way of experiencing his connection with all of human history. We can speak of it in relationship to five general modes.

4   First, the biological mode of immortality, the sense of living on through, but in an emotional sense, *with* or even *in* one's sons and daughters and their sons and daughters, by imagining an endless chain of biological attachment. This mode has found its classical expression in East Asian culture, especially in the traditional Chinese family system, but is of enormous importance in all cultures, and may well be the most universally significant of man's modes of immortality. Nor does it ever remain purely biological, but in varying degrees extends itself into social dimensions, into the sense of surviving through one's tribe, organization, people, nation or even species, that is, living on in any or all of these.

5   The second mode is the theological, as expressed both in ideas put forth by various religions concerning a life after death, and in the more general theological principle of the spiritual conquest of death. One finds expressions of the theological mode in the concepts developed by religions and cultures to suggest the acquisition of a more-than-natural power over death—in the Christian principle of grace, the Japanese idea of *kami,* and the Roman concept of numen.

6   A third mode is that achieved through man's works, whether through specific creative products or broader human impact, through writings, art, thought, institutions, inventions, or lasting influences of any kind upon other human beings. Thus artists, scientists, revolutionaries, social benefactors, and humble purveyors of kindness can all share in a sense of being outlived by what they have done or created.

7   The fourth mode is that achieved by being survived by nature itself, the sense one will live on in natural elements, limitless in space and time. One finds vivid expressions of this mode in Japanese feelings about nature, partly originating in the animism of Shinto tradition, but also in various expressions of the European Romantic movement, including the American cult of the 'great outdoors.'

8   A fifth mode of immortality, somewhat different from the others, depends entirely upon a psychic state—one so intense that time and death disappear. It may therefore be termed the mode of experiential transcendence, and includes various forms of ecstasy and rapture associated both with the Dionysian principle of excess, and with the mystical sense of oneness with the universe that Freud referred to as the "oceanic feeling."

9   What I am suggesting, then, is that the symbolic modes of immortality are not merely problems one ponders when dying. They are constantly perceived inner standards, though often indirect and outside of awareness, by which we evaluate our lives, by which we maintain feelings of connection, significance, and movement so necessary to everyday psychological

existence. And if we return our attention to nuclear weapons, we can now begin to see the threats they pose to our psychological life quite independently of their use. Their very existence in the world is enough.

For, if we anticipate the possibility of nuclear weapons being used, and   10
I believe everyone from about the age of six or seven in some measure does, we are faced with the prospect of being severed from virtually all of our symbolic paths to immortality. Thus in the post-nuclear world (if we can call it that) we can imagine no biological posterity. Without entering into the debate as to whether a general nuclear war would eliminate *all* human life on earth, or only a considerable segment of it, such is our imagery of total biological destruction that we can no longer count upon living on through (or in) family, nation, or even species. It is even quite possible that some of our present fascination with outer space, the moon, and the planets has to do with our present doubts about biological immortality on earth and with the consequent urge to discover the existence of new life, or the means of revitalizing an old life, elsewhere.

Theological immortality is also threatened. The entire modern secular   11
historical experience had thrown it into great confusion, of course, prior to the existence of nuclear weapons. But these weapons have, for many reasons, intensified the theological crisis. In Hiroshima, for instance, people were unable to find an adequate explanation or formulation for their atomic bomb experience in the Buddhism, Shintoism, or in some cases Christianity, they had known. Nor, for the most part, even in the new religions which blossomed all through Japan after the war, and which many of the Hiroshima people embraced. None of these various forms of religious symbolism seemed adequate to the magnitude of the disaster itself.

As for the rest of us and our nuclear weapons, it is quite possible that   12
belief in a spiritual existence beyond death cannot be effectively maintained in association with an imagined world in which there are none, or virtually none, among the biologically living. That is, one may require an assurance of the continuation of ordinary natural life, in order to be able to believe in a supernatural kind. On the other hand the weapons bring a particular insistence, even desperation, to forms of religious practice sometimes referred to as demythologizing or 'death-of-God theology,' especially where these direct themselves to immediate social and ethical issues, including those of war and peace and nuclear weapons.

Immortality through man's works, the third mode, becomes even more   13
dubious. Following nuclear apocalypse, who can be certain of the survival of creative products, or individual kindnesses? And I think that the threat to man's works contributes to various forms of revolutionary impulse: the attempt on the part of the young both to renew these works and to alter the world in which they are so threatened, and the attempt of the old to preserve and purify what they have created—as, for instance, Mao Tse-tung's quest for revolutionary immortality which I shall discuss in a later chapter.

14   Nature, the fourth mode, is much more difficult to destroy, and the revived interest in man's natural environment may be more than merely an overdue reaction to our long-standing tendency to abuse it. It may, in fact, be a form of clinging to those natural forces which preceded man, and which he has always counted upon to outlast him. We might, in fact, anticipate various forms of natural theologies as a consequence of the nuclear age. But given the power of nuclear weapons, and other weapons too including biological ones, even nature is threatened.

15   In discussing Hiroshima, I mentioned the force of one rumor which spread throughout the city immediately after the bomb fell—the belief that trees, flowers, and grass would never again grow there—as an expression of an ultimate form of desolation which not only encompassed human death but went beyond it. Such is the power of imagery concerning the destruction of nature, and of its being lost to man.

16   This leaves only the fifth mode, that of experiential transcendence, which we may now see to take on a new significance. For with all the other modes so threatened, men are likely to resort to precisely this kind of effort to transcend history itself, that is, to find a timeless, 'deathless' dimension. Such things as the drug revolution among the young, and their general stress upon intense experience, or upon what could be called experiential radicalism—whether in politics, art, or life-style—all these may well be quests for new forms of experiential transcendence, quests that are greatly intensified by the other symbolic impairments brought about by nuclear weapons.

17   What I am suggesting in all this is that nuclear weapons alter and blur the boundaries of our psychological lives, of our symbolic space, in ways crucial to our thought, feelings, and actions.

❖ REPLY TO CHICAGO EMANCIPATION MEMORIAL, WASHINGTON, D.C.

Abraham Lincoln

Abraham Lincoln (1809–1865) was president of the United States during the nation's most violent disagreement. Although the war was not caused solely by differences over slavery, much debate focused on the slavery question. Lincoln, known as the emancipator of slaves, did not seek election on an anti-slavery platform. Many influences during his presidency shaped his decision to sign the Emancipation Proclamation, January 1, 1863. Yet, in September 1862, even as he had reviewed preliminary drafts of a proclamation, Lincoln gave this interview to two abolitionists. In an age when there were few reporters assigned a White House beat and no electronic recordings, this transcript of the exchange offers rare insight into Lincoln's deliberations. The two abolitionists are the "we" of the piece, and Lincoln's words are reported as quotations.

"The subject presented in the memorial is one upon which I have thought   1
much for weeks past, and I may even say for months. I am approached with
the most opposite opinions and advice, and that by religious men, who are
equally certain that they represent the Divine will. I am sure that either the
one or the other class is mistaken in that belief, and perhaps in some respects
both. I hope it will not be irreverent for me to say that if it is probable that
God would reveal his will to others, on a point so connected with my duty, it
might be supposed he would reveal it directly to me; for, unless I am more
deceived in myself than I often am, it is my earnest desire to know the will
of Providence in this matter. *And if I can learn what it is I will do it!* These
are not, however, the days of miracles, and I suppose it will be granted that
I am not to expect a direct revelation. I must study the plain physical facts
of the case, ascertain what is possible and learn what appears to be wise and
right. The subject is difficult, and good men do not agree. For instance, the
other day four gentlemen of standing and intelligence (naming one or two of
the number) from New York called, as a delegation, on business connected
with the war; but, before leaving, two of them earnestly beset me to proclaim
general emancipation, upon which the other two at once attacked them! You
know, also, that the last session of Congress had a decided majority of anti-
slavery men, yet they could not unite on this policy. And the same is true of
the religious people. Why, the rebel soldiers are praying with a great deal
more earnestness, I fear, than our own troops, and expecting God to favor
their side; for one of our soldiers, who had been taken prisoner, told Senator
Wilson, a few days since, that he met with nothing so discouraging as the evident sincerity of those he was among in their prayers. But we will talk over
the merits of the case.

"What *good* would a proclamation of emancipation from me do, espe-   2
cially as we are now situated? I do not want to issue a document that the
whole world will see must necessarily be inoperative, like the Pope's bull
against the comet! Would *my word* free the slaves, when I cannot even enforce the Constitution in the rebel States? Is there a single court, or magis-
trate, or individual that would be influenced by it there? And what reason is
there to think it would have any greater effect upon the slaves than the late
law of Congress, which I approved, and which offers protection and freedom
to the slaves of rebel masters who come within our lines? Yet I cannot learn
that that law has caused a single slave to come over to us. And suppose they
could be induced by a proclamation of freedom from me to throw themselves
upon us, *what should we do with them?* How can we feed and care for such
a multitude? Gen. Butler wrote me a few days since that he was issuing more
rations to the slaves who have rushed to him than to all the white troops under his command. They *eat,* and that is all, though it is true Gen. Butler is
feeding the whites also by the thousand; for it nearly amounts to a famine
there. If, now, the pressure of the war should call off our forces from New
Orleans to defend some other point, what is to prevent the masters from

reducing the blacks to slavery again; for I am told that whenever the rebels take any black prisoners, free or slave, they immediately auction them off! They did so with those they took from a boat that was aground in the Tennessee river a few days ago. And then *I am very ungenerously attacked for it!* For instance, when, after the late battles at and near Bull Run, an expedition went out from Washington under a flag of truce to bury the dead and bring in the wounded, and the rebels seized the blacks who went along to help and sent them into slavery, Horace Greeley said in his paper that the Government would probably do nothing about it. What *could* I do? [Here your delegation suggested that this was a gross outrage on a flag of truce, which covers and protects all over which it waves, and that whatever he could do if *white* men had been similarly detained he *could* do in this case.]

3   "Now, then, tell me, if you please, what possible result of good would follow the issuing of such a proclamation as you desire? Understand, I raise no objections against it on legal or constitutional grounds; for, as commander-in-chief of the army and navy, in time of war, I suppose I have a right to take any measure which may best subdue the enemy. Nor do I urge objections of a moral nature, in view of possible consequences of insurrection and massacre at the South. I view the matter as a practical war measure, to be decided upon according to the advantages or disadvantages it may offer to the suppression of the rebellion."

4   Thus invited, your delegation very willingly made reply to the following effect; it being understood that a portion of the remarks were intermingled by the way of conversation with those of the President just given.

5   We observed (taking up the President's ideas in order) that good men indeed differed in their opinions on this subject; nevertheless *the truth was somewhere,* and it was a matter of solemn moment for him to ascertain it; that we had not been so wanting in respect, alike to ourselves and to him, as to come a thousand miles to bring merely *our opinion* to be set over against the *opinion* of other parties; that the memorial contained facts, principles, and arguments which appealed to the intelligence of the President and to his faith in Divine Providence; that he could not deny that the Bible denounced oppression as one of the highest of crimes, and threatened Divine judgments against nations that practice it; that our country had been exceedingly guilty in this respect, both at the North and South; that our just punishment has come by a slaveholder's rebellion; that the virus of secession is found wherever the virus of slavery extends, and no farther; so that there is the amplest reason for expecting to avert Divine judgments by putting away the sin, and for hoping to remedy the national troubles by striking at their cause.

6   We observed, further, that we freely admitted the probability, and even the certainty, that God would reveal the path of duty to the President as well as to others, provided he sought to learn it in the appointed way; but, as according to his own remark, Providence wrought by means and not miraculously, it might be, God would use the suggestions and arguments of other minds to secure that result. We felt the deepest personal interest in the

matter as of national concern, and would fain aid the thoughts of our President by communicating the convictions of the Christian community from which we came, with the ground upon which they were based.

That it was true he could not now enforce the Constitution at the South;   7 but we could see in that fact no reason whatever for not proclaiming emancipation, but rather the contrary. The two appealed to different classes; the latter would aid, and in truth was necessary to re-establish the former; and the two could be made operative together as fast as our armies fought their way southward; while we had yet to hear that he proposed to abandon the Constitution because of the present difficulty of enforcing it.

As to the inability of Congress to agree on this policy at the late ses-   8 sion, it was quite possible, in view of subsequent events, there might be more unanimity at another meeting. The members have met their constituents and learned of marvellous conversions to the wisdom of emancipation, especially since late reverses have awakened thought as to the extreme peril of the nation, and made bad men as well as good men realize that we have to deal with God in this matter. Men of the most opposite previous views were now uniting in calling for this measure.

That to proclaim emancipation would secure the sympathy of Europe   9 and the whole civilized world, which now saw no other reason for the strife than national pride and ambition, an unwillingness to abridge our domain and power. No other step would be so potent to prevent foreign intervention.

Furthermore, it would send a thrill through the entire North, firing   10 every patriotic heart, giving the people a glorious principle for which to suffer and to fight, and assuring them that the work was to be so thoroughly done as to leave our country free forever from danger and disgrace in this quarter.

We added, that when the proclamation should become widely known   11 (as the law of Congress has *not* been) it would withdraw the slaves from the rebels, leaving them without laborers, and giving us *both laborers and soldiers*. That the difficulty experienced by Gen. Butler and other Generals arose from the fact that *half-way measures could never avail*. It is the inherent vice of half-way measures that they create as many difficulties as they remove. It is folly merely to receive and feed the slaves. They should be welcomed and fed, and then, according to Paul's doctrine, that they who eat must work, be made to labor and to fight for their liberty and ours. With such a policy the blacks would be no incumbrance and their rations no waste. In this respect we should follow the ancient maxim, and learn of the enemy. What the rebels most fear is what we should be most prompt to do; and what they most fear is evident from the hot haste with which, on the first day of the present session of the Rebel Congress, bills were introduced threatening terrible vengeance if we used the blacks in the war.

The President rejoined from time to time in about these terms: 12

"I admit that slavery is the root of the rebellion, or at least its *sine qua*   13 *non*. The ambition of politicians may have instigated them to act, but they would have been impotent without slavery as their instrument. I will also concede that emancipation would help us in Europe, and convince them that we are incited by something more than ambition. I grant further that it would help *somewhat* at the North, though not so much, I fear, as you and those you represent imagine. Still, some additional strength would be added in that way to the war. And then unquestionably it would weaken the rebels by drawing off their laborers, which is of great importance. But I am not so sure we could do much with the blacks. If we were to arm them, I fear that in a few weeks the arms would be in the hands of the rebels; and indeed thus far we have not had arms enough to equip our white troops. I will mention another thing, though it meet only your scorn and contempt: There are fifty thousand bayonets in the Union armies from the Border Slave States. It would be a serious matter if, in consequence of a proclamation such as you desire, they should go over to the rebels. I do not think they all would—not so many indeed as a year ago, or as six months ago—not so many to-day as yesterday. Every day increases their Union feeling. They are also getting their pride enlisted, and want to beat the rebels. Let me say one thing more: I think you should admit that we already have an important principle to rally and unite the people in the fact that constitutional government is at stake. This is a fundamental idea, going down about as deep as any thing."

14   We answered that, being fresh from the people, we were naturally more hopeful than himself as to the necessity and probable effect of such a proclamation. The value of constitutional government is indeed a grand idea for which to contend; but the people know that *nothing else has put constitutional government in danger but slavery;* that the toleration of that aristocratic and despotic element among our free institutions was the inconsistency that had nearly wrought our ruin and caused free government to appear a failure before the world, and therefore the people demand emancipation to preserve and perpetuate constitutional government. Our idea would thus be found to go deeper than this, and to be armed with corresponding power. ("Yes," interrupted Mr. Lincoln, "that is the true ground of our difficulties.") That a proclamation of general emancipation, "giving Liberty and Union" as the national watch-word, would rouse the people and rally them to his support beyond any thing yet witnessed—appealing alike to conscience, sentiment, and hope. He must remember, too, that present manifestations are no index of what would then take place. If the leader will but utter a trumpet call the nation will respond with patriotic ardor. No one can tell the power of the right word from the right man to develop the latent fire and enthusiasm of the masses. ("I know it," exclaimed Mr. Lincoln.) That good sense must of course be exercised in drilling, arming, and using black as well as white troops to make them efficient; and that in a scarcity of arms it was at least worthy of inquiry whether it were not wise to place a portion of them in the hands of those nearest to the seat of the rebellion and able to strike the deadliest blow.

15   That in case of a proclamation of emancipation we had no fear of serious injury from the desertion of Border State troops. The danger was greatly

diminished, as the President had admitted. But let the desertions be what they might, the increased spirit of the North would replace them two to one. One State alone, if necessary, would compensate the loss, were the whole 50,000 to join the enemy. The struggle has gone too far, and cost too much treasure and blood, to allow of a partial settlement. Let the line be drawn at the same time between freedom and slavery, and between loyalty and treason. The sooner we know who are our enemies the better.

In bringing our interview to a close, after an hour of earnest and frank discussion, of which the foregoing is a specimen, Mr. Lincoln remarked: "Do not misunderstand me, because I have mentioned these objections. They indicate the difficulties that have thus far prevented my action in some such way as you desire. I have not decided against a proclamation of liberty to the slaves, but hold the matter under advisement. And I can assure you that the subject is on my mind, by day and night, more than any other. Whatever shall appear to be God's will I will do. I trust that, in the freedom with which I have canvassed your views, I have not in any respect injured your feelings." 16

ADDRESSING AUDIENCE

You think. You speak. You write. These activities suggest a sequence from private to public. You naturally keep many of your thoughts to yourself. Yet, people wonder about you if you talk to yourself. And, aside from chore lists and diary, you probably do not write to yourself. Both writing and speaking are expressive; they are signals to others about what you think, feel, and observe. Child psychologists indicate that at one stage of language development children are content to talk aloud whether they have listeners or not. Older children's speech matures by adjusting to a variety of audiences. In like manner, immature writers, especially in school, may complete assignments that express the writers' feelings with little regard for the reader. Self-expression is the main aim. If the aim is to produce what the teacher demands, students may comply with papers that are neither expressive nor communicative, but are merely wooden. Mature writers consider both what they need to say and to whom they say it to.

Clearly, because argument generally involves reader change, an effective argument is not written to oneself, but is a special kind of writing for others. Thus, the writer of argument must know something about his or her audience and use that knowledge, however limited or hypothetical, to shape the argument. Try to imagine an argument that does not assume an audience, listening or reading, being open to or resisting influence.

The subject for argument may be drawn from public or personal issues. Obviously, with such a variety of issues, you may find yourself in argument or agreement with a variety of audiences. Your audience may be general and large in number: Listen, world! Or it may be very specific and limited to a few or one: Dear Skeeter.

Before accepting or rejecting a subject for argument, you need to consider audience. Like you, individual readers have a complex identity that could be drawn as a circle with divisions. Depending on who they are and what facet of their identity you address, the subject you choose to argue may be important or not, comprehensible or not. You may have heard about American agricultural agents trying to sell tractors to nomadic tribes or frozen foods to Arctic dwellers—it is hard to imagine such audiences understanding the sales talk.

You have seen that sometimes an issue lies embedded in a context that has a dimension of value. Using styrofoam cups touches on environmental and economic values. So, even if the cup-use debate is local, it ripples outward. So, too, your audience expands as you consider cups in an expanded context. You can argue locally to change to paper on your campus, or you can argue for more recycling, including cups, and address audiences citywide, statewide, and beyond. A similar adjustment can be made when you come to an issue by way of value. Take, for example, the commandment "Thou shalt not kill." You can train this value on such local issues as whether to picket abortion clinics or what ought to be the proper punishment for a child who kills an abusive parent.

Audiences can be many or one. They can be reached by means of the local issue or the broad, even universal, value. They can be near or far, in this place, in this time, or elsewhere and in the future.

Often, your issue, your stand, and your support bring you to your natural opposites—those who are involved in the debate, yet are skeptical of your view. In such cases, argument is like a drama in which the writer has a well-defined role to play. The writer's tasks are clear. There is no need to cast out a lot of lines hoping for a nibble. The energy of the debate, of the writer's sense of the truth, and of an audience that needs to hear it, triggers engagement and motivates propounding and supporting a view.

EXERCISE 2.8 In *Common Sense,* Thomas Paine opposed peaceful means and urged Americans to take up arms against the British. His audience was a general one. Yet, in one edition of this popular pamphlet, Paine made a special appeal to Quakers, who on principle are pacifists. He especially addressed them about why they should be a part of an armed uprising.

For one argument subject you have worked with so far, sketch possible arguments for an audience of one person, an audience of one group, and a general audience. Note that you may change your thesis to make it exactly what you wish to say to the particular audience you are addressing.

Try to identify values and specifics useful in convincing these audiences. Sketch the three plans in your notebook.

Academic Audiences

For some academic arguments, you may need to plan for two audiences. If you write to the cafeteria manager about the use of styrofoam cups, that argument will be most likely read first—and certainly graded—by your instructor. You have two audiences: the ostensible one to whom the argument is addressed and the writing coach observing from the sidelines. You want to change the manager and show the instructor that your argument might change the manager. Other students reading that paper are not your primary audience, although you may benefit from their evaluations. The students will evaluate not as the manager would but as the instructor would.

Thankfully, most college arguments are not this complex. For a term paper or essay exam, you can assume the primary audience is the instructor and the secondary audience is anyone else interested in the subject. Interest is assumed, and the assertions of your arguments are judged in large measure by how effectively they are supported. Mina Shaughnessy, a pioneer in teaching writing to open-admissions college students, characterized the academic audience as "the least submissive of audiences, committed as it is, in theory at least, to the assessment of new and yet unproven interpretations of events." This is a high standard—perhaps, appropriate to upper division and graduate work—yet, a goal, nonetheless, of introductory work as well. Shaughnessy's "yet unproven" is equivalent to this book's "arguable" interpretation. She continues, "The writer is thus expected to make 'new' or arguable statements and then make a case for them, pushing his inquiry far enough to meet his audience's criteria for fullness and sound reasoning." Is this harder than meeting the criteria of a real-world cafeteria manager? I wonder. Your instructor may or may not agree with your thesis, but he or she is responsible for evaluating the potential effectiveness of your argument. The instructor reads not to be swayed by the argument but to evaluate it.

Let's take a breather—again with Mina Shaughnessy—and simplify the writer/reader relationship her way, because "a simple set of imagined responses from a [reader] may serve to generate a basic essay form." Imagine this dialogue:

READER'S DEMANDS	WRITER'S RESPONSES
What's your point?	Thesis statement
Prove it to me.	Evidence
So what?	Conclusion, application

Notice how the concept of audience helps produce argument. Sometimes you write easily when you imagine a reader responding to your writing. This imagined reader supplies cues about how you might unfold and link your thoughts, cues you do not pick up when you consult your own opinions without regard to audience. The cues might take the form of questions and requests, such as "Explain more about this" or "Where does this come from?"

EXERCISE 2.9 Use the exchange in the previous list to chart reader demands and writer responses in the arguments by Rich and Lifton.

Use the same exchange to summarize both sides of the discussion between Lincoln and the abolitionists.

Use this exchange to improve an argument plan of your own.

The following are two aids to help you plan for audience. The first aid is a set of questions that lets you see how your views and knowledge relate to audience.

QUESTIONS FOR PLANNING AUDIENCE CHANGE

- To whom are your views on this subject important?
- Do your views challenge others to change or to disagree?
- What do you already know or what can you find out that might support your views in a way that will change others?

The second aid is an argument model that is more specialized than the model of written communication presented in Chapter 1.

AN ARGUMENT MODEL

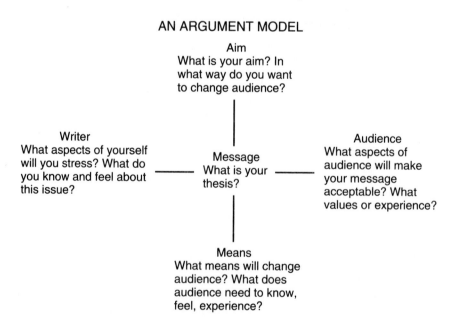

Aim
What is your aim? In what way do you want to change audience?

Writer
What aspects of yourself will you stress? What do you know and feel about this issue?

Message
What is your thesis?

Audience
What aspects of audience will make your message acceptable? What values or experience?

Means
What means will change audience? What does audience need to know, feel, experience?

As you plan your argument, you will fill in some parts of the model more easily than others. The model helps you to include all parts as you plan. Also, the model invites you to consider changing parts and to see how changing any one—audience, for example—may change others, too.

EXERCISE 2.10 As you develop a plan for an argument subject, write answers to the Questions for Planning Audience Change.

EXERCISE 2.11 For the same argument you used in Exercise 2.10, use the just-introduced Argument Model to help you plan the argument. Try to answer all the model's questions. You may want to use the model a second time with the same thesis, but with a different audience. Does using the model help you see argument components? Does it reveal the strengths and weaknesses of your plan?

Planning for Audience Change: Four Approaches

Over the centuries, much has been written about changing audiences— about how to appeal to their reason, their emotions, and their perception of the writer as a credible person. Such effort to define what moves readers is theoretical and still inconclusive, indicating the complexity of the task. Some definitions are cynical and opportunistic; some are hopeful and considerate. Any theory that claims to explain who readers are and what makes them tick is bound to be philosophical—to imply, if not state outright, a broad view of humankind.

The four theorists who will be presented in this section are important because they have helped form the rhetorical tradition that debates the question of how to change audience. Furthermore, these theorists offer some practical tools for causing change. Lastly, these four, although certainly different, provide approaches that use reasons as important parts of the argument. As you plan an argument, you honestly expect to change the audience. Let's consider now the kinds of change you might reasonably plan for.

First, you should reject what I spoof as the mini-max approach or "How I Changed the World in 500 Words!" It would be wonderful if a dime expenditure returned a dollar's profit. It would be great if your letters and memos brought about the changes you sought. Sometimes students get stuck in a naive hope: their short essay on the subject, even though it is a broad one, will open the matter and close it once and for all in several paragraphs. Such an essay will present the last word, implying the writer believes this small effort will trigger the desired change. It is unlikely in argument, or anything else, however, that a minimal effort will produce a maximum result. More likely, maximum efforts, even when repeated, result in small changes. You need to distinguish between wishing aloud and argument. Argument is usually subject to challenge from the skeptical reader. It is usually more difficult than it seems.

Kenneth Boulding Defines Aims

"Image" is Kenneth Boulding's word for our view of the world, for our experience of it. Image is the way we process our experience; it is not just a storehouse of moments. Our next experience—maybe reading an argument, maybe traveling to Bangladesh, maybe a close call on the highway—may change us or not. If an experience changes us, it may change us a little or a lot.

To Boulding, image resembles an atomic structure that is bombarded from outside. The bombardment includes particles that pass through the image, changing nothing—in one ear and out the other! You may hear the siren of a firetruck outside your window, but think nothing of it. Other particles strike the image with little effect. Maybe one tidbit adds to what you already know and upsets nothing. For example, did you know that "Northwest" once referred to land west of the Ohio River, including midwestern states? Or did you know that the word *opossum* comes from the Iroquois word meaning *white beast?* Both tidbits of information may be news to you but will change your image only a little.

Some particles will effect the clarity of what you know, not merely the amount. You will get a clearer or fuzzier picture, a stronger or shakier belief. For example, what happens when you learn about some professional's incompetence in a particular case? That particle may strengthen what you already suspect or it may shake a long-standing confidence. Such bits add and add—drifting in one direction, bringing greater clarity, greater doubt. When enough particles weigh in, you reach a point where your view of the person must change.

If by chance a single particle should strike the nucleus of the knowledge structure, it might cause reverberations, it might set off chain reactions, or it might force a major reconstruction. This type of experience is a conversion. Saul, an early persecutor of Christians, experienced a conversion on his way to Damascus. A light shone around him; he fell to the ground; he heard a voice demanding, "Why are you persecuting me?" He stood up, opened his eyes, and began his calling as a prominent Christian organizer and theologian: Paul. Saul's is a case of taking a direct hit from God! Think of experiences in your own life that have been formative, that turned you around so that afterwards you traveled in a new direction.

What practical use is Boulding's concept of image? The concept shows there are several ways to change a reader. As you learn about your readers, you can estimate what sorts of change your arguments might be designed for. Perhaps an argument will raise a doubt or strengthen a confidence. Perhaps more arguments need to follow the first. Members of Congress, we are told, do not read every letter but stay informed about how many letters favor a debated bill. Boulding shows the good sense of considering degrees of change. Consequently, not all your arguments need be equally ambitious. Nothing is wrong with modest aims. Your guide is "What is achievable?" And that means not "What can I write?" but "What might my audience accept?"

Boulding explains that the knowledge structure was not built in a day and most likely it will not be substantially changed in a day. Indeed, because image includes beliefs and values, readers most likely will not surrender them or willingly trade them for a new set. Boulding explains that image has hierarchies—low-level elements change, whereas higher-level elements remain in place. It is easier to change brand of toothpaste than religious faith, or to change wardrobe rather than friends.

Doesn't this hierarchy indicate something about making progress in argument? Some arguments proceed easily because the issue is not a high-level or core issue. Some issues are low-level or peripheral. People do not object to some changes, says Boulding, if such changes do not unsettle everything else. Image builds symmetry and stability. Whatever threatens these might be resisted. You should not assume, even if you think you have the best reasons, that your readers will accept them and be grateful to you.

Your estimate of what change is possible guides your selection of means to that end. Once you have defined your aim, then you examine how you will achieve it.

EXERCISE 2.12 Read Kenneth Boulding's Introduction to *The Image*. Then use Boulding's ideas about aim to describe the intentions of the arguments by Rich and Lifton. Are the writers' aims the same? Do these writers expect the same kinds of difficulties in changing audience? Record your answers in your notebook.

For your own argument and its possible audience, define aim. That is, define how you wish to change audience. Try using Kenneth Boulding's concepts of image and audience aims to describe what you want to achieve with audience. In your notebook, identify your thesis, your audience, your aim, and your estimate of difficulties in achieving your aim.

❖ Introduction to THE IMAGE

Kenneth Boulding

Kenneth Boulding (b. 1910) is an economist, educator, and writer. Boulding has had a distinguished teaching career at the University of Michigan and the University of Colorado. His belief in human betterment and his view of the world as a whole system motivate his efforts to combine economic theory with other social sciences. Boulding is an articulate pacifist and Quaker. In the Introduction to *The Image:*

Knowledge and Life in Society (1956), Boulding explains how inputs of information and value shape individuals. His theory has been used by speech and writing teachers to account for audience resistance and to help communicators set realistic aims for their writing and speaking.

1   As I sit at my desk, I know where I am. I see before me a window; beyond that some trees; beyond that the red roofs of the campus of Stanford University; beyond them the trees and the roof tops which mark the town of Palo Alto; beyond them the bare golden hills of the Hamilton Range. I know, however, more than I see. Behind me, although I am not looking in that direction, I know there is a window, and beyond that the little campus of the Center for the Advanced Study in the Behavioral Sciences; beyond that the Coast Range; beyond that the Pacific Ocean. Looking ahead of me again, I know that beyond the mountains that close my present horizon, there is a broad valley; beyond that a still higher range of mountains; beyond that other mountains, range upon range, until we come to the Rockies; beyond that the Great Plains and the Mississippi; beyond that the Alleghenies; beyond that the eastern seaboard; beyond that the Atlantic Ocean; beyond that is Europe; beyond that is Asia. I know, furthermore, that if I go far enough I will come back to where I am now. In other words, I have a picture of the earth as round. I visualize it as a globe. I am a little hazy on some of the details. I am not quite sure, for instance, whether Tanganyika is north or south of Nyasaland. I probably could not draw a very good map of Indonesia, but I have a fair idea where everything is located on the face of this globe. Looking further, I visualize the globe as a small speck circling around a bright star which is the sun, in the company of many other similar specks, the planets. Looking still further, I see our star the sun as a member of millions upon millions of others in the Galaxy. Looking still further, I visualize the Galaxy as one of millions upon millions of others in the universe.

2   I am not only located in space, I am located in time. I know that I came to California about a year ago, and I am leaving it in about three weeks. I know that I have lived in a number of different places at different times. I know that about ten years ago a great war came to an end, that about forty years ago another great war came to an end. Certain dates are meaningful: 1776, 1620, 1066. I have a picture in my mind of the formation of the earth, of the long history of geological time, of the brief history of man. The great civilizations pass before my mental screen. Many of the images are vague, but Greece follows Crete, Rome follows Assyria.

3   I am not only located in space and time, I am located in a field of personal relations. I not only know where and when I am, I know to some extent who I am. I am a professor at a great state university. This means that in September I shall go into a classroom and expect to find some students in it and begin to talk to them, and nobody will be surprised. I expect, what is perhaps even more agreeable, that regular salary checks will arrive from the

university. I expect that when I open my mouth on certain occasions people will listen. I know, furthermore, that I am a husband and a father, that there are people who will respond to me affectionately and to whom I will respond in like manner. I know, also, that I have friends, that there are houses here, there, and everywhere into which I may go and I will be welcomed and recognized and received as a guest. I belong to many societies. There are places into which I go, and it will be recognized that I am expected to behave in a certain manner. I may sit down to worship, I may make a speech, I may listen to a concert, I may do all sorts of things.

I am not only located in space and in time and in personal relationships, I am also located in the world of nature, in a world of how things operate. I know that when I get into my car there are some things I must do to start it; some things I must do to back out of the parking lot; some things I must do to drive home. I know that if I jump off a high place I will probably hurt myself. I know that there are some things that would probably not be good for me to eat or to drink. I know certain precautions that are advisable to take to maintain good health. I know that if I lean too far backward in my chair as I sit here at my desk, I will probably fall over. I live, in other words, in a world of reasonably stable relationships, a world of "ifs" and "thens," of "if I do this, then that will happen."

Finally, I am located in the midst of a world of subtle intimations and emotions. I am sometimes elated, sometimes a little depressed, sometimes happy, sometimes sad, sometimes inspired, sometimes pedantic. I am open to subtle intimations of a presence beyond the world of space and time and sense.

What I have been talking about is knowledge. Knowledge, perhaps, is not a good word for this. Perhaps one would rather say my *Image* of the world. Knowledge has an implication of validity, of truth. What I am talking about is what I believe to be true; my subjective knowledge. It is this Image that largely governs my behavior. In about an hour I shall rise, leave my office, go to a car, drive down to my home, play with the children, have supper, perhaps read a book, go to bed. I can predict this behavior with a fair degree of accuracy because of the knowledge which I have: the knowledge that I have a home not far away, to which I am accustomed to go. The prediction, of course, may not be fulfilled. There may be an earthquake, I may have an accident with the car on the way home. I may get home to find that my family has been suddenly called away. A hundred and one things may happen. As each event occurs, however, it alters my knowledge structure or my image. And as it alters my image, I behave accordingly. *The first proposition of this work, therefore, is that behavior depends on the image.*

What, however, determines the image? This is the central question of this work. It is not a question which can be answered by it. Nevertheless, such answers as I shall give will be quite fundamental to the understanding of how both life and society really operate. One thing is clear. The image is built up as a result of all past experience of the possessor of the image. Part of the image is the history of the image itself. At one stage the image, I suppose, consists of little else than an undifferentiated blur and movement. From the moment of birth if not before, there is a constant stream of messages entering the organism from the senses. At first, these may merely be undifferentiated lights and noises. As the child grows, however, they gradually become distinguished into people and objects. He begins to perceive himself as an object in the midst of a world of objects. The conscious image has begun. In infancy the world is a house and, perhaps, a few streets or a park. As the child grows his image of the world expands. He sees himself in a town, a country, on a planet. He finds himself in an increasingly complex web of personal relationships. Every time a message reaches him his image is likely to be changed in some degree by it, and as his image is changed his behavior patterns will be changed likewise.

8   We must distinguish carefully between the image and the messages that reach it. The messages consist of *information* in the sense that they are structured experiences. *The meaning of a message is the change which it produces in the image.*

9   When a message hits an image one of three things can happen. In the first place, the image may remain unaffected. If we think of the image as a rather loose structure, something like a molecule, we may imagine that the message is going straight through without hitting it. The great majority of messages is of this kind. I am receiving messages all the time, for instance, from my eyes and my ears as I sit at my desk, but these messages are ignored by me. There is, for instance, a noise of carpenters working. I know, however, that a building is being built nearby and the fact that I now hear this noise does not add to this image. Indeed, I do not hear the noise at all if I am not listening for it, as I have become so accustomed to it. If the noise stops, however, I notice it. This information changes my image of the universe. I realize that it is now five o'clock, and it is time for me to go home. The message has called my attention, as it were, to my position in time, and I have re-evaluated this position. This is the second possible effect or impact of a message on an image. It may change the image in some rather regular and well-defined way that might be described as simple addition. Suppose, for instance, to revert to an earlier illustration, I look at an atlas and find out exactly the relation of Nyasaland to Tanganyika. I will have added to my knowledge, or my image; I will not, however, have very fundamentally revised it. I still picture the world much as I had pictured it before. Something that was a little vague before is now clearer.

10   There is, however, a third type of change of the image which might be described as a revolutionary change. Sometimes a message hits some sort of nucleus or supporting structure in the image, and the whole thing changes in a quite radical way. A spectacular instance of such a change is conversion. A man, for instance, may think himself a pretty good fellow and then may

hear a preacher who convinces him that, in fact, his life is worthless and shallow, as he is at present living it. The words of the preacher cause a radical reformulation of the man's image of himself in the world, and his behavior changes accordingly. The psychologist may say, of course, that these changes are smaller than they appear, that there is a great mass of the unconscious which does not change, and that the relatively small change in behavior which so often follows intellectual conversion is a testimony to this fact. Nevertheless, the phenomenon of reorganization of the image is an important one, and it occurs to all of us and in ways that are much less spectacular than conversion.

The sudden and dramatic nature of these reorganizations is perhaps a 11 result of the fact that our image is in itself resistant to change. When it receives messages which conflict with it, its first impulse is to reject them as in some sense untrue. Suppose, for instance, that somebody tells us something which is inconsistent with our picture of a certain person. Our first impulse is to reject the proffered information as false. As we continue to receive messages which contradict our image, however, we begin to have doubts, and then one day we receive a message which overthrows our previous image and we revise it completely. The person, for instance, whom we saw as a trusted friend is now seen to be a hypocrite and a deceiver.

Occasionally, things that we see, or read, or hear, revise our concep- 12 tions of space and time, or of relationships. I have recently read, for instance, Vasiliev's *History of the Byzantine Empire*. As a result of reading this book I have considerably revised my image of at least a thousand years of history. I had not given the matter a great deal of thought before, but I suppose if I had been questioned on my view of the period, I would have said that Rome fell in the fifth century and that it was succeeded by a little-known empire centering in Constantinople and a confused medley of tribes, invasions, and successor states. I now see that Rome did not fall, that in a sense it merely faded away, that the history of the Roman Empire and of Byzantium is continuous, and that from the time of its greatest extent the Roman Empire lost one piece after another until only Constantinople was left; and then in 1453 that went. There are books, some of them rather bad books, after which the world is never quite the same again. Veblen, for instance, was not, I think, a great social scientist, and yet he invented an undying phrase: "conspicuous consumption." After reading Veblen, one can never quite see a university campus or an elaborate house in just the same light as before. In a similar vein, David Riesman's division of humanity into inner-directed and other-directed people is no doubt open to serious criticism by the methodologists. Nevertheless, after reading Riesman one has a rather new view of the universe and one looks in one's friends and acquaintances for signs of inner-direction or other-direction.

One should perhaps add a fourth possible impact of the messages on 13 the image. The image has a certain dimension, or quality, of certainty or uncertainty, probability or improbability, clarity or vagueness. Our image of the world is not uniformly certain, uniformly probable, or uniformly clear. Messages, therefore, may have the effect not only of adding to or of reorganizing the image. They may also have the effect of clarifying it, that is, of making something which previously was regarded as less certain more certain, or something which was previously seen in a vague way, clearer.

14   Messages may also have the contrary effect. They may introduce doubt or uncertainty into the image. For instance, the noise of carpenters has just stopped, but my watch tells me it is about four-thirty. This has thrown a certain amount of confusion into my mental image. I was under the impression that the carpenters stopped work at five o'clock. Here is a message which contradicts that impression. What am I to believe? Unfortunately, there are two possible ways of integrating the message into my image. I can believe that I was mistaken in thinking that the carpenters left work at five o'clock and that in fact their day ends at four-thirty. Or, I can believe that my watch is wrong. Either of these two modifications of my image gives meaning to the message. I shall not know for certain which is the right one, however, until I have an opportunity of comparing my watch with a timepiece or with some other source of time which I regard as being more reliable.

15   The impact of messages on the certainty of the image is of great importance in the interpretation of human behavior. Images of the future must be held with a degree of uncertainty, and as time passes and as the images become closer to the present, the messages that we receive inevitably modify them, both as to content and as to certainty.

16   The subjective knowledge structure or image of any individual or organization consists not only of images of "fact" but also images of "value." We shall subject the concept of a "fact" to severe scrutiny in the course of the discussion. In the meantime, however, it is clear that there is a certain difference between the image which I have of physical objects in space and time and the valuations which I put on these objects or on the events which concern them. It is clear that there is a certain difference between, shall we say, my image of Stanford University existing at a certain point in space and time, and my image of the value of Stanford University. If I say "Stanford University is in California," this is rather different from the statement "Stanford University is a good university, or is a better university than X, or a worse university than Y." The latter statements concern my image of values, and although I shall argue that the process by which we obtain an image of values is not very different from the process whereby we obtain an image of fact, there is clearly a certain difference between them.

17   The image of value is concerned with the *rating* of the various parts of our image of the world, according to some scale of betterness or worseness. We, all of us, possess one or more of these scales. It is what the economists call a welfare function. It does not extend over the whole universe. We do not now, for instance, generally regard Jupiter as a better planet than

Saturn. Over that part of the universe which is closest to ourselves, however, we all erect these scales of valuation. Moreover, we change these scales of valuation in response to messages received much as we change our image of the world around us. It is almost certain that most people possess not merely one scale of valuation but many scales for different purposes. For instance, we may say A is better than B for me but worse for the country, or it is better for the country but worse for the world at large. The notion of a hierarchy of scales is very important in determining the effect of messages on the scales themselves.

One of the most important propositions of this theory is that the value 18 scales of any individual or organization are perhaps the most important single element determining the effect of the messages it receives on its image of the world. If a message is perceived that is neither good nor bad it may have little or no effect on the image. If it is perceived as bad or hostile to the image which is held, there will be resistance to accepting it. This resistance is not usually infinite. An often repeated message or a message which comes with unusual force or authority is able to penetrate the resistance and will be able to alter the image. A devout Moslem, for instance, whose whole life has been built around the observance of the precepts of the Koran will resist vigorously any message which tends to throw doubt on the authority of his sacred work. The resistance may take the form of simply ignoring the message, or it may take the form of emotive response: anger, hostility, indignation. In the same way, a "devout" psychologist will resist strongly any evidence presented in favor of extrasensory perception, because to accept it would overthrow his whole image of the universe. If the resistances are very strong, it may take very strong, or often repeated messages to penetrate them, and when they are penetrated, the effect is a realignment or reorganization of the whole knowledge structure.

On the other hand, messages which are favorable to the existing image 19 of the world are received easily and even though they may make minor modifications of the knowledge structure, there will not be any fundamental reorganization. Such messages either will make no impact on the knowledge structure or their impact will be one of rather simple addition or accretion. Such messages may also have the effect of increasing the stability, that is to say, the resistance of unfavorable messages, which the knowledge structure or image possesses.

The stability or resistance to change of a knowledge structure also 20 depends on its internal consistency and arrangement. There seems to be some kind of principle of minimization of internal strain at work which makes some images stable and others unstable for purely internal reasons. In the same way, some crystals or molecules are more stable than others because of the minimization of internal strain. It must be emphasized that it is not merely logical consistency which gives rise to internal cohesiveness of a knowledge structure, although this is an important element. There are important qualities of a nonlogical nature which also give rise to stability. The structure may, for instance, have certain aesthetic relationships among the parts. It may represent or justify a way of life or have certain consequences which are highly regarded in the value system, and so on. Even in mathematics, which is of all knowledge structures the one whose internal consistency is most due to logic, is not devoid of these nonlogical elements. In the acceptance of mathematical arguments by mathematicians there are important criteria of elegance, beauty, and simplicity which contribute toward the stability of these structures.

21   Even at the level of simple or supposedly simple sense perception we are increasingly discovering that the message which comes through the senses is itself mediated through a value system. We do not perceive our sense data raw; they are mediated through a highly learned process of interpretation and acceptance. When an object apparently increases in size on the retina of the eye, we interpret this not as an increase in size but as movement. Indeed, we only get along in the world because we consistently and persistently disbelieve the plain evidence of our senses. The stick in water is not bent; the movie is not a succession of still pictures; and so on.

22   What this means is that for any individual organism or organization, there are no such things as "facts." There are only messages filtered through a changeable value system. This statement may sound rather startling. It is inherent, however, in the view which I have been propounding. This does not mean, however, that the image of the world possessed by an individual is a purely private matter or that all knowledge is simply subjective knowledge, in the sense in which I have used the word. Part of our image of the world is the belief that this image is shared by other people like ourselves who also are part of our image of the world. In common daily intercourse we all behave as if we possess roughly the same image of the world. If a group of people are in a room together, their behavior clearly shows that they all think they are in the same room. It is this shared image which is "public" knowledge as opposed to "private" knowledge. It follows, however, from the argument above that if a group of people are to share the same image of the world, or to put it more exactly, if the various images of the world which they have are to be roughly identical, and if this group of people are exposed to much the same set of messages in building up images of the world, the value systems of all individuals must be approximately the same.

23   The problem is made still more complicated by the fact that a group of individuals does not merely share messages which come to them from "nature." They also initiate and receive messages themselves. This is the characteristic which distinguishes man from the lower organisms—the art of conversation or discourse. The human organism is capable not only of having an image of the world, but of talking about it. This is the extraordinary gift of language. A group of dogs in a pack pursuing a stray cat clearly share an image of the world in the sense that each is aware to some degree of the

situation which they are all in, and is likewise aware of his neighbors. When the chase is over, however, they do not, as far as we know, sit around and talk about it and say, "Wasn't that a fine chase?" or, "Isn't it too bad the cat got away?" or even, "Next time you ought to go that way and I'll go this way and we can corner it." It is discourse or conversation which makes the human image public in a way that the image of no lower animal can possibly be. The term, "universe of discourse" has been used to describe the growth and development of common images in conversation and linguistic intercourse. There are, of course, many such universes of discourse, and although it is a little awkward to speak of many universes, the term is well enough accepted so that we may let it stay.

Where there is no universe of discourse, where the image possessed   24 by the organism is purely private and cannot be communicated to anyone else, we say that the person is mad (to use a somewhat old-fashioned term). It must not be forgotten, however, that the discourse must be received as well as given, and that whether it is received or not depends upon the value system of the recipient. This means that insanity is defined differently from one culture to another because of these differences in value systems and that the schizophrenic of one culture may well be the shaman or the prophet of another.

Up to now I have sidestepped and I will continue to sidestep the greater   25 philosophical arguments of epistemology. I have talked about the image. I have maintained that images can be public as well as private, but I have not discussed the question as to whether images are *true* and how we know whether they are true. Most epistemological systems seek some philosopher's stone by which statements may be tested in order to determine their "truth," that is, their correspondence to outside reality. I do not claim to have any such philosopher's stone, not even the touchstone of science. I have, of course, a great respect for science and scientific method—for careful observation, for planned experience, for the testing of hypotheses and for as much objectivity as semirational beings like ourselves can hope to achieve. In my theoretical system, however, the scientific method merely stands as one among many of the methods whereby images change and develop. The development of images is part of the culture or the subculture in which they are developed, and it depends upon all the elements of that culture or subculture. Science is a subculture among subcultures. It can claim to be useful. It may claim rather more dubiously to be good. It cannot claim to give validity.

In summation, then, my theory might well be called an organic theory   26 of knowledge. Its most fundamental proposition is that knowledge is what somebody or something knows, and that without a knower, knowledge is an absurdity. Moreover, I argue that the growth of knowledge is the growth of an "organic" structure. I am not suggesting here that knowledge is simply an arrangement of neuronal circuits or brain cells, or something of that kind. On the question of the relation between the physical and chemical structure of an organism and its knowledge structure, I am quite prepared to be agnostic. It is, of course, an article of faith among physical scientists that there must be somewhere a one-to-one correspondence between the structures of the physical body and the structures of knowledge. Up to now, there is nothing like empirical proof or even very good evidence for this hypothesis. Indeed, what we know about the brain suggests that it is an extraordinarily unspecialized and, in a sense, unstructured object; and that if there is a physical and chemical structure corresponding to the knowledge structure, it must be of a kind which at present we do not understand. It may be, indeed, that the correspondence between physical structure and mental structure is something that we will never be able to determine because of a sort of "Heisenberg principle" in the investigation of these matters. If the act of observation destroys the thing observed, it is clear that there is a fundamental obstacle to the growth of knowledge in that direction.

27   All these considerations, however, are not fundamental to my position. We do not have to conceive of the knowledge structure as a physico-chemical structure in order to use it in our theoretical construct. It can be inferred from the behavior of the organism just as we constantly infer the images of the world which are possessed by those around us from the messages which they transmit to us. When I say that knowledge is an organic structure, I mean that it follows principles of growth and development similar to those with which we are familiar in complex organizations and organisms. In every organism or organization there are both internal and external factors affecting growth. Growth takes place through a kind of metabolism. Even in the case of knowledge structures, we have a certain intake and output of messages. In the knowledge structure, however, there are important violations of the laws of conservation. The accumulation of knowledge is not merely the difference between messages taken in and messages given out. It is not like a reservoir; it is rather an organization which grows through an active internal organizing principle much as the gene is a principle or entity organizing the growth of bodily structures. The gene, even in the physico-chemical sense may be thought of as an inward teacher imposing its own form and "will" on the less formed matter around it. In the growth of images, also, we may suppose similar models. Knowledge grows also because of inward teachers as well as outward messages. As every good teacher knows, the business of teaching is not that of penetrating the student's defenses with the violence or loudness of the teacher's messages. It is, rather, that of co-operating with the student's own inward teacher whereby the student's image may grow in conformity with that of his outward teacher. The existence of public knowledge depends, therefore, on certain basic similarities among men. It is literally because we are of one "blood," that is, genetic constitution, that we are able to communicate with each other. We cannot talk to the ants or bees; we cannot hold conversations with them, although in a very real sense they communicate to us. It is the purpose of this work, therefore, to discuss the growth of images, both private and public, in

individuals, in organizations, in society at large, and even with some trepidation, among the lower forms of life. Only thus can we develop a really adequate theory of behavior.

Aristotle Defines Means

In the *Rhetoric,* Aristotle urged three methods of effective argument. He urged three because he thought that relying on one was not likely to succeed. Because he understood humans as complex beings, Aristotle thought they could be changed a number of ways. His three appeals address three human dimensions: our reason, our feelings, and our perception of the writer's character. He called these three *logos, pathos,* and *ethos.*

Aristotle, clearly, believed that people could be reached and changed. A speaker or writer could encourage change in audience by building a reasonable case, by stirring the emotions, and by presenting himself or herself believably. Aristotle urged people with good ideas to present their arguments using all three appeals. People, observed Aristotle, are not exclusively reasonable. One who argues with reason alone may lose to those using emotional and character appeals. Aristotle witnessed good ideas and good people losing to worse ideas and worse people. His *Rhetoric* supplies a wide range of methods, a toolbox to be drawn from, to sway audience as Aristotle believed they were swayed in real situations by a combination of logic, feeling, and confidence in the speaker.

EXERCISE 2.13 Identify the elements of *logos, pathos,* and *ethos* in the arguments by Berry (Chapter 1) and Dinesen (Chapter 2). For each essay, describe in your notebook how the elements are developed. Then use Aristotle's three means to help you plan your own argument. How do you expect to use support? How do you expect to use, or avoid the use of, emotion? How do you expect to present yourself as a believable person? Sketch your plan in your notebook.

Stephen Toulmin Defines Shared Assumptions

In *The Uses of Argument,* English philosopher Stephen Toulmin extends the Aristotelian tradition of examining the uses of logic in argument. According to Toulmin, a writer anticipates readers who are ready to oppose the argument but anticipates, as well, readers ready to acknowledge common ground.

Historically, the application of logic to argument has helped map the relationships between thesis and support. The mapping represents symmetry and cogency, often without representing the contending circumstances of arguments, where a moving argument may not be solely a logical one.

Toulmin views argument as a contest similar to a trial in court. The writer is like the lawyer who expects questioning from the opposing lawyer and scrutiny from the jurors. Toulmin creates a planning model that includes the writer's expectations of the readers' reactions, not merely the writer's best arrangement of ideas and support. Toulmin's plan combines logos and pathos; it links them so that the writer's efforts to write a logical argument result in an argument that actually moves readers.

Toulmin renovates the classical, three-part syllogism. He replaces the names of its terms with three new terms. A syllogism is made up of a major premise, a minor premise, and a conclusion:

Major Premise:	Any law that degrades human personality is unjust.
Minor Premise:	Segregation laws degrade human personality.
Conclusion:	Segregation laws are unjust.

The syllogism presents readers with a clear sequence of logical statements, but Toulmin is concerned that logic also be compelling to readers. Toulmin changes the syllogism terms. He renames the conclusion as *the claim*. He renames the minor premise as *the grounds*. Often these two elements make a short form of the argument: Segregation laws are unjust because segregation laws degrade human personality. Toulmin then points out that *the warrant*, the syllogism's major premise, can play a special role in making the argument compelling.

The warrant serves two functions. First, the warrant is an assumption readily shared by writer and reader and, thus, links both parties in agreement. Second, the warrant is a connection between the grounds of an argument and its claim, what you know commonly by the names support and thesis. The warrant guarantees that grounds and claim connect and mean something to readers. The warrant, "Any law that degrades human personality is unjust," may be shared by readers, who then accept a connection between claim and grounds.

TWO FUNCTIONS OF THE WARRANT

Linking Writers and Readers
                  Warrant
        Writer————————Readers

Linking Claim and Grounds
                  Warrant
        Writer's   Writer's
        Claim——————— Grounds

The warrant is an assumption that both writer and readers believe to be true or one that the writer with backing can convince readers to accept. The warrant builds bridges between argument components, between claim and grounds, between writer and readers.

Each of Toulmin's three major terms can be characterized by questions that help remind the writer that arguments need to go forward:

TOULMIN'S THREE MAJOR TERMS

Claim: What are you trying to prove?

Grounds: What do you have to go on?

Warrant: How will you get from your grounds to your claim? How will you get from your assertion of your claim to your readers' acceptance of your claim?

Here is another way to represent Toulmin's approach:

TOULMIN'S PLANNING MODEL

Since this support is true (*Grounds*) and if readers accept this shared assumption, (*Warrant*)

then readers will accept that this (*Claim*) is true.

For example, here is the model with its slots filled:

Since triple-trailer trucks are fuel-efficient, *and* *if* my readers assume that we need to cut fuel waste,

then my readers will accept that triple-trailers should be legal on our highways.

Notice that you can discover other grounds and other warrants to complete this plan for this claim:

Claim: Triple-trailer trucks should be legal on our highways

Grounds and Warrant: Because pollution will be reduced. (We need to reduce pollution.)

Grounds and Warrant: Because fewer trucks will clog our highways. (Our highways are already too crowded.)

Grounds and Warrant: Because only specially trained drivers will drive them. (Our highways should be safe for all to drive.)

Note that some warrants are immediately acceptable to some readers and some are not. This indicates that you will need to discover a warrant that is acceptable to the readers you address. And since warrants link grounds to claims, you will need to consider how your grounds allow certain warrants to be used.

Finally, to the terms *claim, ground,* and *warrant,* Toulmin adds three more to complete his model of argument:

TOULMIN'S THREE MINOR TERMS

Backing: If your readers do not accept your warrant, what can you present to them to make your assumption also their assumption? For example, how can you show that our society does need to cut fuel waste?

Qualifier: Do you need to limit the reach of your claim or warrant so it is stated accurately for your readers? For example, "Triple-trailer trucks should be legal on controlled-access highways." The writer does not want to argue about their use on all roads.

Conditions of Rebuttal: What exceptions to your claim or warrant do you expect your readers to bring up? Readers may know, for example, that not all triple-trailer trucks are fuel-efficient or that some of their drivers are not specially trained. Can you anticipate and be ready to answer such exceptions?

EXERCISE 2.14 In your notebook, define in a sentence or two what warrants are and explain how they are useful in argument.

For the following four sets of claims and grounds, provide the warrant that is implied:

a. You should not buy a rear-engined car. They are not safe.

b. Do not bother to register to vote. Your vote is only one of millions.

c. Do not use a computer to write your argument essays. There are ways to write much more friendly to the environment.

d. Walk your dog off the leash. Your dog needs to run and exercise.

Even without knowing Toulmin's terminology, you have no doubt written arguments that used warrants. Use the following questions to review one of your arguments and take notes in preparation for a class discussion of warrants in arguments. Is your warrant implied or clearly stated? Did you choose it so readers would find it acceptable? Did you use backing for it? Do you think the warrant was an effective part of the argument? Do you see how to make it even more effective?

You know that an argument addresses at least one difference separating writer and reader. By studying and sharpening this difference and others, you learn your tasks. You begin to see how you can assert a view and support it in such a way that you diminish that difference, drawing your audience toward you.

This emphasis on difference, so necessary for defining the task of argument, could distract you from your similarities, what you share in common. These commonalties may be useful in putting your differences into perspective; they may be useful, as Toulmin explains, in diminishing those differences. Here are some questions to help you assess how you are like and unlike your audiences.

QUESTIONS TO ASSESS WRITER-AUDIENCE COMMONALITIES

For any specific argument, use these questions to assess writer-audience commonalities:

Does the audience share my sense of the importance of the issue?

Does the audience know as I do the background of the issue?

Do we have any experience and knowledge that overlap? Have we worked together before?

Do we come to this issue with any shared values? Do we see the issue's history the same way? Do we hope for the same sort of future? Do we have common values that apply to other issues?

Do we share expectations about what argument is? What constitutes reasonable support?

Do we share conventions and traditions of language, organization, and style? Can I assume my way of presenting myself in language will be understood as I intend? How will I need to tailor my use of language to suit audience?

When you find these things in common, you have limited your differences and placed them, possibly, in a context of goodwill and trust.

Carl Rogers Defines Empathy

Operating from his experience as a therapist, Carl Rogers teaches that you often may not convince by good reasons. Rogers has had great influence on other therapists because of his novel approach to listening to clients and holding back his own advice until the client is ready to listen. Rogers has defined this listening as *empathic listening.* It is a type of listening basic to many contemporary discussions of communication between parent and child.

In practice, according to Rogers, your good reasons may threaten a reader because people resist change, even when they know change would be in their best interests. Twenty-four centuries ago, Aristotle defined people as political animals, members of a city-state or close-knit political community. No wonder he believed in the efficacy of reason, feeling, and the speaker's reputation and presentation. Rogers, aware of the effects of mass culture in our time, sees us as guarded creatures, easily isolated, easily threatened, afraid of being proved wrong and of losing. Rogers coaches communicators to appeal to the audience by building trust and mutual respect, an application, really, of Aristotle's emotional and ethical appeals. Rogers calls this appeal *empathy*. In an argument, you might first demonstrate your empathy for the readers' views, that you understand them without judging them. Rogers believes that when an audience feels it is understood, not evaluated or rebutted, it is likely to listen to the writer's views. In Argument Assignment Five, you will practice using empathy in an argument.

EXERCISE 2.15 Read Carl Rogers' "Dealing with Breakdowns in Communications." Take notes so you can summarize what Rogers presents as the major block to communication and his method of overcoming it. Even though Rogers offers no formula for writing argument, list what you feel an argument influenced by Rogers might look like. What Rogerian elements would it include? How might they be organized?

❖ DEALING WITH BREAKDOWNS IN COMMUNICATION

Carl Rogers

Carl Rogers (1902–1987) was a psychotherapist who developed client-centered or non-directive therapy. Rogers' innovations influenced his field. As a humanist, Rogers respected creativity and growth, which he believed could be best developed in each person by "unconditional positive regard." His ideas have been popular among counselors, teachers, and parents. *On Becoming a Person* (1961) sold over half a million copies. Taken from that book, his 1951 address to communications experts, "Dealing with Breakdowns in Communication," provides the foundation for a novel approach to argument that bears his name. Rogerian argument has aims and means unlike those of academic argument. Rogers proceeded differently with his audience because he had views fundamentally different from those of Aristotle and the rational tradition about how people listen and how people change.

1   It may seem curious that a person whose whole professional effort is devoted to psychotherapy should be interested in problems of communication. What relationship is there between providing therapeutic help to individuals with emotional maladjustments and the concern of this conference with obstacles to communication? Actually the relationship is very close indeed. The whole task of psychotherapy is the task of dealing with a failure in communication.

The emotionally maladjusted person, the "neurotic," is in difficulty first because communication within himself has broken down, and second because as a result of this his communication with others has been damaged. If this sounds somewhat strange, then let me put it in other terms. In the "neurotic" individual, parts of himself which have been termed unconscious, or repressed, or denied to awareness, become blocked off so that they no longer communicate themselves to the conscious or managing part of himself. As long as this is true, there are distortions in the way he communicates himself to others, and so he suffers both within himself, and in his interpersonal relations. The task of psychotherapy is to help the person achieve, through a special relationship with a therapist, good communication within himself. Once this is achieved he can communicate more freely and more effectively with others. We may say then that psychotherapy is good communication, within and between men. We may also turn that statement around and it will still be true. Good communication, free communication, within or between men, is always therapeutic.

It is, then, from a background of experience with communication in   2
counseling and psychotherapy that I want to present here two ideas. I wish to state what I believe is one of the major factors in blocking or impeding communication, and then I wish to present what in our experience has proven to be a very important way of improving or facilitating communication.

I would like to propose, as an hypothesis for consideration, that the ma-   3
jor barrier to mutual interpersonal communication is our very natural tendency to judge, to evaluate, to approve or disapprove, the statement of the other person, or the other group. Let me illustrate my meaning with some very simple examples. As you leave the meeting tonight, one of the statements you are likely to hear is, "I didn't like that man's talk." Now what do you respond? Almost invariably your reply will be either approval or disapproval of the attitude expressed. Either you respond, "I didn't either. I thought it was terrible," or else you tend to reply, "Oh, I thought it was really good." In other words, your primary reaction is to evaluate what has just been said to you, to evaluate it from *your* point of view, your own frame of reference.

Or take another example. Suppose I say with some feeling, "I think the   4
Republicans are behaving in ways that show a lot of good sound sense these days," what is the response that arises in your mind as you listen? The overwhelming likelihood is that it will be evaluative. You will find yourself agreeing, or disagreeing, or making some judgment about me such as "He must be a conservative," or "He seems solid in his thinking." Or let us take an illustration from the international scene. Russia says vehemently, "The treaty with Japan is a war plot on the part of the United States." We rise as one person to say "That's a lie!"

This last illustration brings in another element connected with my hy-   5
pothesis. Although the tendency to make evaluations is common in almost all interchange of language, it is very much heightened in those situations

where feelings and emotions are deeply involved. So the stronger our feelings, the more likely it is that there will be no mutual element in the communication. There will be just two ideas, two feelings, two judgments, missing each other in psychological space. I'm sure you recognize this from your own experience. When you have not been emotionally involved yourself, and have listened to a heated discussion, you often go away thinking, "Well, they actually weren't talking about the same thing." And they were not. Each was making a judgment, an evaluation, from his own frame of reference. There was really nothing which could be called communication in any genuine sense. This tendency to react to any emotionally meaningful statement by forming an evaluation of it from our own point of view, is, I repeat, the major barrier to interpersonal communication.

6   But is there any way of solving this problem, of avoiding this barrier? I feel that we are making exciting progress toward this goal and I would like to present it as simply as I can. Real communication occurs, and this evaluative tendency is avoided, when we listen with understanding. What does that mean? It means *to see the expressed idea and attitude from the other person's point of view, to sense how it feels to him, to achieve his frame of reference in regard to the thing he is talking about.*

7   Stated so briefly, this may sound absurdly simple, but it is not. It is an approach which we have found extremely potent in the field of psychotherapy. It is the most effective agent we know for altering the basic personality structure of an individual, and improving his relationships and his communications with others. If I can listen to what he can tell me, if I can understand how it seems to him, if I can see its personal meaning for him, if I can sense the emotional flavor which it has for him, then I will be releasing potent forces of change in him. If I can really understand how he hates his father, or hates the university, or hates communists—if I can catch the flavor of his fear of insanity, or his fear of atom bombs, or of Russia—it will be of the greatest help to him in altering those very hatreds and fears, and in establishing realistic and harmonious relationships with the very people and situations toward which he has felt hatred and fear. We know from our research that such empathic understanding—understanding *with* a person, not *about* him—is such an effective approach that it can bring about major changes in personality.

8   Some of you may be feeling that you listen well to people, and that you have never seen such results. The chances are very great indeed that your listening has not been of the type I have described. Fortunately I can suggest a little laboratory experiment which you can try to test the quality of your understanding. The next time you get into an argument with your wife, or your friend, or with a small group of friends, just stop the discussion for a moment and for an experiment, institute this rule. "Each person can speak up for himself only *after* he has first restated the ideas and feelings of the previous speaker accurately, and to that speaker's satisfaction." You see what this

would mean. It would simply mean that before presenting your own point of view, it would be necessary for you to really achieve the other speaker's frame of reference—to understand his thoughts and feelings so well that you could summarize them for him. Sounds simple doesn't it? But if you try it you will discover it one of the most difficult things you have ever tried to do. However, once you have been able to see the other's point of view, your own comments will have to be drastically revised. You will also find the emotion going out of the discussion, the differences being reduced, and those differences which remain being of a rational and understandable sort.

Can you imagine what this kind of an approach would mean if it were   9 projected into larger areas? What would happen to a labor-management dispute if it was conducted in such a way that labor, without necessarily agreeing, could accurately state management's point of view in a way that management could accept; and management, without approving labor's stand, could state labor's case in a way that labor agreed was accurate? It would mean that real communication was established, and one could practically guarantee that some reasonable solution would be reached.

If then this way of approach is an effective avenue to good communi-   10 cation and good relationships, as I am quite sure you will agree if you try the experiment I have mentioned, why is it not more widely tried and used? I will try to list the difficulties which keep it from being utilized.

In the first place it takes courage, a quality which is not too wide-   11 spread. I am indebted to Dr. S. I. Hayakawa, the semanticist, for pointing out that to carry on psychotherapy in this fashion is to take a very real risk, and that courage is required. If you really understand another person in this way, if you are willing to enter his private world and see the way life appears to him, without any attempt to make evaluative judgments, you run the risk of being changed yourself. You might see it his way, you might find yourself influenced in your attitudes or your personality. The risk of being changed is one of the most frightening prospects most of us can face. If I enter, as fully as I am able, into the private world of a neurotic or psychotic individual, isn't there a risk that I might become lost in that world? Most of us are afraid to take that risk. Or if we had a Russian communist speaker here tonight, or Senator Joe McCarthy, how many of us would dare to try to see the world from each of these points of view? The great majority of us could not *listen;* we would find ourselves compelled to *evaluate,* because listening would seem too dangerous. So the first requirement is courage, and we do not always have it.

But there is a second obstacle. It is just when emotions are strongest   12 that it is most difficult to achieve the frame of reference of the other person or group. Yet it is the time the attitude is most needed, if communication is to be established. We have not found this to be an insuperable obstacle in our experience in psychotherapy. A third party, who is able to lay aside his own feelings and evaluations, can assist greatly by listening with understanding to each person or group and clarifying the views and attitudes each holds. We have found this very effective in small groups in which contradictory or antagonistic attitudes exist. When the parties to a dispute realize that they are being understood, that someone sees how the situation seems to them, the statements grow less exaggerated and less defensive, and it is no longer necessary to maintain the attitude, "I am 100% right and you are 100% wrong." The influence of such an understanding catalyst in the group permits the members to come closer and closer to the objective truth involved in the relationship. In this way mutual communication is established and some type of agreement becomes much more possible. So we may say that though heightened emotions make it much more difficult to understand *with* an opponent, our experience makes it clear that a neutral, understanding, catalyst type of leader or therapist can overcome this obstacle in a small group.

13   This last phrase, however, suggests another obstacle to utilizing the approach I have described. Thus far all our experience has been with small face-to-face groups—groups exhibiting industrial tensions, religious tensions, racial tensions, and therapy groups in which many personal tensions are present. In these small groups our experience, confirmed by a limited amount of research, shows that this basic approach leads to improved communication, to greater acceptance of others and by others, and to attitudes which are more positive and more problem-solving in nature. There is a decrease in defensiveness, in exaggerated statements, in evaluative and critical behavior. But these findings are from small groups. What about trying to achieve understanding between larger groups that are geographically remote? Or between face-to-face groups who are not speaking for themselves, but simply as representatives of others, like the delegates at Kaesong? Frankly we do not know the answers to these questions. I believe the situation might be put this way. As social scientists we have a tentative test-tube solution of the problem of breakdown in communication. But to confirm the validity of this test-tube solution, and to adapt it to the enormous problems of communication-breakdown between classes, groups, and nations, would involve additional funds, much more research, and creative thinking of a high order.

14   Even with our present limited knowledge we can see some steps which might be taken, even in large groups, to increase the amount of listening *with*, and to decrease the amount of evaluation *about*. To be imaginative for a moment, let us suppose that a therapeutically oriented international group went to the Russian leaders and said, "We want to achieve a genuine understanding of your views and even more important, of your attitudes and feelings, toward the United States. We will summarize and resummarize these views and feelings if necessary, until you agree that our description represents the situation as it seems to you." Then suppose they did the same thing with the leaders in our own country. If they then gave the widest possible distribution to these two views, with the feelings clearly described but not expressed in name-calling, might not the effect be very great? It would not guarantee the

type of understanding I have been describing, but it would make it much more possible. We can understand the feelings of a person who hates us much more readily when his attitudes are accurately described to us by a neutral third party, than we can when he is shaking his fist at us.

But even to describe such a first step is to suggest another obstacle to   15
this approach of understanding. Our civilization does not yet have enough faith in the social sciences to utilize their findings. The opposite is true of the physical sciences. During the war when a test-tube solution was found to the problem of synthetic rubber, millions of dollars and an army of talent was turned loose on the problem of using that finding. If synthetic rubber could be made in milligrams, it could and would be made in the thousands of tons. And it was. But in the social science realm, if a way is found of facilitating communication and mutual understanding in small groups, there is no guarantee that the finding will be utilized. It may be a generation or more before the money and the brains will be turned loose to exploit that finding.

In closing, I would like to summarize this small-scale solution to   16
the problem of barriers in communication, and to point out certain of its characteristics.

I have said that our research and experience to date would make it appear that breakdowns in communication, and the evaluative tendency which   17
is the major barrier to communication, can be avoided. The solution is provided by creating a situation in which each of the different parties come to understand the other from the *other's* point of view. This has been achieved, in practice, even when feelings run high, by the influence of a person who is willing to understand each point of view empathically, and who thus acts as a catalyst to precipitate further understanding.

This procedure has important characteristics. It can be initiated by one   18
party, without waiting for the other to be ready. It can even be initiated by a neutral third person, providing he can gain a minimum of cooperation from one of the parties.

This procedure can deal with the insincerities, the defensive exagger-   19
ations, the lies, the "false fronts" which characterize almost every failure in communication. These defensive distortions drop away with astonishing speed as people find that the only intent is to understand, not judge.

This approach leads steadily and rapidly toward the discovery of the   20
truth, toward a realistic appraisal of the objective barriers to communication. The dropping of some defensiveness by one party leads to further dropping of defensiveness by the other party, and truth is thus approached.

This procedure gradually achieves mutual communication. Mutual   21
communication tends to be pointed toward solving a problem rather than toward attacking a person or group. It leads to a situation in which I see how the problem appears to you, as well as to me, and you see how it appears to me, as well as to you. Thus accurately and realistically defined, the problem is almost certain to yield to intelligent attack, or if it is in part insoluble, it will be comfortably accepted as such.

22   This then appears to be a test-tube solution to the breakdown of communication as it occurs in small groups. Can we take this small scale answer, investigate it further, refine it, develop it and apply it to the tragic and well-nigh fatal failures of communication which threaten the very existence of our modern world? It seems to me that this is a possibility and a challenge which we should explore.

EXERCISE 2.16 With classmates who disagree, discuss an issue and use Rogers' "little laboratory experiment" (paragraph 8) as you exchange views.

Discover whether the experiment works as Rogers claims. In your notebook, describe how such an assurance of good listening and suspension of criticism could be used in written form.

This section on addressing audience has explored just the edges of the major questions of any study of argument: Do people change? How do they change? Can I foster and direct their change? You have seen it is easy to over-estimate your ability to persuade. It is easy, also, to write in haste before considering your audience. Every argument challenges you to analyze its components: writer, audience, aims, and means. Discussion of these components thus far has presented you with many options and has encouraged you to choose from them sensitively and shrewdly. In the next chapter, you will learn how to develop and organize the rational appeal used widely in academic and professional writing.

EXERCISE 2.17 Try to remember an issue on which you have changed your mind. Did other people's words, intentionally or unintentionally, cause that change? Do such methods of using words, then, generally move readers and listeners?

Return to the Lincoln selection in this chapter. Consider how the abolitionists tried to change Lincoln. Was Lincoln susceptible to their appeals? What made Lincoln hesitate at that time to proclaim emancipation? Can you infer what it would have taken to get Lincoln to agree? Record your responses for use in class discussion.

ARGUMENT ACTIVITIES

1. Use these four steps to examine an argument in a newspaper or magazine.
   Step One: State what the argument is about.
   Step Two: State it as an issue.
   Step Three: Identify the writer's position.
   Step Four: Identify support for this position.

2. What arguments have you been engaged in that
   Focused on an important issue?
   Focused on an issue whose importance was questionable?
   Drew upon important values of yours?
   Were part of a larger debate, perhaps involving well-known spokespersons and opposing viewpoints already staked out?

3. Formulate issue questions and position statements for the following topics. Formulate at least one reason for each position, then discover a warrant for each thesis/reason or claim/grounds pair.
   • Smoking in public places
   • Identifying AIDS carriers
   • Neutering dogs and cats
   • Allowing women in combat roles
   • Seeking minority representation on the Supreme Court
   • Allowing self-service gas stations
   • Other?

4. Try each of these explorations to discover more about your values and their application to argument.

   Personal Survey Adapted from Carol Bly
   List two values that make life good.
   Identify your first encounter with them.
   List two values that make life hurtful.
   Identify your first encounter with them.
   Name values that as a child you expected to last forever that have actually disappeared from your adult life. List them.

   Personal Survey Adapted from Aristotle
   We argue for the good, against the bad. We argue for the just, the beautiful, the useful and against the unjust, the ugly, the useless. In what situations are good values needing bolstering? What arguments can you make for a specific good?

5. List five ready-made national issues. List five local or personal issues. Can you state them as "should" questions?

6. Can you remember underestimating the complexity of a situation? What happened? How did you discover that you had sized up the situation incorrectly? What did you do to correct your view?

7. What are some complex issues that do not allow for certainty but may demand response and even action? Is there any way to make progress toward agreement on such issues?

8. Discuss an argument aim you plan to achieve by referring to Boulding's image, especially
   Expected change in audience
   Expected resistance to change

9. Think of public arguments that have actually been won, such as our acceptance of the inter-connectedness of the ecological view of our planet. What allowed such arguments to succeed? What impeded them? Refer your discussion to

   Boulding's concept of hierarchy in the image
   Aristotle's three appeals
   Toulmin's shared assumptions
   Rogers' empathy

10. You may begin work on Assignment One, Assignment Two, or Assignment Three in the section of this book entitled Argument Assignments. These are assignments in writing whole essays about issues of your choice. Complete instructions and successful student examples are included with each assignment.

11. You should begin a notebook to save materials for later use, including:
    - Notes from lectures, class discussions, and readings
    - Responses to this textbook's exercises and activities
    - Clippings or copies of arguments and your comments on them
    - Plans for and sketches of your own argument paper assignments

CHAPTER THREE
BUILDING THE ARGUMENT

This chapter is designed to assist the writer who is ready to assert an argument thesis and to begin writing the argument. At this point, you may ask, "How do I find materials addressing the issue I am interested in? How do I use them? Do they clarify or challenge my thesis? Do they support it? How might I organize them?"

Perhaps, in your experience of the writing process, these questions crop up even as you search for an issue or, once you have chosen an issue, before you have formulated your position as a thesis. Often, the writing process is spiral-like rather than linear. In searching for issues and positions, you may consider possible support. In searching for support, for authoritative and compelling material, you reconsider your position on the issue, examining whether or not it is supportable. This shuttling activity is not unusual for the writer who must sometimes write in order to discover what he or she knows or wants to say. Few architects build bridges this way to learn what they might build, but a writer can and often does build an argument this way.

Recognizing, then, that these questions may not always present themselves at the same point in the writing process and that they may crop up in exploratory writing and again in revision, let's examine them now.

BEING INFORMED

You need to be informed about the issue to determine what you know and believe. You need to search for abundant, varied debate to test your hunches and confirm your viewpoints. Listening to such debate, you make use of voices that oppose you and support you. You modify your thesis so that it expresses your best understanding of the issue, creating a thesis that you can support. Then, being informed, you can address readers with debate materials that allow them to understand, respect, and even believe your argument.

You can become informed through recollection and research. Recollection is memory work; it begins with yourself. What do you already know? What personal experience and values support your thesis? What travel, hobbies, or jobs provide you with materials to collect? What courses have you taken or texts have you read? Perhaps you have filled notebooks or written papers that contain pertinent information. How can they be mined for support?

Once you have exhausted your recollections, start to research support for your thesis. Research extends recollection and adds to the breadth of debate on the issue. You may do some reading early in the writing process to find a workable issue and to become informed about it. Such reading should introduce you to a variety of views and allow you to understand them. Such reading may help you to limit your concern to part of an issue or sub-issue that is the right size for a short argument.

EXERCISE 3.1   Turn to Assignment One in the Argument Assignments section of this book. This assignment explains a method of using reading and note taking to explore an issue.

Try a short version of this assignment with two or more essays arguing about the same issue. Your instructor may provide you with the articles or you may find articles in magazines, newspapers, or casebooks such as those in *The Reference Shelf* and *Opposing Viewpoints*. What agreements and differences exist between them? Which argument is more complete and more compelling? What additional materials do you need to be convinced by either argument?

For any of the following exercises, you may wish to use your notebook to record responses and notes. Many of the exercises help you prepare for the fuller writing assignments in this book's Argument Assignments section. It is not too early in the course to be considering issues and approaches for these later assignments.

Once your thesis is established, then research becomes pointed: you read to find what information supports, questions, and refutes your position. You take notes on *all* this information. First, you need to confirm your thesis. Second, you need to gather a variety of support for the thesis. Third, you need to build responses to the opposition you anticipate from your readers because of the views and values they hold. You need to anticipate their questions and objections. You can develop warrants. You can present your reasons with a good awareness of audience needs and skepticism. You can develop a refutation that answers audience criticism directly. Reason tells you, even at a late stage in preparing the argument, that you may have to discard your thesis if recollection and research come up with meager support or with overwhelming evidence against your position.

EXERCISE 3.2   Define in your notebook an argument task with an issue and audience. What is your thesis? What support do you already have? What support do you expect to find in sources? Considering your audience, can you define a warrant or warrants to bridge between your thesis and support? State the warrant or warrants. Then, for each warrant, as you just did for your thesis, list both the support you have and the support you wish to search for.

For example, suppose your thesis is "We should permit triple-trailer trucks on the road because they are extremely safe." What support is there for this thesis? Given an audience of everyday drivers, you can name the warrant: "People want driving to be safe." What support establishes this warrant? That citizens recently passed a seat belt law? That speed limits are generally observed? That car buyers are willing to pay extra for air bags and anti-lock brakes?

Finding Resources

Resources of information abound. For many issues there is more than enough material to help you enter the debate and formulate a supportable thesis. The following resources are common to college libraries, even small ones, and are formatted to allow you to understand contrasting views.

Casebooks that include background and pro and con articles are available on many issues. You can find discussions of smaller issues within such collections. Two such casebook series are *Opposing Viewpoints* and *The Reference Shelf*. Look for the series name in the title section of the card catalog. Each series has fifty or more titles. Under that series name will be listed the titles of all the volumes. Representative topics include energy conservation, the welfare debate, and immigration. For each issue, look for related or sub-issues that are part of the larger issue.

Three other resources present periodical reprints or research derived from periodicals. *The Social Issues Resource Series (SIRS)* groups magazine article reprints by subject. Each binder has a useful index of subheadings and appropriate reprints. This series helps get materials directly into your hands; it enables you to avoid having to search for periodical literature in indexes and on the library shelves. Usually, *SIRS* is in the reference section and cannot be checked out. Sample binder titles include Alcohol, Consumerism, Habitat, Defense, Death and Dying, and Corrections.

The reference section of some libraries contains issues of *The CQ Researcher* (*Editorial Research Reports* before 1991), weekly research reports of about 12,000 words that address narrowly focused, timely issues. Each report sketches background, presents the current debate, forecasts the outlook, and provides bibliographies of the articles used in the report and of additional articles from current periodicals. Recent issues have reported on eating disorders, underage drinking, prescription drug prices, and infant mortality.

Finally, you may be familiar with *Annual Editions,* a publication sometimes used as a reader for lower division courses in the social sciences and business. These volumes are very broad in their coverage—with titles in psychology, geography, criminal justice, and business and management—but they can be useful in defining issues and providing background.

These three sources may be the first stops before you begin to seek additional information in books and periodicals at large. For short arguments, they may be the last stop, too. Do not overlook the assistance offered by the textbooks you use. Most of them include bibliographies and may mention materials that explore issues. Some include pro and con readings. Teachers and librarians on campus can also help direct you to sources, as can professional agencies off campus.

A note of caution about the library: Beware of the naive view that the library has the answer or the truth—just the information you need to support your argument. The library's rich materials can only become your truth or your answer if you work with them as a critical reader, questioner, and evaluator. "I'm going to the library" should trigger curiosity and criticism: You will find much to grapple with; some of it will not be directly helpful, although you may be able to survey an issue broadly and get a clear sense of what thesis you can support.

A survey of library materials on an issue can help you plan and focus. Once you have collected material on the issue—have become informed and then formed a tentative thesis—you may focus exclusively on debate limited to that thesis. The more you bring to the library of your doubts, beliefs, curiosity, and energy, the more you will accomplish. When you carry little or nothing to the library, you run the risk of finding little or nothing there!

EXERCISE 3.3   Find sources discussing an issue that interests you, one you may already have taken a stand on. Consider a mix of books, periodicals, and TV and radio programs that you might check for information. Think of people you might interview. They may provide you with materials or inform you about how to obtain them. List these sources in your notebook. Indicate how you might use these resources to refine and support your thesis.

USING AVAILABLE SUPPORT

The task of supporting your views can sometimes seem overwhelming. Indeed, what do you really know? Can you support your position? What support will convince your readers? Mina Shaughnessy, in *Errors and Expectations,* defines the challenge of writing argument and two related problems:

Probably the most important point to be made about statements of opinion or judgment is that they must be backed up by some kind of evidence or support which assures the reader that what is being said to be true of the real world is indeed true.

Two sorts of problems can arise in this kind of assignment. First, the student lacks information and cannot therefore make his case even though he suspects that a good one might be made. Second, the student is uncertain of how much evidence he needs to make his point with an academic audience.

For most issues, in most situations where values are contested, you can only imagine the complete argument—all or most of the information needed to make a case and, hence, more than enough to convince the reader. Somewhere between the enfeebled position of knowing too little and convincing no one and the opposite extreme of knowing everything and wowing everybody, you address your readers. This vast, uncertain territory is the ground of argument. It is the place where you and others are, indeed, moved to work out your positions and build your cases. Feeling uninformed motivates you to become informed. Feeling uncertain about convincing others motivates you to gather and relate support.

Aristotle believed that in courts, legislature, and academies, people could do no more than use the available arguments—those supports that they recollected from their experience and collected from others' experience. An effective argument need not offer every conceivable support, but should include the support available by some self-searching and some research. Remember that argument is functional; its success is not measured against an ideal (thesis first, 500 words, three sources). An argument succeeds to the extent it changes audience. Hardly ever is exhaustive support demanded. Instead, the writer of effective arguments selects and organizes evidence to sway readers.

And, remember, before you can sway others, you must get their attention and consideration. You strive to be clear. You strive to get a fair hearing and even respect for your efforts. These are worthy aims. Your being daunted by a complex task may be seasoned by this reminder: As you argue, you draw from what is available to you. You are not required to know everything or to present everything you know, just as you are not required to address everyone.

EXERCISE 3.4 Return to the two Rachel Carson selections and the Aldo Leopold essay in Chapter 1. Both of these writers develop a new position on their subjects because they become better informed than they once were. For each writer, state in your notebook the original thesis and then the revised thesis. Identify the new experience or information that changed their views.

For his essay, also in Chapter 1, Wendell Berry appears certain and un-changeable. Speculate on what additional information might change Berry's mind. Try to be specific in your notebook responses.

EXERCISE 3.5   Read the article "Rock Music." Discuss how authors John Gibbons and Steven Schlossman make use of available arguments. How do these scientists make new materials available for their consideration? How do they use such materials to test and support their thesis about the musical rocks? As you consider their article, write your observations in your notebook.

❖ ROCK MUSIC

John Gibbons and Steven Schlossman

John Gibbons and Steven Schlossman published "Rock Music" in *Natural History* in 1970. The article attempts to explain the mystery of certain rocks that, when struck, emit a ringing note. Gibbons and Schlossman refute earlier theories and pro-pose their own explanation. As scientists writing for a general audience, Gibbons and Schlossman explain more than the rocks; they demonstrate how scientists begin with a question, propose a hypothesis, test that hypothesis, and establish a thesis. They also make it clear that they benefitted by crossing scientific disciplines and collaborating with others. Although the argument assignments in this book do not require field studies and laboratory testing, from this article you can learn to ap-preciate scientific questioning and research. Your own efforts in defining your posi-tion on an issue and in searching for support can be guided by similar care and clearsightedness.

1   On a June day in 1890, Dr. J. J. Ott played several musical selections for the Buckwampum Historical Society in Bucks County, Pennsylvania. He was ac-companied by a brass band, but, in the words of one who was there "the clear, bell-like tones" he was playing "could be heard above the notes of the horns." What made the concert different was that Dr. Ott was making music by hitting boulders with a hammer.

2   Dr. Ott had put together an octave of ringing rocks from a boulder field in Bridgeton, one of many dotting eastern Pennsylvania and western New Jersey. The peculiar ability of the rocks in some of the fields to ring like a bell had been known long before, but not until 1965 was a serious attempt made to find out why.

3   Local myths about the boulder fields abound to this day. Little is known about the Indians' opinions, but many early settlers apparently at-tributed the boulder accumulations to the aborigines themselves. A vague picture of the fields as ceremonial sites built by the Indians runs through

many accounts. Nearly all the explanations, in fact, call upon man or some supernatural force for the genesis of the fields; natural origins are rejected altogether. Other explanations invoke witchcraft, arguing that the fields are either the site of a great curse or are areas possessed by witches. The fields have been called the ruins of ancient civilizations, the landing sites of spacecraft from alien planets, and almost anything else that comes to mind. One local maintained that the WPA piled the rocks in a "make-work" effort.

The common thread through most of the region's mythology appears to be a rejection of natural origins for the fields. The failure of science, through some sixty years of intermittent investigation, to provide any better answers must have helped to confirm that idea. Although the fields may have been visited by naturalists long before, the first comprehensive description was not published until 1909.　　4

The ringing rocks fields are not very different from the other boulder fields in the area. Irregular clearings of ten to fifteen acres in the predominantly hardwood forest, the fields are floored by loosely piled boulders varying in size from one to fifteen feet in diameter. The boulders are made up of a dark igneous rock called diabase that is about 180 million years old. There is no soil between the boulders in the field, and they lie on a sloping bedrock surface of the same rock type. Some worts and lichens are the only plants to be found there. The absence of soil to retain rainfall makes the presence of rooted plants impossible. The microclimate of the area has been aptly described as desertlike.　　5

The boulders themselves are usually flat, and their exposed surfaces are often stained reddish by iron oxides. Weathering has sculptured the upper surfaces into a pitted and grooved pattern. The surrounding forest floor contains boulders similar in size and composition to those in the boulder fields. Outside the fields, however, the boulders do not ring, have no reddish stains, and display a peculiar "crazed," or cracked, pattern on their surfaces. One of the persistent observations about the boulders is that they cease to ring if they are removed from the fields.　　6

B. F. Fackenthal published the first scholarly work on the ringing rocks (1909 and 1919). Fackenthal was a naturalist of the breed responsible for much of the early description and exploration of this country. A natural scientist of broad interest and great curiosity, his description of the ringing rocks fields is an interesting and wonderfully informative work. In the 1919 volume of the Bucks County Historical Society Proceedings, he wrote about the geologic setting of the area, and about the then-current explanations of the phenomenon. Venturing a guess of his own about the ringing phenomenon, he said:　　7

"The ringing properties are doubtless due to the texture of the diabase of which they are composed, but why some should respond with a ring and others lying alongside are non-resonant, does not to my mind fully appear.　　8

They were doubtless cooled or annealed differently and therefore the crystalization may have been different."

9   Little more was written about ringing rocks for the next forty-five years, but boulder fields in general were studied enough to be considered a well-understood phenomenon.

10   Boulder fields of the kind found in the Bucks County area are not particularly uncommon throughout the temperate and arctic regions of the world. Under climatic conditions that feature severe temperature variation above and below freezing, along with enough rain or snowfall to keep the ground wet, frost action can easily produce such boulder fields, or *felsenmeer* (literally "stone seas"), as they are called in Europe. Water soaking into the bedrock surface expands upon freezing and breaks up that surface. Frost heave, the movements produced in soil by freezing and thawing, tends to move the boulders toward the surface. If the climate is severe enough to prevent plant cover from developing, the soil may eventually be flushed away by summer rains. The result is a boulder-covered bedrock surface with little or no soil.

11   Huge expanses of boulder-carpeted terrain may be seen today above timberline in most mountainous regions. These *felsenmeer* are more or less permanent features in those regions of high altitude or high latitude having rigorous climates. How, then, can they be related to the temperate, humid climate of the middle Atlantic region? The answer lies in the history of the last Ice Age. Although the glaciers that last retreated from the area about 12,000 years ago never extended to the actual site of the ringing rocks fields, their presence profoundly affected the area's climate. The nearest ice masses are thought to have occurred only about twenty miles northwest of the site. This places the boulder fields well within the range of periglacial, or near glacial, climatic effects. The areas marginal to the glaciers experienced rigorous climates quite analogous to high alpine climates.

12   G. Gordon Connalley, a glacial geologist, proposes that all of the region's hillslopes were shattered by severe frost action during glaciation. After the glaciers retreated and the climate returned to its present state, the boulder seas were gradually reclaimed by the forests. The fields still in existence are the last remnants of once extensive *felsenmeer*. Even these remnants are being encroached upon by the forest. The trees near the edges of the field are younger than the rest of the surrounding forest, and in some places the boundaries are blurred by the advance of shrubs and vines into the fields.

13   In general, none of these ideas about the origin of boulder fields is new. Most geologists have long agreed that most fields originated in the way just outlined. The trick is to explain why the ringing boulders ring.

14   In 1965 Richard Faas, an oceanographer and geologist from nearby Lafayette College, and John Flocks, a student, took up the problem. Faas and Flocks were interested in problems of sound travel in rocks. This interest arose from Faas's studies of sound travel in ocean bottom sediments.

Faas and Flocks demonstrated that the audible tone produced by a   15
blow on a ringing boulder was the product of interference between several
subaudible resonant frequencies. That is, when struck, the boulder vibrates
at several frequencies. None of these frequencies is audible, but the sum of
the interfering and interacting frequencies produces a tone that can be heard
by the human ear. The subaudible vibrations have unusual frequencies
(cycles per second) and attenuation (duration) for rock materials. Faas and
Flocks also pointed out that the tones produced showed some correlation
with boulder size.

We became interested in the problem through Faas and several teach-   16
ing trips to the fields. Our field observations, added to Faas's sonic data, led
us to a tentative hypothesis about the ringing boulders and eventually to a
systematic study. The ringing boulders often spall (flat chips break off from
the surface) when tapped lightly with a hammer. These spalls are surprisingly energetic, sometimes flying past one's ear with a humming sound. If a
ringing boulder, which is very tough, is broken apart with a sledge hammer,
it soon stops ringing altogether. Such breaks produce a peculiar surface pattern often seen in metals that have broken under large internal stresses. The
boulders are unusually absorbent when wet. The outer inch or so of most of
the boulders is noticeably altered in color and texture by weathering, and that
altered zone soaks up water at a surprising rate.

Formation of a workable hypothesis, one that would form a solid foun-   17
dation for research, is a critical matter in such a project. If the hypothesis is
carefully thought out, it has an organizing effect on the whole effort. It is necessary to begin with a question—in this case: Why do the ringing rocks ring?
The next step is to assemble all available information. This information can
then be used to weed out the most likely answer or answers. Once a test hypothesis has been chosen, it is important to state it in the simplest and most
concise terms possible. When that is done the questions needed to test the
hypothesis become clear almost automatically. If the questions are answered
in the affirmative, that is, if the correct hypothesis was chosen, then interpretation of the impact of the hypothesis on other, related questions is the final step.

In the case of the ringing rocks the process went something like this.   18
Question: Why do the boulders ring? Information: The rocks were very energetic (spalling, fracture type); they resonated at a frequency different from
the "natural" frequency; and there was something unusual about the fields'
dry and exposed environment that seemed to produce or at least localize the
abnormal resonance. Our search for a hypothesis seemed to lead back each
time to one focus: How can the resonant frequency of rock be altered by a
natural process?

All materials have what may be called a natural resonant frequency.   19
That is, because of its atomic structure any material has one vibration

frequency at which it resonates, or responds harmonically, to its own vibration. Natural resonance is a well-defined concept that has been thoroughly studied by metallurgists and engineers. The natural resonance of crystalline substances, such as minerals, depends primarily upon the strength of the atomic bonds and upon the atomic spacing.

20   The most feasible way of changing the resonant frequency of a material is to subject it to an elastic strain. Elastic strains are impermanent changes in the shape or size of a body. That is, if a body is elastically strained and the stress is removed, the body returns to its original shape or size. Elastic strain involves no breaking or rearranging of atomic bonds. Rather, the material changes shape by what can be thought of as stretching the bonds. When the stress is removed, the bonds rebound, returning the atomic structure to its original position. While the bonds are stretched, however, the resonant frequency of the material is changed because the atomic spacing is altered. A good example of this principle is the old musical saw act from vaudeville days. The musician changed the tone of the saw by bending (elastically straining) the saw while he stroked it with a violin bow.

21   Now we can modify our original question: Why do the ringing rocks ring? If elastic strain is the most easily visualized means of changing the resonant frequency of a body, the question can be rewritten: Do the ringing rocks ring because they are somehow under stress?

22   We decided the best way to find out would be to dissect the rocks and see if they showed signs of stress. This technique assumes that any body subject to stress over a long period of time will reach equilibrium, a balanced state, if it does not break. Ice in a glass bottle provides a familiar analogy. As the ice expands, tension increases in the glass. The forces are balanced—until the glass breaks. Before the glass breaks, it is possible to measure the stresses in the ice-bottle system indirectly. Melting the ice removes the stress; then the return of the bottle to its original size and shape can be measured. Because the force needed to "stretch" glass (this is known as its elastic constant) is known, it is easy to compute how much stress was required to stretch the glass by the measured amount.

23   Rocks are more complicated than ice in bottles because the balanced forces exist in the same object. But the stress regions tend to lie parallel to the object's surfaces when equilibrium is complete. So by slicing off sections parallel to the surface, we can measure the change as the core returns to its original size and shape. We also have to know the elastic constant of the material involved, but this is either available in published reports or can be easily measured in the laboratory. Then we can say how much stress was present in the rock.

24   To use this technique we sawed the ends and sides from boulders, leaving only central cores. We carefully measured the cores many times over a long period of time to determine whether any change of dimensions took place. The first ringing rock core we measured was almost eleven inches long. A relaxation (contraction) of almost 1/500 of an inch was observed.

That measurement exceeded our wildest estimates and led us to be- 25
lieve that the technique of measurement was introducing a large amount of
error into the data. Therefore we decided to use electronic measurement
with foil strain gauges. These tiny strips of metal and plastic can measure
extremely fine changes of shape on a surface when coupled with the proper
electrical receptors, amplifiers, and strip-chart recorders. They have the
additional advantage of constantly recording the change in shape of the
body as time passes, producing a new kind of information, as well as greater
accuracy and precision.

The sensitivity of foil strain gauges is fantastic. While testing and cal- 26
ibrating the equipment we glued a strain gauge to an old core of very hard
diabase, about one and a half inches on a side and nine inches long. Just for
fun, one of us placed the core over his knee and tried to bend it. The recorder
dutifully recorded 1/100,000 of an inch strain.

Foil strain gauges showed that the cores from ringing boulders relaxed 27
an average of approximately 1/10,000 of an inch per inch of specimen
length. Nonringing boulders from outside the fields showed no relaxation.
In most cases total relaxation required between seventy and eighty hours.
Early relaxation was rapid, followed by a long period of gradual change of
specimen shape. Occasionally, the gradual tapering off was interrupted by
sharp fluctuations; in two cases these could be correlated with the formation
of visible fractures.

Core relaxation as time passed was plotted as a curve on a strip-chart 28
recorder. The various forces that can change the shape of a body tend to produce curves that have characteristic shapes, or "fingerprints." The curves
from the ringing boulders compared well with curves for a type of relaxation
metallurgists call after-working, or anelastic strain. In the field of rock me-
chanics the same phenomenon is called recoverable creep.

Normally the strain magnitudes measured indicate the result of 29
tremendous stresses. By using the experimentally determined elastic constants for diabase, published by Francis Birch, and the relaxation figures that
we obtained, we could compute theoretical values for the stresses stored in
the rock. For some rocks these values were as high as 15,000 pounds per
square inch. Such large stress values are particularly perplexing in boulders
lying in an open field acted upon by no observable external forces.

Creep, or anelastic behavior, is a particularly logical explanation for 30
this apparent paradox. It can produce fairly large strains at relatively low
stresses, with the important qualification that the stresses be applied over
a long period of time. Therefore, the large stresses seemingly indicated by
the computation based on Birch's short-term constants are not particularly
relevant. The strains observed seem to be the result of stresses applied over
very long periods of time.

The origin of the stresses was determined by more conventional geo- 31
logic techniques. We prepared thin sections from several areas within each

boulder and examined them under the petrographic microscope. The outer "skin" of the boulders is, as already mentioned, quite permeable to water. Water combines chemically with minerals and changes them in the process called chemical weathering. New minerals, usually clays, are often produced when the original minerals are broken down by water.

32   Microscopic examination showed that chemical weathering had in some cases advanced two or three inches into the boulders. The most chemically susceptible mineral in diabase is pyroxene. The pyroxenes in the diabase were completely removed at the surface of the boulders. Near the surface the pyroxenes were completely altered to a type of clay known as montmorillonite. Alteration of pyroxenes to clay diminished as distance from the surface became greater.

33   The source of the stresses in the boulders was clear at once. The change from pyroxene to montmorillonite produces a volume change. If a given volume of pyroxene is weathered to montmorillonite, the montmorillonite occupies more space than the original pyroxene. The expansion of many grains of pyroxene during weathering produces an expansion of the outer shell of the boulders and a corresponding tension in the core. The strain resulting from the tension raises the resonant frequency from its natural value to that observed in the ringing rocks.

34   Stresses caused by weathering exist in many rock types. In most, the stresses cause a surface sloughing known as exfoliation. The combination of unusual strength and slow production of stress allows the diabase to accumulate stresses of great enough magnitude to produce the ringing effect.

35   The arguments presented up to this point are entirely internal: they all come from a study of the boulders. Now we needed some external confirmation to make the argument tight. Relaxed cores, which no longer rang, were fitted with steel grips. When restressed in an engineering tensile tester to 10,000 pounds per square inch, the cores rang clearly. With this reasonably independent confirmation of the association between strain and ringing, we were satisfied that our original hypothesis was confirmed.

36   We also wanted to know the role of the special boulder-field environment in producing the ringing effect. Apparently the answer lies in a very delicate balance between weathering rate and rock strength. The boulders in the fields are not buried in soil or shaded by overhanging trees. They are wet only for a short period following a rain or snowfall. This makes the chemical alteration of the minerals and the stresses produced by those alterations accumulate at a very slow rate. Frost action, the breaking of rock by expanding ice, is probably also minimized by the short time water stays in the system. Long periods of time for the establishment of a state of stress equilibrium are thus provided.

37   Those boulders outside the fields exist in a different environment: they are shaded and usually lie on or in water-retaining soil and forest litter. Weathering and frost action proceed much more quickly. Time for adjustment

of the stresses in the rock to an equilibrium state is insufficient, and the boulders "crack up."

This conclusion explains why boulders removed from the field stop ringing. If left outside in a rock garden or other shaded spot the boulders are soon overstressed and break up. Ringing rocks kept dry in geologic collections continue to ring indefinitely. 38

The delicacy of environmental controls on the ringing effect can be illustrated by examining the edges of the boulder fields: the zone separating boulders that ring from those that do not is relatively sharp. The boundary usually lies several feet within the field. The position of the boundary was a puzzle until a botanist friend accompanied us to the site one day. His chance comment about the plants growing along the *shade line* from the bordering trees struck home. The boundary of the ringing boulders area corresponds roughly to the average position of the shade produced by the larger trees about the edges of the field. More shade means less evaporation and thus more moisture retained. Enough apparently, to disrupt the balanced processes that causes the boulders to ring. 39

We therefore propose that the answer to the ringing rocks lies, not in witchcraft or ancient ruins, but in a very subtle and delicate interaction between earth materials and environment over very long periods of time. These are things that cannot be observed in terms of man's unaided senses. The concept of the immensity of geologic time is peculiar enough to most people. The measurements necessary to detect and measure the data presented here are impossible without complex instruments. Faced with phenomena for which there are no observable causes, it is completely logical that supernatural explanations should be proposed. Such proposals are the product of the same curiosity that has produced all sciences, especially the natural sciences. 40

The face of the natural sciences has been changing radically over the past few years, and the proposed solution to the ringing rocks problem presented here is a good example of that change. Once, people like B. F. Fackenthal were naturalists. Their approach to problems could be broad and general because the volume of material to be mastered in the natural and physical sciences was relatively small. Then came the "information explosion." It has become impossible for a man to be acquainted with all the knowledge in his own field, much less in many fields at once. The Renaissance man seems to be lost. Workers with narrow specialties are the rule. This situation has led to many scientific impasses. Problems involving natural systems are often simply too broad and complex to be managed by one man's education. 41

The solution appears to lie in the multidisciplinary approach. The team we put together to solve the mystery of the ringing rocks included three physicists, two engineers, four geologists of varying specialties, two biology students, and one botanist. Once we all got together, those rocks didn't stand a chance. 42

EXERCISE 3.6 In the following reading selection, Amiri Baraka uses what is generally known about jazz to make assertions about what he views as the most influential jazz instrument and its greatest players. Working without collaborators and without scientific apparatus, Baraka, nonetheless, builds a case with available arguments. Read his argument. What materials does he use? How does he relate and combine them to support his thesis? Can you think of what additional support could make his argument more convincing than it is? Record in your notebook your observations of Baraka's use of available support.

 THREE WAYS TO PLAY THE SAXOPHONE

Amiri Baraka

Amiri Baraka (b. 1934), who changed his name from LeRoi Jones in 1957, is an important poet, playwright, and cultural and political leader. He is a professor of Afro-American Studies at the State University of New York at Stonybrook. He wrote about modern jazz in *Black Music* (1968). In that book, "Three Ways to Play the Saxophone" allowed Baraka to present some music history and to argue in an organized way what many of us argue informally in conversation: who the best practitioners are in any given field. Notice how greatly Baraka's persuasiveness depends on his definition of "important musician" and on the neat fit of three acknowledged masters with three modern giants. Baraka illustrates that if readers accept his definition of an important player, they are already tending to accept his choices of individual musicians. Baraka also illustrates how clarity and symmetry of presentation contribute to a convincing argument.

1   I think there are very few people who are close to jazz who would dispute the fact that the three most important saxophonists in all jazz history, up to now, have been Coleman Hawkins, Lester Young and Charlie Parker. There have, of course, been other important jazz saxophonists, but these three men have been more than just brilliant instrumentalists and gifted improvisors; what is most important is that they were innovators, and lasting influences on their contemporaries and every other jazz musician to come after them, no matter what instrument they might play. Just as you once could find (and can still find) piano players or guitarists who patterned their styles on what Louis Armstrong did on trumpet, so you can find diverse instrumentalists making curious, or not so curious, uses of what *Bean, Pres* and *Bird* have done. Charlie Parker's influence is just as important to post-bop piano players as it is to saxophonists. Even a musician as patently individual as vibist, Milt Jackson, must admit to being heavily influenced by the Coleman Hawkins attack. There are guitar players and trombone players whose styles owe a great debt to Lester Young's behind-the-beat, *cool,* definition of jazz. But as

far as jazz saxophone is concerned, it would be almost impossible to find a player who is untouched by what these three masters accomplished.

Of course the ways in which various saxophonists have used Parker's or Hawkins' or Young's influence, have differed quite widely. There are saxophonists who are merely content to imitate, almost exactly, or as closely as they are able, the style of one of the innovators. But the most imaginative hornmen are always able to maintain enough of their own personalities so that any use they make of, say, a Lester Young, is interesting, and even moving, in its own right. Also, there are many very fine players who have been able to utilize two of the major styles at the same time and still come up with something beautifully singular. One thinks immediately of a tenor man like Lucky Thompson who seems to have understood both Hawkins and Young equally, and to have arrived at an astonishingly original use of both those antithetical concepts of tenor saxophone playing. Gene Ammons is another fine tenor player who puts both Young and Hawkins to work in his own playing and manages to emerge as a fascinating stylist. Charlie Rouse, yet another. And, of course, there are many more. The point is that for every Paul Quinichette, say, who was content to utilize merely Lester Young's heavy influence, or Sonny Stitt, who could hear only Parker, or Chu Berry, who was fastened to Hawkins, there were other players who were able to take some of the strongest qualities of two of the innovators, or even all three, after bebop and the emergence of Charlie Parker as the third giant of the jazz saxophone, and fashion their own personal styles.

It is possible to trace the development and ascendancy of the saxophone in jazz by citing just what each of these three men contributed. Coleman Hawkins is known by most jazz people as "The Man Who Invented The Saxophone." It was Bean who first made the sax a respectable instrument, as far as jazz musicians were concerned. Before his appearance, the instrument was used largely for its novelty effect in dance bands and those hotel or theatre groups known as "Mickey Mouse" bands. Hawkins took the horn, and inspired by Louis Armstrong's trumpet technique, developed a huge tone and a smooth, on-the-beat approach to saxophone phrasing that brought the instrument into its own as a jazz solo voice. And for a long time after Hawkins almost anyone who played the instrument sounded like him . . . there was just no other way.

Lester (Pres) Young brought the tenor saxophone to perhaps an even more autonomous position as a solo instrument. Instead of emulating Hawkins' wide-toned, on-the-beat, eighth-note approach, Pres, inspired as he said by the C-melody saxophone of Frank Traumbauer, brought a light, flowing, gauzy tone to the tenor. He also liked to lag just a little behind the beat and accent this penchant by "laying out" or resting at then unusual places in a phrase, and then swooping lazily but impeccably back into the phrase as if he had never stopped playing. Hawkins' saxophone work, as impressive as it was, was really just an extension of the Louis Armstrong trumpet style to another instrument. But Young made for the first time a music that was strictly a "saxophone music," and his flexible, almost uncanny, rhythmic sense provided a model for many of the young musicians who came along in the 40's to produce the music called bebop. Since Young, jazz has become increasingly a saxophone music, in the sense that the music's chief innovators since that time have been saxophonists. From the earliest days of jazz the chief solo instrument had been the trumpet, and trumpet players like the fabled Buddy Bolden, Freddy Keppart, King Oliver and Louis Armstrong, the music's most illustrious soloists. But Hawkins demonstrated how powerfully jazz could be played on a saxophone, and Young made the saxophone potentially the music's most expressive instrument.

5   Alto saxophonist, Charlie Parker was one of the two most exciting soloists jazz has seen so far; the other, of course, being Louis Armstrong. And as such, he made jazz musicians even more saxophone conscious. After Parker, trumpet players, piano players, guitar players, bass players, etc., all tried to sound like him, in much the same fashion as all kinds of instrumentalists had once tried to sound like Armstrong. Parker made the conquest of the music by the saxophone, which Young had begun, very nearly complete. Since Young, we have had Roy Eldridge, Dizzy Gillespie, Fats Navarro, Miles Davis, Clifford Brown, all as brilliant trumpet soloists, but the chief innovators have been saxophonists. And just as Parker was the soul and fire of the bebop era (in fact, most jazz saxophonists are even now heavily indebted to him), it is still saxophonists who are the fiercest innovators in contemporary jazz.

6   Right at this moment (in 1963) three of the most daring innovators in jazz are saxophone players. And a curious coincidence is that like Hawkins, Young and Parker, the proportion remains the same, i.e., two tenor saxophonists and one alto player make up the triumvirate. The tenor men are Sonny Rollins and John Coltrane. The alto player is Ornette Coleman, the most controversial of the three.

7   Of the three, Rollins has been on the jazz scene the longest, having come up with the "second generation" of boppers. Rollins, like everyone else of the period, was deeply affected by Charlie Parker's music, and his style on tenor has always shown Parker's influence. But by the mid-fifties Rollins came into his own and began to play his own horn, and since then he has become an extremely ubiquitous influence himself. In fact Rollins was perhaps the strongest voice of the recent *Hard Bop* trend. It was a trend that was marked by a "return" by many jazz musicians to what they considered their roots (as a reaction to the soft timbres and rigid arrangements of cool jazz). Saxophonists began to utilize wider and harsher tones, of which Sonny's was the widest and harshest and most expressive, and accompanying piano chords became more basic and simplified, often relying on a sort of gospel or *churchy* feeling to emphasize the Afro-American beginnings of the music. This trend still persists in what is called *soul music* or *funky* jazz, which is

still enjoying a great deal of popularity. But Rollins has since gone on to deeper and even more expressive things. Albums like *Way Out West, Freedom Suite* and *Saxophone Colossus* showed that Sonny was interested in being more than fashionable. And he still had more experimenting to do.

John Coltrane, after playing with various rhythm and blues groups, and 8 one of Dizzy Gillespie's big bands late in the 40's, began to be noticed in the middle 50's as a member of the Miles Davis Quartet and Quintet. Coltrane's biggest influence for quite a while was Dexter Gordon, who also influenced Rollins and was one of the earliest people to transfer Parker's approach to the tenor saxophone. Coltrane was also struck quite a bit by Rollins, but by the time he finished playing with Thelonius Monk's wild groups (1957) he was well on his way to becoming one of the most singular stylists in jazz.

The youngest of the three current saxophone innovators is alto man, 9 Ornette Coleman. He is also the one whose innovations have been most challenged by many jazz critics and musicians whose shortsightedness makes it difficult for them to accept the genuinely new. Just as Young and Parker were for a long time considered charlatans or "merely inept," except by a few musicians and critics who tried to understand what they were doing, so young Coleman has had a difficult time of it, but he has been, to my mind, the most exciting and influential innovator in jazz since Parker. And even though Coleman didn't arrive on the "big time" jazz scene until 1959–60, he has already managed to influence, to quite an extent, the other two major innovators, Rollins and Coltrane, not to mention the myriads of other younger players, regardless of their instruments.

Rollins and Coltrane had mature styles before Ornette Coleman was 10 known even to jazz "insiders." Rollins' huge tone, which often sounded like Coleman Hawkins paraphrasing Charlie Parker, and his ability to improvise logically and beautifully from thematic materials rather than chordal, were the things that characterized his pre-Coleman style. Coltrane's sound was and is smaller and less rigid than Rollins', and because of its striking similarity to a human cry it can often raise the hairs on the back of your neck. Rollins seems always to address himself to any extemporization in the most formally logical manner, while Coltrane strings seemingly endless notes and scales together, making what some critics called "sheets of sound."

Coltrane and Coleman have almost diametrically opposing approaches 11 to a jazz solo. Coltrane's music takes its impetus and shape from the repeated chords that harmonically fix the tune. In fact, he plays sometimes as if he would like to take each note of a chord and sound it singly, but at the same time as the overall chord. It is like a painter who instead of painting a simple white, paints all the elemental pigments that the white contains, and at the same time as the white itself. But Ornette Coleman's music has been described as "non-chordal." That is, he does not limit his line to notes that are specifically called for by the sounded chord. The form of a Coleman solo is usually determined by the total musical shape of what he is playing, i.e., the melody, timbre, pitch and of course, the rhythm—all of these moved by Ornette's singularly emotional approach to jazz, in much the same way as the older, "primitive," blues singers produced their music. And this has been his largest influence on the two older men. This *freedom* that Coleman has insisted on in his playing, has opened totally fresh areas of expression for Coltrane and Rollins as well, but in the context of their own demandingly individual conceptions.

12   On Rollins' latest records, e.g., *Our Man in Jazz* (Victor LSP-2612) and club dates, or on Coltrane's recently recorded *Live* (Impulse A-10), or in-person solos, the influence of this revived concept of free improvisation based, finally, on the oldest sense of form in Afro-American music, *the individual,* reaches its most impressive manifestation. And, of course, Ornette Coleman himself, on his records, or in person, continues to excite intrepid jazz listeners all over the country by the fierceness and originality of his imagination. At this point in jazz the most imaginative voices continue to be saxophonists (though the pianist Cecil Taylor has also to be cited in any list of recent innovators). And it would seem that not only have Rollins, Coltrane and Coleman learned from the three original saxophone innovators, Hawkins, Young and Parker, but that they themselves are seriously intent on becoming innovators of the same stature. It is certainly not a far-fetched idea.

MARSHALING SUPPORT

You want to be understood. You want your views to be respected. You want to be believed. Your use of evidence is not haphazard. You marshal evidence so that your audience may understand your views, respect your efforts, and accept your thesis. Even if you cannot achieve all three of these goals—listed here in order of increasing difficulty—you argue by using support purposefully. You use it to explain, to reason, and to persuade. You imagine your readers asking, "What's your point?" Then, you imagine the skeptics challenging, "Prove it to me!" You hear your own voice saying, "This is what I think is right," and then, "Here's why."

When you marshal support, you draw together and organize what you know, your available arguments, in the form of reasons to accept your thesis and in the form of support for those reasons. Thesis and support are clear and connected. Among such ordered ranks, it is easy to see the statement that is out of line.

The following editorial, from *The Register–Guard* (Eugene, Oregon), illustrates the basic argument components of thesis and reasons:

DROP PRIVATE PATROLS

Local homosexual activists are right to be concerned about incidents of gay-bashing that have occurred in Eugene. But they are wrong in planning to form special patrols during the Eugene Celebration to protect gays and lesbians from harassment. Here's why:

- The patrols smack of vigilantism and could very well incite untoward incidents rather than prevent them.
- The individuals forming the patrols have no training in how to properly defuse confrontational situations.
- The presence of the patrols, no matter the legitimacy of their concerns, might prompt other groups to form their own special security squads. A proliferation of such groups would more likely than not lead to confrontations between groups.
- The Eugene Department of Public Safety plans to double its downtown police presence—from four to eight patrol officers on foot—during the Eugene Celebration. Those officers are specifically trained to handle criminal or anti-social behavior. It is appropriate that they, and not private citizens, take care of any problems that arise.

This editorial appeared just before an annual civic celebration. The year before there had been an attack on two men purported to be gay. Activists were planning to set up patrols for this year's event. The writer of the editorial opposes such patrols and gives four reasons, each marked by a black dot. The sentence "Here's why" is the hinge connecting reasons to the thesis. Notice that each reason presents a distinct way to support the thesis. There are really four reasons, not two or three with some repeating of the others.

Consider this analogy: The thesis of an argument and its reasons form a bridge.

Thesis

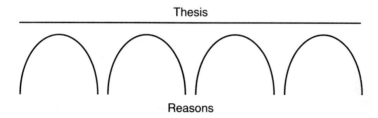

Reasons

Just as the roadway gets supported by archways, so the thesis gets supported by reasons.

EXERCISE 3.7 In your notebook, write a position statement/thesis for three or four issues that concern you. Provide reasons for them, making sure each reason links clearly to the thesis.

Now think about expanding the argument, not with added reasons, but with added discussion of the four reasons given. Whenever a reason seems unsubstantiated or debatable, readers expect further development, which, in bridge imagery, might look this way:

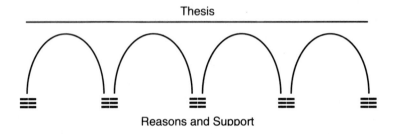

The footings, the third component of the bridge, offer support to the arches, just as supporting material in the argument can bolster the reasons. Skeptical readers should see that your thesis solidly rests on a base and that the archways, in turn, rest on concrete foundations.

A student wrote the following argument for an early assignment for which students were to assert a position and provide reasons. Unlike the previous newspaper editorial, Laurie J. Wright's argument includes this third level of supporting reasons.

SHOULD TROJAN NUCLEAR POWER PLANT RESUME OPERATIONS THIS SPRING?

Dangers associated with Trojan Nuclear Power Plant justify its continued shutdown, though Portland General Electric plans to resume operation in February or March of this year. Questionable safety of operation closed Trojan in March 1991 when physical defects were discovered. Since then, inspections revealed human error in failing to monitor and regulate operations. Recently, the potential for seismologic catastrophe has become a public concern; Trojan's very location poses a risk.

The Trojan plant is located on the Cascadia Subduction Zone, an area in which earthquakes are likely to occur. The facility was not designed to withstand the type of earthquake that has assaulted the subduction zones on the coast of Oregon and Washington in the past couple of years. The Trojan plant would not escape damage from a quake the strength of those occurring on the coast. Along with the potential threat of earthquake, further hazards at Trojan have been unearthed.

Cracks in the conduction pipes which carry high-pressure steam from the core of the reactor were discovered, and Trojan was subsequently closed in March of 1991. As the repair and inspection ensued, a new type of damage, microcracking, was discovered. These microcracks were found in the conducting tubes near steel support plates for the tubes. The microcracked tubes are not going to be investigated or repaired by PGE. In the interest of resuming production, PGE hopes to begin power generation early this year. Earthquake and microcracks in tubes threatening rupture are dangerous enough, yet further disregard for safety exists at Trojan.

Add one more reason to continue Trojan's shutdown: The Nuclear Regulatory Commission discovered the facility's failure to monitor valves, resulting in incorrect settings at the plant. Six other safety violations are currently being researched by the NRC.

The Eugene Water and Electric Board holds a 30% interest in PGE's nuclear generating site. Local interest in safety should not be secondary to interest in power generation at Trojan. Yet Trojan's closure this past year has not caused a notable increase in cost of electricity or a notable loss of supply. Safety for Trojan's employees, area residents, and public lands is too important a concern to cast aside for a surplus of kilowattage. The continued shutdown of Trojan ensures safety. Obviously unsafe operation this spring should not be allowed.

This argument does not use more reasons than the editorial. Each writer has four sections of discussion, four reasons or archways. The difference in length results from the second writer's development of details that support the reasons. This is an extended construction, one with footings fixed on solid ground.

EXERCISE 3.8 Reread the Baraka essay presented earlier in this chapter. Consider the essay in terms of thesis, reasons, and support for reasons. In your notebook, try outlining the essay with at least three levels.

Connecting the Abstract and Concrete

The discussion thus far on thesis, reasons, and support has used an operation so basic to your thought process that you are hardly ever aware of it. That operation is the movement of thought back and forth along lines sketched by seeming opposites:

Concrete ◄──────► Abstract

Specific ◄──────► General

Sometimes this movement is visualized vertically:

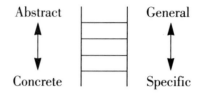

The operation can be compared to climbing up and down a ladder.

Before illustrating, let's define these terms. To be *abstract* is to think about or express ideas or concepts that are "above" the data of the senses, that is, above what you see, hear, taste, smell, or touch. To be *general* is to speak about categories and groupings without attention to the particularities of group members. In contrast, to be *concrete* is to deal with the sand grains of experience—with what gives experience its weight and distinction—all the sense data available to you. To be *specific* is to point to the example, to illustrate, or to name the individual item, person, or event.

Looking broadly at thinking and language, you can see that any noun can be placed on a rung of the abstraction ladder. Then, for that noun, you can find other nouns that are more abstract or general and that are more concrete or specific.

Take the task of defining a simple word: *red.* You can say (up the ladder to the group), "Red is a *color*" and (down the ladder to an instance) "such as found in a *stop sign* or a *St. Louis Cardinal baseball cap.*" What is the definition of a college? It is an institution of education. This answer groups colleges with universities, public and private postsecondary schools and institutes, as well as with secondary and elementary schools. The college offers four years of education, usually without offering graduate degrees. This method of definition brackets the term between a group term and a specifying term. Definition is one kind of workout on the abstraction ladder.

Isolated words cannot be said to be abstract or concrete, general or specific. Like the seeming opposites slow/fast, cold/hot, or small/large, the terms naming the ends of the ladder describe relationships that are relative. Any word is more or less general than some other word. That word can be set on the ladder with other words ranged above it and below it, moving up to greater abstraction and generality and down toward specific detail and concreteness. Here are three ladders for three words:

UNEMPLOYMENT	*WATERMELON*	*LICENSE PLATE ENV 012*
U.S. domestic problems	Foodstuffs	ID numbers
U.S. economic problems	Supermarket produce	ID numbers relating to car use

Unemployment	Fruit	Numbers identifying a car
Unemployed auto workers	Melons	License plates
Unemployed GM auto workers	*Watermelon*	License plates of the family's car
My cousin Serge laid off in Pontiac, MI	$.09 a pound watermelon	*ENV 012*

Clearly, the abstraction ladder provides a view of a mental activity. This activity moves from one level of abstraction to another. This motion, as you will see, is basic to deduction and induction, to definition and analysis. It is basic, too, to many conventional writing structures. The subject of a sentence is specified by the details of its predicate and modifiers. The topic sentence of a paragraph is specified by discussion sentences. The thesis of an argument is specified by discussion paragraphs, which are built of reasons and their support. Graphically, these structures look like at least two or three rungs of an abstraction ladder:

Subject of a sentence	Topic sentence of a paragraph	Thesis of argument
Predicate of a sentence	Discussion of topic	Reasons for thesis
		Support for reasons

You may already have surmised that outlining is a form of laddering, of showing levels of abstraction. The following is an outline of Laurie Wright's essay:

Thesis: Trojan should not be allowed to continue operation
    Reason: Potential for earthquake
        Support: Cascadia subduction zone
                Construction of Trojan
    Reason: Damage to Trojan
        Support: Cracks
                Microcracks
    Reason: Failure to monitor
        Support: NRC findings
    Reason: Unaffected rates and supply
        Support: Safety more important than generation
                of surplus electricity, but no loss of supply
                or increase in rates

The outline charts the sequence of the argument point by point. Also, its indentations show the relative importance of every point. The outline shows the relationships between high-, medium-, and low-level abstractions.

The concepts of thesis, reasons, support; the abstraction ladder; and outlining assist in building argument. They help you discover *what materials* you have brainstormed, gathered, or drafted. They help you find *what relationships* link and organize them. You discover ways to line up or marshal evidence. You may also see what is missing and what you need to add in order to strengthen the argument. You are able to discover *what order* is best for your readers. These same patterns of thinking up and down the abstraction ladder enable you to read and understand other people's arguments, too.

EXERCISE 3.9 Using first the Baraka essay presented in the previous section and then one of your arguments, make one or more lists of terms used in each essay and rank them by abstraction level. Consider how such ranking reveals something about the structure of the writer's thoughts and of the argument's organization. Compare your word list for the Baraka essay with your outline of the same essay completed for Exercise 3.8.

Using Reason to Link Ideas

We have discussed how reasons support a thesis. But what is reason? What is reason's connection to Aristotle's *logos* or the word "logical"? How, in those periods that you manage to be reasonable or rational, do you act? When you are rational, how do you use thought and how do you use language?

These are complex considerations. It is difficult enough to think, let alone think about thinking!

Reason is characteristically linear. As you think rationally, you trace the line of your thought. This line is more than a sequence whose parts are linked by "and." After all, over-the-back-fence gossip proceeds by *and's* and a line of *he said's* and *she said's*. Like the plot of a well-crafted drama, reason sequences ideas and words so they have consequences. Since A is true and B is true, therefore C is true. Or D is true because E and F and G are true. The linking words *since* and *because* supersede *and,* so that reasoning becomes a thinking process that results in a conclusion—a process that arrives somewhere.

In rational sequences each step should be valid. A valid sequence or step reveals how thought has been developed and where thought is going. Rational sequences terminate in a conclusion. If you have studied algebra or geometry, you have probably had instructors who insisted as much on the right steps as on the right answers. Reason provides adequate steps to arrive at the answer. Nothing is left out.

To say a thought sequence is valid is to say the steps taken to reach the conclusion follow logically. When we are illogical—skipping steps, leaping to conclusions—dismayed readers exclaim, "How does that follow? Where did you get that? I don't see what you're driving at!"

Even when all of the steps in the sequence follow expectations of logical thinking, a sequence of thought may be valid but not true. Examine this sequence of statements: *All presidential candidates are opportunists. David Duke is a presidential candidate. David Duke is an opportunist.* In this example, we know David Duke is a presidential candidate. But do we know all such candidates are opportunists? If this were indeed the case, then we could conclude that any particular presidential candidate is also an opportunist. The links in the argument chain are valid, but not every link is true. Let us look at another example: *If we cut taxes, the economy will recover. We are cutting taxes. The economy will recover.* This is a valid set because it follows guidelines for rational thought, and it is true if its assumptions are true. Yet, assumptions are often debatable. How do we know cutting taxes will improve the economy? How do we know the government will actually cut taxes? Consider this pseudorational sequence of graffiti: *Ray Charles is blind. Love is blind. God is love. Ray Charles is God.* However much we worship Ray Charles, the sequence is not a valid one because the links joining the statements play on words and reveal little logical relationship.

Products of reason need to be true as well as valid. In this sense, *true* means that each step of the sequence accurately reflects the world as the reader perceives it. The truth of a thesis is tested against reality. The thesis derived from a scientific experiment needs to be verifiable in similar repeated situations. The thesis of an argument will be believed if it seems evidently true. What makes a thesis evidently true is the kind, amount, and arrangement of evidence or support.

The sequence about David Duke might be true if you can assume that all presidential candidates really are opportunists. The prediction about the economy is true if there really is such a link, as stated, between tax cuts and improvements. If there are few benefits or none, then the sequence is less consequential than it seems. Also, assuming the link between tax cuts and economic improvement, you must also assume that taxes will be cut.

Although statements might sequence logically, they still may be inaccurate for describing the world your readers know. The valid but untrue argument has the shape of reason, yet it is finally unverifiable. An invalid argument, on the other hand, may include many accurate steps, but it lacks the clarity and purpose of consecutive thought. As you can see, crisp handling of reason is a forceful persuader, especially when an argument is both valid (well ordered) and true (well supported).

The concept of warrants opens another possibility. An assumption may not be true, but your audience may believe it is. What if an audience does believe that presidential candidates are opportunists or that tax cuts cause an improved economy? In Toulmin's scheme, statements may very well be true or untrue, but they may be *believed* or *disbelieved*, implying that changing an audience partly depends on their beliefs, true or untrue. This possibility challenges the integrity of reason and its traditional task to map out the truth.

If these last paragraphs described the product of reason, perhaps you now can consider the habits of thinking that help ensure valid and true conclusions. Certainly, haste is an enemy of reason. Think of the people you know who present their arguments without thinking. Much of their poor reasoning results as much from overcrowded schedules and distractions as it does from flaws in reasoning.

Undue haste makes it difficult for you to find the relationships between the parts of your reasoning. You might fail to see the valid connections and true connections. You might not have time to align thesis and reasons or to give reasons support. You build a rickety bridge.

To counteract this haste, you can use the thesis deliberately to help you identify reasons and support. The thesis you argue goes up against opposing views. By considering the opposition, that is, skeptical readers, you can certainly check hasty thinking and flimsy supporting. What do they need to know, feel, and experience before they believe you? What rebuttals to your thesis can you anticipate? How can this realistic expectation of opposition help you sharpen your use of reason, your sense of the argument's validity and truth?

Undue haste can make it difficult for you to evaluate the truth of the support you use. How accurate are the facts you have gathered from others? Do you understand the inferences others have drawn from these facts? And, when others claim a conclusion to be a good or bad one, do you understand from what value system, bias, or special interest they speak? If you receive facts, inferences, and judgments without critical evaluation, you are likely to perpetuate errors, reveal incompetency, and trigger the skepticism of readers. Building arguments usually requires that you use sources, but you must use them with judgment.

Qualifying Your Statements

Qualifying words can help you say more exactly what you wish to say. Instead of saying, "All politicians are opportunists," you might qualify or change the statement to say, "Many politicians are opportunists." Later, in the thought sequence, you will not be able to say, "David Duke is an opportunist." It will be more reasonable to say, "So David Duke may be an opportunist." Here are some absolute terms contrasted with qualifiers:

ABSOLUTE TERMS	QUALIFIERS
All	Many, some
Always	Often, sometimes
Never	Seldom
Certainly	In my opinion, most likely
In all cases	In most cases, in some cases
Will happen	May or might happen
It is	It seems to be, it appears to be

It is fine to be absolute whenever the truth sustains the absolute, but in a world of differences you must often assert your thesis with qualifiers.

Cogent arguments are well made, valid and true, well sequenced, and believably supported. *Fallacious* arguments make mistakes in sequencing and cannot be verified. Chapter 4 presents some common fallacies. As in so many areas of life, there seem to be more ways to be wrong than right. Yet, there are many ways to argue successfully.

EXERCISE 3.10 If reason tracks a line from a problem to a possible solution, or from a tentative thesis to a supported, convincing thesis, try tracing the line of thought developed by the authors of "Rock Music." Try tracking Baraka's line of thought as it leads to clarifying reasons supporting his choices of the great jazz saxophonists. You may represent this line of reasoning as a listing or as a horizontal "time" line with the steps along the way identified. Try various ways of representing this line in your notebook.

EXERCISE 3.11 Using the letters to the editor in Argument Activity 1 at the end of this chapter, underline words that make statements absolute or qualified. For one of your arguments, underline words that signal qualified statements and absolute statements. In your notebook, make a list of qualifiers and of absolute terms. Then describe in a paragraph the possible effects on readers as they encounter absolute and qualified statements. In what circumstances is one or the other kind of statement appropriate?

ORGANIZING SUPPORT

Once you have gathered support and understand its relationships to thesis, you can be satisfied that you know *what* you are going to write. That alone is an accomplishment en route to the finished argument. Now you must determine *in what order* you will present your support.

There is no single formula for structuring argument. The suggestions that follow are meant to be factors in planning, not a recipe for a teacher's favorite order.

Traditional Organization

The trio of introduction, body, and conclusion is familiar. Most academic writing employs this organizational order. The following outline presents that order, elaborated on to suit argument:

Introduction
  Establish the importance of the issue
  Provide necessary background (history, definitions)
  Introduce the writer (credentials, involvement in the issue,
    relationship to audience)
  State the thesis
  Preview support
Body
  Support the thesis (reasons and variety of support)
  Refute opposing reasons
Conclusion
  Restate thesis and support
  Call to action, show application

Traditional argument includes the steps of stating the issue, taking a stand, supporting the stand, refuting the opposition, and exhorting the audience to belief and action.

The traditional organizational pattern can help you plan an argument, even if you do not follow it step by step. This order presents a set of slots which you can fill with material or not, depending on your purpose and ability. You may choose not to refute, or, if your readers know the issue well, you may not need to provide background, just as you may not need to say much about yourself if readers already know about your involvement with the issue.

The traditional order has endured not just because it appeals to our sense of order and tradition, but also because its steps allow the writer to develop appeals to the reader's reason, emotion, and social sense. The heart of the rational appeal is in thesis and its support. The appeal to emotions can be made at the outset, as part of the issue's background and present importance. A restatement in the conclusion is not mere repetition in order to teach; such repetition is often heightened to arouse feeling and involve the reader. It is an opportunity to restate the thesis with feeling. Throughout the argument, the writer can present himself or herself as a person who is informed, concerned, and believable. Yet, again, a special introductory step can be taken to establish the character of the writer as a factor encouraging acceptance of the argument. So, the traditional format allows the writer all of these opportunities: to present the argument, to address the audience, and, as an informed and involved person, to become an asset in achieving argument aims.

EXERCISE 3.12 Read Barbara Howell's "WIC: Investing in Our Future." This argument fills many of the slots of traditional organization. Identify the argument parts and list them in your notebook. Does their order contribute to guiding and convincing readers?

 ## WIC: INVESTING IN OUR FUTURE
Barbara Howell

Barbara Howell wrote "WIC: Investing in Our Future" in 1989 as a background paper for members of Bread for the World, a Christian citizens' group that lobbies Congress on food and foreign aid issues. The paper argues for full funding of a particular program and urges members to write Congress. The paper is typical of many reports seeking support for specific measures. It appeals to reason and to the emotions; it is a detailed report as well as a call for action. Notice the traditional organization that includes sections of explanation, support for the thesis, anticipation of counterarguments, and motivation to action.

> *"Let the children come to me, and do not stop them because the kingdom of God belongs to such as these. . . .* 1
>
> *"Then [Jesus] took the children in his arms, placed his hands on each of them, and blessed them."*
>
> —Mark 10:14–16

The United States is one of the most affluent countries in the world with one 2 of the highest standards of living. Yet almost 13 million U.S. children are poor. Nearly one-quarter of all children born in this nation begin life under conditions of poverty that make it difficult for them to develop to their full potential. Almost one-half of Black children start out with this disadvantage. A recent study showed that children born in the United States are two to three times more likely to grow up poor than children in other western countries such as Sweden, West Germany, Switzerland, Canada and Great Britain. The United States also ranks 19th among industrialized countries in preventing infant mortality.

3   The health consequences of being poor are devastating. Each day in the United States 27 children die from the effects of poverty. Poor families are at high risk of having their babies die in infancy or suffer from mental or physical disabilities that hinder them for the rest of their lives.

4   However, the U.S. government operates an especially effective program—the Special Supplemental Food Program for Women, Infants and Children (WIC)—that could, if fully funded, eliminate or lessen the effects of malnutrition in the first years of life. Currently, though, because of inadequate funding, WIC cannot serve an estimated 3.6 million eligible pregnant women, infants and children.

5   WIC provides a variety of services to its participants and has three main functions:

- To provide supplemental foods for improving the health of low-income pregnant women, new mothers, infants and children up to 5;
- To motivate WIC mothers to pay more attention to the nutritional quality of the food they and their children eat; and
- To be alert to WIC participants' medical needs and refer them to health services for prenatal and well-baby care and child immunizations.

Support for WIC

6   A variety of prestigious panels have urged recently that the United States immediately address child poverty. They all say the WIC program is especially effective and needs to be expanded.

7   In 1987, more than 200 business and education leaders on the Committee for Economic Development (CED) called on citizens and policymakers to invest money in proven programs such as WIC that prevent health and education problems. In CED's report, "Children in Need: Investment Strategies for the Educationally Disadvantaged," CED members argued that neglecting this investment will result in a much greater cost to society by producing an inadequately prepared work force unable to meet future economic challenges.

8   About the same time, the National Governors' Association issued a similar assessment. It called for extraordinary efforts to assure that basic needs such as food and medical care are met in early childhood to allow children to grow and develop fully.

9   In a September 1988 event called "An Historic Day for Children," the National Commission to Prevent Infant Mortality, whose members were appointed by Congress, gathered corporate, government and community leaders to challenge them to end the high level of preventable infant deaths in the United States. The commission's report, "Death Before Life: The Tragedy of Infant Mortality," specifically calls for sufficient funding for WIC to enable all eligible women and children to receive WIC services.

Soon after the 1988 election, a bipartisan panel chaired by former   10
Presidents Gerald Ford and Jimmy Carter presented recommendations to
President-elect Bush in the panel's report, "American Agenda." Their top
domestic priority for increased spending in 1989 was to expand programs of
proven effectiveness for children in poverty. They encouraged the new president to set a goal of full federal government funding for WIC.

WIC Works

Extensive evaluations of the WIC program have shown that low-income preg-   11
nant women who receive WIC benefits are more likely to have healthy babies than women in similar circumstances who are not participating in the
WIC program. WIC reduces fetal death and low birth weight (under $5^{1}/_{2}$
pounds), a major cause of infant mortality. Participants in the program have
diets higher in protein, iron, calcium and vitamin C, which are essential for
optimum development. A pregnant woman's participation in the WIC program also improves her children's later ability to learn. For example, children whose mothers participated in WIC during pregnancy have higher
vocabulary test scores than low-income children whose mothers were not enrolled in WIC.

Not only does WIC prevent many nutrition-related health problems and   12
improve children's development, WIC saves money in the long run. A
Harvard School of Public Health study concluded that for each dollar WIC
spent for prenatal nutrition, $3 were saved in later hospitalization costs. A
similar study by the Missouri Department of Health found that for every WIC
dollar spent, Medicaid saved 49 cents that it would have spent in the first
45 days of a baby's life alone.

Although study results and statistics show the importance of WIC, a   13
personal story gives an even more convincing case for WIC.

Paula did not know about the WIC program when she was pregnant with   14
her first child. She did not receive prenatal care, and her daughter Sarah was
born prematurely, weighing only 5 lbs. 9 oz. A year and a half later, when
Paula was pregnant with her second child, she heard about WIC. But she had
to wait 3 months for an appointment because the clinic was full.

At Paula's first appointment, she found out that Sarah was seriously   15
anemic and needed a special diet. Through her visits with the WIC nutri-
tionist, Paula established new eating habits for herself and her daughter.
Within nine months Sarah's iron level had risen to a normal level.

When Robert, the new baby, was born, he weighed 6 lbs. 13 oz. and had   16
no medical problems. "The WIC program really changed my life," Paula told
BFW staff. "Now I can be a better mother because I know how to care for my
children, and I have good food to give them."

Making WIC Available to All Who Qualify

Bread for the World is spearheading a campaign in 1989 through its Of-   17
fering of Letters to ask Congress to fully fund the WIC program so that all

eligible women, infants and children will be able to receive WIC benefits. Despite its success, WIC is not an "entitlement" program such as food stamps and Social Security, which provide benefits to all those who qualify. Instead, the WIC caseload is limited by the restricted funds Congress provides each year. In 1989 this amount serves about half of U.S. low-income women, infants and children with health problems caused by inadequate nutrition.

18   This BFW campaign is a continuation of the 1987 Offering of Letters that succeeded in increasing WIC funding enough to add 150,000 women, infants and children to the WIC rolls. WIC legislation expires in 1989, and Congress is scheduled to consider revisions in the law as part of the process of continuing or "reauthorizing" the program. This opportunity allows WIC supporters to press for full funding for WIC.

19   Bread for the World members and others will ask Congress to guarantee WIC funding increases for each of the next four or five years, moving toward full funding and enabling WIC to serve all who qualify. Taking into account the need to expand gradually and allow for growth of program administration capabilities, a caseload increase of about 10 percent a year seems practical. If funding is provided to allow this increase, WIC could reach most of the eligible people in four or five years.

20   Other public policy research and advocacy groups have already indicated their interest in joining the WIC campaign, including Interfaith Action for Economic Justice, Food Research and Action Center (FRAC), Center on Budget and Policy Priorities, Children's Defense Fund and World Hunger Year. Other organizations working on child nutrition will be encouraged to support the campaign. Our joint efforts will ensure a broad base of support for the measure.

Expanding WIC's Potential

21   Throughout the year, BFW members will be asked to act on issues in addition to full funding that can improve the WIC program.

22   One of these issues is expanding outreach efforts. Although most WIC agencies provide publicity in their community about WIC, aggressive outreach is not usual. Limited funds make it impossible for most WIC clinics to serve all who are referred by a health professional or come on their own. With full funding, however, more effective measures could be used to reach the women, infants and children who can benefit from WIC services.

23   Another issue to be addressed is revising the proportion of WIC funds that can be used to provide nutrition counseling services. Many women go to WIC clinics needing free food. However, the other services WIC offers through nutrition counseling and referral to health care programs are just as valuable because they provide long-term health benefits.

24   WIC legislation allows up to 20 percent of WIC's funding to be used for nutrition and counseling services and for program administration. The

other 80 percent pays for food. WIC administrators argue that this spending limitation for nutrition services and administration is inadequate and needs to be revised if effective nutrition counseling services are to be carried out.

In most WIC clinics, staff members have too large a caseload for them 25 to give recipients much individual attention. For example, the WIC program provides an excellent opportunity to encourage and support breast-feeding among low-income women. However, this counseling is a time-consuming task, and sometimes WIC staff cannot give it adequate attention. WIC support for breast-feeding and nutrition education must be maintained as a major focus of the WIC program.

In addition to the issues above, Bread for the World recognizes that 26 an expanded WIC program will put more stress on currently inadequate prenatal care and other maternal and child health services. Bread for the World would support legislative opportunities to increase the availability of those services.

Fraud in the WIC Program

There are no data showing widespread fraud in the WIC program, par- 27 ticularly among WIC participants. However, a recent audit by the Office of the Inspector General in the Department of Agriculture (USDA) uncovered some problems with vendor fraud. In six urban areas identified as being at high risk for fraud, significant numbers of non-chain food stores overcharged by as much as 10 percent for WIC foods. It should be noted, though, that purchases from non-chain food stores make up only 15 percent of WIC sales.

In response to the audit, the Food and Nutrition Service of USDA 28 is revising its regulations and will implement tighter vendor monitoring and sanctions against offenders early in 1989. Bread for the World supports these and any other reasonable efforts to reduce fraud in the WIC program.

Investing in Our Future

The time is right for Congress to make the commitment to full funding of 29 the WIC program so that no child in the United States will die in infancy, be born with disabilities, or be malnourished in the early years because of inadequate nutrition.

Bread for the World's 1989 Offering of Letters can be exactly what is 30 needed to persuade the government to make this commitment even when budget deficits demand cuts in other areas, such as military spending.

President Theodore Roosevelt said at the first White House Conference 31 on the Care of Dependent Children in 1909, "When you take care of the children you are taking care of the nation of tomorrow."

Our children are a precious resource, and they need our care today. 32

\

Reader-Based Organization

Traditional organization moves to the thesis as soon as the necessary preliminaries are out of the way. There are uses for this directness. Commonly,
when you pick up a new item, you size it up generally, proceed to its details,
and then refocus on the whole. The manner of your saying, to an extent, follows the manner of your seeing. This conclusion presupposes, of course,
that you are looking foremost at argument content, the shift from thesis to
support and back to thesis. Now, consider what happens if you develop an
argument's organization by studying your readers. Examine the following
four possibilities.

1. What if the audience needs to pay closer attention? Readers may
not be ready for thesis and support if they are inattentive or uninterested. You
probably assume that rational readers, teachers included, will pay attention
to what you write. Yet you may have to provide an interest step or at least a
step that allows readers to settle back with a sense that the show is ready to
begin. The customary jokes introductory to serious addresses and the coming attractions before the feature movie signal to audiences to get ready.
Hamlet begins with a conference about and an appearance of a ghost;
Macbeth starts with a witches' confab. Sometimes you may have to delay your
thesis until after you have secured the attention of your readers. You can get
attention by shock or humor or any personal interest element, usually a specific, which you might present as a statistic, as an anecdote, as a quotation,
or in some other way.

2. What if the audience needs to take you more seriously? How
can you develop your authority on the issue? Before presenting the
thesis, you may wish to introduce yourself in a way that encourages your
audience to listen to you carefully. With some groups, this could be a difficult task.

3. What if the audience needs to begin with the comfort of the safe
and familiar and not be thrust into deep waters? Before presenting your thesis, you can sketch what readers know and believe about the issue and
build on that to arrive at the challenge of the thesis. When you and your
readers both agree—when readers do have a sure grasp of the issue—you
may find commonalities that are useful to establish before moving to your
differences.

Stephen Toulmin's concept of warrant applies. If a warrant is an assumption shared by writer and audience, and if it also guarantees a significant connection between the writer's thesis and support (or *claim* and
grounds), then a writer might start the argument with the warrant, not the thesis. In Exercise 3.2, you examined this argument:

Since they are extremely safe,
(support)
we should permit triple-trailer trucks on our roads.
(thesis)
We want our driving to be safe.
(warrant)

The writer could start with the very point of difference, the thesis, expecting readers to disagree. Or the writer could start the argument with the warrant, a common assumption, establish agreement, and then proceed to the point at issue.

4. What if the audience needs reassurance they will be heard and not bullied? Before presenting thesis, you can sketch out in a nonjudgmental manner the audience's position. This way you can demonstrate that you are a capable listener. You can motivate readers to listen to you in the same manner. Further, you can show yourself to be a person who is not absolute, not a harsh critic intolerant of those who differ with you. You can present your views as being true to you as you understand their views to be true to them. You can demonstrate what Carl Rogers calls empathy. And you demonstrate empathy before you present your own views.

Thus, there is nothing sacred about rapidly presenting thesis and moving at once to support. If your audience needs it, you will take a first step or several steps before stating your thesis.

Also, when you write the conclusion of your argument there are options other than restatement and review. The social needs and niceties may take precedence over concluding with a bald recapitulation. Maybe exhortation is not called for. Instead, you might invite your readers to react to what you have written and to sit down with you soon to exchange ideas and work out a position satisfactory to both of you. Rather than urge action, you might suggest the benefits of continued communication.

This discussion on organization has suggested some of the ways you might reorder, substitute, or delete the steps of the traditional organizational order. Your organization, then, results from a thoughtful analysis of what might work best in a given situation. Organization is not rigid; it is flexible in meeting the various demands of the argument.

EXERCISE 3.13 Arguments vary in their organization. There is variety among the essays by Brody (Chapter 1), Paine (Chapter 2), and Baraka (Chapter 3). Review these arguments and compare the devices used to organize them. List in your notebook how these essays differ in organization. Consider the effectiveness of the organizational choices. What is the connection between organization and intended audience?

Useful Organizing Elements

However unique each argument may be, you will find yourself reusing and adapting several standard elements of organization. Foremost of them, indeed, is the structure of thesis and support, of a higher and lower level bound together by *because.*

Almost as common, and often useful in organizing support, is the simple listing of items. Usually these items are co-ordinate, on the same abstraction level, grouped together by a heading such as *Reasons* or *Examples.* Such a list is a valuable device because you have a sequence of points that relate to the thesis in a similar way. Such a list shows you how to sequence and relate paragraphs and larger chunks of the discussion. Four reasons may need four paragraphs or larger sections. The several supports for any reason may need several sentences each. Listing is a wonderfully simple design tool. And readers easily follow list structures.

Related to the list of points is chronology, a list of moments in time sequence. If an argument lends itself to chronological development, readers easily follow the timeline.

Some issues are prepackaged as pro and con exchanges. Such packaging can be useful. You can create your own pro and con exchange on any issue by imagining the dialogue. You can ask questions and provide answers from the various sides. You can state ideas and counter them. For any statement on the issue, you can raise questions and provide alternatives.

Such a dialogue method of considering views enables you to develop ideas in detail and in relation to your readers' views. It allows you to anticipate objections. It supplies you with an internal voice, that of the skeptical reader who, dissatisfied with unsupported claims and vague connections in thought and writing, is quick to quiz you and to object.

The dialogue method also relates to organization because the shape of the argument grows from your sense of the reader's legitimate resistance to your views and his or her legitimate demand for substantiation. That form develops, as well, from the dialogue within, where reason's proposals are challenged and checked by reason's requirements. Paine's *Common Sense* exemplifies the dialogue format. (See Exercise 2.9 for an outline of this sort of exchange.) Dialogue, therefore, provides tension, and that tension implies basic elements of form: question and answer, comment and criticism, your views and your readers' views, what you believe and why you believe it. This is the actual volley of words and ideas you experience in conversation. If you are ever puzzled about what you should write next in the developing argument, chances are there are directions in what has already been written; chances are there are directions in the responses you believe your readers might give.

EXERCISE 3.14 Elements organizing your essays commonly recur. In at least two of your essays, prepare for a class discussion by finding and labeling some commonly used elements:

Thesis and support

Listing, used to divide support

Chronology

Pro/con contrasts

Dialogue elements

This chapter discussed the building of an argument—from the forming of a thesis, through the gathering of support, to the organization of the whole. Become familiar with this chapter's procedures and tools. Try them out. Add them to your repertoire and your toolbox. Try to find these procedures and tools in the arguments you read, because other writers' achievements can be instructive. Make a unified effort to advance your writing and argument skills.

Chapter 4 focuses exclusively on the varieties of support available for your use. It explains what they are and how to use them. It shows you how to combine them in an argument and to present them to convince your audience.

ARGUMENT ACTIVITIES

1. Read the following letters to the editor of a local newspaper. Outline each one by identifying thesis and reasons. Some letters develop support for the reasons they give. Note that the thesis statement is not always first.

PINE, BEAR GRASS COMMON

Joyce Davis' letter of Feb. 15 in which she implores the Bureau of Land Management to leave out of a timber sale a unique stand of ponderosa pine near Creswell only shows her shocking ignorance of Willamette Valley ecology.

Ponderosa pine is a common tree throughout the Willamette Valley and its foothills. Anyone driving on Fox Hollow Road with his or her eyes open can see thousands of acres of ponderosa pine, both within the city limits and out to Fox Hollow's intersection with the Lorane Highway.

The rare tufted grass she noticed is neither rare nor a member of the grass family. Commonly called bear grass, this tufted plant is a member of the lily family and is quite common in the Coast Range and Cascades.

To the neophyte, a 60 percent slope may be too steep to log and reforest, but such slopes have been routinely managed for decades. The logs will be suspended above the soil during yarding, thus keeping the ground vegetation intact. Reforestation survival rates on such steep slopes average around 90 percent. Within 10 years, the newly planted seedlings will be more than 10 feet tall.

Davis also incorrectly called the harvest unit a clear-cut. Not every tree will be cut. Most of the ponderosa pines she treasures were marked to be left after harvest.

I only hope that Davis will be able to "see the grand picture" and realize that logging can work in harmony with the ecosystem.

Bill Wynkoop

REACH OUT TO OTHERS

I would like to respond to Christine Scherp's Feb. 19 letter in which she made an agonized plea asking how people can start making a difference in children's lives. It's not easy for anyone to deal with the death of a child, especially by violence. We rage inside at the unfairness.

I would like to suggest that people who ache to change a child's life and prevent such violent episodes should volunteer their time. Look first at your own relatives, neighbors and friends and reach out to them. If you truly care and say with sincerity in your voice that you want to help in some way, they will hear that. Take time to babysit, talk, listen and suggest alternatives. The simple act of stepping in and saying, "I care," can prevent negative feelings from escalating. We're talking about patterns and behaviors that can't be changed in a day but only over a period of time. It's scary and hard to get involved in other people's lives, but if they accept your offer of help you've just made the first big step.

If you have time to volunteer for an agency that helps children and parents, look into the Head Start program or volunteer at a crisis center.

You can make a difference, Christine! We all can, but we need to be the ones to reach out and take that step.

Gayla Beanblossom

BAN PLASTIC FOAM

I am writing this letter to question this community's environmental responsibility. I am in no way a radical environmentalist, but I am concerned about the health and future of our planet.

I have lived in Oregon all my life, in the smallest of communities to the larger city of Portland. No community I've come across has ever claimed to be as environmentally concerned as has Lane County, yet I consistently see the use of Styrofoam. I don't believe anyone needs to be told how unsafe this product is for our environment.

I've recently moved here from Portland, where plastic foam is already banned from use in restaurants, etc. How is it that a more conservative and fast-paced city will ban plastic foam long before a smaller community so well known for its liberal environmental concerns?

I think it's time this community starts thinking about what it can do to preserve what we have left of our fragile planet, even if the first step is to ban Styrofoam.

Isla Dane

2. Which of these letters are convincing? What support is offered? What kinds of support do you require in order to be convinced?

3. It is important that reasons for a thesis be distinct and not merely restatements of the same one reason. Which of the following argument outlines repeat and, hence, need trimming?

   a. Desert Storm was a justifiable military action because
      it pushed back aggression
      it contained a threat to uninterrupted oil supply
      it liberated Kuwait

   b. Teenagers should be encouraged to use condoms because
      they help prevent sexually transmitted diseases
      they are a cheaper form of birth control than abortion
      they protect partners from AIDS

   c. The state college and university system should change from a quarter calendar to the semester calender because
      two registrations are cheaper than three
      courses with several weeks added offer a better educational experience than the current courses
      one third fewer courses makes for a more coherent curriculum than the present offerings

4. The following are groups of items listed randomly. Rearrange each group as an abstraction ladder, scaling each item from general to specific.

   a. Supreme Court Justice Sandra Day O'Connor, women in positions of power, powerful women in government, notable women jurists.

   b. The Twins' pitching staff is weakened. The Twins' bullpen has no long-relief pitcher. The Twins will not win the division championship this year. Long-reliever J. T. is on the disabled list.

   c. Oldsmobile Achieva goes head-to-head with Honda Accord. General Motors is responding to Japanese dominance of the compact car market. Oldsmobile has a new import battler. Achieva offers handling, comfort, and economy comparable to the Accord's. Achieva gets slightly better gas mileage in city driving.

5. Examine the organization of the student arguments in the Argument Assignments section of this book. Are any organized traditionally? What steps are included? In what order? Do these examples suggest variety of organization? Pay attention to how each piece begins and ends. Can you suggest more effective ways to organize any of them?

6. In the letters to the editor in Activity 1, examine how each writer appeals to reason and to emotion and presents his or her own character. What is effective? What can be improved?

7. The seventeenth-century French mathematician Pascal collected his notes as *Pensées* or *Thoughts*. Some of Pascal's thoughts reflected on reading and writing, in particular on argument. For each of Pascal's statements, write a brief comment of reaction in your notebook. Does Pascal present you with any new insight about writing argument? Does he restate some points already presented in this book? Are his comments true to your experience of writing argument?

   a. Those who are accustomed to judge by feeling do not understand the process of reasoning, for they would understand at first sight, and they are not used to seek for principles. And others, on the contrary, who are accustomed to reason from principles, do not at all understand matters of feeling, seeking principles, and being unable to see at a glance.

   b. When we wish to correct with advantage, and to show another that he errs, we must notice from what side he views the matter, for on that side it is usually true, and admit that truth to him, but reveal to him the side on which it is false. He is satisfied with that, for he sees that he was not mistaken, and that he only failed to see all sides. Now, no one is offended at not seeing everything; but one does not like to be mistaken.

   c. People are generally better persuaded by the reasons they have themselves discovered than by those which have come into the mind of others.

   d. When we read too fast or too slowly, we understand nothing.

   e. There are some who speak well and write badly. For the place and the audience warm them, and draw from their minds more than they think of without that warmth.

   f. Certain authors, speaking of their works, say, "My book," "My commentary," "My history," etc. They resemble middle class people who have a house of their own, and always have "My house" on their tongue. They would do better to say, "Our book," "Our commentary," "Our history," etc., because there is in them usually more of other people's than their own.

   g. The last thing one settles in writing a book is what one should put in first.

8. The conversations of Socrates (470–399 B.C.) were recorded and no doubt embellished by his student Plato. In the dialogue "Gorgias," Socrates notes the difficulty yet the benefits of arguing well. Use his thoughts to review your own thinking about argument. As you did with

the Pascal selections of Activity 7, use your notebook to record your reactions to Socrates' statements.

a. For it seems to me shameful that, being what apparently at this moment we are, we should consider ourselves to be fine fellows, when we can never hold to the same views about the same questions—and those too the most vital of all—so deplorably uneducated are we!

b. Now you and I are behaving absurdly in this discussion, for throughout the time of our argument we have never ceased returning in circles to the same point in a constant failure to understand each other's meaning.

c. I think we should all be contentiously eager to know what is true and what false in the subject under discussion, for it is a common benefit that this be revealed to all alike.

d. These facts, which were shown to be as I state them some time earlier in our previous discussion, are buckled fast and clamped together—to put it somewhat crudely—by arguments of steel and adamant—at least so it would appear as matters stand. And unless you or one still more enterprising than yourself can undo them, it is impossible to speak aright except as I am now speaking.

CHAPTER FOUR
VARIETIES OF SUPPORT

There are many ways to support a thesis. Although readers seldom require a certain number or combination of supports, your knowledge of the variety of possible support can help you argue effectively.

First of all, a knowledge of the variety of support encourages you to test and to question your position on an issue. As you participate in the debate on an issue, you can understand your own position in terms of what supports it, what questions it, and what is certain and uncertain about it. If evidence raises questions in your mind about your thesis—or refutes it— you may be forced to change it. A primary use of the material you gather is to test once again the solidity of your position and to gauge the need to change it.

If support seems adequate to confirm your position, then you can begin to use this support in your argument. Remember, however, that materials contradictory to your position help you anticipate the objections of readers.

Next, with a variety of support, you are able to consider how to use this variety effectively. How do items of support work together? How do items work with particular readers? Effective arguments weave various strands of support into strong cables. Effective arguments also communicate materials that make a difference to readers—that, ideally, change them. You need to present fresh discussion that challenges readers to consider your position. You connect this support to reader values and needs. Perhaps, readers share with you an appreciation of the importance of the issue or share an assumption or warrant or a similar diagnosis of the problem or desire for a solution. Drawing from a variety of support, you select support that corroborates thesis and communicates to readers.

The following sections of this chapter survey five groups of support. Consider the survey as a menu. Facing many choices can be frustrating, yet such choices allow you to select what is available to you and effective for your readers. For each group, the kinds of supports are defined and illustrated, as are their uses and misuses, including some common fallacies.

In contrast to reasonable arguments, fallacious arguments are basically flawed. The terms *valid* and *true*, introduced in the discussion of reason in Chapter 3, characterize a reasonable argument. Such well-constructed thought contrasts with poor constructions, which are fallacious. Fallacious arguments include mistakes of sequencing and focus. The writers of fallacious arguments often take shortcuts or liberties with supporting materials. Throughout this chapter you will survey fallacies that writers are trapped by or use to trap others.

Listing fallacies and warning against them, however, is about as useful as listing varieties of support and urging their use. More important than such lists is the development of your own critical attitude. To use support well, you must criticize it. Does support test the thesis? Does it work with other support to question or corroborate the thesis? Does it relate to readers? Does it change readers? A critical use of support goes a long way toward preventing fallacies, which, as you will see, often result from haste and expediency. Fallacies can be naive or sophisticated. Although they often result from carelessness, they are sometimes crafted with a deliberate oversimplification or distortion of reasonable thinking.

VARIETIES OF SUPPORT: AN OVERVIEW OF FIVE GROUPS

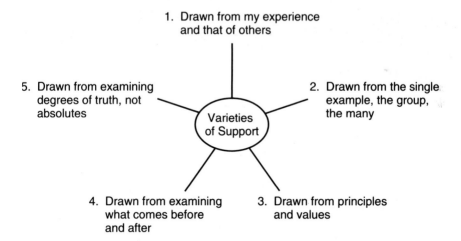

GROUP ONE SUPPORT:
WHAT I AND OTHERS SEE AND SAY

Personal experience, testimony, and authority originate with people who are witnesses or in some other way experienced with the issue. Common sense indicates that those who are closest to or most involved with an issue, who somehow have firsthand experience with it, might give you insights that those who are removed from the issue are not able to give.

Personal Experience

Using reason in arguments does not rule out the "I" of personal experience. Generally, readers demand other kinds of support as well, but personal experience can be effective. It is readily available; it can be vital and sincere. Of course, it needs to be relevant to the thesis. You must fit personal experience to the argument's aims, avoiding mere self-expression and pointless anecdote.

Previously, you saw how Isak Dinesen and Brenda Peterson presented first-person experience to support arguments. It was part of Aldo Leopold's and Wendell Berry's arguments, too.

Testimony

Other people's personal experience may also help you to support a thesis. Commonly, witnesses help build a case in court or win backing for a bill in the legislature. Often, they appear in person, speaking for themselves. Readers value those who have firsthand experience, those who see or hear things pertinent to the debate. You are able to present testimony in direct quotation or as a paraphrase. Because witnesses are often closer to the issues than the writer or the reader, their testimony is at least worth attention. Peterson uses her father's experience—that of a successful hunter and wilderness survivor—to explain and support her thesis.

Authority

Calling on authorities allows you to use the pertinent observations of many qualified people who have published their findings. These people are expert witnesses because, whether or not they have firsthand experience, they have a commitment to understanding the issue. Their interest is not casual, nor is it solely partisan. Such authorities have qualifications related to addressing the issue: academic degrees, subject specialities, and professional affiliations. Jane Brody uses, for example, the work of food scientists and anthropologists to bolster her thesis about diet.

Uses and Misuses of Group One Support

You must ask one important question about testimony, whether of a witness or an expert: How reliable is it? You must consider what may obscure the witness's view of the subject, that is, what personal limitations or biases or special interests the witness may have. The appeal to authority is easily abused. Many commercials employ actors to play doctors or technicians or use real celebrities to endorse products they know little about. Every brand, every administration, every political cause seems to have its authority. You need not pass over using authority because it is so often used poorly. Indeed, using a bona fide authority adds weight to your argument.

The *fallacy of authority* occurs whenever the person presented as an authority really is not one. The so-called authority may have no credentials or no recent experience pertinent to the issue. The person may be expert in some unrelated field, but not clearly connected to the issue. Or, the person, although qualified as an authority, may be compromised by aims (getting money, power, or fame, for example) other than clarifying and telling the truth.

EXERCISE 4.1 How compelling is the use of personal experience in the arguments of Dinesen (Chapter 2), Leopold (Chapter 1), and Berry (Chapter 1)? Would the arguments by Lifton (Chapter 2) and Baraka (Chapter 3) be stronger had they included personal experience? In which of your arguments has personal experience played a supporting role? Write in your notebook a paragraph explaining the uses of personal experience in argument.

EXERCISE 4.2 The following arguments by Susan Faludi and Ed Whitelaw use a variety of authorities. Read these arguments and answer the following questions in your notebook. How integral to the arguments are these authorities? Do the uses of authority help clarify the arguments? Do they also make the arguments convincing? In your arguments, have you used authority to support your thesis? Have you included the voices of authorities who speak against your views? Is there any merit to using opposing authorities?

 BACKLASHES THEN AND NOW

Susan Faludi

Susan Faludi (b. 1959) is a journalist and a winner of a Pulitzer Prize. Her book *Backlash: The Undeclared War Against American Women* (1991) examines reactions against feminism in the light of several historical backlashes. *Backlash* received the National Book Critics' Circle Award for Nonfiction. Faludi argues that not only do Americans have a mistaken notion of the history of women's rights, but that American women unwittingly contribute to the backlashes that impede their progress toward equality. Faludi has a full agenda: her thesis is provocative and her readers expect her to deliver support for it. Indeed, drawing from a number of fields, Faludi offers comprehensive support. The selection from "Backlashes Then and Now" illustrates Faludi's method of focusing a lot of information on her argument point.

A backlash against women's rights is nothing new in American history. Indeed, it's a recurring phenomenon: it returns every time women begin to

1

make some headway toward equality, a seemingly inevitable early frost to the culture's brief flowerings of feminism. "The progress of women's rights in our culture, unlike other types of 'progress,' has always been strangely reversible," American literature scholar Ann Douglas has observed. Women's studies historians over the years have puzzled over the "halting gait," the "fits and starts," the "stop-go affair" of American feminism. "While men proceed on their developmental way, building on inherited traditions," women's historian Dale Spender writes, "women are confined to cycles of lost and found."

2   Yet in the popular imagination, the history of women's rights is more commonly charted as a flat dead line that, only twenty years ago, began a sharp and unprecedented incline. Ignoring the many peaks and valleys traversed in the endless march toward liberty, this mental map of American women's progress presents instead a great plain of "traditional" womanhood, upon which women have roamed helplessly and "naturally," the eternally passive subjects until the 1970s women's movement came along. This map is in itself harmful to women's rights; it presents women's struggle for liberty as if it were a one-time event, a curious and even noxious by-product of a postmodern age. It is, as poet and essayist Adrienne Rich has described it, "the erasure of women's political and historical past which makes each new generation of feminists appear as an abnormal excrescence on the face of time."

3   An accurate charting of American women's progress through history might look more like a corkscrew tilted slightly to one side, its loops inching closer to the line of freedom with the passage of time—but, like a mathematical curve approaching infinity, never touching its goal. The American woman is trapped on this asymptotic spiral, turning endlessly through the generations, drawing ever nearer to her destination without ever arriving. Each revolution promises to be "*the* revolution" that will free her from the orbit, that will grant her, finally, a full measure of human justice and dignity. But each time, the spiral turns her back just short of the finish line. Each time, the American woman hears that she must wait a little longer, be a little more patient—her hour on the stage is not yet at hand. And worse yet, she may learn to accept her coerced deferral as her choice, even to flaunt it.

4   Whenever this spiral has swung closer to equality, women have believed their journey to be drawing to a close. "At the opening of the twentieth century," suffragist Ida Husted Harper rejoiced, the female condition was "completely transformed in most respects." Soon the country would have to open a Woman's Museum, feminist Elsie Clews Parsons mused in 1913, just to prove "to a doubting posterity that once women were a distinct social class." Still later, at the close of World War II, a female steelworker declared in a government survey, "The old theory that a woman's place is in the home no longer exists. Those days are gone forever."

Yet in each of these periods the celebrations were premature. This 5
pattern of women's hopes raised only to be dashed is peculiar neither to
American history nor to modern times. Different kinds of backlashes
against women's mostly tiny gains—or against simply the perception that
women were in the ascendancy—may be found in the rise of restrictive
property laws and penalties for unwed and childless women of ancient
Rome, the heresy judgments against female disciples of the early Christian
Church, or the mass witch burnings of medieval Europe.

But in the compressed history of the United States, backlashes have 6
surfaced with striking frequency and intensity—and they have evolved
their most subtle means of persuasion. In a nation where class distinctions
are weak, or at least submerged, maybe it's little wonder that gender status
is more highly prized and hotly defended. If the American man can claim
no ancestral coat of arms on which to elevate himself from the masses,
perhaps he can fashion his sex into a sort of pedigree. In America, too,
successfully persuading women to collaborate in their own subjugation is
a tradition of particularly long standing. White European women first
entered the American colonies as "purchase brides," shipped into Virginia
and sold to bachelors for the price of transport. This transaction was billed
not as servitude but choice because the brides were "sold with their
own consent." As a perplexed Alexis de Tocqueville observed, the single
woman in early 19th-century America seemed to have more freedom
than her counterpart in Europe, yet also more determination to relinquish it
in confining marriages: "It may be said that she has learned by the use of
her independence to surrender it without a struggle." Such a trait would
prove especially useful in the subsequent periodic campaigns to stymie
women's progress, as American women were encouraged to use what liberty
they did have to promote their own diminishment. As scholar Cynthia
Kinnard observes in her bibliographical survey of American antifeminist
literature, about one-third of the articles and nearly half the books and
pamphlets denouncing the campaign for women's rights have issued from a
female pen.

While American backlashes can be traced back to colonial times, the 7
style of backlash that surfaced in the last decade has its roots most firmly in
the last century. The Victorian era gave rise to mass media and mass marketing—two institutions that have since proved more effective devices for
constraining women's aspirations than coercive laws and punishments. They
rule with the club of conformity, not censure, and claim to speak for female
public opinion, not powerful male interests.

If we retrace the course of women's rights back to the Victorian era, 8
we wind up with a spiral that has made four revolutions. A struggle for
women's rights gained force in the mid-19th century, the early 1900s, the
early 1940s, and the early 1970s. In each case, the struggle yielded to
backlash.

The All-American Repeating Backlash

9 The "woman movement" of the mid-19th century, launched at the 1848
Seneca Falls women's rights convention and articulated most famously by
Elizabeth Cady Stanton and Susan B. Anthony, pressed for suffrage and an
array of liberties—education, jobs, marital and property rights, "voluntary
motherhood," health and dress reform. But by the end of the century, a cultural counterreaction crushed women's appeals for justice. Women fell back
before a barrage of warnings virtually identical to today's, voiced by that
era's lineup of Ivy League scholars, religious leaders, medical experts, and
press pundits. Educated women of this era, too, were said to be falling victim to a man shortage; "the redundancy of spinster gentlewomen," in the
parlance of the time, inspired debate in state legislatures and frenzied
scholarly "research." A marriage study even made the rounds in 1895, asserting that only 28 percent of college-educated women could get married.
They, too, faced a so-called infertility epidemic—this one induced by
"brain-womb" conflict, as a Harvard professor's best-selling book defined it
in 1873. And Victorian women who worked were likewise said to be suffering a sort of early career burnout—"exhaustion of the feminine nervous
system"—and losing their femininity to "hermaphroditism."

10   Then as now, late-Victorian religious and political leaders accused
women who postponed childbearing of triggering a "race suicide" that endangered (white) America's future; they were, in the words of President
Theodore Roosevelt, "criminals against the race" and "objects of contemp-
tuous abhorrence by healthy people." Married women who demanded rights
were charged, then as now, with creating a "crisis of the family." The media
and the churches railed against feminists for fueling divorce rates, and
state legislatures passed more than one hundred restrictive divorce laws
between 1889 and 1906. South Carolina banned divorce outright. And a
band of "purity" crusaders, like the contemporary New Right brigade, condemned contraception and abortion as "obscene" and sought to have it
banned. By the late 1800s, they had succeeded: Congress outlawed the distribution of contraceptives and a majority of states criminalized abortion—
both for the first time in the nation's history.

11   In the early 1910s, women's rights activities resurrected the struggle
for suffrage and turned it into a nationwide political campaign. The word
"feminism" entered the popular vocabulary—even silent film vamp Theda
Bara was calling herself one—and dozens of newly formed women's groups
hastened to endorse its tenets. The National Woman's Party organized in
1916, a campaign for an Equal Rights Amendment began and working
women formed their own trade unions and struck for decent pay and better
working conditions. The International Ladies' Garment Workers Union,
founded in 1900, grew so quickly that it was the American Federation of
Labor's third largest affiliate by 1913. Margaret Sanger led a national birth

control movement. And Heterodoxy, a sort of feminist intelligentsia, began conducting early versions of consciousness-raising groups.

But just as women had won the right to vote and a handful of state leg-   12
islatures had granted women jury duty and passed equal-pay laws, another counterassault on feminism began. The U.S. War Department, with the aid of the American Legion and the Daughters of the American Revolution, incited a red-baiting campaign against women's rights leaders. Feminists like Charlotte Perkins Gilman suddenly found they couldn't get their writings published; Jane Addams was labeled a Communist and a "serious threat" to national security; and Emma Goldman was exiled. The media maligned suffragists; magazine writers advised that feminism was "destructive of woman's happiness"; popular novels attacked "career women"; clergymen railed against "the evils of woman's revolt"; scholars charged feminism with fueling divorce and infertility; and doctors claimed that birth control was causing "an increase in insanity, tuberculosis, Bright's disease, diabetes, and cancer." Young women, magazine writers informed, no longer wanted to be bothered with "all that feminist pother." Post-feminist sentiments first surfaced, not in the 1980s media, but in the 1920s press. Under this barrage, membership in feminist organizations soon plummeted, and the remaining women's groups hastened to denounce the Equal Rights Amendment or simply converted themselves to social clubs. "Ex-feminists" began issuing their confessions.

In place of equal respect, the nation offered women the Miss America   13
beauty pageant, established in 1920—the same year women won the vote. In place of equal rights, lawmakers, labor and corporate leaders, and eventually some women's groups endorsed "protective" labor policies, measures that served largely to protect men's jobs and deny women equal pay. The '20s eroded a decade of growth for female professionals; by 1930 there were fewer female doctors than in 1910. When the Depression hit, a new round of federal and state laws forced thousands of women out of the work force, and new federal wage codes institutionalized lower pay rates for women.

"All about us we see attempts being made, buttressed by governmen-   14
tal authority, to throw women back into the morass of unlovely dependence from which they were just beginning to emerge," feminist Doris Stevens wrote in 1933, in *Equal Rights*, the National Woman's Party publication. "It looks sometimes as if pre-suffrage conditions even might be curiously reversed and the grievance held by women against men be changed into a grievance held by men against women," Margaret Culkin Banning remarked in an essay in *Harper's* in 1935. But like today, most social commentators held that the feminists' tents were folding only because their battle was over—women's rights had been secured. As political science scholar Ethel Klein writes of the 1920s, "The dissipation of interest in the women's movement was taken as a sign not of failure but of completion."

15   The spiral swung around again in the 1940s as a wartime economy opened millions of high-paying industrial jobs to women, and the government even began to offer minimal day care and household assistance. Federal brochures saluted the hardy working woman as a true patriot. Strong women became cultural icons; Rosie the Riveter was revered and, in 1941, Wonder Woman was introduced. Women welcomed their new economic status; 5 to 6 million poured into the work force during the war years, 2 million into heavy-industry jobs; by war's end, they would represent a record 57 percent of all employed people. Seventy-five percent reported in government surveys that they were going to keep their jobs after the war—and, in the younger generation, 88 percent of the 33,000 girls polled in a *Senior Scholastic* survey said they wanted a career, too. Women's political energies revived; working-class women flooded unions, protested for equal pay, equal seniority rights, and day care; and feminists launched a new campaign for the ERA. This time, the amendment won the endorsements of both political parties, and, in the course of the war, for the first time since the ERA had been proposed in 1923, the Senate Judiciary Committee voted it to the Senate floor three times. In a record outpouring of legislative goodwill, the '40s-era Congress passed thirty-three bills serving to advance women's rights.

16   But with the close of World War II, efforts by industry, government, and the media converged to force a female retreat. Two months after a U.S. victory had been declared abroad, women were losing their economic beachhead as 800,000 were fired from the aircraft industry; by the end of the year, 2 million female workers had been purged from heavy industry. Employers revived prohibitions against hiring married women or imposed caps on female workers' salaries; and the federal government proposed giving unemployment assistance only to men, shut down its day care services, and defended the "right" of veterans to displace working women. An anti-ERA coalition rallied its forces, including the federal Women's Bureau, forty-three national organizations, and the National Committee to Defeat the UnEqual Rights Amendment. Soon, they had killed the amendment—a death sentence hailed on the *New York Times* editorial page. "Motherhood cannot be amended and we are glad the Senate didn't try," the newspaper proclaimed. When the United Nations issued a statement supporting equal rights for women in 1948, the United States government was the only one of the twenty-two American nations that wouldn't sign it.

17   Employers who had applauded women's work during the war now accused working women of incompetence or "bad attitudes"—and laid them off at rates that were 75 percent higher than men's. Advice experts filled bookstores with the usual warnings: education and jobs were stripping women of their femininity and denying them marriage and motherhood; women were suffering "fatigue" and mental instability from employment; women who used day care were selfish "fur-coated mothers." Yet another Ivy League marriage study drew headlines: this Cornell University study said

college-educated single women had no more than a 65 percent chance of getting married. Better watch out, the Sunday magazine *This Week* advised its female readers; a college education "skyrockets your chances of becoming an old maid." Feminism was "a deep illness" that was turning modern women into a woebegone "lost sex," the era's leading advice book warned. Independent-minded women had gotten "out of hand" during the war, Barnard sociologist Willard Waller decreed. The rise in female autonomy and aggressiveness, scholar and government officials agreed, was causing a rise in juvenile delinquency and divorce rates—and would only lead to the collapse of the family. Child-care authorities, most notably Dr. Benjamin Spock, demanded that wives stay home, and colleges produced new curricula to train women to be good homemakers.

Advertisers reversed their wartime message—that women could work   18
and enjoy a family life—and claimed now that women must choose, and choose only home. As a survey of women's images in postwar magazine fiction would later find, careers for women were painted in a more unattractive light in this era than at any time since the turn of the century; these short stories represented "the strongest assault on feminine careerism" since 1905. On the comics pages, even the postwar Wonder Woman was going weak at the knees.

Again, a few defenders of women's rights tried to point out signs of the   19
gathering political storm. In 1948, Susan B. Anthony IV remarked that there appeared to be a move afoot to "crack up" the women's movement. Margaret Hickey, head of the federal Women's Advisory Committee to the War Manpower Commission warned that a "campaign of undercover methods and trumped up excuses" was driving women from top-paying government jobs. But most women's rights groups were disowning their own cause. Soon, Hickey herself was declaring, "The days of the old, selfish, strident feminism are over." Meanwhile, a younger generation of women, adrift in a TV-shaped dreamscape of suburban patios and family dens, donned padded bras and denied personal ambition. Soon, the majority of young college women were claiming they were on campus only to find husbands. Their age at first marriage dropped to a record low for the century; the number of their babies climbed to a record high.

The '50s era of the "feminine mystique" is amply chronicled, most fa-   20
mously in Betty Friedan's 1963 account. But in fact the much publicized homebound image of the '50s woman little matched her actual circumstances. This is an important distinction that bears special relevance to the current backlash, the effects of which have often been discounted, characterized as benign or even meaningless because women continue to enter the work force. In the '50s, while women may have been hastening down the aisle, they were also increasing their numbers at the office—soon at a pace that outstripped even their wartime work participation. And it was precisely women's unrelenting influx into the job market, not a retreat to the home, that

provoked and sustained the antifeminist furor. It was the reality of the nine-to-five working woman that heightened cultural fantasies of the compliant homebody and playmate. As literary scholars Sandra M. Gilbert and Susan Gubar observe of the postwar era, "[J]ust as more and more women were getting paid for using their brains, more and more men represented them in novels, plays, and poems as nothing but bodies."

21 These cultural images notwithstanding, the proportion of women working doubled between 1940 and 1950, and for the first time the majority of them were married—forcing the average man to face the specter of the working woman in his own home. Even at the very peak of the postwar industries' expulsion of female workers, women were quietly returning to the workplace through a back door. While 3.25 million women were pushed or persuaded out of industrial jobs in the first year after the end of World War II, 2.75 million women were entering the work force at the same time, in lower-paid clerical and administrative positions. Two years after the war, working women had recouped their numerical setbacks in the job market, and by 1952 more women were employed than at the height of the war economy's output. By 1955 the *average* wife worked until her first child was born and went back to work when her children started school.

22 The backlash of the feminine-mystique years did not return working women to the home (and, instructively, almost none of the wartime *clerical* work force was laid off after V-J Day). Rather, the culture derided them; employers discriminated against them; government promoted new employment policies that discriminated against women; and eventually women themselves internalized the message that, if they must work, they should stick to typing. The ranks of working women didn't shrink in the '50s, but the proportion of them who were relegated to low-paying jobs rose, their pay gap climbed, and occupational segregation increased as their numbers in the higher-paying professions declined from one-half in 1930 to about one-third by 1960. The '50s backlash, in short, didn't transform women into full-time "happy housewives"; it just demoted them to poorly paid secretaries.

23 Women's contradictory circumstances in the '50s—rising economic participation coupled with an embattled and diminished cultural stature—is the central paradox of women under a backlash. At the turn of the century, concerted efforts by university presidents, politicians, and business leaders to purge women from the campus and the office also failed; between 1870 and 1910 both the proportion of college women and the proportion of working women doubled. We should not, therefore, gauge a backlash by losses in women's numbers in the job market, but by attacks on women's rights and opportunities within that market, attacks that serve to stall and set back true economic equality. As a 1985 AFL-CIO report on workers' rights observed of women's dubious progress in the '80s job market: "The number of working women has grown to about 50 million today, but there has been no similar growth in their economic status."

To understand why a backlash works in this contrary manner, we need   24
to go back to our tilted corkscrew model of female progress. In any time of
backlash, cultural anxiety inevitably centers on two pressure points in that
spiral, demographic trends that act like two arrows pushing against the spiral, causing it to lean in the direction of women's advancement, but also becoming the foci of the backlash's greatest wrath.

A woman's claim to her own paycheck is one of these arrows. The pro-   25
portion of women in the paid labor force has been rising with little interrup-
tion since the Victorian era. In a society where income is the measure of
social strength and authority, women's growing presence in the labor force
can't help but mitigate women's secondary standing. But it hasn't brought full
equality. Instead, with each turn of the spiral, the culture simply redoubles
its resistance, if not by returning women to the kitchen, then by making the
hours spent away from their stoves as inequitable and intolerable as possible: pushing women into the worst occupations, paying them the lowest
wages, laying them off first and promoting them last, refusing to offer child
care or family leave, and subjecting them to harassment.

The other straight arrow pressing against but never piercing the back-   26
lash corkscrew is a woman's control over her own fertility—and it, too, sets
up the same paradox between private behavior and public attitudes. As
Henry Adams said of the furor over women's increasing propensity to limit
family growth in his day, "[T]he surface current of social opinion seemed set
as strongly in one direction as the silent undercurrent of social action ran in
the other." With the exception of the postwar baby boom, the number of
childbirths per household has gradually declined in the last century. The
ability to limit family size has certainly improved women's situation, but it,
too, has only inspired countervailing social campaigns to regulate pregnant
women's behavior and stigmatize the childless. In periods of backlash, birth
control becomes less available, abortion is restricted, and women who avail
themselves of it are painted as "selfish" or "immoral."

The 1970s women's movement made its most substantial progress on   27
the twin fronts of employment and fertility—forging historic and record numbers of equal employment and anti-discrimination policies, forcing open the
doors to lucrative and elite "male" professions, and ultimately helping to legalize abortion. And now, once again, as the backlash crests and breaks, it
crashes hardest on these two shores—dismantling the federal apparatus for
enforcing equal opportunity, gutting crucial legal rulings for working women,
undermining abortion rights, halting birth control research, and promulgat-
ing "fetal protection" and "fetal rights" policies that have shut women out of
lucrative jobs, caused them to undergo invasive obstetric surgeries against
their will, and thrown "bad" mothers in jail.

◆   ◆   ◆

The attack on women's rights that has developed in the last decade is per-   28
haps most remarkable for how little it has been remarked upon at all. The

press has largely ignored the mounting evidence of a backlash—and promoted the "evidence" that the backlash invented instead. The media have circulated make-believe data on marriage and infertility that linked women's progress to marital and fertility setbacks, or unquestioningly passed along misleading government and private reports that concealed increasing inequities and injustice—such as the Labor Department's claim that women's wage gap has suddenly narrowed or the EEOC's claim that sexual harassment on the job is declining or a Justice Department report that rape rates are static.

29   In place of factual reporting on the political erosion in women's lives, the mass media have offered us fictional accounts of women "cocooning," a so-called new social trend in which the *Good Housekeeping*–created "New Traditionalist" gladly retreats to her domestic shell. Cocooning is little more than a resurgence of the 1950s "back-to-the-home movement," itself a creation of advertisers and, in turn, a recycled version of the Victorian fantasy that a new "cult of domesticity" was bringing droves of women home. Not surprisingly, the cocooning lady has been invented and exalted by the same institutions that have sustained the heaviest financial hit from women's increasingly noncocooning habits. Traditional women's magazine publishers, television programmers, and the marketers of fashion, beauty, and household goods have all played central roles—all merchandisers who still believe they need "feminine passivity" and full-time homemaking to sell their wares. They have saluted and sold the New Traditionalist's virtuous surrender time and again—in promotional tributes heralding the so-called return of the "new" Clairol Girl, the "new" Breck Girl, the new hearth angel of *Victoria* magazine, and the new lady of leisure in the catalogs of Victoria's Secret.

30   The very choice of the word "cocooning" should suggest to us the trend's fantastical nature. A cocoon is a husk sloughed upon maturity; butterflies don't return to their chrysalis—nor to a larval state. The cultural myth of cocooning suggests an adult woman who has regressed in her life cycle, returned to a gestational stage. It maps the road back from the feminist journey, which was once aptly defined by a turn-of-the-century writer as "the attempt of women to grow up." Cocooning's infantile imagery, furthermore, bears a vindictive subtext, by promoting a retreat from female adulthood at the very time when the largest proportion of the female population is entering middle age. Feminine youth is elevated when women can least ascend its pedestal; cocooning urges women to become little girls, then mocks them mercilessly for the impossibility of that venture.

31   The false feminine vision that has been unfurled by contemporary popular culture in the last decade is a sort of vast velveteen curtain that hides women's reality while claiming to be its mirror. It has not made women cocoon or become New Traditionalists. But its thick drapery has both concealed the political assault on women's rights and become the impossible standard

by which American women are asked to judge themselves. Its false front has encouraged each woman to doubt herself for not matching the image in the mass-produced mirror, instead of doubting the validity of the mirror itself and pressing to discover what its nonreflective surface hides.

As the backlash has gained power, instead of fighting and exposing its force, many women's groups and individual women have become caught up with fitting into its fabricated backdrop. Feminist-minded institutions founded a decade earlier, from The First Women's Bank to Options for Women, camouflaged their intent with new, neutral-sounding names; women in politics have claimed they are now only interested in "family issues," not women's rights; and career women with Ivy League degrees have eschewed the feminist label for public consumption. Instead of assailing injustice, many women have learned to adjust to it. Instead of getting angry, they have become depressed. Instead of uniting their prodigious numbers, they have splintered and turned their pain and frustration inward, some in starkly physical ways.   32

In turn, this female adjustment process to backlash pressures has yielded record profits for the many "professionals" who have rushed in to exploit and exacerbate it: advice writers and pop therapists, matchmaking consultants, plastic surgeons, and infertility specialists have both fueled and cashed in on women's anxiety and panic under the backlash. Millions of women have sought relief from their distress, only to wind up in the all-popular counseling of the era where women learn not to raise their voices but to lower their expectations and "surrender" to their "higher power."   33

The American woman has not yet slipped into a cocoon, but she has tumbled down a rabbit hole into sudden isolation. In Wendy Wasserstein's 1988 Broadway hit *The Heidi Chronicles,* her heroine, Heidi Holland, delivers a speech that would become one of the most quoted lines by women writing about the female experience in the '80s: "I feel stranded, and I thought the point was that we wouldn't feel stranded," the once feminist art historian says. "I thought we were all in this together." As women's collective quest for equal rights smacks into the backlash's wall of resistance, it breaks into a million pieces, each shard a separate woman's life. The backlash has ushered in not the cozy feeling of "family togetherness," as advertisers have described it, but the chilling realization that it is now every woman for herself. "I'm alone," a secretary confides in an article surveying contemporary women, an article that is filled with such laments. "I know a lot of people [are] dealing with the same problems, but I guess we're just dealing with them by ourselves." Both young and old women, nonideological undergraduates and feminist activitists alike, have felt the pain of this new isolation—and the sense of powerlessness it has bred. "I feel abandoned," an older feminist writes in the letters column of *Ms.,* "as if we were all members of a club that they have suddenly quit." "We don't feel angry, we feel helpless," a young woman bursts out at a college panel on women's status.   34

35   The loss of a collective spirit has proven far more debilitating to American women than what is commonly characterized as the overly taxing experience of a liberated life. Backlash-era conventional wisdom blames the women's movement for American women's "exhaustion." The feminists have pushed forward too fast, backlash pundits say; they have brought too much change too soon and have worn women out. But the malaise and enervation that women are feeling today aren't induced by the speed of liberation but by its stagnation. The feminist revolution has petered out, leaving so many women discouraged and paralyzed by the knowledge that, once again, the possibility for real progress has been foreclosed.

36   When one is feeling stranded, finding a safe harbor inevitably becomes a more compelling course than bucking social currents. Keeping the peace with the particular man in one's life becomes more essential than battling the mass male culture. Saying one is "not a feminist" (even while supporting quietly every item of the feminist platform) seems the most prudent, self-protective strategy. Ultimately in such conditions, the impulse to remedy social injustice can become not only secondary but silent. "In a state of feeling alone," as feminist writer Susan Griffin has said, "the knowledge of oppression remains mute."

37   To expect each woman, in such a time of isolation and crushing conformism, to brave a solitary feminist stand is asking too much. "If I were to overcome the conventions," Virginia Woolf wrote, "I should need the courage of a hero, and I am not a hero." Under the backlash, even a heroine can lose her nerve, as the social climate raises the stakes to an unbearable degree and as the backlash rhetoric drives home, time and again, the terrible penalties that will befall a pioneering woman who flouts convention. In the last decade, all the warnings and threats about the "consequences" and "costs" of feminist aspiration have had their desired effect. By 1989, almost half the women in a *New York Times* poll on women's status said they now feared they had sacrificed too much for their gains. The maximum price that their culture had forced them to pay for minimal progress, they said, was just too high.

❖ OREGON'S REAL ECONOMY

Ed Whitelaw

Ed Whitelaw (b. 1941) is a professor of economics at the University of Oregon and President of ECO Northwest, an economic consulting firm. Whitelaw's article, "Oregon's Real Economy," argues for a major new approach to a regional economy. Because Whitelaw challenges popular views of the region's economy, the burden is on Whitelaw to show skeptics that he can support his position. Even in this brief paper, Whitelaw draws on a variety of support. His paper has sparked controversy between proponents of "the old, comfortable economic myths" and of some new approaches.

Ask Oregonians to identify the three most important economic sectors in   1
their state, and most of them will say timber, agriculture and tourism, usually listing them as the Eugene *Register-Guard* did in a recent editorial:
"[Tourism] ranks third behind wood products and agriculture in statewide
economic impact." It is remarkable that such an idea can be so widely held—
and so wrong.

If by "statewide economic impact" the *Register-Guard* meant total em-   2
ployment, it was far off the mark: None of these industries ranks among the
top five Oregon employers, which are health services (about 10 percent of total employment); wholesale trade (about 9 percent); business and professional services (also about 9 percent); finance, insurance and real estate
(about 8 percent); and transportation, communication and utilities (about 7
percent). Agriculture and timber each employs only 4 to 6 percent of the total. And tourism employs only 2 to 4 percent.

The *Register-Guard* is not alone in its ranking assuredness. In his 1991   3
testimony before the Endangered Species Committee—the so-called God
Squad—Con Schallau, chief economist for the American Forest Resource
Alliance, said of Oregon, "[A]lthough the relative importance of the forest
products industry has declined since 1980, it is still the dominant component." Put some real numbers on this claim, and it vanishes. The number of
workers in Oregon's lumber and wood products industry declined by 17 percent (13,500 jobs) between 1979 (the year preceding the national recession
of the early 1980s) and 1989 (the year preceding the current national reces-
sionary period, and long before the spotted owl recovery plan had any impact). By contrast, total employment in Oregon increased by 23 percent
(257,000 jobs) during the same period. Since 1989, timber jobs have continued to decrease while Oregon's total jobs have continued to increase. The
timber industry could not be the dominant component of Oregon's economy
if, as it contracts, Oregon's economy expands.

Maybe the problem is that those who feel compelled to rank-order in-   4
dustries are not simply counting jobs, but have employed some more sophisticated and useful measure. However, if by "statewide economic
impact" the *Register-Guard* meant growth in jobs, growth in pay per worker,
growth in total payroll, or forecasted growth in any of these measures, their
ranking still is wrong. In fact, by these measures timber and agriculture
rank consistently near the bottom. But aren't we replacing relatively high-
paying timber jobs with low-paying jobs in retail stores and fast-food
restaurants? Also wrong: Most of the sectors that have had the greatest
growth in jobs in the recent past pay higher wages than either timber or
agriculture. For example, the high-skill, high-pay business and professional
services (including advertising agencies, software services, engineering and
architectural services and management consulting) have added more jobs
than timber has lost, and these services pay substantially more than timber
pays. Within manufacturing, while the lumber and wood products sector

lost 7,500 jobs between 1986 and 1991, the other manufacturing sectors added 22,500 jobs—and, again, these sectors pay more than the lumber and wood products sector pays.

5   The future promises more of the same. Three of these faster-growing manufacturing sectors—electrical machinery, nonelectrical machinery, and instruments—offer an illustrative contrast with the timber industry. In addition to containing the industries we usually think of as "high tech" (such as computers, semiconductors and instruments to measure electricity), they include the manufacture of power hand tools, pumps, refrigeration equipment, light fixtures, household appliances and dental supplies. Just three years ago these three sectors, with 46,170 employees, were smaller than the lumber and wood products sector, which employed 67,300 workers. But the September 1992 Oregon Economic and Revenue Forecast from the Oregon Executive Department discloses that a historic shift in the rank-order of these sectors is taking place. The Forecast predicts that by 1997 employment in lumber and wood products will have fallen to 50,000, while employment in the mostly high-tech sectors will have risen to 55,500. More important, in 1991, the latest year for which I could obtain the data, payroll per worker in lumber and wood products was slightly less than $26,000, while payroll per worker in the three sectors was slightly more than $33,000—and the latter has been increasing twice as fast as the former.

6   Finally, the sectors that serve tourism, such as lodging and eating places, rank high (though not at the top) in the and expected growth in jobs. But they rank quite low in such measures as pay per worker.

7   It is a bit of a mystery to me why a paper such as the *Register-Guard* or individuals who seem knowledgeable feel compelled to rank-order industries, to find a mythical top dog. I think part of the answer lies with attempting to apply a largely outmoded model of how regional economies grow. This model, which received much attention from regional economists during the immediate post-WWII period, assumed that to grow and prosper, a community, a state or a region had to attract new dollars from the outside. In its simplistic form, which unfortunately most state and local economic-development specialists adopted enthusiastically, the model implied that if a state or local economy failed to expand its exports, it could not grow and prosper. Policymakers became obsessed with identifying the principal exporters and elaborating policies favoring these top dogs, whose barking presumably would rouse the rest of the economy. On too many occasions over the years, I have heard or read the so-called opinion leaders of Oregon—politicians, agency heads, editorial writers and, especially disappointing, educators— announce the currently perceived "leading industry." Most of the time it has been timber. A former state economic-development official, who no doubt would prefer that I remember him for other statements, was fond of referring

to timber as the "mother industry," apparently choosing to ignore that she was trashing her home and abandoning her children.

These economic-development cheerleaders often concluded that only   8
exports mattered, and specifically, only manufactured exports mattered—that attracting or stimulating manufacturing jobs was a necessary and sufficient precursor for growth in other sectors. But as long ago as 1956, economist Charles Tiebout pointed out in the *Journal of Political Economy* that using this logic means that the only way the world economy could grow and prosper is by exporting to celestial economies. Clearly this is absurd. A number of other economists now discount the export-base model, both because it suffers fatal theoretical flaws and because it yields meaningless, even silly, results.

And the emphasis on manufacturing alone is also wrong. Martin   9
Bailey, an economist at the University of Maryland, stated in a recent newspaper interview, " . . . competitiveness is not just machinery and semiconductors but the entire economy. The service sector is terribly important to overall living standards." In other words, neither manufacturing nor services is sufficient for a viable economy; both are necessary.

If we abandon the cherished model of the past, can we replace it with   10
something of value, a different, better model, not one demonstrably wrong in its assumptions, facts and policies? Yes, we can. Oregon's recent strong growth relative to the national economy reflects a multitude of forces and comparative advantages that have been operating in concert for several decades—not the result of the lucky draw of a couple of fast-growing industries. Part of this healthy performance is the evolution of a structure that permits an orderly change: some sectors of the economy mature and decline, while others grow. Nearly 25 years ago the urban and regional economist Wilbur Thompson anticipated part of what explains Oregon's economic performance: " . . . all products wax and wane, and so the long-range viability of any area must rest ultimately on its capacity to invent and/or innovate or otherwise acquire new export bases. The economic base of the larger metropolitan area is, then, the creativity of its universities and research parks, the sophistication of its engineering firms and financial institutions, the persuasiveness of its public relations and advertising agencies, the flexibility of its transportation networks and utility systems, and all the other dimensions of infrastructure that facilitate the quick and orderly transfer from old dying bases to new growing ones."

These economic attributes that Thompson extols all reflect the well-   11
educated, well-trained technical, administrative and professional personnel driving Oregon's economy. Other symptoms illustrate the broad strength of Oregon's economy. The Portland metropolitan economy, accounting for more than half of Oregon's economy and a much greater share of its growth, is among the three or four most diversified metropolitan economies in the

nation. It is an excellent example of a non-rank-ordered economy—an economy that is healthy precisely because it does not have a top dog.

12   To give this structure life, to make it work, one must add a driver, an underlying dynamic mechanism. There is widespread agreement among urban and regional economists in the Pacific Northwest about the extent to which the region's economic growth depends on its reputation for providing residents with a high quality of life. Consider, for example, this recent statement from John Mitchell, chief economist at US Bancorp, and Paul Sommers, research director of the University of Washington's Northwest Policy Center: "Residents and businesses continue to move into the Northwest as more parts of the region are discovered by national and foreign tourists and businesses seeking . . . favorable living conditions for employees. If [Oregon and the other Northwest states] can manage to preserve their unique environmental assets . . . the Northwest will remain one of the strongest regional economies in the country."

13   Not incidentally, Mitchell and Sommers correctly identify here the salient economic impact of tourism, which is not the dollars it brings in or the workers it employs but the number of talented Oregonians it dissuades from emigrating and the number of talented non-Oregonians it persuades to immigrate.

14   Bill Conerly, chief economist for First Interstate Bank of Oregon, summed it up in a newspaper interview this spring. "People are moving here not because of jobs but because of quality of life," he said. "If people want to live here, jobs will follow."

15   Oregonians, therefore, have a choice to make. We must choose between two economic futures. One of these futures—and the policies that get us there—is based on a mistake, a myth, a flawed model. The other reflects reality.

16   Several years ago, several hundred Oregonians, representing business (including the timber industry), labor, academia and local communities looked at alternative ways of solving the state's problems and meeting its challenges. They rejected traditional approaches, such as trying to boost the state's timber industry, in favor of alternatives they deemed better able to yield widespread improvement in the standard of living of Oregonians. The document summarizing the plan is called *Oregon Shines: An Economic Strategy for the Pacific Century.*

17   The heart of the strategy is summarized in three "Key Strategic Initiatives." The first two emphasize private and public investment in these areas:

> • *Invest in Workers.* Oregon can raise the income of its citizens only if communities, businesses and families increase the education and skills of workers.

- *Enhance the Quality of Life.* Oregon's quality of life attracts people and advanced industrial firms. Degradation of Oregon's environmental qualities will jeopardize its most important comparative advantage.

Since the publication of this strategic plan, the Oregon Progress Board, chaired by the governor and advised by the legislature and hundreds of other organizations and individuals, developed a set of measures, published last year as *Oregon Benchmarks,* for monitoring our progress in raising our standards of living. [18]

All this, of course, sounds upbeat. It reflects the optimistic assumption that we can perceive the reality of our condition and improve it. But as long as the *Register-Guard* and others hold onto the old, comfortable economic myths of our past rather than face the realities of today and tomorrow, the assumption is overly optimistic. [19]

In his 1956 book *The Image: Knowledge in Life and Society,* Kenneth Boulding addresses this point: "What I have been talking about is knowledge. Knowledge, perhaps, is not a good word for this. Perhaps one would rather say my Image of the world. Knowledge has an implication of validity, of truth. What I am talking about is what I believe to be true; my subjective knowledge. It is this Image that largely governs my behavior." [20]

The behaviors of the press, the politicians, the policymakers and indeed all of us here in Oregon toward our economy thus are affected by our images of the world. We live in our images. We act on our images. And as long as they fail to reflect reality, our economic policies, and to a disquieting extent our standards of living, will reflect the fading memories of our economic past. Such nostalgia will simply impoverish us. [21]

EXERCISE 4.3 Which do you find more effective, quotation or paraphrase? Do Faludi and Whitelaw use one method of presenting authority more than the other? Is a reference to a study more or less authoritative than a reference to an individual researcher? Record your responses in your notebook.

GROUP TWO SUPPORT: THE ONE AND THE MANY

Support from this group extends from single experiences and single factual items to larger and larger clusters of experience and data. Often a single example or fact is telling, yet such an item can be added to so as to permit new insights and to broaden and solidify support.

Example

Consider the story of Jill as a case illustrating the potential use of example. Jill is a kid who refuses to eat everything at dinner. "Clean your plate," says one parent. "Think of all the starving children throughout the world," states the other. Jill frowns, pauses, jabs back, "Name one!"

Can you claim to be informed yet not muster a single example? One example may be worth a thousand generalities. Specifics drive many successful arguments. You turn to experience, yours and that of others, to recollect or collect vivid instances—the crystals of ideas. Notice in "WIC: Investing in Our Future" (Chapter 3) how Barbara Howell uses the example of one mother and her son to show that the program works.

Be aware that you may present examples in several ways. As you name and present one example, you may present it in its physical details (describe it) or its components (analyze it) or as it reveals itself in time (narrate it, explain its process). Remember, too, your example can be actual—the nitty-gritty bottom rung of the abstraction ladder—"I know an illiterate person who is not able to get work." Or your example can be hypothetical—built from common sense—"It's easy to imagine an illiterate person who is not able to get work."

Statistics

Statistics afford a broader view than do examples. That is because statistics report on many instances, not just one or two. They broaden support. Every side has its witness; every side has its statistics. Some statistics are carefully arrived at. Some are not. As with witnesses, you need to use statistics with an eye to their accuracy, currency, and relevancy. An argument should not seem like a numbers game. But if you can link trustworthy numerical data to your thesis, you have helped support the thesis with the power of many specifics.

In Rachel Carson's selection from *Silent Spring* (Chapter 1), a biologist testifies that in a sprayed area where 100,000 fiddler crabs should have been he counted 100. Barbara Howell, in the WIC argument (Chapter 3), states that because of poor funding WIC cannot serve 3.6 million eligible pregnant women, infants, and children. Statistics, as used in Carson's and Howell's arguments, shift focus from single examples to hundreds and thousands, even millions of cases.

Induction

Induction is a use of reason that moves from a group of related specifics to a concluding insight about them. Inductive support involves collections of tidbits of evidence. From such collections, you can use induction to draw conclusions.

For most inductions, you start with a hunch or hypothesis. You base such a hypothesis on observation. Then, using induction, you draw in more observations and process them to test the hypothesis. A hypothesis, once you have tested and proved it accurate, becomes a theory in science or a thesis in argument. Induction moves up the abstraction ladder from specifics to a generalization.

For example, suppose you have observed for years that hot weather saps some people's energy. You expect high temperatures to floor them. You have discovered that these people have low blood pressure. One of your friends is not like this: in hot weather, she has always been active. But after her doctor prescribed medication to lower her blood pressure, she now feels enervated by 90-degree days. Your hunch is forming: People with low blood pressure suffer from the heat more than people with high blood pressure do. This is a minute induction based on limited examples:

> What is true for some   So maybe it is true
> is also true for her.   for many other people, too.

You can expand the induction by asking a group—let's say your writing class—two questions. What are they? What cause and effect link do you wish to discover? First question: Is your blood pressure high, average, or low? Second question: In very hot weather, is your activity level high, average, or low? From this larger sample, you may be able to predict how people with low blood pressure can be expected to act on hot summer days.

Induction takes you toward what you want to know but may not be able to know directly. With effort, you could test your hypothesis by asking the same questions of many people, but hardly of everybody. A reasonable induction may characterize very large groups; it may predict some aspect of the future.

Less formally, Isak Dinesen uses induction to reach a conclusion about living things. Three vivid experiences help her remember "the saying of a hero in a book," which is her thesis.

If personal experience, testimony, and example provide you with useful bits of support, then statistics and induction help you to process them. Statistics format bits as numbers, giving you a shorthand for handling large groups and a convenient way to summarize and to present. Induction goes further by allowing you to aim in the direction of a new insight as you move from a few to the many or the all—from surface phenomena to an understanding of cause, from the past and present into a partially charted future.

Definition

Induction helps you find the common thread running through instances. Induction is a logical procedure. Definition also works to characterize a group of items: liberals, radiators, roses. Definition, though, is more an act of language than of logic. Humpty Dumpty recognized the importance of naming when he told Alice that whoever has the power to name has the power to rule. Often you argue with others about terms because how people name things is crucial. Wendell Berry refuses to buy a computer. Whereas his friends define the computer as a helpful tool, Berry defines it as harmful and unnecessary. The Haitian boat people take risks to sail to the United States, even though our immigration service allows only those who might suffer for their political views in Haiti to stay here. The others, defined as economic refugees seeking a better standard of living, are sent back. Some human rights groups argue that those who are returned to Haiti may face intimidation, so they are truly political refugees. Whose definition is the correct one? Whose will prevail?

Definitions can be highly charged, small arguments. They often are used to add value to or devalue what is being named. Perhaps you have seen these two animal rights bumper stickers: Animal Breeders Are Pimps and Fur Is Dead. In American Cancer Society ads against smoking, grungy people shown puffing cigarettes are ironically identified with the caption "Smoking is glamorous." If you accept any of these definitions, you are accepting a thesis as well. When you use definitions acceptable to your readers, you have established important common ground.

When Aristotle urges people to argue for the good, who is to say what may be good or what may be just, useful, or beautiful? You can foresee differing over terms. Such disagreement can degenerate into wrangling and hairsplitting, into fighting over whose terms to use.

Yet, to the extent that words contain any meaning that people can agree on—and especially a meaning that conveys a sense of values or principles—arguing about terms and seeking agreement on them is worth the effort. As you argue, you try to define terms to the satisfaction of readers so that with those terms the argument can develop. When you use a term that is either highly personal or highly technical, you need to define it and stipulate that you will use the term this way throughout your argument. Wendell Berry defines what a tool should be, and by his definition, the personal computer falls short. Amiri Baraka defines the most important jazz musicians as great players *and* great innovators with lasting influence. We might argue with his definition, but, if we accept his method of choosing, we move closer to accepting his actual choice of musicians. Remember the discussion of the definition of argument in Chapter 1? You might question my definition of argument, but its use in this book, once I have defined it, should always be clear. Finally, do not assume you can nail down agreement about a term by writing, "according to Webster . . ." The meanings of words are not in dictionaries, but in the uses to which people put them.

Analysis

Definitions may be subjective, technical, or, perhaps, even misleading. A leading baker of cookies advertises "No Tropical Oils" because such oils are notoriously high in saturated fats, which are shunned by health-conscious shoppers. Well, what is the fatty ingredient? Lard! This is, of course, not a tropical oil, but it is the granddaddy of bad fats! Because language is a cover or wrapper, people can more easily change it than the thing it wraps. A new, improved deodorant looks larger than its predecessor, but it actually contains less deodorant. No wonder one should learn to read labels analytically, noting the ingredients, weight, percentages, and so forth.

Analysis permits you to examine a whole item in terms of its constituents. It breaks the unit apart. In her argument, Jane Brody analyzes the structure of our teeth and our digestive tract to find they are better suited to consuming plant foods than meat. She also analyzes the American diet to find that 70 percent of the protein we consume is derived from animals. And, on this point, she analyzes the history of American eating habits: 70 percent is more than double the percentage of animal protein consumed in the year 1900, showing that Americans have come to rely more and more on meat as their protein source. Brody's analysis supports her thesis about the need to change our diet.

Comparison and Contrast

Your earliest arguments probably used the support of comparison and contrast. Comparing—lining up two or more related items to study and rank them—is a human habit. Babies look at their hands as if to choose a favorite. When young, you probably ranked your friends, toys, and favorite songs. You appealed to your parents when you felt you were wronged by not getting the allowance or privileges of a sibling or playmate.

Comparison and contrast have argumentative force because any item in debate can look better or worse by comparison. For example, the breakfast cereal Nutri-Grain Nuggets looks a lot like the original Grape Nuts. The cereal box invites comparison: "It looks the same, but is it? In a word—no." In a taste test, people preferred Nutri-Grain 2 to 1. "That's quite a difference." The ad also claims that Nutri-Grain is "the only whole grain nugget cereal."

This ad sketches lines of contrast that are suggestive, but never substantive. Most comparisons and contrasts in rational argument need to be filled in with detail to be clear and compelling. Both Isak Dinesen and Brenda Peterson developed support for their positions by showing contrasts between what is natural and what is overcivilized, between grateful use and consumerism. Aldo Leopold contrasted a mountain with wolves to a mountain without wolves. Robert Jay Lifton contrasted a traditionally secure sense of immortality to a threatened sense of it in the present nuclear age. You urge people to accept your position on its own merits, yet also because it will be safer, cheaper, fairer, and easier to implement than opposing positions.

Analogy

Drawing analogies is a way of comparing. The comparison is figurative or imaginative, not factual. The item considered is compared to an item from a different category. You might be as "wise as your mother"—that's a straight-forward comparison—but if you are as "wise as serpents and as harmless as doves," comparison becomes novel and, possibly in argument, forceful.

In their arguments, both Susan Faludi and Thomas Paine used analo-gies. To clarify her thesis about the twists and turns in the progress of women's rights, Susan Faludi used the analogy of the corkscrew. Thomas Paine stressed the importance of present deeds by comparing them to a pin's engraving on the bark of a young tree: The characters will get larger with time and posterity will read them, to our shame or glory.

Think of the argumentative power of this analogy: Just as the head controls the body, so the monarch controls the body politic. Or this analogy: As a captain must command a ship in a storm, so a storm-tossed nation re-quires strong leadership with no bickering or disobedience among the sailors. Can you see how these analogies argue for central control? Closer to the present, the domino theory of foreign affairs was a dominant—some would say a tragic—analogy in Cold War political debates. As a row of dominoes, arranged in a line, all topple after the first one falls, so nations fall one after the other if the first is allowed to fall to the enemy. This anal-ogy presented a readily understood picture of a political possibility—such a picture shaped U.S. interventions in Vietnam and Latin America throughout the post–World War II period.

The key to a rational use of analogy is to recognize not only how two items are comparable but how they are different, and how many individual circumstances ought not to be easily clumped together by vivid and appeal-ing picture language.

Uses and Misuses of Group Two Support

Any single example, fact, or element of analysis may be useful to an argu-ment. Nonetheless, you should not give any one item more importance than it deserves—beware the *fallacy of exaggerated importance.* Examples are of-ten vivid and emotional, yet it is fallacious to suggest that one item neces-sarily represents the whole group or proves the thesis conclusively. The case of one TV-watching child, for example, cannot alone drive an argument about the effects of TV on reading ability. Likewise, it is fallacious to exaggerate the importance of one element and overlook others. A review of a luxury car might make a mountain out of a molehill by discussing the deficient sound system, never giving attention to comfort, styling, or warranty. A motel ad might tout a convenient downtown location, but say nothing about noise, lack of a view, or limited parking. The unbalanced selection from a larger slate of items is closely related to slanting: Salespeople predispose a shopper to consider a camera or computer by listing only its strengths. Campaigners discourage votes for a ballot measure by listing only its weaknesses.

The *fallacy of hasty generalizations* results from a careless handling of one or a few examples or other argument items: parts of analysis, numerical data, a sampling of testimony. From the specifics you do have, what can you reasonably conclude? What support do these few specifics really supply? Such questions help check the rush to generalize or to exploit what is known in order to reach for statements possibly true for the larger group or at a higher level on the abstraction ladder. Is it reasonable to predict future use of U.S. military forces or to form U.S. policy about military use on the basis of our nation's experience in Grenada, Panama, and Iraq? Shouldn't policy makers consider Vietnam, Korea, and World War II? Your being critical of evidence checks the urge to generalize hastily. When you are aware of opposing views, of examples and other data that do not lead to a generalization, you are not likely to jump to conclusions.

The *fallacy of equivocation* threatens the clear understanding of terms. To equivocate is to speak ambiguously, so that a repeated term appears to mean different things in different uses. Abstract terms such as "masterpiece," "excellence in education," and "recession" allow for ambiguity more readily than "Emily Dickinson's poetry," "small classes," "12 percent unemployment." A letter to a newspaper defended the execution of a murderer, saying such executions "deter" capital crimes. The letter said the deterrence was obvious, because the executed criminal would never kill again. This is a shifted, even shifty, use of the usual sense of deterrence.

In using comparisons, two pathways may be alluring. One is the *fallacy of incomplete comparisons,* often seen in an advertiser's use of the word "better." "Better than what?" you ask. In argument, a thesis cannot bask in the sunshine of "better" or "best" without a demonstration of its superiority. Comparisons should be completed and, if challenged, supported.

The other path, *the fallacy of false dilemma,* is made easy with the assumption that any issue has only a pro side and a con side, two sides and only two sides. You can avoid this fallacy by looking for alternatives. Bumper stickers—brief and bold as they must be—implore you to love it or leave it, to use it or lose it. Are these the only choices? Sometimes there are well-argued positions between the extremes. Also, opposing views, as you study them, sometimes reveal common themes. There is often common ground in the heated debates of jobs versus environment, of wage war against drugs versus legalize drugs, or pro-life versus pro-choice.

The *fallacy of false analogy* stems also from faulty comparison, but this time the comparison involves literally dissimilar items. Can Faludi really show that progress in women's rights is like a corkscrew when there are so many real dissimilarities? Can Paine show that actions today really resemble carvings in bark? An analogy works effectively in argument when readers can concentrate on similarities and not be distracted by differences between the compared items. When a politician introduces another politician as his friend and discusses the rapid growth of their friendship as a cancer, listeners might shudder at the inept analogy. How could a friendship be like a disease? In using analogy, you must be sensitive to unlikeness and to connotation, and then judge if the analogy is worth using at all.

EXERCISE 4.4 Read the following essay by Victor Papanek, "Our Kleenex Culture." Papanek wrote the essay in 1971, so some of his references are dated. From your viewpoint, you can judge to what extent the changes Papanek predicts have come to pass. Also, your distance on the subject allows you to criticize Papanek's use of logic. Once you have read Papanek, answer the following questions in your notebook.

How reasonable is the Kleenex analogy that is introduced in Paragraph 2?

How reasonable is the listing of accidents? Is the list's connection to the thesis clear? Do the Christmas items add to the argument?

Explain how Papanek avoids the fallacy of false dilemma in his discussion of disposable products.

Explain the effect of the closing example of *The New York Times.*

What do you think of Papanek's 1971 predictions about a typical moving day in 1999? Was there support in the argument that would have made the predictions seem likely in 1971? What do you know about product longevity and obsolescence that Papanek could not know in 1971? Did Papanek make solid use of available support to make his predictions?

❖ OUR KLEENEX CULTURE: OBSOLESCENCE, PERMANENCE, AND VALUE

Victor Papanek

Victor Papanek (b. 1926) is an Austrian designer, educator, and writer who moved to the United States in 1939. He is a professor of design at the University of Kansas School of Architecture. *Design for the Real World: Human Ecology and Social Change* (1971), from which this selection is drawn, argues for the economical, environment-friendly design of buildings and products. Because Papanek makes predictions about the 1990s, you are in a good position to examine the strengths and weaknesses of his argument.

In all likelihood it started with automobiles. Dies, tools, and molds that are   1
used in manufacturing cars wear out after about 3 years of usage. This has
provided the Detroit automobile makers with a timetable for their "styling
cycle." Minor cosmetic changes are performed at least once a year; because
of the need for rebuilt and redesigned dies, a major style change is plugged
in every 2½ or 3 years. Since the end of World War II, the car manufacturers have sold the American public on the concept that it is stylish and "in"
to change cars every 3 years, at the very least. With this continuous change
has come sloppy workmanship and virtually non-existent quality control.
For a quarter of a century American national administrations have proclaimed their tacit approval or enthusiastic support of this system. Some of
the economic and waste-making results of this policy have been documented in other chapters. But what is at stake here is an expansion: from
changing automobiles every few years, to considering everything a throw-
away item, and considering *all* consumer goods, and indeed, most human
values, to be disposable.

When people are persuaded, advertised, propagandized, and victim-   2
ized into throwing away their cars every 3 years, their clothes twice yearly,
their high-fidelity sets every few years, their houses every 5 years (the average American family was moving once every 56 months as I was writing this
book), then we may consider most other things fully obsolete. Throwing away
furniture, transportation, clothing, and appliances may soon lead us to feel
that marriages (and other personal relationships) are throw-away items as
well and that on a global scale countries, and indeed entire subcontinents,
are disposable like Kleenex.

In spite of its shrill and horrifying overtones, Vance Packard's *The*   3
Wastemakers tells the story of forced obsolescence and the death-rating of
products like it is.

That which we throw away, we fail to value. When we design and plan   4
things to be discarded, we exercise insufficient care in designing or in considering safety factors.

On April 8, 1969, the Health Department of Suffolk County, New York,   5
reported on their study of color TV sets. Studying sets of all sizes, prices and
makes, they discovered that minimally 20 percent of all color TV sets emit-
ted harmful X-rays at a distance of from 3 to 9 feet. In other words, at least
one in every 5 color television sets being used may sterilize the viewer, or
subject his or her children to genetic damage after prolonged exposure.

As of April 1, 1969, General Motors was recalling one out of every 7   6
automobiles and trucks for "remedial repairs" as these vehicles proved
themselves clearly unsafe in operation.

More than $750,000 has been awarded to plaintiffs or *their survivors* by   7
a jury in Sacramento because of the negligent design of the gas tank on the
early Corvette. A jury in Los Angeles gave more than $1 million to several
people because of the Volkswagen's poor cornering capability.

8   On June 29, 1967, Ernest Pelton, a seventeen-year-old playing football for his high school in Sacramento County, California, received a head injury. The depression of the subcortical layers of his brain have plunged him into a permanent coma, and he is not expected ever to regain consciousness. Medical costs for the remainder of his lifetime have been estimated to run in excess of $1 million. What makes the story relevant is that Mr. Pelton wore the best and most expensive ($28.95) football helmet being manufactured. Every year 125,000 of these helmets are sold, yet *they have never been tested for absorption of kinetic energy!* In fact, of the 15 million safety helmets, hard hats, football helmets, etc., sold annually in this country, none have ever been tested in kinetic energy situations!

9   And the examples, culled from various news accounts over recent years, go on:

> A young man is paralyzed for life because the power on his workbench is accidentally activated;
>
> A mother of 3 is killed because her chest is crushed by the steering column in a car crash;
>
> The boom of a large construction crane collapses, and 5 families are left without husbands or fathers;
>
> Six hundred women (a year) lose their hands in top-loading washers;
>
> A young girl leaving a drugstore is literally cut into ribbons because the plate glass door fails to pivot properly after a pebble gets caught in its track;
>
> A crooked union boss fails to see that safety laws on cableways are enforced: a cable shears and 3 miners are crushed;
>
> A tank car carrying carbon dioxide at −20° C. explodes in the middle of a Midwestern town;
>
> Three children are paralyzed from the neck down because they went down a slide head first (slides are badly designed, yet no attention has been given to redesigning them);
>
> A gymnast is made into a quadriplegic because his portable horizontal bar is inherently unstable;
>
> A baby drinks a toxic household cleaner and is brain-damaged for life.

10   It is probably impossible to make even a ballpark guess regarding the number of deaths and injuries caused by design. There are a few figures we can start with, however. According to the National Safety Council, we kill an average of 50,000 Americans annually and maim a further 600,000 each year in traffic accidents. According to a report by Dennis Bracken (radio station KNX, Los Angeles, November, 1970), we kill and injure 700,000 children through unsafe toys each year in the United States. According to

the National Heart Association, the lives of approximately 50 per cent of all industrial workers are shortened by 5 years or more through heart stress caused by noisy equipment. Unsafe home appliances account for 250,000 injuries and deaths annually. Even the design of so-called "safety equipment" imposes further and greater hazards: "Approved" fire escapes tend to fry people trying to use them. Eight thousand people have died this way over the years when they were trapped by the escape mechanism.

Recently the control panel of stoves has been moved to the rear of both   11
gas and electric units. The manufacturer's explanation is that this will make control knobs more difficult for small children to reach. In reality, a merchandising gimmick is at work here: by running wiring straight up the back of the stove, the stove can be built less expensively, yet sold for more money. The control unit is still there, an attractive nuisance, and children merely have to climb upon a stool and balance precariously while trying to play with the pretty knobs. Often they may fall and burn their arms or faces. A design solution would be simple: a double-security switch that requires both hands to engage "on" (similar to "Record" switches on tape recorders). Instead, appliance manufacturers woo the public with such felicitous confections as a recent Hotpoint range, the oven of which played "Tenderly" whenever the roast was ready. (!)

(Since I collect examples of the idiocies dreamt up by fellow designers,   12
I found myself enchanted by two new offerings for the 1970 Christmas gift market. One of these was an electric, dial-a-matic Necktie Selector for the home. You push a series of buttons, specifying shirt color, suit color, and other pertinent data, then a little wheel moves forward and presents the 6 or 10 ties that fit in with your particular color choice. This gadget mounts on the inside of the closet door, comes in a choice of "modernistic" or "Early American," and is only $49.95. The other, alas, was still in the developmental stages in 1970, but they were promising it by *next* Christmas. It was an *electronic* necktie selector that uses a colorimeter and a scanning device to assess your entire wardrobe. No longer will you have to feed color specifications to the gadget and push buttons: instead, the tie selector will take a good hard look at you, scan your "ensemble," and then hand you the tie that is good for you. It seems we will be privileged to buy this for a mere 300 bucks a throw.)

There is no question that the concept of obsolescence can be a sound   13
one. Disposable hospital syringes, for instance, eliminate some of the need for costly autoclaves and other sterilizing equipment. In underdeveloped countries, or climatic situations where sterilization becomes difficult or impossible, a whole line of disposable surgical and dental instruments will become useful. Throw-away Kleenex, diapers, etc., are certainly welcome.

But when a new category of objects is designed for disposability, two   14
new parameters must enter the design process. For one thing, does the price

of the object reflect its ephemeral character? The 99¢ paper dresses cited before are excellent answers to changing fashion or to travel needs, or in the area of temporary protective clothing. But this is not the case with the $149.50 paper dress.

15   The second consideration deals with what happens to the disposable article after it has been disposed of. Automobile junkyards follow our highways from coast to coast. And even these appalling smears on the landscape at least have a (painfully slow) rusting process in their favor, so that five or twenty years hence they will have turned to dust. The new plastics and aluminum will not disintegrate, and the concept of being up to our armpits in discarded beer cans is not a pleasant prospect for the future.

16   It is here that bio-degradable materials (i.e., plastics that become absorbed into the soil, water run-off, or air) will have to be used more and more in the future. The Tetra-Pak Company, responsible for the distribution of seven billion milk, cream, and other packages a year, is now working on an ideal self-destructive package in Sweden. A new process, developed in collaboration with the Institute for Polymer Technology in Stockholm, accelerates the decomposition rate of polyethylene plastics. Thus, packages will decompose much more rapidly after they have been discarded without having their strength and other properties affected while still in use. A new disposable, self-destructive beer bottle called "Rigello" is already on the market. Much more than these Swedish experiments will have to be done to save us from product pollution.

◆   ◆   ◆

17   To return to the primary concept of a disposable society: With increasing technological obsolescence, the exchange of products for newer, radically improved versions makes sense. Unfortunately, as yet there has been no reaction to this new factor on the market level. If we are to "trade in" yesterday's products and appliances for today's, and today's for tomorrow's at an ever-accelerating rate, then unit cost must reflect this tendency. Slowly, two methods of dealing with this problem are beginning to emerge.

18   Leasing rather than owning is beginning to make headway. There are a number of states in which it is less expensive to lease an automobile on a 3-year contract than to own one. This concept has the added motivation built in that the man who leases his automobile is no longer bothered by maintenance cost, insurance, fluctuating trade-in values, etc. In some of our larger cities it has become possible to lease such large appliances as refrigerators, freezers, stoves, dishwashers, washer and dryers, air-conditioning units, and TV sets. This trend has grown even more pronounced in manufacturing and office situations. Maintenance and service problems surrounding the hardware in the computer, research lab, and office-filing fields make the leasing of equipment more and more rational. Property tax laws in many states are also helping to make the concept of "temporary use" rather than "permanent ownership" more palatable to the consuming public.

It now becomes necessary only to convince the consumer that, in point   19
of fact, he *owns* very little even now. The homes which make up our suburbs
and exurbs are purchased on 20- or 30-year mortgages, but (as we have seen
above) with the average family moving every 56 months, are sold and resold
many times over. Most automobiles are purchased on an installment plan
lasting 36 months. They are usually traded in 4 to 6 months before the contract is completed, and the still partially unpaid-for car is used as a trade-in.
The concept of ownership, as it applies to cars, homes, and large appliances
in a highly mobile society, becomes a mere polite fiction.

This is indeed a major volte-face regarding possessions. It is a change   20
of attitude often condemned out of hand by the older generation (who are sub-
limely unaware of how little they themselves, in fact, ever own). But this
moral condemnation is not really relevant and never has been. The "curse of
possessions" has been viewed with alarm by religious leaders, philosophers,
and social thinkers throughout human history. And the concept of being
owned by things, rather than owning them, is becoming clear to our young
people. Our greatest hope in turning away from a gadget-happy, goods-
oriented, consumption-motivated society based on private capitalist acquis-
itive philosophies, lies in a recognition of these facts.

A second way of dealing with the technological obsolescing of products   21
lies in restructuring prices for the consumer market. On Sunday, April 6,
1969, *The New York Times* carried an advertisement for an inflatable easy
chair (imported from England) at a retail price of $6.95 (including shipping,
taxes and import duties). Within 5 days mail and telephone orders were received for 60,000 chairs. A few years ago hassocks and occasional chairs
made of plastic-reinforced cardboard were available at such discount outlets
as Pier I and Cost Plus at prices ranging from 59¢ to $1.49. Such items, com-
bining usefulness, bright color, modish design, comfort, extremely low cost,
light weight, and easy "knock-down factors" with eventual nonchalant disposability, naturally appeal to young people and college students. But their
appeal is filtering down to larger and more "settled" segments of the population as well.

Mass production and automation procedures should make an increas-   22
ing number of inexpensive, semi-disposable products available to the public. If this trend continues (*and does not lead to waste-making and pollution*),
it is a healthy one. If further justification were needed for this throwaway society on moral grounds, a corollary trend has already begun to make its appearance. A home containing inexpensive plastic dinnerware will, often as
not, also contain one or two pieces of fine craftsman-produced ceramics. The
99¢ paper dress will be dramatized with a custom-designed, custom-made
ring created specifically for the wearer by a silversmith. One of the inexpensive cardboard easy chairs (bought a few years ago at Cost Plus) may well
contain a $60 hand-woven cushion (bought at a prestigious craft shop or a
gallery). In fact, the current renaissance of the crafts is partially traceable to

consumer money liberated for investment in these custom-made art objects through the reduction of prices for everyday goods.

23   This trend is by no means in full force as yet. But if we look to moving day in 1999, we may well see a family loading their car with a few boxes full of art and craft objects, ceramics, hand-woven cushions and wall-hangings, books and cassettes while nearly all of the so-called "hard goods" have either been returned to the lessor or thrown away, to be replaced by newly leased appliances and inexpensively purchased furnishings at the point of destination.

24   If we summarize, we see readily that certain aspects of our Kleenex Culture are unavoidable and, in fact, beneficial. However, the dominance of the market place has so far delayed the emergence of a rational design strategy. Obviously, it is easier to sell objects that are thrown away than objects that are permanent, and industry has done little or nothing to decide what should be thrown away and what should not. It is also much pleasanter (for shareowners, and vice-presidents in charge of marketing) to sell throwaway things that are priced as if they were to be kept permanently. The two alternatives to the present price system, leasing, or lower prices combined with the customers' investment recovery through meaningful trade-in or "model-swapping," have not been explored. Technological innovation is progressing at an ever-accelerating pace while raw materials disappear. (Thus it is instructive to note that it takes about 850 acres of Canadian timber to print one Sunday's *New York Times*. To which may be added: *The New York Times* Sunday edition sells for 50¢ and contains more paper and typography than an unillustrated novel retailing for $7.95. While the *Times* carries about 500 photographs and drawings in its Sunday edition, and a novel does not, book-binding costs average 22¢ per book. It costs the city of New York nearly 10¢ per copy each week to clean up discarded copies of the Sunday *New York Times*.)

25   The question of whether design and marketing strategy is possible in these areas under a system of private capitalism remains experimental. But it is obvious that in a world of need, answers to this question must be found.

EXERCISE 4.5 A very common analogy these days in discussing action about a public problem is the analogy of war. We have a war against drugs and a war against AIDS. In what ways is this war analogy useful in argument? How might it be fallacious?

Would you apply the analogy to efforts to solve other problems? In your notebook, record your opinion about the effectiveness of the war analogy.

EXERCISE 4.6 Monitor for one week the newspaper or radio or TV coverage of one issue. Keep track in your notebook of how supports from Group

One and Group Two are used. List the support types you find. Indicate if their uses are rational or fallacious. For the issue you chose, what is your impression of the medium you tracked as a source of reliable information and opinion?

GROUP THREE SUPPORT: PRINCIPLES

Group three support differs from the other groups because it draws support from materials more general than the thesis. These materials—values, principles, generalizations—take the reader up, not down, the abstraction ladder. Because you have had a lot of experience using detail in supporting a thesis, you may be surprised that values can be used as supports. As you argue, you can apply values to your specific issue and thesis. This group provides you with a strong, new dimension of support.

Personal Values

You have your own values and sense of what is axiomatic for you. You derive these from experience, from training, and from faith and hope. Such personal values most likely suffuse your position statements on a variety of issues. If argument is, as Aristotle said, taking a stand for the good, then argument is inextricably bound to values.

The concepts of reason—of thesis and of support—are not neutral in value. You can think of reason in argument as a demonstration of thought connecting various points: the point of the thesis, the many factual points of support, the points of other available arguments, including points of principle and value.

For example, consider the argument favoring the use of animals in medical research. A writer could list many discoveries made through such experimentation, the time and expense saved, and so on. This sounds familiar: reasons tucked in under a thesis, the reasons providing archways for tucking in more specific support. *Which* discoveries? *How much* time and money saved? Now, what if one of the reasons was the principle that animals are here on earth to serve and provide for humans? This is a different sort of reason. As a value or principle, it is broader than the other reasons. It is higher on the abstraction ladder and requires support unlike that required for the other reasons.

Value and principle are general, yet they have many specific applications. The principle that animals are here for human use can be applied to arguments about wearing fur, eating meat, using ivory, hunting, and, of course, doing medical experiments with animals. Support for such a value will usually not include statistics and dollar amounts, but instead will show the source and tradition of the value, prime examples of the value in use in this context and others, prominent spokespersons for the value, and so on.

Cultural Values

Often many of your values express those of your culture, so it is hard to distinguish between what you believe and what others in your culture believe. Much of your personal core of beliefs comes from your culture.

If your thesis is based on a personal value that you assume your readers do not share, then you need to argue in support of the value. If, however, you and your readers share a value that supports your thesis, a thesis your readers do not share, then the shared value, or warrant, can be very useful in helping draw you both together.

Is the United States such a multicultural nation that its citizens assume no common values? I suspect there are values that late twentieth-century North Americans share: freedom of choice, equality of opportunity, individual initiative. A common Japanese adage says, "The nail that sticks out gets hammered down." My discussions with students indicate strong disagreement with this statement. My students offer contrasting North American maxims: Just Do It, Do Your Own Thing, and The squeaky wheel gets the grease.

Arguments express values, both personal and cultural, because they often aim to reach agreement about what is good. Bill McKibben recognizes our need to be informed, Wendell Berry acknowledges our fascination with technology, and Barbara Powell assumes readers share the value that "our children are a precious resource." Imagine how identifying a common value in support of thesis—how using a warrant—can pull readers into the current of your argument.

Deduction

Deduction is the fraternal twin of induction. Deduction, like induction, is a reasoning process relating general and specific statements. The direction of thought in deduction moves down from the general to the specifics, down the abstraction ladder to make an application of value to guide your understanding of a particular situation. For example, the core of Martin Luther King's appeal to white clergy in "Letter from Birmingham Jail" was derived from principles and was expressed deductively. Each deduction illustrated below is presented in the form of a syllogism, a three-part sequence including a major premise, a minor premise, and a conclusion. Each syllogism shows a different kind of major premise or starting point, simply to demonstrate what you can use as you write your own syllogisms. The names of the different types of syllogisms refer to their different starting points. Note that the major premise of the first syllogism characterizes a group or category, in this case law (any law, all laws).

A CATEGORICAL SYLLOGISM

Any law that degrades human personality is unjust.

Segregation laws degrade human personality.

Therefore, segregation laws are unjust.

Another way to reach this conclusion starts with a major premise that states alternatives (either/or):

AN ALTERNATIVE SYLLOGISM

A law is either just or unjust.

Segregation laws are not just.

Therefore, segregation laws are unjust.

Then, in his line of reasoning, King presented a related deduction drawn from the earlier deduction. This time the major premise describes a hypothetical situation (if) and a consequence:

A HYPOTHETICAL SYLLOGISM

If segregation laws are unjust, we must disobey them.

Segregation laws are unjust.

Therefore, we must disobey them.

Thus, deduction allows your readers to see how you build an argument from principles and assumptions and connect them to the issue of the argument, touching specific situations with general and personal truths. If a syllogism is logical, it helps you clarify your ideas, yet a good syllogism, like a good induction, also has the force to compel, because its conclusion is the outcome of earlier steps that, hopefully, your readers have agreed to take with you. Once the audience accepts the earlier steps—the two premises—the conclusion seems inevitable. As King illustrates, your first syllogism may produce a conclusion that supplies the next syllogism with its major premise, producing a chain of reasoning.

Uses and Misuses of Group Three Support

Because values are inherent in people and associated with social grouping, class, and nation, it is not surprising that they are easy to manipulate. To an extent, appeals to value "work the audience." Aristotle recognized this in speeches of praise and blame: "Whatever quality the audience esteems, the speaker must attribute to the object of his praise."

The *fallacy of popular appeals* connects thesis very loosely to popularly held values and beliefs. If voters want a tough approach to crime, the candidate delivers the buzzwords "law and order" and assumes an identity with audience. This is fallacious if the candidate does not have a clearly stated and supported anti-crime platform, but reaps the benefits of having one with very little effort and without obligating promises. The appeal to popular values allows the candidate to seem more like the locals than he or she may really be.

The *fallacy of tradition* is another easy, yet mistaken, way of connecting a thesis to a value that has broad appeal. In this case, because audiences accept traditional values or ways of doing things, they may be pleased with a thesis that does not overturn tradition and that helps confirm it. Audience may trust the tried and true, but the fallacy here is that what has been tried may not really be true. Consider traditional wisdom about diet, health care, and raising children. What has been tried by one era may not be useful for the next. Both Jane Brody and Thomas Paine refuse to play along with traditional values; they challenge them. And the scientists of "Rock Music" show that new explanations displace old explanations and that knowledge in many disciplines is dynamic, not fixed.

The *bandwagon fallacy* is yet another illogical appeal to what is popular. This fallacy centers on what is trendy. Because everyone is doing it, audience should, too—the implication being that "it" is good and that people ought to keep up with what others are doing. If a running shoe has many imitators, is it necessarily good? The bandwagon fallacy equates popularity with merit. Both qualities may, indeed, be joined in one idea or product, but there is no necessary connection between them.

The *fallacy of false premises* upsets the progress of deductions. In deduction you cannot draw conclusions better than your premises. Readers need to understand and accept your premises. They accept them because they know they are solid, either from their own experience or from the support you present. Readers will not let you pass from premises to conclusions when your premises are questionable.

Consider the premises of an argument you have read in this book. Isak Dinesen's thinking can be presented in syllogism form:

Premise	If in possessing a beautiful thing we diminish it, then we should leave it alone.
Premise	In possessing it we do diminish it.
Conclusion	We should leave it alone.

Looking at the premises, you might say, "Oh, really? Show me!" For you might be thinking, "No, when I buy a fur hat, I don't expect to get a rabbit. I accept the diminished thing and use it for what it is." Or you might react this way: "Possessing something doesn't necessitate diminishing it. This Navaho ring is rich with memories of my first trip to Arizona."

Dinesen's premises are not false, especially as her essay presents support for them. But her conclusions can be no better than her premises. In such informal deductions, readers do not require absolute proof. Readers often supply qualifiers, if the writer does not, noting, "This may be so in many cases, if not all." Scientific deductions, such as those explaining the mystery of the rocks in "Rock Music," need to be verifiable in repeated tests with other similar rocks. Most readers expect more rigor from scientific uses of logic than from personal uses of logic.

One more example illustrates the need to avoid using false premises. Suppose you argue for Americans to do something to boost their own economy. You might use the principle or premise that any activity that boosts their economy is worth supporting. The next premise, suggested by the tobacco industry, is that selling more cigarettes will help build the economy. Do you conclude that you should accept this strategy? Not necessarily! But the tobacco industry argument has some momentum—it is pushing you because you accepted the first premise without seeing it open the door to the next premise and to a conclusion far from what you had in mind.

EXERCISE 4.7 Read the following essay by Bill Woolum. Identify the cultural values Woolum uses to develop his argument. Are they values his audience shares? Does Woolum make these values appealing? Are they values you share? Without sharing these values, could you be convinced by Woolum's argument? Once you have answered these questions, write a paragraph observing how values can be used in argument.

❖ MATERIALISM REVISITED: LOVING THE HUNDRETH SHEEP

Bill Woolum

Bill Woolum (b. 1953) is an English professor at Lane Community College. Woolum wrote this article in 1989 when he edited *The Run Off,* the newspaper of a Sierra Club chapter. Woolum acknowledges a debt to Wendell Berry in his use of terms and ideas. In his argument, Woolum steers away from statistics and examples and develops support with a parable, definitions of values, and deductions. The argument's tone and method derive from the sermon tradition, not the tradition of the scientific report. Indeed, Woolum "preaches to the converted," to the members of his environmental group. Yet, even within the group, Woolum recognizes differences about terms and perspectives. From a pep-talk motive, Woolum develops strongly felt and reasoned encouragement.

1   In the biblical parable of the lost sheep, a shepherd discovers that one of his one hundred sheep is missing and he leaves the other ninety-nine to search for the one who is lost. Theologically, this parable tells of God's active, persistent love for the alienated. Morally, the parable teaches us, in Wendell Berry's words, that each is more precious than all. If all were more precious, the shepherd would count himself fortunate to have ninety-nine percent of his sheep in tow, but because he prizes each, he cannot rest until his hundreth sheep is found and celebrated.

2   If applied to the material world of nature, to particular trees, individual species (snail darters, louseworts, Northern spotted owls), drops of water, and grains of sand, we are reminded that this love for and commitment to the particular embodies the most noble and laudable materialism, a materialism that loves and defends all of nature's particularity.

3   If seen this way, our resistance must not be to materialism, but mercantilism. A materialism that cherishes the miracle of nature's ability to replenish its own material life by producing its own nutrients, beauty, and chemical basis for life is the moral bedrock of the environmental cause. Environmentalists celebrate the material particularity of the material world and desire to preserve and protect its self-sustaining integrity: the each is more precious than the all.

4   Mercantilists abstract nature by regarding it as a resource, a commodity. Regarding nature in terms of board feet, sustainable yield, resource development, and acceptable levels of vandalism and pollution, desecrates the love of material things by giving love of quantities precedent over the love of their qualities. The moral measure of mercantilism is money. Money governs the conscience of mercantilism.

5   Some might argue that I am being generous in using the word "conscience" in the same sentence with "mercantilism." But the etymological roots of "conscience" tell us otherwise. The word conscience derives from the Latin prefix *con*, meaning "together", combined with the Latin word *scire*, meaning "to know". Making choices of conscience involves knowing together two things: a general principle in relation to the particular matter at hand. The general principle governing mercantilism is profitability. When faced with the fact that smelting lead endangers the health of children, the mercantilist can conscience it if lead smelting makes money and provides jobs: the all is more precious than the each. Not all children will be made ill, although a few will be, and those few children are not as important as the mercantile returns of smelting lead.

6   Likewise, when faced with the fact that logging old growth forests will extinguish the Northern spotted owl, the mercantilist can conscience this consequence of money making because the all is more precious than the each: an individual species of bird is seen as dispensable (all species are not lost; only one) and less important than the quantitative value of the trees.

The mercantilist also has great faith in technology. A central tenet of 7
mercantilist faith is that what humanity has destroyed, technology can repair.
Smelting lead might poison children within a certain proximity of the smelter,
but, believes the mercantilist, medical technology certainly exists or can be
developed to cure the child or make the poison tolerable.

Likewise, the mercantilist cannot (or will not) believe that some other 8
kind of habitat cannot be created for the Northern spotted owl that will not
only sustain the bird, but might even be superior to what the owl has known.
After all, mercantilist foresters believe they can employ technology to create
a single crop "forest" superior to what nature created despite the rampant
destruction and intolerance of countless various and particular vegetative
life forms. The all, the creation of a money crop, is deemed more valuable
and precious than the incalcuable richness of nature's infinite variety, its fe-
cund eachness.

Culturally, we continue to more deeply absorb and more readily legit- 9
imize mercantilism. Consequently, we become increasingly alienated from
the sacred qualities of the material world, even allowing "materialism" to become a perjorative word. We must insist that our opponents understand that
our outrage at the desecration of the earth is rooted in our knowledge of the
sacramental nature of the material world more than in quantitative measures
of trees logged, amount of air spoiled, number of species lost, or barrels of
oil spilled. Like the shepherd of the parable, our sacramental respect for the
material world is rooted in our love for each: each rock, each plant, each
breath of air, each spray of mist, each drop of rain, each flake of snow. We
must resist expressing our outrage in mercantile terms. Instead, we must
proudly confront our opponents' clumsy, greedy destruction with our love,
reverence, and respect for the sacred eachness of the natural world.

EXERCISE 4.8 Examine the use of deductive reasoning in the arguments
by Woolum and Brody (Chapter 1). Try to follow the line of reasoning used in
each essay. Try summarizing the reasoning by writing syllogisms in your
notebook. Try all three forms presented in this chapter's section, "Deduction," and reviewed below.

THREE SYLLOGISM FORMS

Form 1. *Categorical.* Major premise begins with *all*, describing a
category.
   All colleges should have an affirmative action officer.
   University of Q is a college.
   University of Q should have an affirmative action officer.
Form 2. *Alternative.* Major premise begins with *either*, presenting an
alternative.

Either University of Q will hire an affirmative action officer or it will leave the post vacant.

University of Q will not leave the post vacant.

University of Q will hire an affirmative action officer.

Form 3. *Hypothetical.* Major premise begins with *if,* presenting a hypothesis.

If University of Q intends to follow the law, then it should hire an affirmative action officer.

University of Q does intend to follow the law.

University of Q should hire an affirmative action officer.

GROUP FOUR SUPPORT: LOOKING BEFORE AND AFTER

Whereas your time sense makes both narration and process description familiar and comfortable modes of writing, it also allows you to use preceding events to establish cause and to explain or even predict later events.

Precedent

Our nation's most celebrated speech begins "Fourscore and seven years ago our fathers brought forth on this continent a new nation. . . ." At Gettysburg, November 19, 1863, Abraham Lincoln was counting back to the events of 1776. As he dedicated a battlefield as a cemetery for huge Union losses, Lincoln pointed back to battlefields where the life of the nation was won. The short address concludes, "We here highly resolve that these dead shall not have died in vain; that this nation, under God, shall have a new birth of freedom. . . ." In Lincoln's reasoning, as great deeds for freedom have been done before, and not in vain, so the dead soldiers of 1863 had done great deeds for freedom, to the degree that their labors have effected a new birth of national identity.

Lincoln's speech is primarily ceremonial; it was not addressed to dissenting audiences. Yet, at the time, Lincoln could not be sure that the Union would win the war. In argument, too, the urging of a present-day plan can draw force from a precedent, a parallel situation of the past that might be used to help decide a similar case in the present. Imagine you are constructing an argument in favor of legalizing most drugs. You can point to the Prohibition Amendment of 1919 and its failings and then suggest that just as America was better off with the repeal of this 18th Amendment, the nation would be better off by ending its current prohibitions on drugs. Using the same tactic, people who display the bumper sticker that proclaims "No Vietnam in Latin America" urge a present thesis in terms of a past event.

Arguments based on precedent are as strong as the resemblance between the two situations. Such arguments should not result from the unexamined traditionalism expressed by "If it was good enough for Grandpa, it's good enough for me." Most situations, in their particulars, are truly unprecedented; history seems to have no necessity to produce identical episodes. The question is, rather, when you find similar episodes, how does the earlier episode help readers understand the present or future? You need to demonstrate the lesson the past event teaches.

Cause and Effect

A precedent comes before the event in question, but it may not be a cause. We recognize that children are fascinated with the word *because* long before they understand causal relationships. Since *because* is a basic connector in many arguments, you, too, appreciate A causing B and B, in turn, causing C. Many of your reasons are stated as *because's*.

Scores of arguments are based on causal relationships. If the nation's economy is lagging, politicians, business leaders, and economists analyze why it is lagging or what is causing the slowdown. They disagree about the causes of a problem just as they disagree about its solution. Should there be more or fewer taxes? Should trade be freer or more restricted? Should government spend more money or less money? Should Americans buy goods or invest their savings? Answers to such questions are often based on interpretations of cause and effect. How do you know any particular policy will actually work? You need to support assertions that something will cause something else or be the effect of something else. Your support may take the form of statistics, comparisons or precedents, testimony of authority, personal experience, warrants or common values, and so on. Barbara Howell used several kinds of support to establish that WIC actually results in benefits important enough to justify expanding the WIC program.

You should note that an effect may have more than one cause and that a cause or causes may have one or more effects. This complicates your search for lines of causality, linking causes to effects.

Uses and Misuses of Group Four Support

A commonplace adage warns that if you do not understand the events of the past you will be condemned to repeat them. A statement like this sends you searching the past for precedent, as if many precedents existed, like pebbles on the shore.

The *fallacy of false precedent* resembles the fallacy of false analogy: whereas some likenesses exist between a past event and a present event, more differences than likenesses are often apparent. Precedents can construct a valuable tradition, as court decisions do in the field of law. Cues from the past inform many other fields. Yet to argue from precedent is fallacious when the two or more cases have little in common. Does Lincoln "stretch it" to identify the Civil War as a second birth of freedom? Is prohibition of alcohol to the culture of alcohol what drug enforcement is to the culture of drugs? How alike are the 1920s and 1990s? Does it follow in Brody's argument that if early humans ate mainly a vegetarian diet that we should also? Haven't food gathering and production radically changed over time? The record of events is so rich that you could probably find precedents for anything. Do the Vietnam War and Desert Storm encourage or discourage introducing large numbers of U.S. soldiers on foreign soil?

A rational use of precedent builds on likenesses between the events. In a sense, these likenesses show readers whether your use of precedent to support thesis is reasonable or not.

The *fallacy of false cause,* often called the post hoc fallacy, states that A is the cause of B simply because A preceded B. But your good sense warns that when something occurs before something else it is not necessarily its cause. Fallacies of false cause do not establish that a preceding occurrence was a cause. For example, perhaps a neighborhood was safe until an immigrant group moved in. It is easy to say the new group changed the neighborhood, although there are probably neighborhoods that are less safe even though they have had no change in population. Or, perhaps, a deer population prospered until wolves were shot. It is easy to say the killing of the wolves caused the decline of the deer population because of overgrazing and subsequent starvation.

Aldo Leopold recognized in "Thinking Like a Mountain" (Chapter 1) that causes and effects come in chains: the removal of wolves allows deer to overproduce and this increased population causes overgrazing, which, in turn, starves the deer. Did Leopold really establish or merely assert these effects? Could there be other, even more important, causes of such changes? Such questions can be applied to every link in the causal chain.

Whenever you assert something is a cause or effect, you must look deeper than chronological order. You need to establish cause by giving support to your interpretation of events.

EXERCISE 4.9   Analyze cause and effect in the arguments by Lifton (Chapter 2), Faludi (Chapter 4), and Whitelaw (Chapter 4). Are causes established convincingly? Are they merely asserted, perhaps with the assumption that readers have analyzed causes the same way the writer has? Record your evaluations in your notebook.

GROUP FIVE SUPPORT: DEGREE

Because you cannot settle most arguments with certainty, you often argue the degree of certainty involved. You show how your proposal is more likely to be implemented or is more worthy of being implemented than other proposals. You grant that other proposals have possibility and merit, but you support your view by degree to show that your proposal, although not perfect, is better than the others. If your thesis is not absolutely true, you can at least demonstrate that it is truer than other thesis statements.

Likelihood

In the previous discussion on qualifying words, you saw that arguments seldom pit views that are 100 percent right against those that are 100 percent wrong. Most arguments, like most elections, are won by degrees: no politician gets all or none of the votes. In argument, you cannot assign absolute winners and losers because most issues are uncertain. This is especially true when you argue about the future. So, instead of asking if one side is right and the other is wrong, you might ask "How likely are these arguments?"

If you cannot have certainty, you must settle for likelihood, the higher degree of probability. When you hear a proposal to build a highway linking a port city to a populated inland corridor, you hear the claims that such a road will create trade, increase local manufacturing, and produce jobs. Are these things likely to happen? Will this proposed road actually affect the port these ways? Are other cheaper and simpler proposals as likely to produce these benefits? What is the likelihood that any proposal will achieve what its proponents claim? No one can answer these questions for sure. Yet the strong argument can show its answers are likely to be true. Howell believes WIC has a very good chance of helping poor American families; Rogers is not so sure whether his methods will ever be applied to social and political problems, yet there is enough promise in such methods that Rogers, nonetheless, urges their wide use.

Merit

You are not the first or the last to take up almost any issue; you realize that your side does not have all the good people and all the right answers. Reason tells you that your opponents, as imperfect as they are, can most likely teach you and help you articulate the issue and move all sides toward a conclusion.

In such a mixed world, your argument must shun attributions of total praise or total blame. Your argument needs to demonstrate how your position is better than opposing views. Your position may not be a perfect one, but you argue that it is better than, or the best of, what has been offered. What are the merits of your argument? What are the demerits of opposing views? Can you show that your view has greater merit than the views you oppose? You build such an argument to demonstrate that your view has an edge over any other. Arguing merit is useful in situations when no one view can claim a monopoly on truth and cogent support; that is, arguing merit is useful in most arguments. Lincoln, in his discussions with abolitionists, saw merit and demerit in signing an emancipation proclamation. No doubt, the manufacture of a typewriter uses resources and energy, but Berry asserts the typewriter is a better tool than a word processor because the typewriter does not need further energy/resource inputs to operate.

Uses and Misuses of Group Five Support

Using arguments of degree frees you from the pressure to be certain and complete, but such arguments lead to their own fallacies.

In a recent Senate campaign, the incumbent accused his challenger, who was a member of the House of Representatives, of having the worst attendance record of the entire state's Congressional delegation. The challenger's attendance may have been the worst of the delegation—a group of only six—but he attended more than 80 percent of the time and the best attendance was little over 90 percent. In arguments of degree, clearly, something may be worse than something else but still good, or it may be better than something else but still poor. This is a *fallacy of degree:* to state or imply something is good or bad merely by pointing to its relative position in the group or pair. Readers may think they hear "good" or "bad" when an argument really states "better" or "worse." If, as Wendell Berry writes, PCs use more energy than manual typewriters, does Berry mean they use an indefensible amount of energy and are, thus, poor machines? How much energy do they use? And shouldn't Berry measure energy expended to work with a manual typewriter?

Another fallacy of degree is the *fallacy of the slippery slope.* This fallacy occurs when someone opposes an action because it is a bad step that leads to even worse steps. The fallacy disparages taking this first step without ever showing how it will actually lead to the next steps. The name of this fallacy suggests irreversible decline. The fallacy plays on audience fears and insecurities. It is illustrated by the familiar adage. "If we give them an inch, they'll take a mile." The usher at the concert says, "If I let you cut into this line, then I'll have to let everyone cut in!" This fallacy is a variation of the domino effect, except each step leads to an even worse one. One question to ask about the slippery slope—or about any prediction, even if it is well stated—is "How likely is this?" If the step is taken, will the next step necessarily be worse? Will the next step even be necessary?

EXERCISE 4.10   Return to Carl Rogers' argument (Chapter 2) and identify where Rogers discusses the merits and likelihood of people's using his methods of communication. Would Rogers have been more convincing had he not mentioned the difficulties inherent in his proposals?

Have you developed an argument of degree? When is such an approach useful? How do writers signal that their arguments are of degree and are not absolute? Are arguments of degree necessarily weak arguments? In your notebook, record your observations about arguments of degree.

EXERCISE 4.11 In 1971 Victor Papanek (presented earlier in this chapter) made some predictions about 1999, so you may be in a better position than Papanek to criticize them. What were his predictions? Was he guilty of presenting a slippery slope? Answer these questions in your notebook.

USING VARIETY TO SUPPORT THESIS

This chapter offers a menu of varieties of support. You will find a checklist of these varied supports at the end of this chapter. You will use many of these varieties as you build your argument. Yet, even though you appreciate the possible range, the limits of what you know about a subject may, in turn, limit the items you can actually use. That is fine. You can consider each variety of support as a separate thread or wire, which wrapped with others—as many as are available—makes a stronger and stronger cable. Your case rests on many supports, not just one or a few.

Two selections taken from Howard Zinn's *The People's History of the United States* follow. Because he attempts a controversial revision of history, Zinn must employ argument to state and support his points. As you read, notice how Zinn winds together various supports to challenge, if not convince, you.

 ## From THE PEOPLE'S HISTORY OF THE UNITED STATES

Howard Zinn

Howard Zinn (b. 1922) is professor emeritus of political science at Boston University. He specializes in the history of civil disobedience, having written books about the civil rights movement and about opposition to the Vietnam War. *A People's History of the United States* is Zinn's attempt to write history from the point of view of minority and working class groups. Because he propounds a debatable thesis about American history, Zinn provides a multitude of support in his book-length argument. These excerpts about American courts and prisons illustrate Zinn's method of assertion and documented discussion. Note that he uses a variety of support to make his claims clear and convincing.

This first passage from Zinn asserts a thesis about the Supreme Court at the end of the nineteenth century: The Supreme Court favored the rich over the poor. Notice how Zinn supports his thesis with an analysis of cause and effect, with examples, with testimony, and with precedent.

Meanwhile, the Supreme Court, despite its look of somber, black-robed fairness, was doing its bit for the ruling elite. How could it be independent, with   1 its members chosen by the President and ratified by the Senate? How could it be neutral between rich and poor when its members were often former wealthy lawyers, and almost always came from the upper class? Early in the nineteenth century the Court laid the legal basis for a nationally regulated economy by establishing federal control over interstate commerce, and the legal basis for corporate capitalism by making the contract sacred.

2   In 1895 the Court interpreted the Sherman Act so as to make it harmless. It said a monopoly of sugar refining was a monopoly in manufacturing, not commerce, and so could not be regulated by Congress through the Sherman Act (*U.S.* v. *E.C. Knight Co.*). The Court also said the Sherman Act could be used against interstate strikes (the railway strike of 1894) because they were in restraint of trade. It also declared unconstitutional a small attempt by Congress to tax high incomes at a higher rate (*Pollock* v. *Farmers' Loan & Trust Company*). In later years it would refuse to break up the Standard Oil and American Tobacco monopolies, saying the Sherman Act barred only "unreasonable" combinations in restraint of trade.

3   A New York banker toasted the Supreme Court in 1895: "I give you, gentlemen, the Supreme Court of the United States—guardian of the dollar, defender of private property, enemy of spoliation, sheet anchor of the Republic."

4   Very soon after the Fourteenth Amendment became law, the Supreme Court began to demolish it as a protection for blacks, and to develop it as a protection for corporations. However, in 1877, a Supreme Court decision (*Munn* v. *Illinois*) approved state laws regulating the prices charged to farmers for the use of grain elevators. The grain elevator company argued it was a person being deprived of property, thus violating the Fourteenth Amendment's declaration "nor shall any State deprive any person of life, liberty, or property without due process of law." The Supreme Court disagreed, saying that grain elevators were not simply private property but were invested with "a public interest" and so could be regulated.

5   One year after that decision, the American Bar Association, organized by lawyers accustomed to serving the wealthy, began a national campaign of education to reverse the Court decision. Its presidents said, at different times: "If trusts are a defensive weapon of property interests against the communistic trend, they are desirable." And: "Monopoly is often a necessity and an advantage."

6   By 1886, they succeeded, State legislatures, under the pressure of aroused farmers, had passed laws to regulate the rates charged farmers by the railroads. The Supreme Court that year (*Wabash* v. *Illinois*) said states could not do this, that this was an intrusion on federal power. That year alone, the Court did away with 230 state laws that had been passed to regulate corporations.

7   By this time the Supreme Court had accepted the argument that corporations were "persons" and their money was property protected by the due process clause of the Fourteenth Amendment. Supposedly, the Amendment

had been passed to protect Negro rights, but of the Fourteenth Amendment cases brought before the Supreme Court between 1890 and 1910, nineteen dealt with the Negro, 288 dealt with corporations.

The justices of the Supreme Court were not simply interpreters of the   8
Constitution. They were men of certain backgrounds, of certain interests. One of them (Justice Samuel Miller) had said in 1875: "It is vain to contend with Judges who have been at the bar the advocates for forty years of railroad companies, and all forms of associated capital. . . ." In 1893, Supreme Court Justice David J. Brewer, addressing the New York State Bar Association, said:

It is the unvarying law that the wealth of the community will be in   9
the hands of the few. . . . The great majority of men are unwilling to endure that long self-denial and saving which makes accumulations possible . . . and hence it always has been, and until human nature is remodeled always will be true, that the wealth of a nation is in the hands of a few, while the many subsist upon the proceeds of their daily toil.

This was not just a whim of the 1880s and 1890s—it went back to the   10
Founding Fathers, who had learned their law in the era of *Blackstone's Commentaries*, which said: "So great is the regard of the law for private property, that it will not authorize the least violation of it; no, not even for the common good of the whole community."

Control in modern times requires more than force, more than law. It re-   11
quires that a population dangerously concentrated in cities and factories, whose lives are filled with cause for rebellion, be taught that all is right as it is. And so, the schools, the churches, the popular literature taught that to be rich was a sign of superiority, to be poor a sign of personal failure, and that the only way upward for a poor person was to climb into the ranks of the rich by extraordinary effort and extraordinary luck.

This second passage by Zinn states that American prisons reflect American class interests. Again, notice the variety of supports: comparison, definition, value, cause and effect, statistics, authority, example, testimony, and induction.

The prisons in the United States had long been an extreme reflection of   1
the American system itself: the stark life differences between rich and poor, the racism, the use of victims against one another, the lack of resources of the underclass to speak out, the endless "reforms" that changed little. Dostoevski once said: "The degree of civilization in a society can be judged by entering its prisons."

It had long been true, and prisoners knew this better than anyone, that   2
the poorer you were the more likely you were to end up in jail. This was

not just because the poor committed more crimes. In fact, they did. The rich did not have to commit crimes to get what they wanted; the laws were on their side. But when the rich did commit crimes, they often were not prosecuted, and if they were they could get out on bail, hire clever lawyers, get better treatment from judges. Somehow, the jails ended up full of poor black people.

3   In 1969, there were 502 convictions for tax fraud. Such cases, called "white-collar crimes," usually involve people with a good deal of money. Of those convicted, 20 percent ended up in jail. The fraud averaged $190,000 per case; their sentences averaged seven months. That same year, for burglary and auto theft (crimes of the poor) 60 percent ended up in prison. The auto thefts averaged $992; the sentences averaged eighteen months. The burglaries averaged $321; the sentences averaged thirty-three months.

4   Willard Gaylin, a psychiatrist, relates (*Partial Justice*) a case which, with changes in details, could be multiplied thousands of times. He had just interviewed seventeen Jehovah's Witnesses who refused to register for the draft during the Vietnam war, and all had received two-year sentences. He came to a young black man who had notified his draft board he could not in conscience cooperate with the draft because he was repelled by the violence of the Vietnam war. He received a five-year sentence. Gaylin writes: "Hank's was the first five-year sentence I had encountered. He was also the first black man." There were additional factors:

5   "How was your hair then?" I asked.
          "Afro."
          "And what were you wearing?"
          "A dashiki."
          "Don't you think that might have affected your sentence?"
          "Of course."
          "Was it worth a year or two of your life?" I asked.
          "That's all of my life," he said, looking at me with a combination of dismay and confusion. "Man, don't you know! That's what it's all about! Am I free to have my style, am I free to have my hair, am I free to have my skin?"
          "Of course," I said. "You're right."

6   Gaylin found enormous discretion given to judges in the handing out of sentences. In Oregon, of thirty-three men convicted of violating the draft law, eighteen were put on probation. In southern Texas, of sixteen men violating the same law, none was put on probation, and in southern Mississippi, every defendant was convicted and given the maximum of five years. In one part of the country (New England), the average sentence for all crimes was eleven months; in another part (the South), it was seventy-eight months. But it wasn't simply a matter of North and South. In New York City, one judge handling

673 persons brought before him for public drunkenness (all poor; the rich get drunk behind closed doors) discharged 531 of them. Another judge, handling 566 persons on the same charge, discharged one person.

    With such power in the hands of the courts, the poor, the black, the odd,   7 the homosexual, the hippie, the radical are not likely to get equal treatment before judges who are almost uniformly white, upper middle class, orthodox.

EXERCISE 4.12 In the Susan Faludi argument (presented earlier in this chapter), identify the uses of varied supports. Use the checklist of varieties of support at the end of this chapter to guide your search and to record your findings.

For any of your arguments, do the same identification of support. Are there some varieties you have not used? Do you understand how to use them? Can you add any of them as you revise your arguments? Use the checklist at the end of this chapter to record the varieties you have used and to make a note of the varieties you may want to try using in revised or new arguments.

USING SUPPORT TO CHANGE AUDIENCE

The explanations about support varieties and the cautions about avoiding fallacies may give you the impression that building arguments occurs in a workplace sealed off from audience. This is a false impression because ultimately, argument is your effort to reach audience. Even as you build an argument and determine uses for varied support, you need to face your readers.

    In the Howard Zinn selections, support is pertinent to thesis; it is also abundant and varied. If Zinn's work is impressive, it is not only because his assertions about American courts and prisons initiate parades of detail. What is impressive is that his effort attempts to change readers—that is why arguments include support. Surely, logic demands it, but so do readers. Zinn knows that support has compelling force.

    Let us examine a part of Susan Faludi's book *Backlash: The Undeclared War Against American Women.* Faludi writes to change readers, and her use of support serves this aim. The selection printed earlier in this chapter appears toward the beginning of Faludi's book, so it deals with preliminaries. The selection aims at readers who, Faludi believes, need to see the recurrence of backlashes in the history of American women's movements and who need to see that each backlash succeeded, in part, because women unwittingly cooperated with it. Faludi indicates that the "popular imagination" fails to understand the pattern of repeated backlash. This may be Faludi's polite way of telling her readers that they can learn something they do not know and that they will be on the receiving end of her argument.

How does Faludi use support to change audience? Even before this selection, Faludi works to establish common ground with her readers. She introduces the thesis of the entire book: The movement of backlash against women's rights charges women with all the crimes the backlash perpetrates. This backlash appalls Faludi. She is impelled to argue that women need to be aware that they cooperate with the backlash. Fundamental to her book's argument is the establishment of a bond between writer and readers that affirms the value of women's rights and the need to continue the struggle for them. To map this argument in ways you are already familiar with:

Because women have not
attained equality (grounds),

the women's movement must
continue to struggle (claim).

and since we believe that justice
demands that women attain
equality (warrant),

The warrant—a social bond between writer and readers—guarantees that support adds force to the claim. After this preliminary, Faludi's next step is to examine what discourages the women's movement from continued struggle. The selection presented in this chapter argues that the perception of women's history, mistaken as it is, serves to muffle protest. One way to map this step is:

Because our popular view of history
prevents our activity,

we need to change that
view of history.

and since we believe we need to be active,

In addition to building common ground through warrants, Faludi uses analogy to persuade her readers to re-envision women's history. Their history is not a flat, dead line, but a corkscrew line, which represents moving forward and nearing goals, but also represents repeated turnings back, or backlashes. This analogy challenges Faludi's readers.

The discussion in this section of her book is detailed because Faludi must establish the laborious, frustrating pattern represented by the corkscrew. Faludi examines four backlashes. The reader's image of a dormant past with a sudden, recent surge is questioned by the dynamic, restless turning of the corkscrew. For each backlash, Faludi develops illustrations to show the progression and the turning back. She uses abundant, varied resources. She quotes men and women, radicals and conservatives. She examines popular culture, labor history, and demographics.

Throughout the welter of data and opinions, Faludi sustains the pattern of progress and backlash—she presents it four times. Throughout, she uses the corkscrew analogy. The two camps of competitors remain clear, even as Faludi explains that women themselves contribute to the backlash. The rest of the book, its major part, presents the elements of the most recent backlash, still in progress, and still unperceived and unchallenged.

Let this brief analysis of Faludi's work serve as a summary of Chapters 3 and 4. You build arguments, indeed, to clarify your own views on an issue. You gather debate materials and weigh them. You establish a viewpoint and take a stand. And, ultimately, this stand involves you in a dramatic situation because you take a stand before readers who will test and question and answer what you offer. In this role of one who argues, you see the use of your study, of finding a thesis and supporting it, of presenting varied support to readers, and of seeking change.

EXERCISE 4.13 Select one argument from the readings in this chapter and one from your own work. First, in one sentence, define the aim of each argument in terms of audience change. Next, make a note of the various supports used in each argument. Use the following checklist. Then, explain how such variety might bring about the intended change.

CHECKLIST OF VARIED SUPPORT

Personal experience
Testimony
Authority

Example
Statistics
Induction
Definition
Analysis
Comparison and contrast
Analogy

Personal values
Cultural values
Deduction

Precedent
Cause and effect

Likelihood
Merit

ARGUMENT ACTIVITIES

1. In small group discussion, help one another use a variety of supports for a thesis. Each writer can take turns reading a thesis aloud. For each thesis, the group can suggest useful supports. Use the previous checklist to help make the suggestions varied.

2. Choose an argument you have written. Use the previous checklist to help identify supports you used. Did you make use of variety? What kind of support can you add now? Where in your argument would you place it? Draft an outline of an expanded argument that shows the new variety of support and its position in the argument.

   For this activity, you can change the checklist items into questions, "What *precedent* supports my thesis? "What is the *likelihood* of my thesis?" "How can I use *induction* to support my thesis?"

3. Consider the following quotations to help you reflect on popular and formal uses of information.

   "Popular induction depends upon the emotional interest of the instances, not upon their number."

   Bertrand Russell

   "Some kinds of information that the scientist regards as highly pertinent and logically compelling are habitually ignored by people. Other kinds of information, logically much weaker, trigger strong inferences and action tendencies. We can think of no more useful activity for psychologists who study information processing than to discover what information their subjects regard as information worthy of processing."

   Richard E. Nisbett

4. In group discussion, examine the following questions about using support:

   When you write an argument, do you spend more time trying to sequence materials logically than you do trying to use materials to change readers?

   How are these two tasks different?

   Have you been able to combine them both in writing an argument?

5. Compare with other students your experiences of searching for sources of support. When did you feel outside sources were necessary? How strong would your argument have been without them? Before looking for sources, how concretely did you define what you sought for? Did you find what you wanted? What methods did you use to find sources? Do you have some advice about what to do and what not to do?

6. For any course you are taking, name a debate about the subject discipline—What are psychologists arguing about? What do journalists debate? What about economists?

In the debate you chose, name the main positions and their spokes-persons. Where do you stand on the issue? Which spokespersons are successful in mustering support? Do they use support to change audience? What are the strengths and weaknesses of the spokespersons? What can you suggest to make the debate clear and the various sides convincing? What would it take to conclude the debate?

7. Chapter 4 directly relates to Argument Assignment Four, Argument with Varied Support. Read about that assignment and examine the student examples. Is it clear how footings of varied support help advance the thesis? Can you detect strong appeals to values and principles? Can you identify warrants?

8. You may begin writing Argument Assignment Four. This assignment asks you to write an argument on any issue you choose and to build your case with a variety of support.

CHAPTER FIVE
STYLE AND ARGUMENT

THREE VIEWS OF STYLE

If this were a book about baking cakes, you would expect a late chapter to explain how to ice the cake and serve it. Sometimes style seems simply the finishing touches. Stylists of clothing and hair present options to try. Without modifying the basic self, these options usually involve how people present themselves to others. Perhaps style would not be so important if people were not conscious of others who see them, hear their conversations, or read their essays.

Matters of style, in this chapter, are matters of choice. You become a stylist in writing—or other pursuits—because you are able to make some choices, one by one or in an ensemble, and then remake them. As you will see, style elements are not merely add-ons: a coat of paint, a layer of icing, or a change of clothing. For the small or the large elements of an argument, you make your choices in accord with your position on an issue, your audience, the kinds of support available, or the type of organization you find workable.

From small to large, the elements you choose among are words, sentences, paragraphs, and schemes of organization. Largest of all, present everywhere, but sometimes hard to pinpoint, is the writer's persona. Obviously, such elements are not cake decoration. They are, rather, the building blocks as well as the head and heart of any essay.

As a writer, what motivates you to make choices? Partly, like a supermarket shopper, you choose for the sake of choosing: a choice was there, so you made it! Sometimes, weary of choices, you fall back on familiar, customary options. Three other motives—often combined, sometimes separate—may encourage you to choose deliberately: adding your signature to the argument, crafting its elements, and making it effective for an audience.

Personal Signature

As with your choices of personal effects—from wristwatch to sunhat—you choose language to express who you are. Writing reflects and expresses your character. You wish to write sincerely, uniquely, and personally: This is the writer speaking; I have something special to tell you, in a way not quite like anyone else's. Just as your voice print or your fingerprints identify you, so does your writing stand as your signature, your personal flag, or coat-of-arms.

Even when completing other people's assignments—those of your teachers or supervisors—you have a chance to stamp the product with your own style. When asked about a certain word choice or choice of introduction, you might say, "That's my way. That's really me!"

Craft

Jonathan Swift, author of *Gulliver's Travels*, reduced the definition of style to "the proper words in the proper places." This definition leaves you on your own to puzzle out what are proper words and what is the exact or fitting place for each and every word of the essay. This short definition is easier to remember than to practice: it demands finesse and know-how like that of a watchmaker or surgeon. In short, the emphasis is on craft, on how to use language so it achieves a standard that appears fixed and universal. Such a definition, such expectation of craft, is a yardstick to measure your individual efforts. Perhaps this definition, so certain and obvious at first glance, but really elusive and even harsh, may trigger that old distaste for writing to please English teachers and others who seem to know what good writing is. These critics tell you about your improper choices—as if that alone could show you how to make the proper ones!

Yet, whatever your skills or successes, you probably do take pains to write essays that are well crafted, easy to read, and even noteworthy for what they say and how they say it. The word *how* draws out the builder in you. A piece of writing challenges you to snap together all of its parts and to make it function smoothly.

Appropriateness

You can choose language to express yourself. You can also choose language to craft the essay. Or you can choose language to succeed in your aims with readers, language that is appropriate to your purpose.

The following anecdote illustrates how a writer has to choose and choose again to find language his or her audience will understand:

A plumber once wrote to a research bureau pointing out that he had used hydrochloric acid to clean out sewer pipes and inquired,

"Was there any possible harm?" The first reply was as follows: "The efficacy of hydrochloric acid is indisputable, but the corrosive residue is incompatible with metallic permanence." The plumber then thanked them for the information approving his procedure. The dismayed research bureau tried again, saying, "We cannot assume responsibility for the production of toxic and noxious residue with hydrochloric acid and suggest you use an alternative procedure." Once again the plumber thanked them for their approval. Finally, the bureau, worried about the New York sewers, called in a third scientist who wrote: "Don't use hydrochloric acid. It eats hell out of the pipes."

Edgar Dale, "Clear Only If Known," *The News Letter,* Ohio State University (Cited by R. E. Young, A. L. Becker, K. L. Pike, *Rhetoric: Discovery and Change,* Harcourt Brace, 1970)

Even as you complete someone else's assignment, you may feel a strong pull to speak effectively to your readers. In some cases, your desire to communicate works alongside your desire to express yourself in your own way and to write to a standard of craft. When these desires do not work together, you will need to decide which of them to serve. When people say an essay is *by* an author, they recognize personal accomplishment, something the author has made. Yet when they think of the essay as coming *from* an author, they recognize it as an effort of self-expression or a useful service for an audience. In some essays, you will indeed be lucky to satisfy your drives to be original, skillful, *and* useful.

Perhaps, when you write arguments to change readers, writing appropriately may appear more important than writing artistically or uniquely. These latter two aims need not be thwarted; they can serve appropriateness, as well. A major concern, then, is that your style choices work for readers.

EXERCISE 5.1 Examine the approach to style of two arguments: one by Jane Brody (Chapter 1) and the other by Isak Dinesen (Chapter 2). Did these writers choose to style their essays with their personal signature, to achieve a high standard of craft, or to make their arguments appropriate to audience? In your notebook, point to specific choices and indicate, in general, which of the three approaches seems dominant.

Keeping in mind why you make style choices, let us examine several areas of choices. Our discussion begins with choices that influence the relationship between writer and audience. Then, we examine some building blocks of the essay, starting with organization and moving to the smaller units of paragraphs, sentences, and words.

CHOICES OF PERSONA AND TONE OF VOICE

As you listen to someone in conversation, you are alert not only to what the person says but how he or she says it. As you read an essay, you find yourself engaged by the writer's subject and, also, by the writer's character and tone of voice. Any piece of writing reveals much about its writer. For discussion purposes, let's call the character that the writer projects in a certain piece of writing the writer's *persona*.

The writer's persona impacts readers. This messenger helps or hinders the acceptance of the message. An appealing persona can help convince readers. An unappealing persona can alienate them. Aristotle called this appeal the ethical appeal because the writer's *ethos,* his or her presentation of self in the writing, does influence readers. Aristotle urged public speakers to combine the ethical appeal with logical and emotion appeals—what Aristotle called *logos* and *pathos.*

The persona reveals itself by what it says and how it says it. As someone in conversation speaks in a certain tone of voice, and is able to move from one tone to another, so the writer communicates with a voice of a particular tone, something you sense with your ear even as you read silently. You might sense that one writer has a friendly voice and another has a threatening one. Another writer may begin an argument in an objective, dispassionate tone of voice and conclude with a voice that expresses deep concern and agitation.

Any consideration of persona and tone of voice is a study of human character. To describe a writer's persona and tone of voice, you can use adjectives that describe character: "This writer has a _____ persona. She speaks in a _____ tone of voice." You can use words such as "enthusiastic," "peevish," "brusque," "cordial," "sincere."

EXERCISE 5.2   Read the following quotations and consider for each selection what is being said and how it is being said. In your notebook, describe the persona and tone of voice of each writer. Try to make the descriptions exact. List the elements of each selection that lead you to describe the persona as you do.

1. It doesn't help you all for me just to speculate on this, but we want him brought to justice. It's only fair and right for these kids lying here that that happens, and I'm determined to see that that happens. So, we'll keep working on the problem. But I can't help you because it's a lot of diplomatic effort going on.

> —President Bush, after a visit to wounded American soldiers, answering journalists' questions about the likelihood of capturing Panamanian General Noreiga

2. Read this notice: Limit of Liability. Submitting any film, print, slide, negative, or video tape to this firm for processing, printing, or other handling constitutes an Agreement by you that any damages or loss by our company, subsidiary or agents, even though due to the negligence or other fault of our company, subsidiary, or agents, will only entitle you to replacement with a like amount of unexposed film or video tape.

—Notice on film developing envelope

3. Mathematics is important in every aspect of our lives today, but few Americans understand mathematics or feel confident using math.

When I tell people I am a mathematics teacher, I am treated as if I am an auditor for the IRS. People think I might ask them for a quadratic formula, and they are sure they have forgotten it.

—Iris Carl, President, National Council
of the Teachers of Mathematics

4. I have just resigned my position as a full, tenured professor of neuro-surgery at Stanford University Medical School. I did so because I was tired of being treated as less than an equal person. I was tired of being condescendingly called "Hon" by my peers, of having my honest differences of opinion put down as a manifestation of premenstrual syndrome, of having my ideas treated less seriously than those of the men I work with. I wanted my dignity back.

—Dr. Frances Conley

5. Marking individual bees with daubs of paint, the researchers set them free to forage. The bees began by randomly visiting flowers. With their keen color vision able to discriminate between blue and yellow, they needed only a sample of five or six flowers before they started focusing on the predictable blue flowers.

—Natalie Angier, science article,
The New York Times

6. Will the pot contend with the potter, or the earthen ware with the hand that shapes it? Will the clay ask the potter what he is making? or his handiwork say to him, "You have no skill"? Will the babe say to his father, "What are you begetting?" or to his mother, "What are you bringing to birth?" Thus says the Lord, Israel's Holy One, his maker: Would you dare question me concerning my children, or instruct me in my handiwork?

—Isaiah, Chapter 45, 9–11

Perhaps this sampler of voices struck you with its diversity. You should be aware that choices exist in matters of style. You have great variety and un-numbered combinations to choose from.

The persona of your writing is sometimes deliberate or, at other times, just "out there" without deliberation. In either case, you express yourself by means of a persona. As you present a persona, you are not being dishonest. You are not assuming an alias to avoid detection. Your chosen persona is part of your strategy, and, at the same time, your persona represents a true aspect of yourself. You wear one of your hats. Remember the discussion of values in Chapter 2 when you drew a circle and divided it into your various selves? Such roles are not make-believe; they are truthful aspects of the self. Just as you act in a variety of capacities, so you write from one capacity or another. For example, you might write addressing the issue of increasing college tuition from your role as a college student or as a voter/taxpayer concerned about methods of financing college education. Maybe you could employ both of these roles in one argument?

Also, you may identify your persona as you consider the voices available to you. How do you feel about the issue? About your audience? About yourself? In the college tuition debate, should you be conciliatory or combative, more certain or less certain about your position, more like or unlike your readers, more or less evaluative or emphatic? Voice tone emerges from complex considerations, and that tone affects readers—disposes them to listen or not, to accept the writer's views or not, to respond or not.

Certainly, writers and speakers sometimes do dishonestly assume a persona; that fact should keep you alert. You often weigh the character of the one who wants to change you: Is he for real? Does she really mean what she says? Is this, indeed, the kind of person the writer is? Often, you will select a persona and develop it to instill confidence, because if readers question or doubt your persona, they may question and doubt your thesis as well.

EXERCISE 5.3 Return to the essays by Berry (Chapter 1) and Peterson (Chapter 2) to examine how these writers present themselves. In your notebook, describe for each essay the writer's persona and tone of voice. Is there ever a shift in tone of voice or a revelation about the writer that makes you reconsider your initial sense of persona?

This use of persona and tone of voice, which ought to reveal who you are, has significant consequences. The main consequence you aim for in argument is to be believed. And that consequence follows your being understood and respected. Imagine trying to convince an audience as diverse as all America. This is the job of presidential hopefuls. Each one of them brings assets and deficits to the job. Running for the Democratic presidential nomination, Bill Clinton, then the governor of Arkansas, was observed by the chairperson of the Democratic party in Texas: "He plays well down here. But, shoot, he's got the same accent we got, and he could be the boy next door over in East Texas." With his knowledge of neighbors and his assumption of being much like them, Clinton, according to this observer, had an effective persona for a Texas campaign. But how did Clinton modify that persona to reach voters in other regions? What did Clinton do to present himself as other than the governor of a rural state, a regional favorite, or, even more challenging, a political animal with the nickname "Slick Willie"?

In the lingo of media, Clinton may have had an image problem. This book uses, instead, the terms *persona* and *tone of voice* and includes a demand for honesty in using them, avoiding cynicism and opportunism.

EXERCISE 5.4 Two inaugural addresses, those of President Kennedy (1961) and President Bush (1989), reveal choices of persona and tone of voice. After you read them carefully, compare their choices of persona and voice tones (which may vary within one piece). What do you know about the historical circumstances of each address, and can you see how each president attempted to make choices appropriate to his time? Summarize your reactions in a paragraph or two in your notebook and be ready to discuss them in class.

❖ INAUGURAL ADDRESS
John F. Kennedy

John F. Kennedy (1917–1963) was the thirty-fifth president of the United States. Narrowly defeating Richard Nixon in 1960, Kennedy, at age 43, became the youngest person to be elected president. His inaugural address was an eloquent one, well crafted and economical, rekindling American idealism and striking a note of challenge. Most inaugurals share similar aims; inaugurals are occasions to tell Americans where they are and where they must go. They are occasions for the new president to look back and ahead and to confirm, criticize, and extend American political traditions. Read this inaugural with a sense of how Kennedy shapes a conventional speaking occasion to fit the particularities of his time.

My Fellow Citizens:

1   We observe today not a victory of party but a celebration of freedom—symbolizing an end as well as a beginning—signifying renewal as well as change. For I have sworn before you and Almighty God the same solemn oath our forebears prescribed nearly a century and three quarters ago.

2   The world is very different now. For man holds in his mortal hands the power to abolish all form of human poverty and to abolish all form of human life. And yet the same revolutionary beliefs for which our forebears fought are still at issue around the globe—the belief that the rights of man come not from the generosity of the state but from the hand of God.

3   We dare not forget today that we are the heirs of that first revolution. Let the word go forth from this time and place, to friend and foe alike, that the torch has been passed to a new generation of Americans—born in this century, tempered by war, disciplined by a cold and bitter peace, proud of our ancient heritage—and unwilling to witness or permit the slow undoing of

those human rights to which this nation has always been committed, and to which we are committed today.

Let every nation know, whether it wish us well or ill, that we shall pay 4 any price, bear any burden, meet any hardship, support any friend or oppose any foe in order to assure the survival and success of liberty.

This much we pledge—and more. 5

To those old allies whose cultural and spiritual origins we share, we 6 pledge the loyalty of faithful friends. United, there is little we cannot do in a host of new cooperative ventures. Divided, there is little we can do—for we dare not meet a powerful challenge at odds and split asunder.

To those new states whom we now welcome to the ranks of the free, we 7 pledge our word that one form of colonial control shall not have passed merely to be replaced by a far more iron tyranny. We shall not always expect to find them supporting our every view. But we shall always hope to find them strongly supporting their own freedom—and to remember that, in the past, those who foolishly sought to find power by riding on the tiger's back inevitably ended up inside.

To those people in the huts and villages of half the globe struggling to 8 break the bonds of mass misery, we pledge our best efforts to help them help themselves, for whatever period is required—not because the communists are doing it, not because we seek their votes, but because it is right. If the free society cannot help the many who are poor, it can never save the few who are rich.

To our sister republics south of our border, we offer a special pledge— 9 to convert our good words into good deeds—in a new alliance for progress— to assist free men and free governments in casting off the chains of poverty. But this peaceful revolution of hope cannot become the prey of hostile powers. Let all our neighbors know that we shall join with them to oppose aggression or subversion anywhere in the Americas. And let every other power know that this Hemisphere intends to remain the master of its own house.

To that world assembly of sovereign states, the United Nations, our last 10 best hope in an age where the instruments of war have far outpaced the instruments of peace, we renew our pledge of support—to prevent its becoming merely a forum for invective—to strengthen its shield of the new and the weak—and to enlarge the area to which its writ may run.

Finally, to those nations who would make themselves our adversary, we 11 offer not a pledge but a request: that both sides begin anew the quest for peace, before the dark powers of destruction unleashed by science engulf all humanity in planned or accidental self-destruction.

We dare not tempt them with weakness. For only when our arms are suf- 12 ficient beyond doubt can we be certain beyond doubt that they will never be employed.

But neither can two great and powerful groups of nations take comfort 13 from their present course—both sides overburdened by the cost of modern weapons, both rightly alarmed by the steady spread of the deadly atom, yet both racing to alter that uncertain balance of terror that stays the hand of mankind's final war.

14   So let us begin anew—remembering on both sides that civility is not a sign of weakness, and sincerity is always subject to proof. Let us never negotiate out of fear. But let us never fear to negotiate.

15   Let both sides explore what problems unite us instead of belaboring the problems that divide us.

16   Let both sides, for the first time, formulate serious and precise proposals for the inspection and control of arms—and bring the absolute power to destroy other nations under the absolute control of all nations.

17   Let both sides join to invoke the wonders of science instead of its terrors. Together let us explore the stars, conquer the deserts, eradicate disease, tap the ocean depths and encourage the arts and commerce.

18   Let both sides unite to heed in all corners of the earth the command of Isaiah—to "undo the heavy burdens . . . (and) let the oppressed go free."

19   And if a beach-head of cooperation can be made in the jungles of suspicion, let both sides join in the next task: creating, not a new balance of power, but a new world of law, where the strong are just and the weak secure and the peace preserved forever.

20   All this will not be finished in the first one hundred days. Nor will it be finished in the first one thousand days, nor in the life of this Administration, nor even perhaps in our lifetime on this planet. But let us begin.

21   In your hands, my fellow citizens, more than in mine, will rest the final success or failure of our course. Since this country was founded, each generation has been summoned to give testimony to its national loyalty. The graves of young Americans who answered that call encircle the globe.

22   Now the trumpet summons us again—not as a call to bear arms, though arms we need—not as a call to battle, though embattled we are—but a call to bear the burden of a long twilight struggle, year in and year out, "rejoicing in hope, patient in tribulation"—a struggle against the common enemies of man: tyranny, poverty, disease and war itself.

23   Can we forge against these enemies a grand and global alliance, North and South, East and West, that can assure a more fruitful life for all mankind? Will you join in that historic effort?

24   In the long history of the world, only a few generations have been granted the role of defending freedom in its hour of maximum danger. I do not shrink from this responsibility—I welcome it. I do not believe that any of us would exchange places with any other people or any other generation. The energy, the faith and the devotion which we bring to this endeavor will light our country and all who serve it—and the glow from that fire can truly light the world.

25   And so, my fellow Americans: ask not what your country will do for you—ask what you can do for your country.

My fellow citizens of the world: ask not what America will do for you, 26
but what together we can do for the freedom of man.

Finally, whether you are citizens of America or of the world, ask of 27
us the same high standards of strength and sacrifice that we shall ask of
you. With a good conscience our only sure reward, with history the final
judge of our deeds, let us go forth to lead the land we love, asking His bless-
ing and His help, but knowing that here on earth God's work must truly
be our own.

 ## INAUGURAL ADDRESS

George Bush

George Bush (b. 1924) was the forty-first president of the United States. Unlike
Kennedy, Bush followed a president of his own party, for whom Bush had served eight
years as vice president. In the almost three decades since Kennedy, America had
become a more complex society. After Vietnam and Watergate, after a decline in
American competitiveness and persistent tensions of race, gender, and class, politicians seemed unable to sound a single, clear, unifying note. Instead, they tried building bridges to many different constituencies. As you read this inaugural address,
consider how Bush reached out to many audiences. Even as the speech includes the
basic elements of inaugurals, Bush's address reflects a particular moment and a
newly elected leader's sense of his role.

THANK YOU, ladies and gentlemen. 1

Mr. Chief Justice, Mr. President, Vice President Quayle, Senator 2
Mitchell, Speaker Wright, Senator Dole, Congressman Michel, and fellow
citizens, neighbors and friends.

There is a man here who has earned a lasting place in our hearts—and 3
in our history. President Reagan, on behalf of our nation, I thank you for the
wonderful things that you have done for America.

I have just repeated word-for-word the oath taken by George Washing- 4
ton 200 years ago; and the Bible on which I placed my hand is the Bible on
which he placed his.

It is right that the memory of Washington be with us today, not only be- 5
cause this is our bicentennial inauguration, but because Washington remains
the father of our country. And, he would, I think, be gladdened by this day.
For today is the concrete expression of a stunning fact: Our continuity these
200 years since our government began.

We meet on democracy's front porch. A good place to talk as neighbors, 6
and as friends. For this is a day when our nation is made whole, when our
differences, for a moment, are suspended.

And, my first act as president is a prayer. I ask you to bow your heads: 7

8   "Heavenly Father, we bow our heads and thank You for your love. Accept our thanks for the peace that yields this day and the shared faith that makes its continuance likely. Make us strong to do Your work, willing to heed and hear Your will, and write on our hearts these words: 'Use power to help people.' For we are given power not to advance our own purposes, nor to make a great show in the world, nor a name. There is but one just use of power, and it is to serve people. Help us remember, Lord. Amen."

9   I come before you and assume the presidency at a moment rich with promise. We live in a peaceful, prosperous time, but we can make it better.

10   For a new breeze is blowing, and a world refreshed by freedom seems reborn; for in man's heart, if not in fact, the day of the dictator is over. The totalitarian era is passing, its old ideas blown away like leaves from an ancient lifeless tree.

11   A new breeze is blowing—and a nation refreshed by freedom stands ready to push on: there is new ground to be broken, and new action to be taken.

12   There are times when the future seems thick as a fog; you sit and wait, hoping the mists will lift and reveal the right path.

13   But this is a time when the future seems a door you can walk right through—into a room called Tomorrow.

14   Great nations of the world are moving toward democracy—through the door to freedom.

15   Men and women of the world move toward free markets—through the door to prosperity.

16   THE PEOPLE of the world agitate for free expression and free thought—through the door to the moral and intellectual satisfactions that only liberty allows.

17   We know what works: Freedom works. We know what's right: Freedom is right. We know how to secure a more just and prosperous life for man on earth: through free markets, free speech, free elections, and the exercise of free will unhampered by the state.

18   For the first time in this century—for the first time in perhaps all history—man does not have to invent a system by which to live. We don't have to talk late into the night about which form of government is better. We don't have to wrest justice from the kings—we only have to summon it from within ourselves.

19   We must act on what we know. I take as my guide the hope of a saint in crucial things—unity; in important things—diversity, in all things, generosity.

20   America today is a proud, free nation, decent and civil—a place we cannot help but love. We know in our hearts, not loudly and proudly, but as a simple fact, that this country has meaning beyond what we see, and that our strength is a force for good.

But have we changed as a nation, even in our time? Are we enthralled   21
with material things, less appreciative of the nobility of work and sacrifice?

My friends, we are not the sum of our possessions. They are not the   22
measure of our lives. In our hearts we know what matters. We cannot hope
only to leave our children a bigger car, a bigger bank account. We must
hope to give them a sense of what it means to be a loyal friend, a loving parent, a citizen who leaves his home, his neighborhood and town better than
he found it.

And what do we want the men and women who work with us to say when   23
we're no longer there? That we were more driven to succeed than anyone
around us? Or that we stopped to ask if a sick child had gotten better and
stayed a moment there to trade a word of friendship.

No president, no government, can teach us to remember what is best in   24
what we are. But if the man you have chosen to lead this government can help
make a difference; if he can celebrate the quieter, deeper successes that are
made not of gold and silk, but of better hearts and finer souls; if he can do
these things, then he must.

America is never wholly herself unless she is engaged in high moral   25
principle. We as a people have such a purpose today. It is to make kinder the
face of the nation and gentler the face of the world.

My friends, we have work to do. There are the homeless, lost and roam-   26
ing—there are the children who have nothing, no love, no normalcy—there
are those who cannot free themselves of enslavement to whatever addiction—
drugs, welfare, demoralization that rules the slums. There is crime to be conquered, the rough crime of the streets. There are young women to be helped
who are about to become mothers of children they can't care for and might
not love. They need our care, our guidance, and education; though we bless
them for choosing life.

THE OLD SOLUTION, the old way, was to think that public money   27
alone could end these problems. But we have learned that that is not so. And
in any case, our funds are low. We have a deficit to bring down. We have more
will than wallet; but will is what we need.

We will make the hard choices, looking at what we have, perhaps allo-   28
cating it differently, making our decisions based on honest need and prudent safety.

And then we will do the wisest thing of all: we will turn to the only re-   29
source we have that in times of need always grows: the goodness and the
courage of the American people.

And, I am speaking of a new engagement in the lives of others—a new   30
activism, hands-on and involved, that gets the job done. We must bring in the
generations, harnessing the unused talent of the elderly and the unfocused
energy of the young. For not only leadership is passed from generation to

generation, but so is stewardship. And the generation born after the Second World War has come of age.

31   I have spoken of a "thousand points of light"—of all the community organizations that are spread like stars throughout the nation, doing good.

32   We will work hand in hand, encouraging, sometimes leading, sometimes being led, rewarding. We will work on this in the White House, in the Cabinet agencies. I will go to the people and the programs that are the brighter points of light, and I'll ask every member of my government to become involved.

33   The old ideas are new again because they're not old, they are timeless: duty, sacrifice, commitment, and a patriotism that finds its expression in taking part and pitching in.

34   And we need a new engagement, too, between the executive and the Congress.

35   The challenges before us will be thrashed out with the House and Senate. And we must bring the federal budget into balance. And we must ensure that America stands before the world united: strong, at peace, and fiscally sound. But, of course, things may be difficult.

36   We need compromise; we have had dissension. We need harmony; we have had a chorus of discordant voices.

37   For Congress, too, has changed in our time. There has grown a certain divisiveness. We have seen the hard looks and heard the statements in which not each others' ideas are challenged, but each others' motives.

38   And our great parties have too often been far apart and untrusting of each other.

39   It's been this way since Vietnam. That war cleaves us still. But, friends, that war began in earnest a quarter of a century ago; and, surely, the Statute of Limitations has been reached. This is a fact: The final lesson of Vietnam is that no great nation can long afford to be sundered by a memory.

40   A NEW BREEZE is blowing—and the old bipartisanship must be made new again.

41   To my friends—and yes, I do mean friends—in the loyal opposition—and yes, I mean loyal: I put out my hand.

42   I am putting out my hand to you, Mr. Speaker.

43   I am putting out my hand to you, Mr. Majority Leader.

44   For this is the thing: this is the age of the offered hand.

45   And we can't turn back clocks, and I don't want to. But when our fathers were young, Mr. Speaker, our differences ended at the water's edge. And we don't wish to turn back time. But when our mothers were young, Mr. Majority Leader, the Congress and the executive were capable of working together to produce a budget on which this nation could live.

46   Let us negotiate soon—and hard. But in the end, let us produce.

The American people await action. They didn't send us here to bicker. 47
They ask us to rise above the merely partisan. "In crucial things, unity"—
and this, my friends, is crucial.

To the world, too, we offer new engagement and a renewed vow: We will 48
stay strong to protect the peace. The "offered hand" is a reluctant fist; once
made, strong and can be used with great effect.

There are today Americans who are held against their will in foreign 49
lands, and Americans who are unaccounted for. Assistance can be shown
here, and will be long remembered. Good will begets good will. Good faith
can be a spiral that endlessly moves on.

Great nations like great men must keep their word. When America says 50
something, America means it, whether a treaty or an agreement or a vow
made on marble steps. We will always try to speak clearly, for candor is a
compliment. But subtlety, too, is good and has its place.

While keeping our alliances and friendships around the world strong, 51
ever strong, we will continue the new closeness with the Soviet Union, con-
sistent both with our security and with progress. One might say that our new
relationship in part reflects the triumph of hope and strength over experience. But hope is good. And so is strength. And vigilance.

HERE TODAY ARE tens of thousands of our citizens who feel the un- 52
derstandable satisfaction of those who have taken part in democracy and
seen their hopes fulfilled.

But my thoughts have been turning the past few days to those who 53
would be watching at home.

To an older fellow who will throw a salute by himself when the flag 54
goes by, and the woman who will tell her sons the words of the battle hymns.
I do not mean this to be sentimental. I mean that on days like this, we remember that we are all part of a continuum, inescapably connected by the
ties that bind.

Our children are watching in schools throughout our great land. And to 55
them I say, thank you for watching democracy's big day. For democracy belongs to us all, and freedom is like a beautiful kite that can go higher and
higher with the breeze . . .

And to all I say: No matter what your circumstances or where you are, 56
you are part of this day, you are part of the life of our great nation.

A president is neither prince nor pope, and I don't seek "a window on 57
men's souls." In fact, I yearn for a greater tolerance, an easy-goingness about
each other's attitudes and way of life.

There are few clear areas in which we as a society must rise up united 58
and express our intolerance. And the most obvious now is drugs. And when
that first cocaine was smuggled in on a ship, it may as well have been a
deadly bacteria, so much has it hurt the body, the soul of our country. And

there is much to be done and to be said, but take my word for it: This
scourge will stop.

59   And so, there is much to do: and tomorrow the work begins.

60   And I do not mistrust the future; I do not fear what is ahead. For
our problems are large, but our heart is larger. Our challenges are great,
but our will is greater. And if our flaws are endless, God's love is truly
boundless.

61   Some see leadership as high drama, and the sound of trumpets calling.
And sometimes it is that. But I see history as a book with many pages—and
each day we fill a page with acts of hopefulness and meaning.

62   The new breeze blows, a page turns, the story unfolds—and so today a
chapter begins: a small and stately story of unity, diversity and generosity—
shared, and written, together.

63   Thank you.

64   God bless you. And God bless the United States of America.

Let me draw examples from a domain humbler than presidential ceremony.
In my writing classes, I ask students to write me a note whenever their papers are late. These letters share similar aims of explaining and excusing,
but they make interesting contrasts in their uses of persona and tone. Here
are three samples of this vast correspondence:

I've been KO'ed by Mr. Virus. Will have it for you soon.

I am, once again, forced to turn in my paper late. Sometimes I have difficulty in putting my ideas on paper. It is not that I haven't tried, I have,
but I seem to be struggling with this essay. I will most likely turn in the
essay on Friday.

My argument that was due today is nearly complete and will be turned
in Friday, 11/8. Also, I am returning herewith my "Racism" argument,
per your request. You wanted to review some of your comments before
I re-edit.

How free are you to choose your persona and tone of voice? Certainly,
you do not have the detachment of a ghostwriter. Your character and
feelings show through. Even so, as you are varied in your roles and in your
attitudes and emotions, you are able to consider choosing persona and voice
for your arguments. From the range of your true selves and your honest
voices, you may select those you think are appropriate. Even if you are
limited to the persona and voice that the argument situation draws from
you, you can still be aware that your persona and voice have an impact
on readers.

EXERCISE 5.5 Look over one of your arguments. How do you think a reader who does not know you would perceive you solely on the basis of this essay? Characterize your persona and voice. What elements of the essay present persona and voice? Considering your aim and your audience, do you think you made effective choices of persona and voice? Record your reactions in your notebook. Bring to class your notebook comments and the argument you examined.

CHOICES OF ORGANIZATION

This book has already presented some elements of organization. In Chapter 3, you examined ways to organize an argument to help you clarify your reasons and to convince your readers. This discussion shows how you can discover options for organization early in the writing process and then use them purposefully in later drafts.

Serving Purpose

Beyond the one or two formulas you have learned, you can organize essays in many other ways. You can choose an organization suited to the specific argument. If you wish to appeal to the reader's reason, you know you must be organized. You must structure a paper that clearly connects thesis and support. That structure must accommodate the kinds of varied, detailed support expected by the rational reader. You must provide clarity, clarity, clarity! You labor to focus on main points, to subordinate details, to make transitions easy to follow, and to provide a wealth of support and to document it.

Deductive and Inductive Order

Traditional argument takes readers through familiar steps: introduction, thesis and support, refutation, conclusion. The introduction names the issue, provides background, motivates interest, presents the writer, and establishes a relationship with readers. The thesis and support section asserts the position statement and develops support for it, including any warrants and support for them. The refutation answers anticipated opposition. The conclusion restates thesis, reviews main supports, urges acceptance, and points out the next step. To review these concepts, see Chapter 3 "Organizing Support: Traditional Organization."

This traditional order follows the movement of deduction: the most important point, the thesis, precedes its supporting reasons. Each reason precedes its supporting details. Thus, the shape of the traditional argument looks like and feels like orderly thinking about the issue, showing that all units are related by subject matter and by abstraction level and held in place by the most general term. To review the ideas of the abstraction ladder, see Chapter 3, "Connecting the Abstract and Concrete." Such a structure has a familiar shape, where numbers indicate abstraction level:

1. Thesis
    2. First reason
        3. Support
        3. Support
    2. Second reason
        3. Support
        3. Support
        3. Support

Now imagine, instead, that in thinking about the issue, you do not start with a position but with numerous specifics. Perhaps you are interested in the debate, but do not yet have a position. What if you think first about your reading and experience and then arrive at your position? Often writers think this way: inductively. Thus, you can, if you choose, structure an argument that moves readers through a discussion toward thesis. Such an order, which Isak Dinesen used in "The Iguana," delays thesis, allowing readers to follow a line of details and reasons leading to thesis. Inductive order can convey your progress toward discovery. It invites readers to experience your formulation of a position.

        3. Support
        3. Support
    2. First reason
        3. Support
        3. Support
        3. Support
    2. Second reason
1. Thesis

Both deductive and inductive organization help demonstrate logos, the cogency of thought essential to rational argument.

EXERCISE 5.6 Select an argument you have organized traditionally with thesis first or nearly first. What steps do you need to take to convert the argument to an inductive organization? Would the argument be stronger? Would it express your views and affect audience in different ways? Either rewrite the argument or outline it in your notebook. Record your estimate of the value of the changes.

Organization and Persona

Now suppose, in addition to presenting your thought, you are concerned with presenting your persona in the argument. Persona, like thought, can be revealed by organization. A rational writer controls materials by using the patterns you have just reviewed here. The Rogerian writer, sensitive to the emotional value of the issue, checks the urge to present his or her own thesis first (deduction) or to funnel the entire essay toward the thesis (induction). Rogerian organization is untraditional because it serves an untraditional aim and persona. The Rogerian requirement to empathize demanded this novel order.

If you write for readers who are easily threatened, you might demonstrate empathy before you present your thesis. If you address readers who are in agreement with part of your support, you might first develop that part—a warrant, for example. You might move from the familiar to the unfamiliar. You might move from less to more weighty matters. Let me illustrate with a personal anecdote.

One evening I caught the last bus from campus and noticed three or four homeless men getting aboard with me. I suppose they had drifted up from the river and were headed to town for a meal and a bed somewhere. I sat near them, close enough to hear that they had no money and that the mission in town was closed to latecomers at this hour. We got to talking, and one of the men, the spokesperson, presented me with three proposals. I still marvel at the shrewdness of his order. He gave three pitches: "Why don't you come with us, since we have a lot of fun?" No. "Well, why don't we come over to your house and I'll cook us all supper?" No. "But, what if you give us some money so we can get something to eat?" I said no a third time; the spokesperson's smiling eye showed me the pleasure he took in grading his three requests from the wildly improbable to the quite possible. He was a strategist.

Your sense of audience informs your choice of organization. Organization is more than a tidy arrangement, reflecting actual thought or chains of reasoning. Your ordering can be strategic—not logical, but psychological—shaped by your sense of what might be an effective order for playing the cards you hold in your hand.

EXERCISE 5.7   Read the funeral orations of Brutus and Antony from Shakespeare's *Julius Caesar*. Although these speeches are different in many ways, notice how Antony orders his materials. Notice the strategic ordering as Antony names the perpetrators of each stab wound and as he delays reading the will. Describe in your notebook Antony's strategy. After examining his oration, turn to the arguments by Jane Brody (Chapter 1) and Robert Jay Lifton (Chapter 2). Surely less dramatic and less manipulative than Antony, still Brody and Lifton order their arguments to serve aims. In your notebook, describe how their organization of materials serves aims. Examine the placement of thesis and the ordering of discussion sections.

❖ JULIUS CAESAR, Funeral Orations

William Shakespeare

William Shakespeare (1564–1616) drew from Plutarch's *Lives* for the history and characters of *Julius Caesar* (1599). For the scene reprinted here, Shakespeare used Plutarch in a general way. He had Brutus give Antony permission to speak, which both Plutarch and Shakespeare thought was a mistake, and he followed up on Plutarch's hint that Brutus' own speech was short and understated. Shakespeare invented the speeches and developed their influence on a volatile audience. Drama, in general, is a superb medium for exploring conflict, and *Julius Caesar* is full of contention. Although assassination, war, and suicide mark off stages of the plot, the characters' speeches reveal their reasons for conflict and are aimed at convincing other characters. Both Brutus and Antony are practiced orators. Yet each speaker chooses a different strategy to make his case. The speeches are fiction, but they are nonetheless famous examples of argument. They illustrate varied appeals and varied uses of organization and content to sway audience.

[Scene II.   The Forum.]

Enter *Brutus* and *Cassius,* with the *Plebeians.*°

Plebeians. We will be satisfied! Let us be satisfied!
Bru. Then follow me and give me audience, friends.
Cassius, go you into the other street
And part the numbers.
5 Those that will hear me speak, let 'em stay here;
Those that will follow Cassius, go with him;
And public reasons shall be rendered
Of Cæsar's death.
1. Pleb.   I will hear Brutus speak.
10 *2. Pleb.* I will hear Cassius, and compare their reasons
When severally° we hear them rendered.
[*Exit Cassius, with some of the Plebeians.*] *Brutus*
goes into the pulpit.°
3. Pleb. The noble Brutus is ascended. Silence!
Bru. Be patient till the last.

Plebeians: common citizens.   *severally:* separately.   *the pulpit:* raised platform.

Romans, countrymen, and lovers,° hear me for my cause, and be silent, that you may hear. Believe me for mine honor, and have respect to mine honor, that you may believe. Censure° me in your wisdom, and awake your senses, that you may the better judge. If there be any in this assembly, any dear friend of Cæsar's, to him I say that Brutus' love to Cæsar was no less than his. If then that friend demand why Brutus rose against Cæsar, this is my answer: Not that I loved Cæsar less, but that I loved Rome more. Had you rather Cæsar were living, and die all slaves, than that Cæsar were dead, to live all freemen? As Cæsar loved me, I weep for him; as he was fortunate, I rejoice at it; as he was valiant, I honor him; but—as he was ambitious, I slew him. There is tears for his love; joy for his fortune; honor for his valor; and death for his ambition. Who is here so base that would be a bondman?° If any, speak, for him have I offended. Who is here so rude° that would not be a Roman? If any, speak, for him have I offended. Who is here so vile that will not love his country? If any, speak, for him have I offended. I pause for a reply.

All. None, Brutus, none!

Bru. Then none have I offended. I have done no more to Cæsar than you shall do to Brutus. The question of his death is enrolled° in the Capitol; his glory not extenuated,° wherein he was worthy, nor his offenses enforced,° for which he suffered death.

Enter *Mark Antony* [and others], with *Cæsar's* body.

Here comes his body, mourned by Mark Antony, who, though he had no hand in his death, shall receive the benefit of his dying, a place in the commonwealth, as which of you shall not? With this I depart, that, as I slew my best lover for the good of Rome, I have the same dagger for myself when it shall please my country to need my death.

All. Live, Brutus! live, live!

1. Pleb. Bring him with triumph home unto his house.

2. Pleb. Give him a statue with his ancestors.

3. Pleb. Let him be Cæsar.

4. Pleb.   Cæsar's better parts

---

lovers: friends.   *Censure:* judge.   *bondman:* slave.   *rude:* uncivilized.   *enrolled:* recorded.   *extenuated:* diminished.   *enforced:* exaggerated.

Shall be crowned° in Brutus.

    1. Pleb. We'll bring him to his house with shouts and
55   clamors.

    Bru. My countrymen—

    2. Pleb.   Peace! silence! Brutus speaks.

    1. Pleb. Peace, ho!

    Bru. Good countrymen, let me depart alone,
60 And, for my sake, stay here with Antony.

Do grace to° Cæsar's corpse, and grace° his speech

Tending to Cæsar's glories which Mark Antony,

By our permission, is allowed to make.

I do entreat you, not a man depart,
65 Save I alone, till Antony have spoke.   *Exit.*

    1. Pleb. Stay, ho! and let us hear Mark Antony.

    3. Pleb. Let him go up into the public chair.

We'll hear him. Noble Antony, go up.

    Ant. For Brutus' sake I am beholding to you.

                      [Goes into the pulpit.]
70   *4. Pleb.* What does he say of Brutus?

    3. Pleb.   He says for Brutus' sake

He finds himself beholding to us all.

    4. Pleb. 'Twere best he speak no harm of Brutus here!

    1. Pleb. This Cæsar was a tyrant.
75   *3. Pleb.*   Nay, that's certain.

We are blest that Rome is rid of him.

    2. Pleb. Peace! Let us hear what Antony can say.

    Ant. You gentle Romans—

    All.   Peace, ho! Let us hear him.
80   *Ant.* Friends, Romans, countrymen, lend me your ears;

I come to bury Cæsar, not to praise him.

The evil that men do lives after them;

The good is oft interred with their bones.

So let it be with Cæsar. The noble Brutus
85 Hath told you Cæsar was ambitious.

If it were so, it was a grievous fault,

And grievously hath Cæsar answered it.

Here, under leave of Brutus and the rest

(For Brutus is an honorable man;
90 So are they all, all honorable men),

Come I to speak in Cæsar's funeral.

He was my friend, faithful and just to me;

But Brutus says he was ambitious,

---

crowned: perfected.   *Do grace:* pay respect.   *grace:* listen to courteously.

And Brutus is an honorable man.
He hath brought many captives home to Rome,   95
Whose ransoms did the general coffers fill.
Did this in Cæsar seem ambitious?
When that the poor have cried, Cæsar hath wept;
Ambition should be made of sterner stuff.
Yet Brutus says he was ambitious;   100
And Brutus is an honorable man.
You all did see that on the Lupercal°
I thrice presented him a kingly crown,
Which he did thrice refuse. Was this ambition?
Yet Brutus says he was ambitious;   105
And sure he is an honorable man.
I speak not to disprove what Brutus spoke,
But here I am to speak what I do know.
You all did love him once, not without cause.
What cause withholds you then to mourn for him?   110
O judgment, thou art fled to brutish beasts,
And men have lost their reason! Bear with me,
My heart is in the coffin there with Cæsar,
And I must pause till it come back to me.
    1. Pleb. Methinks there is much reason in his sayings.   115
    2. Pleb. If thou consider rightly of the matter,
Cæsar has had great wrong.
    3. Pleb.   Has he, masters?
I fear there will a worse come in his place.
    4. Pleb. Marked ye his words? He would not take the   120
        crown;
Therefore 'tis certain he was not ambitious.
    1. Pleb. If it be found so, some will dear abide it.°
    2. Pleb. Poor soul! his eyes are red as fire with weep-
        ing.   125
    3. Pleb. There's not a nobler man in Rome than
        Antony.
    4. Pleb. Now mark him. He begins again to speak.
    Ant. But yesterday the word of Cæsar might
Have stood against the world. Now lies he there,   130
And none so poor to do him reverence.
O masters! If I were disposed to stir
Your hearts and minds to mutiny and rage,
I should do Brutus wrong, and Cassius wrong,
Who, you all know, are honorable men.   135

Lupercal: a feast day. *dear abide it:* dearly pay for it.

I will not do them wrong. I rather choose
To wrong the dead, to wrong myself and you,
Than I will wrong such honorable men.
But here's a parchment with the seal of Cæsar.
140 I found it in his closet; 'tis his will.
Let but the commons hear this testament,
Which (pardon me) I do not mean to read,
And they would go and kiss dead Cæsar's wounds
And dip their napkins° in his sacred blood;
145 Yea, beg a hair of him for memory,
And dying, mention it within their wills,
Bequeathing it as a rich legacy
Unto their issue.
       4. Pleb. We'll hear the will! Read it, Mark Antony.
150   *All.* The will, the will! We will hear Cæsar's will!
       Ant. Have patience, gentle friends, I must not read it.
It is not meet you know how Cæsar loved you.
You are not wood, you are not stones, but men;
And being men, hearing the will of Cæsar,
155 It will inflame you, it will make you mad.
'Tis good you know not that you are his heirs,
For if you should, O, what would come of it?
       4. Pleb. Read the will! We'll hear it, Antony!
You shall read us the will, Cæsar's will!
160   *Ant.* Will you be patient? Will you stay awhile?
I have o'ershot myself° to tell you of it.
I fear I wrong the honorable men
Whose daggers have stabbed Cæsar; I do fear it.
       4. Pleb. They were traitors. Honorable men!
165   *All.* The will! the testament!
       2. Pleb. They were villains, murderers! The will! Read
the will!
       Ant. You will compel me then to read the will?
Then make a ring about the corpse of Cæsar
170 And let me show you him that made the will.
Shall I descend? and will you give me leave?
       All. Come down.
       2. Pleb. Descend.
       3. Pleb. You shall have leave.
                     [*Antony comes down.*]
175   *4. Pleb.* A ring! Stand round.
       1. Pleb. Stand from the hearse! Stand from the body!

napkins: handkerchiefs.   *o'ershot myself:* overstepped bounds

    2. Pleb. Room for Antony, most noble Antony!
    Ant. Nay, press not so upon me. Stand far off.
    All. Stand back! Room! Bear back!
    Ant. If you have tears, prepare to shed them now.   180
You all do know this mantle. I remember
The first time ever Cæsar put it on.
'Twas on a summer's evening in his tent,
That day he overcame the Nervii.°
Look, in this place ran Cassius' dagger through.   185
See what a rent the envious Casca made.
Through this the well-beloved Brutus stabbed;
And as he plucked his cursed steel away,
Mark how the blood of Cæsar followed it,
As rushing out of doors to be resolved°   190
If Brutus so unkindly knocked or no;
For Brutus, as you know, was Cæsar's angel.
Judge, O you gods, how dearly Cæsar loved him!
This was the most unkindest cut of all;
For when the noble Cæsar saw him stab,   195
Ingratitude, more strong than traitors' arms,
Quite vanquished him. Then burst his mighty heart;
And in his mantle muffling up his face,
Even at the base of Pompey's statuë°
(Which all the while ran blood) great Cæsar fell.   200
O, what a fall was there, my countrymen!
Then I, and you, and all of us fell down,
Whilst bloody treason flourished over us.
O, now you weep, and I perceive you feel
The dint° of pity. These are gracious drops.   205
Kind souls, what, weep you when you but behold
Our Cæsar's vesture wounded? Look you here!
Here is himself, marrred as you see with traitors.
    1. Pleb. O piteous spectacle!
    2. Pleb. O noble Cæsar!   210
    3. Pleb. O woeful day!
    4. Pleb. O traitors, villains!
    1. Pleb. O most bloody sight!
    2. Pleb. We will be revenged.
    All. Revenge! About! Seek! Burn! Fire! Kill! Slay!   215
Let not a traitor live!
    Ant. Stay, countrymen.

Nervii: a Belgian tribe.   *to be resolved:* to discover.   *Pompey's statuë:* statue of a former rival of Caesar.
dint: impact.

    1. Pleb. Peace there! Hear the noble Antony.

    2. Pleb. We'll hear him, we'll follow him, we'll die
220 with him!

    Ant. Good friends, sweet friends, let me not stir you up
To such a sudden flood of mutiny.
They that have done this deed are honorable.
What private griefs they have, alas, I know not,
225 That made them do it. They are wise and honorable,
And will no doubt with reasons answer you.
I come not, friends, to steal away your hearts.
I am no orator, as Brutus is,
But (as you know me all) a plain blunt man
230 That love my friend; and that they know full well
That gave me public leave to speak of him.
For I have neither wit, nor words, nor worth,
Action, nor utterance, nor the power of speech
To stir men's blood. I only speak right on.
235 I tell you that which you yourselves do know,
Show you sweet Cæsar's wounds, poor poor dumb mouths,
And bid them speak for me. But were I Brutus,
And Brutus Antony, there were an Antony
Would ruffle up your spirits, and put a tongue
240 In every wound of Cæsar that should move
The stones of Rome to rise and mutiny.

    All. We'll mutiny.

    1. Pleb.   We'll burn the house of Brutus.

    3. Pleb. Away then! Come, seek the conspirators.
245   *Ant.* Yet hear me, countrymen. Yet hear me speak.

    All. Peace, ho! Hear Antony, most noble Antony!

    Ant. Why, friends, you go to do you know not what.
Wherein hath Cæsar thus deserved your loves?
Alas, you know not! I must tell you then.
250 You have forgot the will I told you of.

    All. Most true! The will! Let's stay and hear the will.

    Ant. Here is the will, and under Cæsar's seal.
To every Roman citizen he gives,
To every several° man, seventy-five drachmas.
255   *2. Pleb.* Most noble Cæsar! We'll revenge his death!

    3. Pleb. O royal Cæsar!

    Ant. Hear me with patience.

    All. Peace, ho!

    Ant. Moreover, he hath left you all his walks,

every several: every single.

His private arbors, and new-planted orchards,   260
On this side Tiber; he hath left them you,
And to your heirs for ever—common pleasures,
To walk abroad and recreate yourselves.
Here was a Cæsar! When comes such another?
  1. Pleb. Never, never! Come, away, away!   265
We'll burn his body in the holy place
And with the brands fire the traitor's houses.
Take up the body.
  2. Pleb. Go fetch fire!
  3. Pleb. Pluck down benches!   270
  4. Pleb. Pluck down forms, windows, anything!
    Exeunt Plebeians [with the body].
  Ant. Now let it work. Mischief, thou art afoot,
Take thou what course thou wilt.

    Enter *Servant.*

      How now, fellow?
  Serv. Sir, Octavius° is already come to Rome.   275
  Ant. Where is he?
  Serv. He and Lepidus are at Cæsar's house.
  Ant. And thither will I straight to visit him.
He comes upon a wish. Fortune is merry,
And in this mood will give us anything.   280
  Serv. I heard him say Brutus and Cassius
Are rid like madmen through the gates of Rome.
  Ant. Belike they had some notice of the people
How I had moved them. Bring me to Octavius.
    Exeunt.

Discovering Order

What prompts you to organize a certain way? Your awareness of traditional formats? Your sense of the argument moment, of your possible persona, and of readers' needs? Perhaps all of these?

  Some early steps as you plan and draft an argument can help you try out organizational ideas. You might wish to draft freely about your position, jotting down anything that comes to your mind as you fill the page. *Focused free writing* can begin to reveal the relation between thesis and support; it can begin to reveal possible choices of persona and voice.

Octavius: adopted son of Caesar

Such an early collection of thoughts is far from finished, but you can use a highlighter to set off items that look like keepers. Then, lifting some of these onto a fresh page, you may be impelled to write more, perhaps with a sharper focus or sense of mission. This carryover technique is called *looping*. Or, if you have listed ideas and specifics in a brainstorming session, you can begin to sort them according to what goes together or apart. You can sort them by finding or creating the general term for some of the concrete items. You can find or add concrete items. These *clusters,* in their relationships among themselves, may suggest thesis-level ideas and sections, or paragraph groups. As you advance toward stating your thesis and outlining the main supports and the details supporting them, your organizational plan is evolving.

Your writing teachers have taught you to organize ideas neatly, but not necessarily in the service of argument, that is, communicatively and persuasively. Your several reasons may be clearly marked, but shouldn't you consider in what order to present them to readers? And shouldn't you consider where they appear in relation to thesis, before or after? You might take cues from the line of reasoning. You might take cues from audience. Your outline, a blueprint of organization, should be evaluated: How effective might this argument actually be? It takes more than order to create a strong argument, although it is hard to imagine a disorderly effort succeeding. Will this organization work for readers?

EXERCISE 5.8 For any issue you plan to write about, do some focused free writing and looping in your notebook. Or do some listing and clustering. Use this early drafting to discover possible ways to organize the argument. Consider the search for organizing principles as the search for logical connections between ideas and for strategies to help change readers.

Revealing Order

Papers that seem disorganized often prevent readers from moving easily up and down the abstraction ladder. Many of these arguments appear flat or circular: it is not evident what is important, nor is it evident how parts relate. Everything seems equal in emphasis and interchangeable in sequence.

Let the structures you use be simple. You can think in terms of thesis (big box) and reasons (the next smallest box). If these units relate logically, you already feel order emerging. But how can you reveal this order to others?

Simple structures accomplish what organization must do:

FOUR TASKS OF ORGANIZATION

1. Show the connection between thesis and support.
2. Divide the support so its richness, variety, and relatedness are evident.

3. Provide a clear line for readers to progress along.
4. Order materials strategically for readers.

Sometimes planning in paragraphs or in groups of paragraphs helps you see the progression of the argument, stepping stone by stepping stone. Looking at the whole pathway helps you check the argument's scope, order, and appropriateness. It is much more efficient to change a plan than to change a detailed draft. Try outlining by paragraph before or after the first full draft.

Signals alert readers to the place of each paragraph or sentence in the whole argument. You can signal likeness and unlikeness using words like *and, like, but, however,* and *in contrast.* You can signal time and space relationships by using *then, later, now, finally, here, there, inside,* and *beyond.* You can signal cause and effect with *because, as a result,* and *so.* You can signal level of generality by using *for instance, for example, in summary, in principle,* and *the main point being.*

You also can signal parts of the argument: use *another reason, the argument is strengthened by,* or *in conclusion.* You can preview and review materials too. The argument can look forward or backward to any or all sections. Often, a place where readers stumbled becomes smoother in recapitulation. Or a difficult section is easier for readers to travel with a previewing road map in hand.

EXERCISE 5.9 Choose either the essay by Brody (Chapter 1) or the one by Dinesen (Chapter 2) and one of your own. For these essays, list in your notebook the names of the largest, simplest structures. Can readers easily see them? What reveals them? Previews? Reviews? Transitions? Topic sentence and paragraphing? Could other structures work as well as or better than the original structures? In your notebook, record your findings about simple structures and bold signals.

Using Emphasis

How is emphasis useful? A reader needs to see the connections you make between ideas and details. Imagine a reader feeling that your paper was all ideas or all details or a mixture of both but without a clue as to how they interrelate. The main clue to such relationships is thesis. Some parts of your essay are central, and some are peripheral. Without a clear sense of this, the reader cannot make sense of the essay. It seems all center, all edge, all important, all unimportant.

Transitional signals are in themselves emphatic and noteworthy, like road signs to the expectant driver. But emphasis is created other ways also. Let us consider placement, length, and repetition and restatement.

Consider placement as emphasis. Placement is the writer's equivalent of the sign painter's brightest colors. Readers attend to the beginnings and endings of units, whether of the whole paper, the paragraph, or the sentence. Emphatic spots are shaded in the following diagrams:

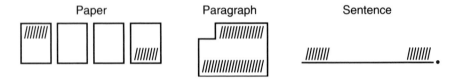

You can manage the middles of structures—even as I am doing in this sentence—to call attention there. Or, more commonly, you can use beginnings and endings, of which an essay fortunately has so many because of its paragraphs and sentences. Thus, you have many opportunities to avoid writing unemphatically.

Consider length emphatic. Surprisingly, it is the short unit that stands out. Look at the short paragraphs in an essay. They work to emphasize a main point, to preview, to review, to connect, and to mark a departure. And short sentences, too, jump out from a backdrop of longer sentences. And so may short words when you put them next to long ones. Such short structures can be compared to the sign painter's bold lettering.

Consider repetition as emphasis. The sign painter's billboard design is repeated all over town. Consider restatement as emphasis. What those billboards want you to buy is unmistakable even though some signs vary the way of saying it. Although you have been told to shun repeating words and to seek new equivalents in a thesaurus, such advice is questioned by the practice of good writers. Why does Carl Rogers repeat the word "communication" a dozen times in his first paragraph? And later, when he does not repeat the same word, Rogers uses related ones, stitching together sections of his paper, like quilting squares joined by a common thread. Readers easily pick out his main concerns.

EXERCISE 5.10 For the two essays you chose for Exercise 5.9, make lists in your notebook of the three or four most important ideas. Then examine the essays to see how they emphasize the importance of these ideas. Is emphasis created by placement, length, or repetition and restatement? Write a paragraph explaining how the essays give emphasis to important ideas.

CHOICES OF PARAGRAPHS

In discussion of style, paragraphs do not get the attention they deserve. Compared to sentences and words, paragraphs may seem humdrum and predictable, so workaday there is nothing to say about them.

You were taught once, when such matters might have held a spark of novelty, that paragraphs are groups of sentences related by a single topic, structured usually by a topic sentence and followed by details. Knowing this much got you to college and through a variety of papers.

Think of writing as a technology that succeeded by symbolizing speech graphically. Early writing systems did not come complete with capital and lower-case letters, or with conventions of punctuation or paragraphing. Imagine reading a manuscript (the word means *handwritten*) with no capitals, no punctuation, no paragraphing, and no guides for separating words from each other or dividing them at the ends of lines! Imagine reading lines of letters that just snaked along!

So the paragraph (a mark *para* or *beside* the *graph* or *writing*) is a tool. Often, you use it without thinking. As there are no hard-and-fast rules about stopping one paragraph and starting the next one, you keep writing and you paragraph almost automatically. You edit to prevent run-on sentences and fragments, but you may never have looked at paragraphs this way. "Run-on" paragraphs need division or clearer internal connections. "Fragmentary" paragraphs need connection to other paragraphs or further development.

Using Paragraph Length and Structure

Considered as an element of style, what can be said about paragraphs? Already you have considered something about paragraph length. An extremely short paragraph arrests readers. It gives emphasis to an idea or detail, to a connection or change of direction.

Middle-sized to long paragraphs are the workhorses of discussion and development. In argument, they pull the weight of various supports. When you write a string of short paragraphs in a discussion, you should check to see if some of them need combining or if some need further development. The paragraph can contain many details and accommodate numerous shifts up and down the abstraction ladder. As a sentence can carry more than a single thought, so, too, a paragraph can include more than one topic, especially when the aim of the paragraph is to interrelate such topics.

As you would never introduce a paper with care and then unload support randomly, so you would not introduce a paragraph and dump the details in. The principles for structuring support are the same for the larger or smaller unit: details are related to one another, to the topic or thesis sentence, and to even finer details. Thus, they are coordinate with some content and subordinate or superordinate to other content. A crafted paragraph, no matter how casual it appears, stows every sentence in its place so it can work with the others to achieve its task. And, on a larger scale, a sequence of paragraphs locates each member paragraph in the place where it can contribute to the task of the entire sequence.

EXERCISE 5.11 Return to a section from Howard Zinn's history in Chapter 4, "Using Variety to Support a Thesis." Look at the six paragraphs numbered 11–16. Zinn writes page after page of paragraphs like these. They assert and develop ideas. Observe how this sequence of paragraphs works, noticing paragraph length and function, as well as the transitions linking paragraphs. Jot down your observations in your notebook.

EXERCISE 5.12 Examine the single, long paragraph from Brenda Peterson's essay "Growing Up Game" which follows. Number each of the sentences. The paragraph begins with a topic sentence that links to the previous paragraph. Then, Peterson opens the discussion. She presents many details and many ideas. Can you follow them? What signals en route help you hold these ten sentences together? In your notebook, list the transitional signals and try outlining the paragraph.

> My father had also taught us as children that animals were our brothers and sisters under the skin. They died so that we might live. And of this sacrifice we must be mindful. "God make us grateful for what we are about to receive," took on a new meaning when one knew the animal's struggle pitted against our own appetite. We also used *all* the animal so that an elk became elk steaks, stew, salami, and sausage. His head and horns went on the wall to watch us more earnestly than any babysitter, and every Christmas Eve we had a ceremony of making our own moccasins for the new year out of whatever Father had tanned. "Nothing wasted," my father would always say, or, as we munched on sausage cookies made from moosemeat or venison, "Think about who you're eating." We thought of ourselves as intricately linked to the food chain. We knew, for example, that a forest fire meant, at the end of the line, we'd suffer too. We'd have buck stew instead of venison steak and the meat would be stringy, withered-tasting because in the animal kingdom, as it seemed with humans, only the meanest and leanest and orneriest survived.

EXERCISE 5.13 Look at passages of long paragraphs in the essays by Francis Bacon (Chapter 1) and Virginia Woolf (Chapter 1), passages of short paragraphs in the pieces by Wendell Berry (Chapter 1) and John F. Kennedy (Chapter 5), and passages of middle-sized paragraphs in the essays by Isak Dinesen (Chapter 2) and Robert Jay Lifton (Chapter 2). Look at the paragraphing in one of your arguments. Where would you place yourself among these writers of paragraphs of varied lengths? With these examples before you, do you see any reason to write paragraphs much longer or shorter than you customarily do? In your notebook, write a paragraph—and not a short one—summarizing your observations about paragraph length and your handling of it.

Specialized Paragraphs

There are some specialized functions for paragraphs, too, as the discussion about emphasis indicated. Every argument has an agenda. Paragraphs help introduce and conclude the agenda; they preview and review it and connect its various items.

Various ways to start and conclude an argument are presented in the following list. Although these variations may not require a whole paragraph, you may want to plan introductory and concluding paragraphs that do more than or other than state the thesis. Sometimes you can improve your argument simply by adding on to the original draft a new start and a new finish.

WAYS TO VARY YOUR INTRODUCTIONS
AND CONCLUSIONS

Introduction

State thesis, preview reasons and support

Establish context, present background

Introduce writer's involvement and qualifications

Introduce persona, establish tone of voice

Establish social bonds with readers
 Common concerns
 Common values
 Common affiliations

Generate interest
 Arresting specifics
  Fact
  Quotation
  Anecdote

Conclusion

Restate thesis, review support

Point to new context, to future

Employ persona, tone of voice
 Intensification
 Audience involvement

Reemphasize common bonds with readers

Generate commitment to thesis
 Appeal to emotions
 Call to action
 Use specifics
  Fact

Quotation
Anecdote

EXERCISE 5.14 Compile a list of as many varieties of introductions and conclusions as you can find in arguments in this book or among the essays by writers in your class. Using the list and the examples from other writers, try adding or rearranging opening and closing steps for one of your arguments. Do such changes strengthen the argument? In what ways?

CHOICES OF SENTENCES

As we move to smaller units of composition, more and more might be said, especially about sentences and words. The challenge here is to apply advice about these units to the writing of argument.

Sentence Variety

Already you have seen that sentences vary in length. You saw that short sentences tend to be emphatic in a setting of relatively longer sentences. Remember how Dr. Conley concluded her paragraph: "I want my dignity back." These five words secure the theme and tone of the passage, achieving emphasis in contrast to the preceding forty-one-word sentence. Such a contrast—a reduction times eight—seems to set in the hook of the short sentence. Carl Rogers, in his address, uses short sentences to lead into discussion: "Let me illustrate my meaning with some very simple examples," "Or take another example," "Stated so briefly, this may sound simple, but it is not." Rogers is able to summarize well, but allows for the complexity of his subject. Examine the graduation to longer sentences as Rogers develops this paragraph:

> Stated so briefly, this may sound absurdly simple, but it is not. [12 words] It is an approach which we have found extremely potent in the field of psychotherapy. [15 words] It is the most effective agent we know for altering the basic personality structure of an individual, and improving his relationships and his communications with others. [26 words] If I can listen to what he can tell me, if I can understand how it seems to him, if I can see its personal meaning for him, if I can sense the emotional flavor which it has for him, then I will be releasing potent forces of change in him. [51 words]

Next, Rogers writes another listing of if's, this time using seventy-four words! His clincher sentence is a mere thirty-one words. He begins the next paragraph with a relatively short sentence of twenty words.

Rogers did not count words this way. But he may have felt his sentences fill and overflow as he developed his ideas. And he may have sensed the value to the audience of sentences reined in for summary and for emphasis. One effect of this variety on audience is to be swept up in the discussion and to touch down periodically with the summarizers and transitions that help direct the rush of the essay. Such sentence crafting builds Rogers' persona as a thinker and communicator and helps carry readers along the course of his address.

Notice the many short sentences in the following news article that explains and defends the shooting of a black bear in a populated area:

> On the basis of these considerations, the decision was made to remove the bear. Live trapping was out of the question. The bear was not feeding and could not be baited into a trap.
>
> Tranquilizing the animal was a second best choice. [Three sentences, one 13, one 19, and one 28 words, reject this option.]
>
> The one remaining option was to kill the animal. To have done otherwise would have amounted to gambling the potential loss of livestock and human lives against the life of a black bear. With the odds of a tragic encounter increasing every day, there was only one choice to make. The black bear population in Oregon is healthy, especially in the Cascades and Coast Range, and the loss of one animal, while unfortunate, will not make a significant difference.
>
> Pat Wray,
> Information Supervision,
> Oregon Department of
> Fish and Wildlife

Some of the longest sentences of this article reach almost forty words, and the short ones are as short as five words. The clarity and certainty of the writer's views are striking, in part because of the strings of relatively short sentences. No doubt, what sentences say does more than length to establish thesis, persona, and tone. Sentence length, though, is one method a writer employs to express and enhance content.

Sentences vary in length; they also vary in function. Very simply, most sentences declare something, ending with a period. Other, rarer ones, hence useful in creating variety, question and exclaim, and are punctuated by a question mark or an exclamation point. In the paragraph that follows, Pat Wray closes the bear article with a question and with some questioning sentence fragments. They are additionally interesting because they are quoted (yet another sentence function):

> Dean Wheeler, Assistant Regional Supervisor in Corvallis, summed up the bottom line for the Department of Fish and Wildlife. "We knew going in that some people would not agree with our decision to destroy the

bear, but what could I say to the mother of a young boy that had been killed by the animal? That we were sorry? That we'd known something like this might happen but we didn't want to take the heat?"

These are rhetorical questions because, for the speaker, they are already answered. Rhetorical questions elicit a desired response, in this case, "Of course not!"

Another kind of question clearly asks for an answer unknown to either the reader or the writer. Rogers uses questions this way, advancing his discussion by posing questions that his readers may be asking and that he attempts to answer: "But is there any way of solving this problem, of avoiding this barrier?" There are some genuine unknowns in Rogers' thinking about communication. He is truly questing. His questions help to structure the argument, involve readers, and present an inquiring, striving persona.

Have you used questions this way, rhetorically or searchingly? Try using them.

Exclamations are used infrequently in rational and Rogerian argument, perhaps because firecrackers are not suited to either. Rational readers do not want distractions, and Rogerian readers do not want surprises or shocks. I have used exclamations in these last pages about sentence length and type. Did you notice? Stay alert!

EXERCISE 5.15 Examine the length and function of sentences in two arguments, including one of your own. List the varieties you find and be ready to point to examples of each variety. If you have not already included them, try writing some short sentences and some questions. How does variety contribute to each of the arguments? Record your observations for class discussion.

Writers lengthen sentences by adding single words and word groups that are less than sentences. Grammarians call such add-ons "modifiers." You can change or modify your sentences by adding modifiers. If you heavily modify, you will write much longer sentences. If you lightly modify, you will write slightly longer ones. You probably write sentences somewhere between the world's shortest sentence ("Go!") and the world's longest sentence (yet to be written!). There is no grammatical limit to lengthening a sentence. Common sense and the reading abilities of audience limit sentence length.

You can create variety by how much modification you add and by where you add it to your sentences, at the beginning, middle, or end. So you have the choice to add and to position modifiers.

MODIFIER TYPES AND PLACEMENT

Sentences Modified by Single Word Modifiers

Adjectives

Adverbs

Sentences Modified by Word Group Modifiers
Phrases
Subordinate clauses

Modifiers Placed
Before the sentence subject and verb
After the sentence subject and verb
Between the sentence subject and verb

Taking together the kinds and positions of modifiers, you have the possibility of great choice and great variety.

Imagine a sentence-making kit containing a subject-verb platform and a bunch of modifiers, a basic Lego set. Notice how the underlined modifiers work in the following examples.

1. Platform: Civilization does not have faith.

   Modified Sentence: <u>Our</u> civilization does not <u>yet</u> have <u>enough</u> faith <u>in the social sciences</u> <u>to utilize their findings.</u>   *Carl Rogers*

2. Platform: We observe not a victory but a celebration.

   Modified Sentence: We observe <u>today</u> not a victory <u>of party</u> but a celebration <u>of freedom</u>—<u>symbolizing an end as well as a beginning</u>—<u>signifying renewal as well as change.</u>   *John F. Kennedy*

3. Platform: Education is education.

   Modified Sentence: <u>A liberal</u> education is <u>an</u> education <u>in ideas</u>—<u>not merely memorizing them, but learning to move among them, balancing one against the other, negotiating relationships, accommodating new arguments, and returning for another look.</u>   *Wayne Booth*

4. Platform: What makes me sad is inability.

   Modified Sentence: <u>And</u> what makes me sad <u>about the women's movement in general</u> is <u>my own</u> inability, <u>and that of so many other women, to get across such gulfs, to join hands, to unite on anything.</u>
   Nora Ephron

5. Platform: Never be afraid.

   Modified Sentence: Never be afraid <u>to raise your voice for honesty and truth and compassion, against injustice, lying and greed.</u>
   William Faulkner

6. Platform: Politics has been described.

   Modified Sentence: <u>By my calculations,</u> politics has been described <u>as the great American sport ever since the first election was called a race and the candidate became a winner.</u>   *Ellen Goodman*

All these writers elaborate on simple platforms. Their sentences show a variety of modifier type and placement. Their sentences show how modifiers help specify and enrich meaning.

Consider some alternatives to one writer's choices. In sentence 6, Ellen Goodman adds modifiers to the end of the sentence, a common, easy-to-read practice. Look at the option that places modifiers at the head of the sentence:

> By my calculations, ever since the first election was called a race and the candidate became a winner, politics has been described as the great American sport.

The next option modifies within the sentence:

> Politics, by my calculations ever since the first election was called a race and the candidate became a winner, has been described as the great American sport.

Look at sentence 3 again and imagine it starting, "Not merely memorizing them . . ." and ending "a liberal education is an education in ideas." Try reordering other of these sentences. Be aware of options as you craft sentences in your arguments. Try similar recastings of sentences in your arguments that you feel deserve special care because they are important to you. Also, recast any sentences in your arguments that are not as clear or as forceful as they could be.

One other tool for lengthening sentences is combining a sentence with another sentence. This is not modifying, but compounding, adding two or more sentences together with appropriate linking words or punctuation.

> In that moment time was suspended; the world to which I belonged did not exist and I might have been an onlooker from outer space.
> *Rachel Carson*
>
> Write, comb it out, rewrite, keep combing.   *Peggy Noonan*
>
> Soon, the majority of young college age women were claiming they were on campus only to find husbands. Their age at first marriage dropped to a record low for the century; the number of their babies climbed to a record high.   *Susan Faludi*

These examples compound complete sentences; the first uses the semicolon and *and* to link them. The second uses commas to link a series of four. The third, uses the semicolon to link the two sentences. The next example intrudes a complete sentence between the subject and verb of another sentence:

> His eyes—they were pale blue, around an aquiline nose over a trapper's moustache—search the woodlot for a proper tree.   *John McPhee*

EXERCISE 5.16 Take two well-developed paragraphs, one from the text readings, one from an essay of yours. Copy them into your notebook. Underline all the modifiers in the two passages. Which writer modifies more heavily? Which writer uses more variety in placing modifiers? Can you suggest effective changes in the modification in both passages? Should you cut, add, reposition? Write alternate versions for both paragraphs. If you cannot make them better, at least exercise well and make them different! Be prepared to discuss your choices in class, to give and receive advice about rewriting sentences.

Using Sentence Variety

Your choice of sentence types can help your arguments. You want to succeed on the level of simply being understood. You also want your persona and your sentences to be appropriate to the task, that is, well suited to you as a writer, to your subject, and to your audience. You want the craftsmanship of your sentences to be obvious, too.

Here is a passage—hard or impossible to understand—and a revision of it. If the writer had written his sentence to suit a truly helpful persona and not a technocrat, these sentences would not have been so difficult:

> Meanwhile, reconfiguring presently owned electronic keyboards, or normal attritional replacement of old equipment with new machines having keyboards which can be arranged to suit individual needs, is the option which managers, teachers, and all prospective buyers of word processing equipment should consider.

This sentence concludes a paper about speech recognition and keyboard design. It is stunning for the wrong reasons. Why is it so hard to read? Contrast it to this rewrite:

> Meanwhile, some electronic keyboards can be reconfigured. As equipment wears out, it can be replaced by machines with keyboards that can be arranged to suit individual needs. Those options should be used while the speech-recognition designers perfect their product.

Somehow, more sentences work better here. The pacing becomes slower; there's room to breathe. Reading the first version, you don't know what you are being told until the end of the sentence. The new version's first sentence is short and easy. Subjects and verbs are placed nearer the beginnings of sentences and are not interrupted by word group modifiers.

The original sentence has its verb as its twenty-seventh word! Its platform is "Reconfiguring or replacement is the option." The platform elements are strung apart by modifiers. Jargon clogs the way: "normal attritional replacement" is rephrased in the revision to read "equipment wears out." So, sentence writing is a craft in the service of speaking clearly, and word choice is a part of the craft.

Do you appreciate what makes reading a passage difficult? Reading formulas are used to determine the grade level of textbooks. One often-used formula developed by Edward Fry estimates readability by sampling three passages of one hundred words each and counting the number of syllables and sentences in each passage, averaging them, and finding grade level on a special graph. (See Argument Activity 5 for an application of the formula.) For Fry, longer words and longer sentences definitely make reading difficult. Of course, such a simple measure does not factor in the reader's motivation and interest in the subject matter. Nor does Fry's formula distinguish between well-made and poorly made sentences, whatever their length.

In what ways—other than measuring level of reading difficulty—can you examine how sentences help or hinder the task of argument? Reconsider for a moment some writers whose articles you have read. Did their sentence choices seem appropriate to their persona? Carl Rogers used many questions. You have seen how they help make transitions, and these questions are also thoroughly Rogerian as they invite readers to become involved and to inquire along with Rogers himself.

Pat Wray, defending the bear shooting, used many short sentences to set up headings for support and to communicate certainty about the decision. Such sentence choices communicate both the position and the persona. Also, because Wray writes for the broadest possible readership—newspaper readers—his directness and simplicity seem deliberate. Newspaper readers, on average, read less well than readers of technical journals, and whatever their abilities, they are likely to be interrupted as they read. Thus, some features of an argument exist because the writer wishes to reach particular readers. And among those features are sentences.

EXERCISE 5.17   Of all the reading selections you have encountered in this text, which ones were easy and which were difficult? What creates ease and difficulty of reading? Consider factors of word choice and sentence length, as Fry did, but consider what other factors influence how approachable an essay seems. In your notebook, write a paragraph summarizing your findings and opinions about reading with ease or difficulty.

Five Special Opportunities for Crafting Sentences

This section examines five opportunities for crafting sentences—opportunities that can be used well when the writer sees what is special about each of them. You will examine sentences that pair and list, that compare, that fit subjects to strong verbs, that clearly modify, and that use and cite sources.

Pairs and Lists

First, let's examine two boasts, not even sentences, on the label of a liquid soap bottle: *Kills Germs. Mild to Skin.* Although these are not sentences, they do present two positive aspects that can be restated to reveal this close pairing of the soap's virtues: *Kills Germs. Soothes Skin.* Or, *Tough on Germs. Mild to Skin.* Parallelism is the principle of these rewrites.

When your sentence presents units of parallel content, you should express them by using parallel grammatical units:

> We all strive for safety, prosperity, comfort, long life, and dullness.
> *Aldo Leopold*

> Studies are for delight, for ornament, and for ability.   *Francis Bacon*

> Our society is moving steadily from natural sources of information toward electronic ones, from the mountain and the field toward the television; this great transition is very nearly complete.   *Bill McKibben*

> In an orchard there should be enough to eat, enough to lay up, enough to be stolen, and enough to rot on the ground.   *Samuel Johnson*

When parallelism is not managed well, the results are awkward and unclear:

1. We often hear or witness children abusing alcohol at an early age.

   Revised: We often hear *about* or witness children abusing alcohol at an early age.

2. I believe a person should have the right to die without legal difficulties and the wishes of the family carried out.

   Revised: I believe a person should have the right to die without legal difficulties and *with* the wishes of the family carried out.

3. The monkeys showed signs of nervousness, depression, and they would cling to anything that was put in their cage, thinking it was their mother.

   Revised: The monkeys showed signs of nervousness *and* depression, and they would cling to anything that was put in their cage, thinking it was their mother.

Use parallelism to show off the matching relationships between pairs and among list items.

Comparisons

Many ads claim a product is better. Isn't it fair to ask, "Better than what?" Academic writing completes comparisons and compares like items. Consider how to improve the following:

This cigarette has less tar.

Here our winters are as mild as Georgia.

My income is smaller than my husband.

Your nose is a lot like your parents.

Completing comparisons is only reasonable (so is comparing noses with noses!). Here is a sentence that completes its comparison, showing that comparison is a form of parallelism:

It's better to raise a question without deciding upon it than to decide upon it without raising it.

Strong Verbs

The following are problem sentences using weak verbs and some revisions using strong verbs:

1. The importance fluid power plays in industry is beyond our imagination.

   Revised: We cannot imagine the importance of fluid power in industry.

   Note: The noun *imagination* can be changed to a strong verb *imagine,* replacing the weak *is.*

2. The person who has the sole responsibility for feeding the computer that contains the necessary steps required to derive a solution for a given problem is the programmer.

   Revised: The programmer has the sole responsibility for feeding the computer the steps required to solve a problem.

   Note: The original seems backwards and slow: So-and-so who blah blah *is* the programmer. *Is* is weak! Say the programmer *feeds,* or use some other direct and active verb.

For the following flawed originals, use strong verbs and place them close to their subjects.

1. The issue about log exports is a big concern to Westerners.
2. The reason behind the brand's widespread popularity lies in the quality of its boots.
3. The need for me to get feelings inside of me out is what leads me to being an artist.
4. Another hardship experienced by fast-food employees is lack of benefits.
5. The fact that the nonsmoker is involuntarily forced to breathe toxic cigarette smoke is an infringement of the nonsmoker's rights.

Note how these sentences lead off with the wrong foot: the abstract subject assures roundabout progress and a weak verb. In sentence 5, for example, rather than using the verb *is* with the abstract subject *The fact that,* try a verb such as *impinges* or *forces* and fit it to the best subject. What impinges or forces? These flawed sentences pile up nouns and use weak verbs. Do you see how to revise sentences like these? Select strong subject and verb platforms for the sentences you modify.

Clear Modifiers

Some modifiers can move to several spots in a sentence; others cannot:

As a farmer, I do almost all of my work with horses.   *Wendell Berry*

OK   I do almost all my work as a farmer with horses.
OK   I do almost all of my work with horses as a farmer.

Although the alternate sentences may not sound as natural as the original, they are clear because *as a farmer* conveys the sense of the original even when it is relocated. This is not always the case:

The place of the fiddler crab in the ecology of the world it inhabits is a necessary one, not easily filled.   *Rachel Carson*

Only because this sentence begins with "the place" can this next version express the original meaning, even though it expresses it awkwardly:

OK   Not easily filled, the place of the fiddler crab in the ecology of the world it inhabits is a necessary one.

But, look at what happens if the modifier is relocated to another spot:

Not OK   The place of the fiddler crab in the ecology of the world it inhabits, not easily filled, is a necessary one.

What is not easily filled? The world? The ecology? Clearly, for some modifiers, some places in the sentence are better than others.

If the modifier does not modify the entire sentence, then you must place it exactly. Because it could modify more than one part of the sentence, you must make its purpose clear by positioning it or rephrasing it so it modifies what you intended. Look at the underlined modifiers in the following sentences. Change their positions and, if need be, their wording so they modify exactly.

1. The change was made in spite of the enormous popularity <u>because the cars were outdated.</u>
2. <u>Having rotted in the cellar,</u> the farmer could not sell the potatoes.
3. I feel as if I let my whole team and every fan <u>personally down.</u>
4. <u>After being found guilty and sentenced to life,</u> the jury decides how many years the convicted murderer is sentenced to prison.
5. Over a thousand suits were initiated by NOW against U.S. corporations <u>charging sex discrimination.</u>

As you add modifiers to sentence platforms, you add complexity, possibly at the risk of losing clarity. Therefore, modify with care.

Quotes, Paraphrases, and Citations

When you quote or paraphrase sources, you often write sentences with added parts. You need to know the conventions of such special tasks.

Make it a practice to connect your use of sources to your thesis, not simply scatter them throughout the argument. You can reveal the connection of source material to thesis by introducing it so it fits into the paragraph and by leading away from it so its significance is emphasized and connected to your next sentence. In paragraphs 8 and 9 of his essay in Chapter 4, Howard Zinn steers the reader toward and then away from source material: "In 1893, Supreme Court Justice David J. Brewer, addressing the New York State Bar Association, said. . . ." This is Zinn's second quotation showing that justices do not simply interpret the Constitution. Then, following the quote, Zinn writes, "This was not just a whim of the 1880s and 1890s—it went back to the Founding Fathers. . . ."

Another example of embedding source material in the argument, not just sprinkling it on top, comes from Ada Louise Huxtable's article at the end of this chapter:

> Equally disturbing is the church's odd illusion that it is engaged in an act of preservation. "We have agreed that we will accept no offer, however big, that would in any way harm our magnificent church building . . . ," says the official statement. To which the only response is amen. The harm that will be done to the landmark church by this decision will be irreparable.

Huxtable leaves no doubt that the official statement is both odd and harmful. If Huxtable chose to paraphrase the official statement, she would use her own language to present the original material. She would strive to be objective in her rewording of it: The official statement says the church will accept no bid, no matter how high, that would harm the existing church building.

When do you quote? When do you paraphrase? No formula determines when, but consider for a moment what quotes and paraphrases contribute to argument:

USES OF QUOTES AND PARAPHRASES

Quote to:

Exhibit authentic material, especially if readers might question the accuracy and objectivity of a paraphrase

Emphasize positions or support with particularly distinctive or eloquent original wording

Vary the weave of sources, when most will be presented by paraphrase

Paraphrase to:

Present the majority of source material

Help keep your writing uniform in style

Allow you to use sources with greater convenience than the actual quotation allows

Remember, as you take notes, you should make clear for later use what materials you have quoted verbatim and what you have already paraphrased in your notes. You may choose later to paraphrase any materials, but you cannot choose to quote unless you have recorded exactly or have access to the original. So, if you are uncertain about whether you will actually quote a source in your argument, take down the exact wording. You will then be able to quote it or paraphrase it. For most of your notetaking, paraphrasing goes faster than quoting, and in the argument, you will most likely be paraphrasing more than quoting. Try to limit copying sources verbatim to those materials you are sure to quote or to those you need to consider later for use as quotations.

You need to cite your use of sources in most college writing. As you take notes, be sure to identify the sources you draw from. You will need an identification for each use of source material in the argument. This convention of identifying sources is a tedious, clerical chore, but it helps prevent plagiarism, which is the writer's intentional or unintentional use of source language and source content as his or her own. In this culture, an author has ownership interest in the content and the language of his or her original work. So, any use of a source—quoted or paraphrased—must be identified.

Quotes, obviously, are marked by quotation marks or set off in a special way if they are extended, like the section I just quoted from Huxtable. You indent and single-space the quotation, omitting the quotation marks. It is easy enough to tag the writer or speaker. Paraphrases are harder to mark, because you have nothing comparable to quotation marks to indicate where they start and end. You can mark the start of a paraphrase, as Ed Whitelaw does in his article in Chapter 4, with the identification of the source: "But as long ago as 1956, economist Charles Tiebout pointed out in the *Journal of Political Economy* that using this logic means. . . ." Ed Whitelaw signals the end of the paraphrase with a shift to an evaluation of Tiebout's idea: "Clearly this is absurd." If the Tiebout material had been extensive, Whitelaw would need to keep using the author or title to keep readers alert to the continuation of the paraphrase: "Tiebout also pointed out . . ." "Tiebout's article stressed that. . . ." Whitelaw effectively uses source materials, leading into and away from them, varying quotation and paraphrase, and identifying their sources.

A compact book such as this one cannot explain the details and options of documenting sources. You know there are several conventions of documentation, and you are most likely experienced using at least one. Your instructors in writing or other subjects will indicate their preference for documentation styles. Most handbooks of writing explain the options.

Once plagiarism is not the issue, you can appreciate how identifying sources helps a writer of argument to build a case. Using sources makes clear that your argument incorporates other voices, some more authoritative or more eloquent than yours, and your readers give you credit for drawing together diverse materials in a clear, compelling way.

EXERCISE 5.18 Check the sentence crafting of one of your arguments. Place an asterisk next to any use of pairs, lists, or comparisons. For each sentence, underline subject and verb twice and modifiers once. With this analysis complete, you can check how well you used these features. Rewrite, as necessary, to make lists parallel, to complete comparisons, and to ensure that you use strong verbs and clear modifiers.

EXERCISE 5.19 Review how the following essays use source materials in argument. Note how they lead into and away from each source, how they use quote and paraphrase, and how they identify the source.

Jane Brody (Chapter 1)

Barbara Howell (Chapter 3)

Ed Whitelaw (Chapter 4)

Mike Taskey (Argument Assignment Five)

Review one of your arguments for its use of sources. Did you integrate them? Did you present them as quotations or paraphrases? How did you identify sources? Overall, have you used source materials effectively? Write a paragraph in your notebook describing successful uses of source materials in writing by you and others.

CHOICES OF WORDS

Writing is really easy; it is just a matter of words! In no other area of the craft are the choices so abundant. Successful choices require your deliberation.

Isak Dinesen describes iguanas that "shine like a heap of precious stones or like a pane cut out of an old church window." Brenda Peterson recalls that one of her earliest memories is of "crawling across the vast continent of crinkled linoleum in [her] Forest Service cabin kitchen, down splintered back steps, through wildflowers growing wheat-high." Such language permits us to see what the writer sees.

"I've been KO'ed by Mr. Virus," writes a student whose paper is late. "I have just resigned my position as a full, tenured professor of neurosurgery at Stanford University Medical School," announces Dr. Frances Conley. "I did so because I was tired of being treated as less than an equal person." Such language allows us to hear the writer's voice.

Toward the end of his address, Carl Rogers observes, "Even with our present limited knowledge we can see some steps which might be taken, even in large groups, to increase the amount of listening *with,* and to decrease the amount of evaluation *about.*" Introducing each of four paragraphs about American justice, Howard Zinn writes these sentences:

> The prisons in the United States had long been an extreme reflection of the American system itself. . . .

> It had long been true, and prisoners knew this better than anyone, that the poorer you were the more likely you were to end up in Jail.

> Willard Gaylin, a psychiatrist, relates (*Partial Justice*) a case which, with changes in details, could be multiplied thousands of times.

> With such power in the hands of the courts, the poor, the black, the odd, the homosexual, the hippie, the radical are not likely to get equal treatment before judges who are almost uniformly white, middle-class, orthodox.

Such language permits us to follow the writer's thought, from theory to application, from generalization to specifics, from one step to the next.

Rachel Carson, in *The Edge of the Sea,* recounts an experience of a beach at night. She comes to understand "life itself" symbolized by "the little crab alone with the sea."

> There was no other visible life—just one small crab near the sea. I have seen hundreds of ghost crabs in other settings, but suddenly

> I was filled with the odd sensation that for the first time I knew the creature in its own world—that I understood, as never before, the essence of its being. In that moment time was suspended; the world to which I belonged did not exist and I might have been an onlooker from outer space.

Not hushed and awed, but indignant, Wendell Berry gives one strong reason why he will not use an electric-powered machine to write his essays:

> A number of people, by now, told me that I could greatly improve things by buying a computer. My answer is that I am not going to do it. I have several reasons, and they are good ones. . . . I would hate to think my work as a writer could not be done without direct dependence on strip-mine coal. How could I write conscientiously against the rape of nature if I were, in the act of writing, implicated in the rape?

Such language allows us to feel what the writer feels. Like the writers of the other selections, Carson and Berry make something of their choices. Their feelings, their ideas, their voices, and their experiences direct their selections of language sufficient to the task.

Using Synonyms or Near Synonyms

Faced with such variety, you need to consider your choices. Many words are so much alike in sound and spelling you may easily confuse them. Other words, while naming the same or related things, have quite different connotations, which you can use to influence a reader. A wide choice of synonyms or near synonyms offers you opportunities to be exact or inexact, objective or evaluative.

Consider for a moment these treacherous sound- and look-alikes: *infer, imply; affect, effect; disinterested, uninterested.* When do you use *reticent* or *reluctant*? When is behavior *aberrant* or *abhorrent*?

Examine in the following lists some words that overlap in meaning, but connote very differently:

ghetto	gravedigger	politician
slum	undertaker	public servant
inner city	mortician	diplomat
	funeral director	statesman
		(statesperson!)

A good dictionary or thesaurus can help explain gradations of meaning. For example, here is part of a dictionary entry for the word *servile.*

"servile": see synonyms at *obedient*

synonyms: obedient, compliant, acquiescent, submissive, docile, amenable, obsequious, servile, tractable, dutiful

Obsequious and *servile* refer to slavish, truckling obedience in persons. *Tractable* applies to persons, animals, and things with the capacity for being handled or led; *dutiful* signifies a scrupulous sense of responsibility. . . .

(Excerpted from *The American Heritage Dictionary of the English Language*)

Being Clear and Concise

Choosing your words carefully helps your readers to see your subject, hear your voice, follow your reasoning, and sense your feelings. Before examining some special opportunities for crafting language, consider two aims that are important for most arguments: clarity and conciseness. These aims can help you select specific words, as well as cut some.

Inaccurate word choices chip away at rational argument. Sometimes the blurring occurs in reasoning, organizing, or development. Sometimes it occurs in isolated words.

Some errors in word choice stem from ignorance of accepted usage. One writer used the phrase "financially despondent" when he or she really meant "financially dependent." One writer described Star Wars, or the Strategic Defense Initiative, as "a defense mechanism"! Another writer let stand, "From the time I was young my parents have *installed* in me a belief in. . . ." The accurate choice is *instilled*.

Other inaccuracies may result from "lazytalk," an informal style adequate for many exchanges, but not rigorous enough for argument. In lazytalk, an issue, say capital punishment, is described as having "been around as long as recorded history." Such talk produces a vague answer to a question about how the student will use the next few weeks of classes: "Broadening my general whatever." Lazytalk allows mistakes with even the simplest words.

Both must work 60 hours per week *to support* their apartment rent. (*to pay?*)

Parking problems continue at the university despite measures to curb traffic, which included raising the *price* of *traffic* meters. (*fees? rates? parking meters?*)

Other mistakes that threaten clarity are misprints, typos, and glitches:

Whose to say my *sedements* are any more correct than yours? (*who's? sentiments?*)

Of course, you still have to debug *the any* program.

As the Spanish philosopher George Santayana warned: "Those who do not remember the past are condemned to *relieve* it." (*relive* it?)

Was President Bush misquoted in an article headlined, "Bush laments crisis in education"? The article noted that Bush would attend an adult-education commencement to promote the idea that "you're never too old to stop learning"! Strive to be clear and accurate in your expression. Expressing thought is not an easy task.

Conciseness, the second aim in choosing words for an argument, should not imply writing in a telegraphic style. The arguments assigned in college require development and benefit from detailed, varied support. College papers ought to be richly developed, but sentences should be concise, saying what they mean.

It is easy to pad even short sentences. Ready-made words and phrases intrude unless you check your drafts critically. A state governor says she is "certainly uncertain" about raising taxes. A student arguing about access to hypodermic needles begins, "There are good and bad points about over-the-counter needles." Another writer discusses "the current system now intact." Such redundancies and unfortunate echoes do not allow for crisp statements.

Sometimes a serious persona verges on pomposity. You may find yourself writing like someone else. Instead of simply writing, "The eye cannot easily detect counterfeits," you write "Counterfeits are not easily detected by the visual process." You may overwrite because you want to sound better than you believe you might if you wrote directly, honestly, and naturally. How would you change the following wordy sentences?

Many people are under the opinion that smoke doesn't affect others.

The desire for more power and quickness is exemplified by the expense people accept to buy the higher octane gasoline.

In these examples, whatever the persona or tone may be, the writer starts a sentence that demands completion, no matter how wordy. For the first sentence, you could write many people *think.* For the second sentence, you could try starting the sentence with *People desire power and speed so much that they. . . .*

A shaky choice of subject leads to writing around the point, rather than to the point. You may think you need to finish what you start, rather than trying another subject that opens a direct course for the sentence. How can you improve the following sentences by using another subject and verb platform?

I learned that by cutting trees it helps wildlife prosper in those areas.

At First Interstate they have several checking account plans.

With the three 8-hour shifts, it would require more officers.

All three sentences unnecessarily rename the subject as a weaker pronoun. Put the noun in the independent part of the sentence and use the pronoun, if you still need it, in the dependent part. Rather than writing, "In Dinesen's article, *she* describes . . ." write "In *her* article, Dinesen describes. . . ."

Examine how subject choices in the sentences below lead to wordiness. Can you see other ways to start these sentences and to rewrite concisely?

The *reason* for more officers is because the last shift receives more calls for service than the others.

What methanol is is basically a wood alcohol that is turned into a powerful fuel to be burned.

To review the importance of subject and verb choices for writing clear, concise sentences, return to this chapter's section, "Strong Verbs."

EXERCISE 5.20   Examine the word choices in the two Rachel Carson selections in Chapter 1. Underline word choices that are especially effective in expressing what the writer sees, thinks, and feels. Write in your notebook what you have discovered makes a word effective or ineffective.

Examine how you have chosen words for the same purposes. For your argument, underline effective choices and circle choices you want to reconsider and improve on. For the circled words, write one or two better options.

EXERCISE 5.21   Check through an entire argument of yours, evaluating word choice for clarity and conciseness. Use an asterisk to mark particularly successful passages. Create alternatives for passages that could be clearer and more concise. Be prepared to discuss in class your specific word choices.

Four Special Opportunities for Crafting Words

This section identifies some special opportunities for crafting words. First, consider using simple words. Second, consider the virtues of repetition and variation. Third, study using pronouns that establish your relationship to audience, including pronouns of gender. And, fourth, understand how several techniques can produce bright work, fresh word choices, and an end to the trite or cliched.

Simple Words

Brenda Peterson chose simple language to summarize her family's relationship to game animals: "They died so that we might live." The simple word choices are direct, yet they also reverberate with the elemental simplicity of religious ritual. Isak Dinesen used simple language that reflected her own simple motives—motives that she later discovered were naive: "Once I shot an Iguana. I thought that I should be able to make some pretty things from his skin." She also used simple language to phrase this warning to settlers of East Africa: "For the sake of your own eyes and heart, shoot not the Iguana."

The point to consider is the power of such elemental words, especially in passages where you express ideas ardently. Columnist William Raspberry concluded a warm tribute to the Cosby Show at the time of its final episode:

> And it taught us as television has rarely managed—and as too few of our leaders even attempt—how much alike we really are, and how little money, class and race have to do with it.
> Thanks, Coz.

Other writers of conclusions—the place to be eloquent if you ever will be—also employ simple diction. Bill McKibben, discussing Henry Thoreau's protest against the Mexican War, closed his essay this way:

> His protest was based on small amounts of information fed, in long hours of wilderness reflection, through the mill of principle. True, he went to jail only for a night. And his calm stand went unreported, save in his essay. And yet it has come down to us through generations, a model for much that followed. We say "information" reverently, as if it meant "understanding" or "wisdom," but it doesn't. Sometimes it even gets in the way.

Barbara Howell closed her argument for funding WIC with a forthright quotation and the simplest of final paragraphs:

> President Theodore Roosevelt said at the first White House Conference on the Care of Dependent Children in 1909, "When you take care of the children you are taking care of the nation of tomorrow."

> Our children are a precious resource, and they need our care today.

Repeated Words and Variations

Urging the defense of Britain against German attack, Winston Churchill employed emphatic repetition: "Never, never, never, never give in." Shakespeare's dying King Lear speaks five never's in one line! The civil rights activist Fannie Lou Hamer turned despair into indignation by playing twice on the same phrase: "I'm sick an' tired o' bein' sick an' tired!" This is simple compared to the blues that Muddy Waters crafts with variation: "I live the life of lovin', I love the life I live."

Consider the force of repetition and the surprise of variation. Look for them in others' writing; practice them in your own.

Several other examples are hard to resist sharing:

No one cares how much you know until they know how much you care. *Church signboard*

The earth doesn't belong to us. We belong to the earth.   *Chief Seattle*

We're here to help you get there.   *Transit system slogan*

Rose is a rose is a rose is a rose.   *Gertrude Stein*

EXERCISE 5.22 Examine how writers use simple words and repetition and restatement. Review the essays by Carl Rogers (Chapter 2) and Robert Jay Lifton (Chapter 2), George Bush's inaugural (Chapter 5), and Antony's speech about Caesar (Chapter 5). Use your notebook to describe successful uses of simple and repeated words. Copy your favorites.

Check your own writing for effective use of simple words and repetition and restatement. Try simplifying word choices by using simple words and repeating them. Use these devices to give emphasis to major ideas. Be prepared to discuss in class your new word choices.

Pronouns

The writer often steps into the argument as "I," addressing the reader as "you." These two pronouns establish distance, separateness, and difference. Writer and reader stand opposite as in a duel or other contest. One recurring aim in argument is to bring together the "I" and the "you" in "we." The pronoun "we" establishes union and like-mindedness.

Sometimes the conflict is between "us" and "them": Your audience is already on your side, and you exhort it to do something about "them." Your use of pronouns in writing establishes what is obvious in a direct exchange: who is who, who addresses whom, which people are together and which are at odds. Pronouns can establish, also, attitudes about gender. Throughout the 1980s and into the 1990s, readers and listeners have been paying close attention to sexist language. A contemporary writer cannot start an essay of definition as E. B. White started "The Essayist" in 1977:

The essayist is a self-liberated man, sustained by the childish belief that everything he thinks about, everything that happens to him, is of general interest. He is a fellow who thoroughly enjoys his own work. . . .

This outmoded convention of referring to a person whose gender is unknown or unimportant as "he" has been replaced by a convention that acknowledges that women write essays, too, and that they are not *fellows*! Often, the new convention feels awkward. Must a revision avoiding sexist pronouns become "He or she is a man or woman who thoroughly enjoys his or her work"? Perhaps White's essay could begin, "Essayists are self-liberated people" and use the gender-neutral "they" to represent essayists throughout the piece.

Commonly, nonsexist names for occupations now replace the sexist names:

Men Working	Workers Ahead
Flagman	Flagger
Waiter/Waitress	Waitperson, Server

It may be a while before we have replacements for *hitman* and *cleaning woman*. And although doctor and nurse, lawyer and secretary have no necessary gender, you may bring to such terms the residue of the years when men had the important, well-paying assignments.

Some attempts to avoid sexist pronouns create problems of pronoun agreement:

Every person has a time in their life when they're doing something they dislike.

Many times it has been said that the victim's life flashes before their eyes.

Perhaps these writers failed to see the singular number of *every person* or *the victim*. Perhaps, though, they sensed that using *his life* or *his eyes* would wrongly exclude women. Sometimes a correct grammatical alternative could be a social blunder:

Every attorney values his client's testimony.

Whoever designed the new Saturn automobile really knew what he was doing!

Most college handbooks of writing explain how to avoid sexist language. In using pronouns, you need to limit *he, him,* and *his* to refer to a male person. You may have to employ the evenhanded "he or she," but it is awkward. You can switch the entire passage to the plural "they." Or if you use "he" generically, be sure to alternate it with "she," referring to the writer, for example, as "she" or "he" in different sections.

EXERCISE 5.23 Check any one argument in this text for its use of pronouns. Is the writer "I"? Is the audience "you"? Does the writer use "we" or "us"? Is there also a "they" or "them" in the argument? When referring to an unnamed party of one, does the writer use "he" or "she"? Does the writer's use of pronouns help clarify ideas and convince audience? Record your findings in your notebook.

Examine some specific uses of pronouns in the readings identified below. Record your observations in your notebook. Write a paragraph summarizing your observations about pronoun use in arguments.

Carl Rogers (Chapter 2)	Use of "we" in opening and concluding paragraphs. Use of "I" and "you" in paragraph 2.
Bill McKibben (Chapter 1)	Use of "we" and "you" in paragraph leads.
Barbara Howell (Chapter 3)	Use of "our" in concluding paragraph.
Thomas Paine (Chapter 2)	Use of pronouns for countries in paragraphs 7 and 8.
William Shakespeare (Chapter 2)	Use of pronouns in Hamlet's "What a piece of work is man!"
Mina Shaughnessy (Chapter 2)	Use of pronoun for the writer.
Francis Bacon (Chapter 1)	Use of man/men and male pronouns.

Bright Work: Avoiding Cliches

Bright work is a name for language that sparkles. Such language is at once apt and unexpected. Writers cannot count on writing sentence after sparkling sentence, but their striving to do so can lift up the weakest, dullest of sentences to acceptable levels and promote competent sentences to a superior level.

Metaphors can be sparkling, inept, or trite. Here are some bright ones. First Marian Anderson, the great singer, speaks about racial prejudice:

> Sometimes, it's like a hair across your cheek. You can't see it. You can't find it with your fingers. But you keep brushing at it because the feeling of it is irritating.

Another musician, Gerald Schwartz, describes his work in a symphony orchestra:

Being a trumpet player is like flying by jet: there are long passages of boredom punctuated by moments of panic.

Do you doubt the sincerity or expressive skills of these speakers? How do the following two examples strike you? The writers' use of metaphor is both confusing and hackneyed:

The sky's the limit. We've just scratched the surface.

America should adopt an increase in the minimum wage due to several economic downshifts. The overall cost of the American pie has gone up while the current minimum wage has remained depressingly low.

Many slots in sentences are filled with predictable and near-useless words. Certain adjectives seem to get stuck with certain nouns and lose their original snap through overuse:

An unforgettable character
An historical moment
A heated dispute
The tough questions
Quality time
As long as recorded history
A solid faith

Look at the following sentences about abortion. The underlined sections are so trite they could be used to discuss anything:

The *only viable* solution for *over a million* women every year is abortion. Hopefully, women will make the *right* decision, *one they can live with the rest of their lives.*

This is far from bright work. Even if the ideas were lively, the words would deaden them. Crisp imagery and authentic, energetic word choices polish commonplace observations and may even release the dazzle of insight. You know when you are a beneficiary of such skill with language. Read the following two passages. Which sentences are bright work? Which could be polished even more?

Let me give you word of the philosophy of reforms. The whole history of human liberty shows that all concessions yet made to her august claims have been born of struggle . . . If there is no struggle there is no progress. Those who profess to favor freedom and yet deprecate agitation are men who want crops without plowing the ground. They want the ocean without the roar of its many waters.

Frederick Douglass, 1849, letter to a white abolitionist, cited by Howard Zinn, *A People's History of the United States*

Most, if not all, human lives are full of fantasy—passive day-dreaming which need not be acted on. But to write poetry or fiction, or even to think well, is not to fantasize, or to put fantasies on paper. For a poem to take shape, there has to an imaginative transformation of reality which is in no way passive. And a certain freedom of the mind is needed—freedom to press on, to enter the currents of your thought like a glider pilot, knowing that your motion can be sustained, that the buoyancy of your attention will not be suddenly snatched away.

Adrienne Rich, 1971, from *On Lies, Secrets, and Silence*

EXERCISE 5.24 Peggy Noonan was a speechwriter for Ronald Reagan and George Bush. She wrote Bush's speech accepting the presidential nomination. This speech included the campaign's first mention of "a thousand points of light," a phrase that pleased Noonan because "its power is born of the fact it sounds like what it is describing: an expanse of separate yet connected entities sprinkled across a broad and peaceful sky, which is America, the stretched continent." The phrase immediately became a campaign theme and soon supplied material for political cartoonists.

Have you ever labored over a phrase, trying out variations, as Noonan did, so that it had "power" generated from the particular words? Identify such a phrase in an argument of yours. Or find an opportunity to craft such a potent phrase. Record in your notebook your memorable phrases.

EXERCISE 5.25 Read the next argument by Ada Louise Huxtable. After you read it, examine the stylistic elements listed below. How effective are they in the argument? Do Huxtable's choices contribute to making a clear, convincing essay? In your notebook, write a paragraph describing Huxtable's word choices and their connection to her thesis.

- Religious language of temptation, devil, tempter, saints, poverty, the desert, the forces of darkness
- Reference to Faust
- Tone of voice of "turn a profit," "flushing out the highest bidder," "use their eyes instead of their calculators," "orgasmic tremors"
- Contrasts between the commercial and spiritual, between the sun-filled and flowering garden and the congested commercial heart of the city

- The progression in paragraphs 4–8 from the beauty of the buildings, architecture, and garden to the neighboring structures
- The imagining of changes, using "you" to direct readers, using specific steps of visualizing, using words such as "one arm lopped off," "wipe out the garden," "encroaching blockbusters," "windswept, sterile," "bulk, overwhelm, wall up," "destructive, jarring"
- The string of closing questions, their tone and their return to religious terms

❖ THE TEMPTATION OF ST. BARTHOLOMEW'S

Ada Louise Huxtable

Ada Louise Huxtable (b. 1921), former architecture critic for *The New York Times*, received a Pulitzer Prize in 1970, the first one given for distinguished criticism. From 1981–1986, Huxtable was a Mac Arthur Fellow, compiling two books of her essays about urban life, city planning, and building design: *Goodbye History, Hello Hamburger* and *Architecture, Anyone? Cautionary Tales of the Building Art.* "The Temptation of St. Bartholomew's," describes the efforts of a church in New York City to raise money by selling some land—very valuable land—adjacent to the church building. Huxtable was opposed to the scheme, not only because of the loss to the neighborhood, but because she felt that the plan betrayed values essential to sustaining life in a great city. Like most people who argue, Huxtable makes something big out of what a reader might consider trivial or someone else's private concerns. Huxtable pulls readers into her argument by her frequent use of words drawn from religious life and by her emotionally charged descriptions. The selling of real estate is not business as usual; for Huxtable, it is a temptation that can have grave consequences.

1   If Faust exchanged his soul for immortality, the temptation of St. Bartholomew's is a more pragmatic lure: financial security being offered by a most appropriate modern devil, New York real estate. The testing of moral fiber against sensory gratification or material gain is as old as biblical history, and this time the tempter came in the form of a "prestigious corporation" offering $100 million for the church's prime Park Avenue property as the site for a new office tower. In these days of shrinking congregations and growing deficits, $100 million is an attractive sum. The trials of conscience that have sent saints into poverty and the desert have delivered St. Bart's into the hands of the real estate brokers and developers.

2   Or a part of St. Bart's, since the agreement now rests on a compromise; the rector and the vestry believe that they have found a way to keep the church and turn a profit, too. This revelation was apparently arrived at

through divine guidance. The announcement was made, "after weeks of prayerful consideration," that the church is not for sale. What is for sale, or lease, instead, is only a portion of the land, which will destroy only part of the building complex. St. Bartholomew's is considering disposing of its community house and garden, or about one third of the site. At the least, the buyer will get a coveted Park Avenue address and room enough to build a substantial and enormously profitable structure. Actually, that $100 million offer was peanuts.

The forces of darkness are persistent; a second offer evidently followed 3 the first. Not surprisingly, church officials have voted to put the negotiations into the hands of "outside consultants" professionally adept at flushing out the highest bidder. The availability of this choice corner site at Fiftieth Street, virtually the only open space left on an almost solidly corporate Park Avenue in midtown, is sending orgasmic tremors through New York's real estate community. The church sees no loss of spiritual values in its decision. Temptation comes complete with convenient, if confused, rationalizations about people and buildings, missions and mortar. Brick and stone are called secondary to human needs; it is said that cash will serve society better than beauty. And solvency has a beauty of its own.

That the beauty of the St. Bartholomew block contributes to the welfare 4 of the city and all of its inhabitants are not part of the reckoning. The close link between the spirit and the environment is denied. False and irrelevant equations are made between dealing in real estate and dealing with poverty. Although the quality of the church's art and architecture is well known, the serenity and public availability of its sun-filled and flowering garden in the congested commercial heart of the city are a less acknowledged contribution to all the people of New York. Only in a culture where commercial values have vanquished spiritual values would such a church and its setting not be considered a legacy beyond price from the past to the present and the future.

Equally disturbing is the church's odd illusion that it is engaged in an 5 act of preservation. "We have agreed that we will accept no offer, however big, that would harm in any way our magnificent church building . . . ," says the official statement. To which the only possible response is amen. The harm that will be done to the landmark church by this decision will be irreparable. Perhaps it is time for church officials to take a walk outside and use their eyes instead of their calculators.

The architecture of St. Bartholomew's consists of a church building and 6 a community house that form an integrated **L**-shaped whole. Functionally, the structures are separate, but visually, all the parts are unified. The church was built to the design of Bertram Grosvenor Goodhue in 1918, incorporating a 1903 porch by McKim, Mead and White from an earlier building. The community house was added in the 1920's by Goodhue's firm, after his death. The familiar flat dome of the Byzantine-inspired complex was completed in

1930. Handmade salmon-colored brick and Indiana limestone were used throughout, enriched by skilled carving, rare marbles, and fine details; the church contains numerous works of art. With all the exterior elements meticulously matched in scale and style, the complex is meant to look like one building, and it does.

7   This two-part construction wraps around the garden, embracing and sheltering it with an architecture of agreeable human dimensions, against the backdrop of skyscrapers beyond. The planting acts not only as a frame and setting for the church, but also buffers it from the street and the impact of the larger buildings. The destruction of the garden, which protects and enhances the church at the same time that it opens the corner to the street, is a loss all too easy to understand and deplore. However, it would do more than remove rare open space of great beauty and amenity; it would destroy an essential part of the architectural composition, leaving the truncated church like a jewel without a setting.

8   The quality and relationships of the buildings and landscaping have been recognized and respected by the architects of neighboring structures. Both the Art Deco General Electric building, designed by Cross and Cross in 1931, and the otherwise standard new commercial offices behind the church and community house, demonstrate the considerable care taken to find a sympathetic match to the color of St. Bartholomew's brick. Fortunately, their location on the Lexington Avenue side also makes them background buildings. The entire block works extremely well as one of the city's better examples of urban design.

9   To understand what the changes would be like, it is necessary to look at the church complex from the street. First, imagine one arm of the garden enclosure lopped off. Next, mentally wipe out the garden. Then try to see the church minus the planting to the south that frames the building and insulates it against the march of encroaching blockbusters. Next, visualize an immense tower filling most of the space now occupied by the community house and the garden. Give or take the questionable amenity of a windswept and sterile plaza or arcade with some token planting at its base—features that permit a builder to add more height—the bulk of this tower, no matter how designed, will overwhelm the church beside it; at worst, it will wall up the corner. Consider the truly destructive scale and jarring impact of this construction. Think really big: the kind of building that can, and will, be put up under the present zoning, combining the permitted avenue size and bonuses and the church's air rights, is monstrous. Why else would anyone offer that kind of money?

10   But a bargain is a bargain, and this brutally disfiguring transformation comes along with the cash. Has anyone really thought about it in these terms, prayerfully or otherwise? Is this irreversible sell-off of art and urbanity something the church should knowingly sanction? Is this kind of destruction just too difficult for the nonvisual nonspecialist in urban design to

"see" or imagine? Is no one able to understand what will happen before it actually takes place? Can it really be a matter of equating the beauty of a building with idolatry, an incredibly warped interpretation of the role of architecture in the physical and spiritual life of centuries of civilization which moves the church back to a position so small that there is barely room for the spirit at all? Or is the temptation just too great? The threats to the integrity and even to the survival of the city's art and history today are as devastating as any posed by the bulldozer; they are just wrapped in real estate clothing. Can the church no longer understand or afford the gift of urban grace?

PLANNING AND CHECKING
STYLE CHOICES

As you write, you make a wide variety of style choices, choices of persona and organization, paragraphing, sentence writing, and individual wording. You make these choices at various stages in the writing process. Some you make as you plan, some as you draft, and some as you revise your argument. Some of these choices are unconscious, resulting from habit and from your understanding of the demands of the writing task on a tacit level—a level on which you do not articulate goals and means to achieve them, but write and rewrite until you are generally satisfied with the passage or the whole argument.

As you write an essay, you do not usually follow a single line of thought and expression. Rather, you manage many choices, and for you, such choices become sure and purposeful as you determine the aim of the entire writing task. You make choices, weigh them, and confirm them or change them. What is your subject? Who is your audience? What is your thesis? Your early choices make tangible the various possibilities of the essay. Choosing is clarifying. Once you see the whole task clearly, your choices are better informed: they move from planning to implementing. Then you can manage the whole range of choices so they work, finally, to achieve the aim of the argument.

What follows is a list of the style choices presented in this chapter. You can use this list to help plan your argument. You will make some of these choices early in the writing process. Your persona may be identified from the start with your choice of issue. You can use this list as you draft when you will be able to make choices you could not have made earlier. Also, in the light of further drafting, you will change some choices you made earlier. You will discover better choices. Indeed, you can use this list to help you revise the argument.

This list follows the chapter's discussion from "big" to "small" style elements; however, you should not make your decisions about style from the top of the list down. Rather, use the list to check the progress of your style choices at any stage of the writing. Consider, especially, how your choices support your aim, how they work together. Scan the list to remind yourself of the style elements you still need to consider. Think of it as a packing list; the finished paper includes, sooner or later, choices about all of the following:

CHECKLIST OF STYLE CHOICES

Motives for style choices
    Personal signature
    Craft
    Appropriateness

Persona and tone
    Revealing attitude toward
        Subject
        Audience
        Self

Organization
    Serving purpose
    Serving persona
    Using deductive or inductive order
    Revealing order
        Preview
        Review
        Transitions
        Paragraphing
    Using emphasis
        Placement
        Length
        Repetition

Paragraphs
    Short and long
    Integrating sentences in the paragraph
    Integrating paragraphs in the essay
    Specialized paragraphs
        Varied introductions
        Varied conclusions

Sentences
    Using variety

ARGUMENT ACTIVITIES

1. Referring to this chapter's discussion of "Three Views of Style," consider how you are a stylist. What have your goals been as a stylist in any activity? In the activity of writing?

2. Who of the communicators you know uses an effective persona? Who is able to enhance the message? Who diminishes it? What, in your analysis of communicators, reveals persona?

3. Review some instances of how you reached a conclusion. Did you think inductively? Deductively? If you were to write about any of these experiences, how would you organize your essay? Where would you place your thesis?

4. Have you ever organized a presentation, spoken or written, using an order that reflected the natural order of the subject itself? Have you ever organized to suit your sense of what the audience needed, that is, strategically?

5. Apply Fry's Readability Formula, on the following page, to passages of your own.

GRAPH FOR ESTIMATING READABILITY,
BY EDWARD FRY

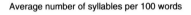

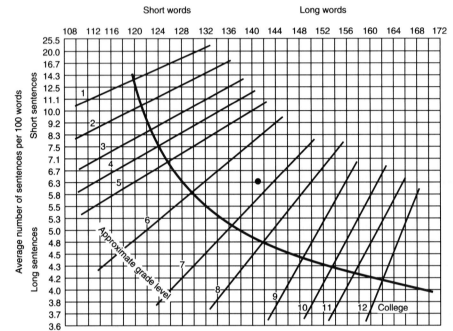

Directions:

Randomly select three 100-word passages from a book or an article. Plot average number of syllables and average number of sentences per 100 words on graph to determine the grade level of the material. Choose more passages per book if great variability is observed and conclude that the book has uneven readability.

Example:

	Syllables	Sentences
First hundred words	124	6.6
Second hundred words	141	5.5
Third hundred words	158	6.8
Average	141	6.3

Readability 7th grade (see dot plotted on graph)

Then copy, double-spaced, about six of your sentences that form a coherent part of one of your arguments. Count the words in each sentence. Study the use of long and short sentences.

Underline all modifiers. Then rewrite the passage, drastically altering the use of short and long and modified and unmodified sentences.

6. In your notebook, make a section available to record passages that you admire for what they say and how they say it. Copy the passages as you find them in your reading and comment on them. Be prepared to share your collection with other writers in your class.

7. As you write Argument Assignments Five and Six, the Rogerian Argument and the Refutation, put into practice what you have learned about making style choices integral to a clear, convincing argument. In the section of Argument Assignments you will find complete instructions for these assignments, as well as some successful student examples.

ARGUMENT ASSIGNMENTS

This section presents six assignments in argument. In completing some or all of them, you will be using approaches and tools introduced elsewhere in this book. Please return to earlier chapters when advised to do so or when you feel the review of a technique or a professional essay might help you succeed with your argument. These assignments encourage you to put theory and advice into practice.

Assigned writing can, at first, appear arbitrary and perhaps ill-suited to the writer's own interests and aims. One key to doing well in such assigned tasks, academic and job-related, is to take time to consider how they can be made useful to you. Inside the teacher's lesson, what is the lesson for you? How, specifically, can assignments in argument reflect your arguments? Consider the notion that you might find an issue that concerns you, or an audience needing to hear from you, or a style of writing that is novel to you, expanding your abilities and repertoire.

Derived from "motive" and related to "motion," the word *motivation* is wedded to most discussions of student effort. For any assignment, at the same time you feel the limits and compulsion of someone else's task making, you can ask, "What moves me? In what direction can I take the assignment, keep it alive, and make it a challenge?"

Each of the six assignments follows the same format. First, the writing task is identified. Second, the purpose of the writing task is explained. Third, the assignment's specifications are listed. Such specs distinguish one writing task from the others. Fourth, student examples are included to illustrate successes with the assignment. Finally, under the headings of planning, drafting, and revising, advice is given about the process of writing each assignment.

PREPARING MANUSCRIPT
AND TYPESCRIPT

Your instructor will no doubt make clear if he or she requires machine-produced papers or will accept handwritten work. In setting up either kind of product, be sure to adhere to the following guidelines for manuscript preparation:

- Use standard-sized paper (remove tractor guides and separate printer pages).
- Use one side only.
- Use wide margins on both left and right.
- Double-space typewriting and handwriting.
- Use ink—pen, ribbon, or printer—that produces legible work.
- Number your pages.
- Staple or paper clip multiple pages.
- Hand in, when instructed, plans and drafts of the essay; if you use a word processor, you will need to print at one or two stages in process.
- Use a title page that includes the following items:

Item	*Example*
Title of the paper	Neglected Horses
Writer's name	Lisa Kocian
Course name and number	English Composition WR122
Date	February 12, 1993
Assignment Task	Paper #3 Argument from Value

CITING SOURCES: A REMINDER

For any assignment in which you use sources, be sure to be clear about what sources you use and how you use them. Although a list of references or a bibliography may be helpful to your readers and your instructor, you need to show how you use sources. Be sure to use quotation marks for quoted materials, to name the source of both quotations and paraphrases, and to identify clearly any use of another person's words, data, or opinions. If you have questions about citing sources and avoiding even a suspicion of plagiarism, review "Quotes, Paraphrases, and Citations" in Chapter 5 and seek the advice of your instructor.

ASSIGNMENT ONE:
DECISION-MAKING KIT

This first assignment asks you to explore an issue without necessarily having or forming an opinion about it. You may think of this assignment as pre-argument, as an attempt to gather materials that enable you—and perhaps others—to become informed and then, later, to develop a position on the issue. Such an assignment asks you to increase your knowledge about the issue by gathering data and views from all sides and keeping an open mind.

This assignment is not really an argument task because you may complete it without taking sides or concentrating on audience change. Although a decision-making kit may change audience, such change is determined less by the writer than by the readers who use the kit to make their own decisions. However, without the kind of hard work and grasp of a range of opinions and support basic to making this kit, a writer's arguments might be merely self-expression, not a thesis essay supported thoughtfully and critically from the discussions of others.

Perhaps you can appreciate the value of a decision-making kit if you can imagine for any issue the existence of packets of information attempting not to promote one thesis, but to provide you with the building blocks of your own decision making. Such blocks might include statistics, testimony, case studies, history, predictions, and evaluations whose limitations and biases were clearly identified. It sounds ideal; the so-called information age is only creeping toward this capability. The question is who would want to present such a kit without putting on it his or her special thesis spin?

To be well informed as you vote, consume, or educate yourself or others takes tremendous effort. Only where you feel inadequate, yet needy, and perhaps do not trust others to decide for you—the salesman, the doctor, the teacher—do you get motivated to dig into the materials available to you. And, in some cases, you may wish that by digging for yourself you might provide others with the materials to help them make up their own minds. Maybe more writers should tell others not what to do and think. Maybe they should provide others with materials that will feed their intelligent decision making.

Task: To make a decision-making kit for an issue. To provide readers with a variety of materials helpful in forming an opinion.

Purpose: To present a variety of materials addressing an issue so the reader is able to make an informed decision. To present materials without prejudice, materials on all sides of the issue that deserve a reader's consideration. To remain objective in your making of the kit. To give the reader pros and cons, if the issue shapes that way, or varied sides of the issue. To include facts, statistics, examples, testimony, and all manner of helpful materials. To organize these materials for easy understanding and use.

Specifications: Readers need to know the assignment's scope (what issue you choose) and its aim (why you are supplying such materials). The "body" of the paper is not discussion or support, but a holding tank for materials you believe are pertinent to decision making. You must present such materials as quotes, paraphrases, or summaries, and you must document sources. You may want to point out materials that agree or disagree on the philosophical or factual level. You should organize the material to make it clear and useful. Charts, tables, headings, and lists may help. You may include an appendix of documents to be read in their original form or a list of references for further reading. The kit may be a stepping stone to extended study.

Example: In "Oregon Education Act," Larry Johnson presents an act that at the time of writing was being debated. Later it was approved. The student draws from some readings about American education and a packet of news clippings about the act itself.

OREGON EDUCATION ACT
Larry Johnson

American education has been in crisis reportedly for many years. According to test scores, since the 1950's Americans have been gradually declining in their ability to read and write and do arithmetic. Japanese and European students score much higher on academic achievement tests. Most of the blame for this decline falls upon public school education.

Some authors have written about this problem. John I. Goodland in his 1982 article "Can We Have Effective Schools?" refers to seven conditions affecting the conduct of schooling that make it hard for schools to reach their goals. These conditions range from lack of cooperation between schools and family to discord among educators. Nat Hentoff in his early 1980's article "The Dumbing of America" puts the blame on the textbook industry. He states that this industry compromises the intellectual integrity of its products rather than lose a sale. So the kids in the classrooms get damaged goods. Jamie M. O'Neill in his article "No Allusions In the Classroom" puts the blame on teachers and students who play games with each other. The teacher tries to find the areas in which students need help, so he or she can help students improve. The students, worried about grades and self-image, hide their ignorance any way they can. Students never ask the questions they need to ask. And the teacher assumes the students are trained in the basics when they really are not. As you can see, many people feel something needs to be done with education in America.

The legislature of Oregon has proposed an education act, House Bill 3565. You may be asking: What is it? What are its benefits? What are its drawbacks? Who supports it? Who opposes it? The purpose of this article is to present the Oregon Education Act to help you, the reader, to formulate your own opinion about it, and to assist you in deciding whether or not you should support it.

What Is the Oregon Education Act?

The act would accomplish many things. It would expand Head Start Programs to all eligible children to ensure that students start school ready to learn. It would combine kindergarten through third grades in shared classrooms. It would do away with traditional grading at that level. It would require a completion of basic academic training by age 16 or the 10th grade. It would test academic and technical skills in grades three, five, eight, and ten. It would separate students into two groups after the 10th grade—college preparatory and academic-technical. It would provide dropouts with special assistance in mastering basic skills. It would lengthen the school year from 175 days to 220 days. It would allow talented teachers to train less productive teachers, and it would allow parents to move students to other schools if academic progress is unsatisfactory. A new system would replace the current high-school diploma. At the 10th grade students would be expected to earn a Certificate of Initial Mastery. Vocational students would continue in school as long as six years, and college preparatory students would continue for two more grades. Students in both categories would earn a Certificate of Advanced Mastery with a college preparatory endorsement or an academic-vocational endorsement. Students with endorsements would then be able to enroll in a two- or four-year college. Vocational students would also be able to enter the workplace.

Support for the Act

Vera Katz, a Democratic representative from Portland, and the sponsor of the bill, stresses that the bill will help prepare an educated workforce for the 21st Century. Future schools will work with business, labor, parents, and educators to create a curriculum that helps graduates get jobs. Katz says that the workforce will be better educated to compete in a global economy. She observes that now 30% of students who begin first grade never graduate from high school. Many who do graduate lack many skills. The same system, Katz believes, will not help our children's future. Katz states that the reform bill holds schools accountable for the progress and performance of students. The new schools will discourage dropping out or passing through without attaining significant academic and employment skills.

State Superintendent of Schools Norma Paulus supports the bill, especially praising its provisions that call for continued education for teachers and for classroom involvement by parents and volunteers.

Officials of Eugene's schools say that the bill mirrors what they have been working toward. Martha Harris, the district's director of curriculum and instruction, says the bill assumes students can learn in a variety of ways not provided for in the present curriculum. Harris says the bill places responsibility for education on parents and community, assumptions the Eugene schools have operated under for some time. Superintendent Margaret Nichols supports the bill, saying, "I think it really speaks to our vision of what education should be."

The Oregon House of Representatives passed the bill by a vote of 55-5. It now goes to the Senate, where thirteen members co-sponsored it. It needs just 16 votes to pass in the Senate.

Larry Campbell, Republican House Speaker, guarantees that $2 million will be available to implement the bill's first stages.

Criticism of the Act

Critics and opponents of the bill raise the issues of tracking, funding the longer school year, using the European system as a model for our schools, and forcing students to choose between two options in the 10th grade.

Critics consider the bill an endorsement of tracking. Tom Mason, a Portland House Democrat, says the bill makes law of a tracking practice many are opposed to. He says minorities still will be pushed into vocational programs and wealthy, middle-class whites will be pushed into pre-college programs.

Judith Grosenick, Associate Dean at the University of Oregon's School of Education, warns, "We've gone through court cases in special education that have said tracking is illegal." She says, "I worry about the subtle problem of discrimination and stereotyping."

The state's biggest teachers union, the Oregon Education Association, is not enthusiastic about the bill. Its president, Karen Famous, is not opposed to change, but she has seen many fads come and go with little effect upon student achievement during her 21 years in education.

Eugene Board of Education Chairperson Paul Harrison said he has serious reservations about so much emphasis on training for the workplace. "Education isn't just to get the best possible job," he said, but should prepare students for citizenship and enhance their appreciation for life. Over a century ago, Cardinal Newman wrote that the principal work of a university is to provide a liberal education, not merely professional education. This idea can be applied to public schooling as well. A liberal education, wrote Newman, gives a person "a clear, conscious view of his own opinions and judgments, a truth in developing them, an eloquence in expressing them, and a force in urging them—it prepares him to fill any post with credit and to master any subject with civility."

Tom Mason opposes the fact that the measure follows the European model. Oregon should not, Mason believes, imitate Western Europe's elitist society or its educational underpinning.

Nor is the longer school year desirable for some. The Eugene Register-Guard indicates that the expanded year ought to be studied further, since the school year is locked into the state's agriculture and its need for labor.

A final criticism aims at the bill's lack of a funding plan. Estimated costs for the next four years are $5.3 million, and that only includes ten days of extending the school year, not the 35 the bill would mandate for the year 2010.

Conclusion

The substance of and opinions about the proposed Oregon Education Act are presented here to benefit you, the reader. They can help you determine your stand on this important bill.

Process:

PLANNING

- Select an issue that you are or can readily become informed about. If you are undecided about your stand on an issue, here is a chance to learn more and to discover your position.

- You may want to select a relatively simple issue or part of a more complicated one. Obviously, a kit could be a booklet. Select your issue with an eye to what is compact and achievable.
- Select an issue that an audience needs help with.
- Take notes about the issue. Take notes purposefully by asking if the material can help readers reach a decision about the issue.
- Document sources as you take notes from them.
- Reformulate your task in terms of scope or even of the issue as you learn about what useful materials are available to you.
- As your notes develop, consider possible formats for your kit. Are pro-con contrasts the only ways of presenting the information you find on the issue?

DRAFTING

- Begin the kit by introducing the issue and the purpose of the materials to follow.
- Use an outline keyed to your source notes to help you keep track of what to include and where.
- Maintain objectivity. You may point out the significance of what you present and the ways of using it to reach a decision, but do not advocate any side.
- Conclude the kit with a restatement of aim and, if possible, with leads for further study or suggestions for reaching a decision.

REVISING

- Read the kit from the reader's viewpoint. Is it useful? Does the organization help? Is it clear how the parts fit together? Is the tone right for the task?
- Check for balanced coverage. If there are not enough materials for a fair representation of the sides of the issue, add more.
- Check all parts of the kit for accuracy.
- Check all parts of the kit for objectivity.

ASSIGNMENT TWO: THESIS AND REASONS ARGUMENT

Task: To write a short argument (400–600 words) setting forth your position statement and supporting reasons.

Purpose: To practice asserting your position on an issue and supporting it with reasons.

Specifications: Make sure your position statement or thesis is prominent. Be sure each reason you offer relates clearly to the position statement. Start a new paragraph for each reason. Make sure each reason is distinct from the others.

Examples: Both of the following essays use traditional structure. They name the thesis and support it with reasons. Note that both essays end with some review, but use the restatement to urge readers to accept the thesis. Jim Garner's argument "Pro Football in Portland" has a civic aim, whereas Melissa Kojima's argument "Letter to a Theater Manager" is addressed to a supervisor.

PRO FOOTBALL IN PORTLAND
Jim Garner

The National Football League is looking to expand in a couple of years. On the list of cities being considered are St. Louis, Missouri, and Birmingham, Alabama. Out of all the cities on the list, there is one city that is very qualified but seems to keep being overlooked. That city is Portland, Oregon, and there are many reasons why it should be looked at by the NFL. Based on the city's business reputation, the support it gives its professional basketball team, and the fact that other less prestigious football leagues have shown interest, I feel Portland should be given serious consideration as a future site for the NFL.

Portland is considered one of the best places in the country to do business. It is always receiving high honors nationally and this year placed in the top ten among great locations for business. However, when you start talking about getting an NFL team, you must show that you can support this team. When I talk about support, I am talking in terms of market size or, in plain English, the city's size. If you compare the population of Portland with that of other successful franchises, you'll see that it has a large enough market. The Pittsburgh Steelers' home has a population of 420,000. The Green Bay Packers from Green Bay, Wisconsin, have a home market of 88,000. The population of Portland is 410,000.

For an example of the kind of fan support you'll probably get, just look at the Trail Blazers. Trail Blazer fans are wild, crazy people. The Blazers play in Memorial Coliseum, and the games have been sold out since 1977. Now you can buy Blazer cable too. I'm sure this cable was created by the popularity of the team, the demand to see them, and the fact that the games have been sold out for so long. I've seen many Blazer games and the atmosphere in the coliseum is always exciting. I think you'd see the same with a professional football team.

Finally, we can look at other less prestigious professional football leagues. The WFL and the USFL, both defunct leagues, had teams in Portland, and they were both supported well. The well-established Canadian Football League has shown great interest in the city. In fact, Portland was their first choice for expansion, but they postponed a decision because there was not enough time to get things going before the league's deadline. Starting March 1, you can see the Oregon Lightning Bolts of the Professional Spring Football League. They will play in Portland's Civic Stadium. So, as evidenced from the interest of other leagues, Portland appears to be a popular choice for professional football.

To all the National Football League owners and their expansion committee: the next time businessmen from Portland are in town to talk expansion, listen to them seriously. There might be a great opportunity for you.

LETTER TO A THEATER MANAGER
Melissa Kojima

Now that Bill has been fired from the box office, you are short one person. I've seen that one less worker can make your job really rough. I know that you've had to fill in during rushes. And I know you've had to have ushers fill in because no one else was available to work. As general manager, you have many, many duties; one less worker makes your job even more complicated. Because you need a permanent worker and because I have a back problem and a school commitment, you should transfer me to the box office.

First of all, you probably didn't know, but, yes, I have a back problem. I was in an automobile accident last January. From that accident, I received compression fractures in my lower back. I have a permanent back problem now. It's not that I can't take it, but carrying ice buckets, bending over sinks to do dishes, arching over to sweep, and pulling and lifting the black floor mats do make my back hurt and ache. Simply put, concession work isn't good for my back. Selling people tickets, recording data on computers, and giving people information about movies would be much easier on my back. I'd be doing my back a big favor by working in the box office. Box office duties aren't as straining as concession duties.

Second of all, I'm a full-time student at Land Community College. As you know since you went to Ricks College and BYU, college is very demanding on students. I have many papers to write and many books to read. Work makes these tasks even harder to accomplish. I'm not saying I want to quit, nor am I saying I don't want this job. I am saying that getting off work at 10:30 PM is very different from getting off at 12:30 AM. Box office workers get to leave after the last movie tickets have been sold about 10:30 PM. Concession workers must stay two hours longer to clean and close the snack bar. They get to leave about 12:30 AM. To get off and sleep, or to get off and do homework, either way two extra hours for me would make a big difference in the life of this college student. Getting off earlier would help me a lot.

Third and last of all, you need a permanent worker in the box office. You need someone who is reliable and responsible. You already know what type of worker I am. You've seen me work, and you know I am reliable and responsible. Your wife told me you said I am quiet but a good worker. Instead of hiring someone you know little about, instead of taking a gamble on someone you don't know, why not transfer me? I am smart and have worked with computers before. I read a lot and know about the newest movies. You know I can be trusted with customers and money. I am the someone you need.

I should be transferred to the box office. We both have a problem and can help each other. You need another employee in the box office. And I need a less straining job. If we get together, we can do what is good for both of us: You can transfer me.

Process:

PLANNING

- Use the questions of Exercise 2.5 to help you find subjects for argument.

- Once you have an interesting subject, answer these questions:
     What is your argument about?
     Can you state it as an issue?
     What is your position?
     What supports your position?

- Use a simple outline of the argument to check for cogency, to avoid duplicating reasons, and to guide drafting. See Chapter 5, the heading Choices of Organization, the subsection Deductive and Inductive Organization.
- Plan a conclusion that does more than restate. See options for conclusions, Chapter 5, the heading Choices of Paragraphs, the subsection Specialized Paragraphs.

DRAFTING

- Briefly introduce the issue; then proceed to your thesis.
- Start a new paragraph for each new reason.
- Use the lead sentences of support paragraphs to name the reasons.
- Develop each reason with as much support as this short assignment allows.

REVISING

- Rewrite, if necessary, to make your position statement evident.
- Rewrite, if necessary, to make reasons distinct and connected to the thesis.
- Add details to support reasons, or
- Trim for compactness and clarity.
- Craft an appropriate closing paragraph.

ASSIGNMENT THREE: ARGUMENT FROM VALUE

In Chapter 4, the third group of varieties of support, Principles, presented ways to develop arguments from personal and cultural values. One application of such values starts with principle and moves toward specific issues.

Task: To write an argument (500–750 words) presenting a position statement supported by a personal or cultural value or belief.

Purpose: To discover that many of your positions on issues derive from your values or beliefs. To understand that what you assert about a specific issue often expresses what you generally assert as true. To use value or belief as a forceful support for thesis.

Specifications: This argument has a position statement of thesis. Major support comes from a principle or principles. You can explain such values by showing their source, their tradition, and their usefulness to you. You may also show how you developed such values, keeping in mind that your main task is supporting the thesis. Any autobiographical material you use should serve the argument.

Examples: Lisa Kocian writes in "Neglected Horses" that humans are responsible for the animals they adapted for their use. She argues from a sense of what is fair.

"A Fresh Look at the Abortion Debate" makes a contribution to the abortion debate because writer Matthew Glencoe steps back to discover something fundamental to his outlook: frankness and openness. This student hopes to bring a value to the debate, one that, perhaps, is acceptable to all sides because it respects individual rights and needs as it reduces the demand for abortion. Note that this argument uses deduction. "If it works for the Dutch, it will work for us. It does work for the Dutch. It will work for us."

NEGLECTED HORSES
Lisa Kocian

Three horses stand in a small barren lot; they are so skinny one can count every bone in their bodies. One horse stands picking at the dirt; another horse gnaws at the already chewed fence, both horses hoping futilely to find some small morsel of food or minerals. The third horse just stands, head drooping. He has given up. All of the horses have dull, shaggy coats with open festering sores on their backs. They have no food and no shelter. This is neglect. Man must take the responsibility to care for and protect horses.

Man domesticated the horse two-thousand years ago. To domesticate means to adapt an animal or plant to life in intimate association with and to the advantage of man or another species, usually by modifying growth and traits through provision of food, protection from enemies, and selective breeding during generations of living in association and often to the extent that the domesticated form loses the ability to survive in nature. By this definition we changed horses from their natural state. We used horses to our benefit. They carried us to battle, helped us hunt, provided transportation, and were an important commodity. With the coming of the Industrial Age, horses are no longer vital for human survival. How do we repay their servitude?

Unlike the buggies and wagons of yesteryear, horses cannot be stored away in museums (except, of course, Trigger, Roy Rogers' famous horse). We must continue to care for and protect horses.

The definition of domesticate illustrates another reason man should care for horses: we made horses dependent on us. Once we took away their ability to survive on their own, we took on the responsibility to care for them.

Although most horses are well cared for, some are neglected.

For me, neglect is not distant, something read about in the newspaper. I have witnessed it. It is not usually the hardened criminal who commits these crimes; it's your neighbor, your friend, or maybe it's you.

My friend committed this crime. He was going out of town and asked me to care for his horse, Camel. I gladly accepted, and I was excited about seeing Camel again. (I had ridden Camel last fall and summer.) I was shocked when I saw him. The only resemblance to the horse I knew as Camel was his color. The former well-conditioned, sleek horse was now a skeleton. His coat was lusterless and coarse. His once well-defined muscles were deteriorating. He had only a spark of his previous high spirits. He was well on his way to starving to death. Fortunately, I was able to save him. His owner is now informed about the proper care of a horse. Camel is fat and sassy. He was lucky. Three years ago in west Eugene, two horses were not so lucky. They died from starvation. The perpetrators were prosecuted, but fines and jail sentences cannot restore life.

Horses are not always in the public eye where one can see the neglect. They are in the backyards, pastures, and barns, private places where only the owners see them. Owners, you must become aware of your animal's health. He depends on you. Society, we must live up to our responsibility.

A FRESH LOOK AT THE ABORTION DEBATE
Matthew Glencoe

The values at the heart of this nation's endless debate over abortion are whether a woman's right to choose not to carry a pregnancy to term outweighs the right of a fetus, as a potential human, to be born. Our society has come to value highly individual freedoms and choice, which is the banner under which one side of this issue gathers. The other side of this issue points to the destruction of life or, at least, the denial of the potential for life. I honestly do not believe that we will come to a satisfactory resolution of the debate, short of divine intervention. It is my feeling, then, that rather than going around and around in endless and unproductive bickering, both sides of the issue should work instead to reduce the need for abortion and abandon the unresolvable debate over the ideologies of this issue.

Here in America we still have many of the moral values of our Puritan forefathers at work in our culture. Now, there is nothing wrong with trying to lead a moral life, but if working for these ideals causes us to turn a blind eye to certain of life's realities, then it can become counter-productive.

In this country, sex, despite how often and how graphically we see it portrayed, is still somewhat of a taboo topic. It is difficult for us to discuss in an open, rational manner. Even when it is talked about, it is almost always handled as something lewd or something sensational, rather than as a basic and simple fact of life. Among other things, this has fostered many sex-myths and misconceptions which are poor substitutes for open, rational discussion and education.

As harmful as myths and misconceptions are, what they have led to is far worse: a generally irresponsible approach to the handling of what is, in fact, the greatest power on earth, the power to create new life.

I had the opportunity to live in the Netherlands for close to two years and found there an interesting comparison to our own culture. In Holland, as in the U.S., abortion is legal and it is relatively easy to have one. There are many Dutch who feel as many Americans do that it is immoral to abort a pregnancy. To them, however, the real problem is not abortion itself, but the cause of abortion, which is the irresponsible use of procreative powers.

From this standpoint, the Dutch have nurtured an openness toward sexual issues and education about them that has led to a responsible approach to the facts of life among its people. In the U.S., as in Holland, birth control is easy to obtain with or without parental consent. Despite the ease of accessibility, American youth who are sexually active make use of it far less than do their Dutch peers. The Dutch position of frankness towards sex has not resulted in the rampant sexual activity among their youth that many here in the U.S. might think it would. Teenaged girls in Holland are no more sexually active than are American girls; however, the incidence of pregnancy among them is only a fraction of that of girls in the U.S. Thus, far fewer girls in the Netherlands are ever confronted with the issue of whether to have an abortion or not. It is within their rights to seek one, but since fewer are faced with the need, fewer abortions take place. This satisfies one side of the issue, as a woman still has that option, if she so chooses, and it also addresses the side of the issue which guards the sanctity of life by protecting a life <u>before</u> it is conceived.

Either way we may change the law, it will not put the debate to rest. The only thing which will bring any resolution to the issue is to change people's values. It is not likely, however, that the fanatics on either side of the uproar will defect to the other camp, and, really, it's not their values which need to change. The change needs to come in how we raise our children. We need to teach them to approach sex responsibly, be that by employing the available precautions or by teaching them restraint. When we live up to this, then far fewer women will be faced with what to do in the event of an unwanted pregnancy.

Process:

PLANNING

- Be sure you have an argument. This is not merely autobiography. Use personal experience to develop the thesis.

- Be sure to identify the value clearly. Develop discussion that shows the reader the force of that value. What is the authority of the value? What is its source, its history, its application? How did you come to understand the issue because of the value?

- You may plan to add other varieties of support as long as you do not obscure your use of value.

DRAFTING

- While you can structure this argument traditionally (here are the three values which lead me to oppose the death penalty), you may want to emphasize aspects of the personal and anecdotal. You may wish to delay thesis until after the opening steps.

- Be sure your autobiographical writing relates to the issue and supports your position.

REVISING

- Because the argument blends strongly felt values with a specific issue, be sure the connections between them are clear. Give the thesis adequate emphasis—by its placement and repetition—to show it is the purpose statement of the entire argument. Also, check the development so that it is clearly supportive, not just loosely linked to thesis.

• Consider organizing the essay so that you establish the interlocking of thesis and value. Try alternate beginnings with thesis, with value, or with specifics.

• If you have more than one value to present, check to see that the reader can easily distinguish each one.

ASSIGNMENT FOUR: ARGUMENT WITH VARIED SUPPORT

Chapter 4 provides a menu of varied supports. It is not necessary to use them all, but this assignment encourages you to use a number of them. Be prepared to refer to Chapter 4 and to search for varied supports. See the Checklist of Varied Support at the end of Chapter 4.

Task: To build an argument (750–1000 words) with a variety of supports and to seek a number of different ways to substantiate thesis by recollection and research.

Purpose: It is unlikely any one kind of support will be decisive in an argument; however, one strategy is to weave together, cablelike, all the varied strands of support available to you. This assignment helps you be resourceful in discovering such supporting threads and in integrating them in a purposeful argument.

Specifications: This argument has a position statement supported by reasons. Each reason, in turn, needs specific support. Review the argument structure of Chapter 3, Marshaling Evidence. The variety of supports should include recollected and researched items. The aim is to write a clear, unified essay with multiple corroborations.

Examples: Two writers have worked hard to develop a convincing argument. Corina Meininger, "A Rash of Diapers," and Jacque Crombie, "Turn Down the Noise," have used a variety of supports for their thesis statements. Refer to the Checklist of Varied Support at the end of Chapter 4 to identify the kinds of support they used.

A RASH OF DIAPERS
Corina Meininger

How many diapers do you think you soiled as a baby?
According to Benning, author of HOW TO BRING UP YOUR

CHILD WITHOUT SPENDING A FORTUNE, the average baby runs through 10,000 diapers before he or she is toilet trained. Ninety percent of the diapers used by children in the United States are the disposable, nonbiodegradable, one-shot, plastic type. Where do all these little bundles of ecological disaster end up? Why are they so popular? Why are they dangerous? What is the best alternative to using them?

First of all, there are plenty of reasons why parents prefer to use disposable diapers. A friend of mine who has a seven-month-old baby points out that cloth diapers are not as absorbent as plastic and they tend to leak. So much technological energy has gone into improving plastic diapers that scientists have invented a material that will wick moisture away from the baby's skin, making it safe to leave them on longer. When my friend is taking care of the baby herself, she uses cloth diapers and changes them often, but if her mother is babysitting, she feels it is too much of an imposition to expect her to do the same.

Another reason for the use of plastic diapers, then, is convenience. Cloth diapers must be changed more often and they must be rinsed out in the toilet (an odious and unsavory job) before they can be washed and reused, whereas plastic ones are simply thrown away. For most people the substantially higher cost of buying new diapers for every change is worth it.

But what exactly is the difference in cost? A package of 48 disposable diapers will cost roughly $10.00. If a baby needs 10,000 diapers in all, that will cost $2083.33! A household that uses cloth diapers will need to buy four or five dozen (depending on how often the parents want to wash them), which will cost approximately three dollars apiece. The total cost of cloth diapers for one baby is about $150–180, but the same diapers can be used for another baby at no additional cost. (After the second baby, though, the diapers will be worn out.) At this point the family using cloth diapers has saved $1903.33—nine-tenths the cost of plastic diapers. What's more, a diaper service can be hired to take away all the soiled cloth diapers and bring them back fresh and clean for three years for only $1080.00! The family using cloth diapers still comes out $823.33 ahead.

Sadly, the higher cost for parents using plastic diapers instead of cloth is only the beginning. Most plastic diapers end up in landfills, which are simply not made to handle human waste. Scientists, such as P. H. Jorgenson and M. L. Peterson, have done extensive studies concerning the hazards of burying disposable diapers and found that viruses from the feces can leak into the earth and pollute underground water supplies. This problem is more serious than one might think, since many of the run-away viruses are live vaccines from routine immunizations, such as polio, diphtheria, whooping cough, tetanus, German measles, and a host of other diseases. The sheer number of discarded diapers that contribute to this problem each year is staggering: 16 billion as estimated by Whole Earth Review (Fall '89). Five percent of the diapers are burned rather than buried. This method of disposal eliminates the possibility of bacterial contamination, but replaces it with air pollution. Plastic diapers are converted to energy when burned, but a better procedure would be to recycle them because "the value of the material when used as fuel is only one-eighth the value of the materials when reused" (Whole Earth Review).

When one considers the extra money and the profound environmental consequences associated with "disposable" diapers (an ironic name for them considering how hard they are to dispose of safely!), it is hard to understand why people persist in using them. The best way to diaper one's children is with cotton; it's reusable, cheap, and biodegradable, and it feels nice next to the skin. Furthermore, it is just as easy to have the diaper service haul cloth diapers away. Last year 4,275,000 tons of diapers were added to this nation's landfills for no reason. That's too many dumps for the dumps!

TURN DOWN THE NOISE
Jacque Crombie

In many urban areas in the United States, the arrival of a new day is announced by the sounds of the garbage collector. For apartment dwellers, clanking pipes, flushing toilets, the sounds of pets and television gradually blend in with the sounds of garbage disposals, dishwashers, vacuum cleaners, washers and dryers. For suburb dwellers on their way to work, the freeway and subway sounds reach a volume that is punctuated by jackhammers, air compressors, bulldozers, and other equipment used for street repair and construction projects.

Offices are filled with the noise from air conditioners, heaters, computers, typewriters, office machines, and ringing telephones. Factories deafen their workers with industrial machinery. After a noisy trip home, workers may experience the sounds of power lawn mowers, leaf/snow blowers, motorbikes,

or loud stereos. A person's nighttime sleep can be interrupted
by barking dogs, passing planes and helicopters, sirens, automobiles, and the sounds of fans and air conditioners. Even
people who escape to the wilderness for solitude may find the
sounds of trailbikes, snowmobiles, and chain saws.

At least nineteen million Americans suffer from acute
hearing loss, and about thirty million have significant hearing
loss. Industrial workers top the list, with about 20% of their
work force having hearing damage. Equally disturbing is the
fact that five million U.S. children under age eighteen have im-
paired hearing. Noise now adversely affects the lives of 40% of
the U.S. population. It is estimated that if environmental noise
continues at its present rate, by the year 2000 almost no one
in the U.S. over age ten will have normal hearing. The United
States must reduce and control its noise pollution more dili-
gently and effectively.

Excessive noise is a form of stress that causes both physical and psychological damage. Noise effects fall into four general categories: annoyance, disruption of activity, partial
or total hearing loss, and physical or mental deterioration.
Continued exposure to high sound levels destroys the microscopic hair cells in the fluid-filled inner ear, hairs which convert sound energy to nerve impulses. The hearing specialist
and ear surgeon Samuel Rosen states that in addition to causing psychic shock, sudden noise automatically constricts blood
vessels, dilates pupils, tenses muscles, increases the heartbeat,
and causes wincing, holding of breath, and stomach spasms.
He explains that the constriction of the blood can become permanent, increasing blood pressure and contributing to heart
disease. Migraine headaches, gastric ulcers, and changes in
brain chemistry can also occur. Research in the United States,
England, and Japan has revealed that the occurrence of birth
defects, high blood pressure, and admissions to mental hospi-
tals is more frequent among those who live around airports.

Noise is probably the easiest kind of pollution to control.
We have both the means and the money; we only need the incentive to enforce tougher regulations. Noise control can be accomplished in three major ways: reducing noise at its source,
substituting less noisy machines and operations, and reducing
the amount of noise entering the listener's ear. The United
States didn't begin to take serious action against noise pollution before 1970. The implementation of the regulations has
been quite lax, allowing fines rather than more serious consequences for the violators.

The USSR and many Western European countries are ahead of the U.S. in noise control. We could follow many of their examples. Several European countries have developed quiet jackhammers, pile drivers, and air compressors that don't cost much more than their noisy counterparts. These countries also muffle construction equipment noise by using small sheds and tents. Some countries use rubberized garbage trucks. Montreal and Mexico City have put rubber wheels on their subway cars. Vehicles in France have separate city and highway horns. Switzerland and West Germany have enforced maximum day and night sound pressure levels in certain areas. Noise control standards need to be set and provisions need to be standardized and written into U.S. building codes. It is the responsibility of the citizens to insist on such laws.

The Environment Protection Agency (EPA) has become involved in noise control regulations for everything from construction to transportation equipment (except aircraft) down to some things as small as air conditioners. Unfortunately, these regulations apply only to equipment manufactured after 1972, and enforcement of these regulations has been almost nonexistent. One step in the right direction occurred when Congress passed the Quiet Communities Act of 1978. This act authorizes the EPA to develop programs to help state and local governments combat excessive noise. By 1980 the EPA had helped 26 states launch noise control programs.

As medical technology improves and allows us to live longer, we must take better care of ourselves, and this includes preventive measures to ensure better hearing in our later years. The public and industry must realize that human considerations are to come before economic considerations. The man-made environment is to be adapted to the needs of living creatures, not the reverse.

The United States can make important progress in controlling noise pollution, but it seems that this will happen only if citizen pressure forces lawmakers to enact and enforce much tougher legislation. We must effectively promote the reduction and control of noise pollution in our society.

Process:

PLANNING

- Estimate possible support of your thesis by listing varieties of support available from memory and outside sources. Your thesis must be well supported.

- Because the thesis must have strong, varied support, one way to ensure this is to start with rich discussion about the issue and then formulate a supportable thesis from it. You might assemble the materials of a decision-making kit. Do not commit to a position that cannot be supported. Consult Chapter 3, Being Informed, for help in locating support.

- Use the outlining device of thesis, reasons, and support to examine what you can already do to argue your point. Such an outline reveals which reasons need additional development; hence, the outline points out useful lines of research.

- Because the argument is made of many parts, some needing to be documented, take careful source notes in preparation to load the outline with detailed support.

- You do not need to answer the opposition, as that is the task of another assignment, refutation.

DRAFTING

- Be aware how your assertions of thesis and supporting reasons demand development by more specific supports.

- Try to weave together a variety of supports for every reason you present. Include specifics: examples, statistics, quotations. Use direct quotations to show you draw from voices other than your own. Be sure to identify sources you use.

- You may have a three- or four-reason argument, but you may not be able to equally support each reason. Consider finding additional support. Consider dropping the weakest reason. Consider including all the reasons but signalling to readers your awareness that all your reasons are not equally supported.

- Within sections, be sure transitions link together the varieties of support. Let the reader see that an assertion is believable because of a, b, c, and d. Pull the varied specifics together.

- Use a bold, crisp order so that connections among paragraphs and larger chunks are easy to follow. Build in adequate transitions at the beginning and ends of paragraphs. If useful, take a whole paragraph to make a transition, or use a whole paragraph to preview or review discussion segments.

REVISING

- This paper has a lot of components. There is a risk that it may clog with details or fly apart with diversity. Check the purpose, order, and emphasis of every part so the reader, coming to the essay for the first time, will be able to follow your argument easily.

• Although a thesis-discussion-conclusion organization can work well, you should check on options for the opening and closing statements. See Chapter 5, Specialized Paragraphs. Often, new steps can simply replace the original steps or be added with little or no change in the paper's discussion.

• You may be dissatisfied with the number and variety of your supports. Add more support to the argument's existing order of reasons.

• Make sure you have used your sources accurately. Doublecheck names, titles, dates, figures, and quotes. Make sure source material is smoothly integrated. Ensure this by introducing the resource, presenting it, and then commenting on its significance. Use enough mortar to hold the bricks in place.

ASSIGNMENT FIVE: ROGERIAN ARGUMENT

Most of this book develops approaches to rational or academic argument. You will find such argument useful in many school assignments: essay exams, term papers, reviews, proposals. All of them require that you take a stand and develop it with support. This is increasingly familiar, isn't it? This is writing based on a view that people are or can be reasonable, that they are interested in your conclusions and how you arrived at them, and that they will give you a fair hearing or reading and then use the opportunity to answer you, presenting points of agreement or disagreement, of further support or counter-support. This kind of exchange informs many domains, not just academics. Many people value open exchange, access to information, the ability to take sides and speak their mind, and the likelihood that someone will hear them, appreciate their efforts, and respond, provoking, in turn, another round of assertion and evidence. You might spoof this evolution of an issue toward greater elaboration and attenuation, but you can also point to informed exchanges, however elaborate, that have led to insight, agreement, and some closure. Consider the recent progress of negotiations, for example, in reducing nuclear arms.

Imagine, however, a situation where these expectations of reasonableness do not pertain. Imagine a situation where people do not listen carefully or respectfully and where they respond with evaluations that inhibit further communication, perhaps even threatening the listener, who is not the confident debater of the rational mode, but the all-too-human person who may remain silent, giving no indication of being willing to change, to compromise, or even to exchange words on the subject.

Psychologist Carl Rogers studied and wrote about overcoming such blocks to communication and change. From his work, teachers and theorists of argument have developed methods they call *Rogerian.*

In a 1951 address at Northwestern University, Carl Rogers attempted to connect what he had learned about communication in his therapy to the unblocking of communication in other public and private realms. This address is included in Chapter 2.

First of all, Rogerian argument is different from rational argument because it draws from a different philosophy. For Rogers, human beings are not predominantly rational. They are defensive, even fearful. They are made uncomfortable by differences of opinion. Rather than argue, they choose silence and retreat. As Rogers says, change is risky, yet nonjudgmental responses might allow people to feel understood and to risk listening to views unlike their own.

Clearly, the crisp competence of rational argument will not work for people who feel evaluated, attacked, and fundamentally misunderstood. So, this second point about Rogerian argument is more strategic than philosophic. The strategic key to Rogerian argument was revealed in Rogers' therapy and later formulated as a test of effective listening: Each person can speak for himself or herself only *after* he or she has first restated the ideas and feelings of the previous speaker accurately and to that speaker's satisfaction.

In academic argument, you'll remember, you address the opposition mainly to critique and refute, and you usually do this after you have presented your views. Rogers challenges you to turn argument end for end, thus starting with the readers, not the writer—with them, not you.

Such restatement of the readers' views does not necessitate your agreement with them. To understand is not the same as to approve. The key, at least at first, is to be nonevaluative, to say you neither agree nor disagree. You develop a credible empathy in order to demonstrate to readers that you understand their views and that you sense how their views feel to them, trying to achieve their frame of reference for the issue. Such empathy, Rogers asserts, allows readers to change: "We know from our research that such empathic understanding—understanding *with* a person, not *about* him—is such an effective approach that it can bring about major changes in personality."

Well, changing someone's views on an issue seems less daunting than the therapist's task. Empathy in Rogerian argument triggers reciprocation. The reader might think, "If you have listened so carefully and understood me so well on this issue, without putting me down, the least I can do is listen to you with an open mind."

Rogers' theory is the starting point for this assignment. By bringing to bear what you know about rational argument, you also will be able to see the distinctive features of both methods. The following chart below summarizes some of the main differences:

TWO KINDS OF ARGUMENT:
RATIONAL AND ROGERIAN

Rational Argument	Rogerian Argument
1. Aims to win over audience	1. Aims to keep communicating with audience
2. Audience as opponent	2. Audience as counterpart
3. Audience often general	3. Audience often specific
4. Assertive, evaluative	4. Empathic, nonevaluative
5. Writer finds truth, asserts and supports it	5. Writer finds frame of reference of audience, presents it, then presents his or her own
6. Thesis and support, maybe a refutation step	6. Audience view, and then writer's view, compare views and possibly combine views
7. Wins assent or serious consideration	7. Allows audience to consider alternative views, invites further exchanges

Now you are ready for the assignment of a Rogerian argument.

Task: To write a Rogerian argument (750–1000 words).

Purpose: To employ Rogerian argument methods to encourage readers to listen to and be changed by your ideas. To establish and keep open lines of communication. To seek agreement based on compromise or synthesis of views.

Specifications: This is an argument; its main aim is to change readers so they accept, or at least hear and understand, the position statement. The initial task is to show readers that they are understood. As much as half the argument can be developed by representing readers' views on the issue. Such representation should be nonevaluative and empathic—show you understand by providing details. Before moving to your views, you may, if able, identify those aspects of the readers' views you agree with. You might share the same concern, the same value or awareness, or some common particulars of experience or data. Note that, at this point, you do not stress what you disagree with. The views of the readers fill the cup half way; they do not leave the cup half empty.

Be sure to agree only where you truly agree. You are Rogerian, not careless or sleazy.

Next, you may present your views, acknowledging that they are yours and that they differ from those you have taken pains to represent. Your presentation should be characterized by the same objectivity, evenhandedness, and fine detail as the first section.

In your conclusion, you may attempt to synthesize views or seek some middle ground only if such moves seem right to you. At least, you can invite readers to respond to your views. Ask if you have been clear, if you need to add or restate anything, if readers have reactions to the discussion of the issue so far.

Examples: Following are two student essays that use Rogerian methods. Although they differ in subject, audience, and structure, they share in common the following characteristics:

1. Argument aim to change audience
2. First sections of empathy
3. Second sections of thesis and support
4. Respectful, careful voice tones
5. Open-ended conclusions with a degree of uncertainty and an invitation to readers to continue to consider, even react to, the writer's position

In "Not Another Prerequisite!" Lisa Kocian writes a letter to an audience of one. Mike Taskey, author of "Holistic Attitudes," writes to anyone who doubts the value of nontraditional medicine.

NOT ANOTHER PREREQUISITE!
Lisa Kocian

Dear Tom:

After our conversation, I believe I have an understanding of your position. You feel that students have had enough prerequisites; the prerequisite of Math 95 for Chemistry 204 is adequate. You feel that this system has been in existence for years and that it is effective. And, why not? While some students have dropped out or received poor grades, many have succeeded. You feel the reason for the poor grades and dropouts is a lack of dedication. After all, chemistry is a difficult subject, no matter how prepared students are.

Am I right when I say your main reason for not wanting to change the current prerequisite is that many students do not want to take the time or spend the money to take one more required course, if they can bypass it? A majority of the students are headed for four-year universities; many are here to save money. Most students want to spend as little time here as possible so they can progress with their degree.

You also feel the extra requirement would not be fair to students who can and do do well in Chemistry 204 without a basic introduction. It also would not be fair to students who had chemistry in high-school and feel they are ready to go directly into the main course. There are also those students who have the ability to assimilate the large dose of chemistry in one shot. You feel these students would suffer under a change in the prerequisite.

I hope I have stated your viewpoint clearly and shown that I understand your position. There are many points that we agree on. As a student, I have seen many examples of the situations that you have described.

I have had friends who dropped out of Chemistry 204 because they did not realize how much work it would take. I have also seen, with amazement, fellow students excel in Chemistry 204 with little or no chemistry background. I also agree with you that chemistry is difficult.

Before talking with you, I had decided that an additional prerequisite should be implemented. I felt the preparation prescribed by the school was inadequate. I wanted you to make Chemistry 101 a prerequisite.

I had come to this conclusion after I had a near-failure in Chemistry 204. Before taking Chemistry 204, I talked with counselors to see if I needed to take a basic chemistry course, maybe Chemistry 101. I had no previous chemistry experience. They said they didn't think it would be necessary; Chemistry 101 was usually for nursing students or non-science majors who did not need to go any further. They said science majors like me usually went right into Chemistry 204. I followed their advice.

After struggling in Chemistry 204 for three weeks, I realized I did not have enough background in chemistry; I was sinking. I took stock of my choices. I could stay in Chemistry 204 and drown. Oh, maybe I could have achieved a C, but to what purpose? I need to understand chemistry because it is the basis of the veterinary degree for which I am striving. Excellent grades are also required to get accepted into the veterinary program. I could drop out, forget my dream, and choose some easier-to-attain career. This was not a valid choice either; I am not a quitter. The only feasible alternative was to switch mid-term into Chemistry 101. Although the switch was difficult, I am glad I did it. It gave me a little more time to assimilate a difficult subject. With the basic introduction, I have since entered Chemistry 204 again, and I am receiving A's. More importantly, I am understanding.

Other students from Chemistry 101, now in 204, have expressed that they benefited greatly from their basic introduction to chemistry. I have also seen some students in my Chemistry 204 class that were drowning. Like me, they hadn't had much chemistry before; they were confused and lost.

Tom, after listening to you, I realized that you were right; it would not be fair to students who did not need the extra background in chemistry to impose a prerequisite. I have re-evaluated my position. Here are some options I have considered:

One is to create a proposed chemistry prerequisite, but have a test available to give students the opportunity to bypass the course. The problem with this option is that it does not help the students who can excel in chemistry without a previous introduction. Such a test would also create more stress on already taxed science majors. The cost to hire someone or pay current personnel to create and administer the proposed test would be a significant factor. Where in our tight budget would we find the funds? This option, in retrospect, does not seem feasible.

The other option seems too simple and easy; I almost overlooked it. Why not simply put a recommendation, not a requirement, in the class schedule for taking Chemistry 101 before Chemistry 204? The cost would be next to nothing. How much do a few added lines to the class schedule cost? Students who feel they are able could ignore the recommendation. Students who are unsure, as I was, could slow down and make a more informed decision on where they should start. I believe a recommendation such as this would be a great benefit. What would it hurt?

Tom, I appreciate your taking the time to listen to my point of view, and I hope you understand. If you have any questions, please contact me. I am very interested in your reaction to my proposal. If I can be any help, please let me know.

Thank you, sincerely,
Lisa Kocian

HOLISTIC ATTITUDES
Mike Taskey

I know the concept of natural remedies for the treatment of acute and chronic diseases may seem farfetched to you. Holistic procedures such as acupuncture, herbalism, and homeopathy sound questionable and ambiguous. You haven't heard any scientific proof of their effectiveness. When you're sick, why should you take a chance on an unproven treatment or prescription?

Everywhere you turn, someone is trying to make a profit from you. Quacks and charlatans are usually the ones behind such practices. You believe anyone who wants to stick needles in you to cure your ailment has obviously got a few screws loose. How can you expect an herb or plant growing in the woods or out your front door to cure your disease? You oppose homeopathy because you think putting more toxins into your body that are similar to the ones you're suffering from will only cause you to be even more sick.

You want to be cured as fast as possible. Your illness is much too severe for such impotent medicine. Modern conventional medicine is recommended by your doctor. Your doctor knows best. Why go against his word?

These modern conventional medicines have been scientifically proven to cure and holistic treatments have not. The American Medical Association (AMA) doesn't even recognize these practices as being beneficial or practical. In fact, the American Medical Association has recently tried to put a ban on any kind of complementary medicine in the United States (Wistler 46). Without the AMA's approval, why should you approve?

You've heard there may be risks in taking herbal remedies. For example, chamomile, which is taken as tea, is now thought to cause vomiting if taken in large doses. Comfrey, which was once taken for the relief of ulcers, is now linked with liver cancer in rats (Wistler 47). These reports make you even more skeptical about holistic approaches in medicine.

Being concerned with what is being put into our bodies, especially when it comes to toxins or medicines, is a good idea. Without scientific evidence of the effectiveness of holistic medicine you could be wasting valuable time. I know when I'm sick I want a remedy that works fast and one that's proven to cure.

There are, however, some positive characteristics of holistic medicine that you might consider. Holistic medicine looks at each of us as a unique individual, whole and complete, functioning as a totality in relation to the universe surrounding us. All states of disease must be viewed in this context. To the extent that we deviate from this perspective, we experience disharmony and disease. The holistic approach believes the most effective, indeed the only, way to cure illness is to increase the health of the afflicted person. Focusing on building up the body's immune system and endurance before such illnesses occur can surely benefit us (Vithoulkas 6).

For most of man's existence, plants were the basic source of medicine. Historically, holistic medicine stretches back to Hippocrates and before, but with the advent of technology and the strictly materialistic worldview, it became lost for a time. Its return is believed to be inspired by the high level of education achieved in modern times. Modern societies such as China, Japan, and other Asian countries are currently using all sorts of complementary medicine including acupuncture, herbalism, and homeopathy. In Europe and Canada, homeopathy is a firmly established form of treatment for acute and chronic illness. For instance, in France, one out of four physicians regularly prescribes homeopathic remedies (Lust 7, Vithoulkas 4).

Maybe you aren't quite sure of what some of these holistic medical treatments entail. Homeopathy is probably the most sophisticated form of holistic medicine and probably the most misunderstood. In a basic definition, homeopathy means "to treat with something that produces an effect similar to the suffering." This system of medical treatment is based on treating diseases with microdoses, which are microscopic doses of herbal drugs which cause symptoms of that same disease and which, thus, toughen your immune system against the disease. Homeopathy, therefore, is designed to reinforce symptoms instead of combating them. Homeopathy does sound a little overwhelming, but tens of millions of people today rely upon homeopathic medicine to treat their acute and chronic conditions (Vithoulkas 3-17).

Another form of holistic medicine is herbalism. Historically, the most important uses of herbs were medicinal. Plants were the basic source of therapeutic products for professional and folk medicine from the earliest days until the twentieth century. They still play a big role in our society. For instance, morphine comes from the opium poppy, quinine from cinchona bark, and taxol comes from the yew tree; all are major contributions to medical technology (Lust 3-9).

A third important form of holistic medicine is acupuncture, a technique in which needles are carefully and systematically placed in the skin in strategic locations so as to stimulate the flow of energy channels or pathways known as meridians. In this system, illness is viewed as an obstruction or imbalance in the flow of your energy or "vital force," which can be rebalanced by the insertion of needles (Vithoulkas 7).

I know these approaches seem somewhat confusing, but maybe with these definitions you are able to understand them better. Modern medicine is also confusing, in fact, far more so than these older practices. Medicine today is mostly comprised of various drugs, which can also have side effects. If one was to sit down and try and figure out the ingredients of some of these drugs and the possible side effects they could have, one might feel a little skeptical towards them too.

Modern medicine waits for you to catch your disease or illness and then tries to cure the symptoms by using drugs, radiation, or surgery. Holistic approaches focus on the body's health and vitality before such a disease can get a firm grip on your immune system. It's my belief that one of the main causes for all the new diseases our country is facing is all the chemicals we promote in our prescription drugs (Wistler 46).

I believe modern conventional medicine has become so in-grained in our society's medical treatment that makers of these drugs have become too dependent on the revenue from their sales. The pharmaceutical industry is trying to hold on to the whole market so badly that it wants to stop other medicine or cures from competing. Dana Ullman, author of numerous books on homeopathy, says, "The serious threat that the micro-dose phenomena and homeopathy poses to science and medi-cine is clear and evident by the strong antagonism against such practices. The fact that critics ignore the numerous other studies which support the action of homeopathy is further evi-dence of this denial and ultimately of an unscientific attitude" (Wistler 47).

The American Medical Association will get its way if we don't voice our opinion on pure and simpler forms of medicine. Medicine is getting very complex, maybe too complex. The side effects of modern medicine play a big role in our country's growing cancer and disease rates. Many cancers are known to stem from the high level of toxins in our environment.

I definitely believe modern medicine plays an important role in our country's health. What I'm suggesting is that we keep an open mind to other possibilities for medicine. We obvi-ously need all the help available with our country's growing disease rate. Since one of your biggest complaints is that holis-tic approaches have not been scientifically proven, why don't we start giving them the necessary attention they deserve? If we can figure out which ones really work, then we won't have to worry about quacks who give holistic medicine a bad name.

If we start focusing on staying healthy and keeping our bodies in tune by using simpler remedies and by avoiding all the harmful chemicals in our foods and medicines, we can reverse the growing rate of incurable diseases.

Works Cited

Lust, John. The Herb Book, New York: Bantam, 1983.

Vithoulkas, George. Homeopathy: Medicine of the New Man. New York: Arco, 1981.

Wistler, Anne. "Faith and Doubt." East West (February, 1989): 46-47.

Process:

PLANNING

- As you select an issue and an audience for the Rogerian argument, consider the following:

    Is the issue likely to arouse strong feeling, to make rational argument difficult, if not impossible?

    Do you know your audience (one person or many) well enough, especially on this issue, to represent their views with convincing empathy?

    Is this an issue which you can be moved on? If you are adamant, then you will have difficulty being nonevaluative and offering compromise.

    If you can answer "yes" to these questions, you may have found an audience and issue for which Rogerian argument works. Consider several such Rogerian situations before selecting one to address in writing.

- Remember that your audience can be one person or more than one. The audience you choose will make a difference, especially in the empathy section. You may find it easier to address one, not a group.

- You may use letter form, with the greeting "Dear_____ ." The direct address of the greeting and letter reminds you that you are writing to someone concerned about the issue.

- Gather as much detailed information as you can about your audience's views. Gather supporting detail for your views as well.

DRAFTING

- Adopt at once the pronouns "you" and "I" so that the argument is personal. Your voice is important to the argument. For Rogers, at least, the truth is personal; it does not exist separately from the believer or knower. Using "you" and "I" signals this condition.

- Development of the readers' views is essential. What can you write to show the readers that you understand? Include the feelings, the experiences, and the values, as well as the reasoning, that make up the readers' position on the issue. Do not use the cliche, "I understand you, but . . . " to turn rapidly from readers to yourself. This cliche makes the reader's views useful only as a bridge to yours. Avoid that.

- Rogerian argument is relatively new and not yet a formula; however, here is a suggested order for its main components:
  1. An introduction naming the issue and recognizing the existence of more than one stand on the issue. (Do not present your thesis here.)
  2. A section demonstrating your empathy for audience views on the issue. (If possible, show what you agree with in such views. Still delay thesis. Do not state your differences here.)
  3. A section presenting your thesis and support. (Do not present your views *against* those of readers; lay them *beside* the others. You are not trumping what the readers have played first. Do not make your effort here seem to cancel out the empathy section.)
  4. A conclusion reconciling or synthesizing views and keeping the lines open for reader response. (Indicate what the next step might be in the exchange between you and your readers.)

REVISING

- Check tone of voice throughout. Rogerian argument voice is respectful, not fawning. The empathy section does not butter up readers. Avoid a buttery tone. Also, avoid evaluating views. You are not necessarily saying you like or agree with your readers; you are hoping to understand them. Be straightforward about the task. Recognize its difficulties and even your inadequacies. You should not sound like a know-it-all or a manipulator. When you present your views, do it in the spirit of the modest tag, "I may be wrong, but here's my opinion." As you revise, underline the absolute, evaluative, and threatening language and then replace it with more conciliatory, qualified wording.

- Be sure you have equally developed both your readers' section and your section. Be sure you did not give your views more attention than you gave to those of your readers. Did you provide details to show you understand? Did you provide details in order to be understood?

- Make sure you accurately stated what you agree with in your readers' views. Be sure you were not carried away by good feeling, thus praising what you do not condone. Also, in your section, check that you did not minimize your differences. Have you been thoughtful and specific about suggestions to compromise or combine views?

ASSIGNMENT SIX: REFUTATION

If Rogerian argument handles readers with kid gloves, refutation handles them with boxing gloves. The verb *refute* means to disprove an argument with evidence. Refutation is counterargument, even a counterattack, as the word's derivation—to drive back—implies. Another term, *rebut,* means much the same, and its etymology is transparent: to butt back, with head or horns!

Many rational arguments contain a refutation element. One traditional organization of argument places refutation after the writer's presentation of thesis and support. The writer anticipates objections or counterarguments with a preemptive strike. Many strategies for argument, especially rational argument, use combative terms. *Strategy* itself comes from the Greek word for generals and what generals plan. They marshal troops (line them up, deploy them); writers marshal evidence. Metaphorically, rational argument, like chess, is a battle or contest. And part of winning may include a crushing counterattack.

There are less martial ways of considering refutation. To some degree, you are always reacting to other opinions. You seldom have the first word on an issue. You become aware of an issue and find yourself in the middle of debate (a word meaning to fight against). Your views do not develop in isolation. Argument swarms with opposing views. And these views are often shaped by their opposites or opponents. Indeed, without a sparring partner on any issue, your views might be flabby and flatfooted. Contesting ideas sharpen discussion. You are often motivated to speak out against views you disagree with. Other people's wrongheadedness can be your starter motor. You are moved to build your case because you have found a view worthy of your opposition. Without an opponent, you cannot debate.

Task: To refute an argument (750–1000 words). To use appeals to reason with a variety of support to present a counterargument.

Purpose: To answer an already stated position. To offer an alternative position. To support an alternative position by showing the weakness of the refuted position and the strength of the alternative. To enter into the debate on an issue by refuting and proposing.

Specifications: The refutation must characterize the views under criticism in a fair manner. To make the views you oppose into something less than they are is fallacious. The strawman fallacy makes a lifeless scarecrow of the opposition. That is illogical, although it may lead to effective satire and humor, the stuff of political cartoons. Because refutation is a component of rational argument, you need to know the opponent's view and present it fairly. You take that view seriously to the extent you study it and answer it.

Refutation, like presentation of a view, examines the thesis and reasons of the opposed view. It is analytical. A good refutation does more than state unhappiness with an opponent's thesis. It examines the weakness of the reasons. It shows that such reasons and support do not argue for the thesis. It offers, whenever possible, other reasons and uses its own varied specifics to build its case.

Your refutation may directly address readers who hold the views you oppose. More frequently, refutation addresses general readers, perhaps undecided or confused, and the writer points out to them the flaws in someone else's view. That is certainly less threatening than direct address.

Examples: Linda Harper-Clausen, "Sexual Harassment Is Not Yet Understood by All Men," refutes the views of a letter writer. She presents the letter and answers many of its points. Her audience is more general than the letter writer; it is any man who does not understand harassment. Stacey Pritchett, "A Matter of Choice," pushes back against popular trends. She demonstrates the rightness of her choice of rejecting the persuasions of the federal government and feminists.

SEXUAL HARASSMENT IS NOT YET UNDERSTOOD BY ALL MEN
Linda Harper-Clausen

I recently read the following letter to the Editor in a recent issue of The Register-Guard:

Men Harassed Too

After reading and hearing days of discussion regarding the sexual harassment of women by men, I thought there should be some mention of sexual harassment of men by women.

I have been sexually harassed by women most of my adult life. When women use strong perfumes, wear short skirts, expose their breasts, wear tight pants, etc., I can feel harassed. Some women use makeup that causes their pupils to appear dilated, their cheeks to appear flushed, and their lips to seem fuller—all biological signs of arousal, which may not be the case under the makeup. It is harassment to appear attracted to someone when you are not interested in that individual.

I visited a trade show recently where models were used as sexual lures to get potential customers into booths— that is harassment.

Women who wish to be considered mainly for their personalities might think carefully about the clothing styles some cultures use—styles that cover all but a woman's personality.

I am tired of being lured by false offers.

This letter clearly illustrates to me that even in the wake of the Clarence Thomas/Anita Hill hearings, the meaning of sexual harassment still isn't understood by all men. "They just don't get it" keeps resounding over the airways of my feminine psyche.

The author of the letter apparently feels women sexually harass him when they dress and make themselves up to look sexually exciting, and excited, but have no interest in him.

I hardly find this behavior comparable to the sexual harassment most women experience. My experiences with harassment have always been calculated, intimidating sexual advances (physical and verbal) made by males toward me when I clearly was not interested. There was usually a hostage issue. That is, these males usually had some power over my job, which they could threaten if I did not comply with their wishes.

One incident of sexual harassment occurred while I was a waitress in a restaurant. I did not agree to meet the married head cook for a sneaky New Year's Eve after-work rendezvous at the motel next door. His flirtatious attitude toward me changed thereafter. He became verbally abusive, calling me "asshole" when I put up orders for him to cook (that was my job), and he made continuous references toward how big my "butt" was. I could do nothing about this. I believe this type of intimidation is much different from the letter writer's idea that women's sexual advertising is a form of harassment.

Animals, plants, and humans all advertise their sexuality. The flowers' brilliant hues summon bees in order to spread pollen. The male peacock fans his gorgeous iridescent tail feathers to attract a mate. In some cultures human males paint and decorate themselves. In our culture, females and males alike advertise their sexuality to attract partners and to keep them interested. How a person goes about it says a lot about what the person is like. A woman who wears a lot of makeup and skimpy clothing might be unsure of her attractiveness and is therefore trying hard to compete for attention. Some women wear little or no makeup and simple clothing in order to let their natural image represent them; they may be less competitive for attention. Whatever their technique, they attract men who are attracted by what they like to see in a woman at first glance. Throughout this process of attracting and competing and drawing each other in, men and women are making choices about whom they do or do not want.

It is true that sexuality is used in commercial advertising to draw attention. It's a mass media technique to manipulate consumers into thinking the product will somehow enhance their own sexuality. Perhaps the letter writer is offended that this technique has an effect upon him. However, the use of sexuality to lure individuals is more a form of exploitation than harassment. The letter writer seems particularly perturbed that he is vulnerable.

It seems he is angry also because the women in short skirts, with perfume and pouting lips, aren't interested in him. If they were, of course, he wouldn't be complaining. This is the opposite of how a sexually harassed woman might feel, when someone is interested in her, but she does not want him to be.

Finally, I object to his next-to-last statement: "Women who wish to be considered mainly for their personalities might think carefully about the clothing styles some cultures use—styles that cover all but a woman's personality." He must be speaking of Middle Eastern women who by law must cover their bodies, except for eyes, at all times. This man is so focused on woman's anatomy that he can't see the personality unless the body is totally hidden. Is there little wonder in the implication that women are not interested in him?

Men could find themselves experiencing sexual harassment too if they were similarly approached by a female who held some aspect of their lives hostage. It probably happens occasionally. More women are making gains in executive positions—perhaps if the tables were turned men would finally gain insight into the trauma this behavior creates. I am not advocating this should happen, even to the letter writer. Perhaps with enough discussion those men who don't yet understand the meaning of sexual harassment will "get it" without having to experience it.

A MATTER OF CHOICE
Stacey L. Pritchett

Family-owned farms. Family-owned ranches. Once these were symbols of the American way of life. Now, due to a multitude of social and economic factors, they are slowly being phased out of business. I saw a story on TV the other night about two brothers who were trying to save a ranch that had been in the family for four generations. Said one, "They keep telling me I should sell out, but how can I? This is my life."

I know how he feels. I, too, follow a way of life that is being threatened with extinction, because I am a full-time homemaker, and, due to a multitude of social and economic factors, my way of life is being threatened.

Traditional families make up only 10–14% of American households, and that number is expected to become even smaller. Some estimates say that by the year 2000 we will make up only 2% of American households.

There are many reasons for the small number of traditional families. Divorce is one reason, with 27% of American households headed by women. Other reasons are financial. Many families simply cannot make it on one income, and our government gives them little incentive to try. While a working woman receives tax credits for childcare, a homemaker receives no special tax breaks. Working women are often eligible for higher social security and pension benefits while a homemaker is generally only eligible for one half of her husband's social security benefit, and, if she outlives him, one half of his pension benefits. Even in an I.R.A., while two-income families can contribute $2000 for each spouse, one-income families can only contribute $2000 for one and a mere $250 for the other.

Many women work because they enjoy the higher standard of living a second paycheck brings them. A friend of mine, who recently got a paying job, told me, "I like not having to pinch pennies. Now we can have the extras we want. Besides, my husband appreciates me more now, since I'm bringing in part of the money. He's more willing to help at home. We're both happier now."

Of course, many women have paying jobs because they wouldn't have it any other way. They consider their careers challenging and fulfilling and would be bored and frustrated as homemakers. They like what they are doing. They have fought long and hard for the right to the career of their choice. I applaud them. The problem is, as more and more families become two-income families, our society leans more and more toward thinking, "This is the way it should be. This is the right way." The feminist movement especially seems to have forgotten that some women prefer a traditional role, and in their eagerness to promote their own lifestyles they have made it more difficult for those of us who wish to stay at home.

Financial considerations aside, the biggest problem for many homemakers is that we are constantly criticized and devalued for what we do. The great irony is that the very women who fought for choices are the ones criticizing ours. They call us "victims of a patriarchal society." They disparage the work we do in the home. They covertly imply, and openly state, that we would be freer, healthier, and happier if we did things their way. Instead of providing a support network, they make us feel isolated, unimportant, and guilty for what we do.

I like my job. I feel I am the best person to care for my family. I also enjoy having the time to help my friends and family. When my friend's babysitter was sick, I watched her kids. When my mother hurt her back, I cleaned the house and fixed her meals. When my sister-in-law got a divorce, I had the time to be there for her and to provide the love and support she needed. There are a lot of things I do that I wouldn't have time for if I worked outside my home, and I like doing them. They are worthwhile. The reason I am a homemaker is not because I am dumb and downtrodden. The reason I am a homemaker is because that is the choice my husband and I made for our family, and we are happy with that choice.

Yes, I would like to see more financial incentives from our government for one-income families. Right now, all we get is lip-service from our politicians. But even more, I would like the feminist movement to recognize the worth of what I do. To quote economist Sylvia Ann Hewlett, "The chic liberal women of NOW have mostly failed to understand that millions of American women like being mothers, and want to strengthen, not weaken, the traditional family structure. For them, motherhood is not a trap, divorce is not liberating."

The best career for a woman is one that makes her happy. After all, it's _her_ choice.

Process:

PLANNING

- Find a view you oppose. Locate who has presented it and where. Make sure it is a view that motivates you to answer back.

- Analyze the thesis, reasons, and support of the argument you plan to refute. If you are not familiar with them, or cannot find them, select another issue.

   To help develop your analysis, fold a sheet in half and write the thesis and reasons you oppose on one side. Write your counterthesis and reasons on the other side. Some of your reasons will go head-to-head with the ones you oppose. Some of your reasons will be new to the argument. And you may leave some of the reasons unopposed. The following is an example of this kind of analysis.

View You Oppose	*Your View*
The sexual attitudes survey should not be funded.	The sexual attitudes survey should be funded.

Because	Because
It is versus the family	It is *not* versus the family
It is too costly	It is costly, but the cost is justified
It invades privacy	It does not invade privacy

- Decide what your strongest answer is to the views you oppose. Consider the variety of support you have for your counterassertions. You may need to conduct research to strengthen your case.

DRAFTING

- Remember, refutation is part of rational argument, so your opposing argument can be strong without being offensive. Try for a tone that is appropriate for the task, the issue, and the audience.
- If refutation is an activity of reason, it should be structured. What are the major sections of your refutation? What order will work for this task? As with the argument using varied supports, you will need to weave together many strands. For each part, small and large, draft transitions to reveal its connection to the whole.

REVISING

- Have you addressed the view you oppose? Is it clear what that view is and why you wish to refute it? Make sure a reader cannot confuse your paraphrase of it with your presentation of your view. Have you structured and supported your reasons?
- To what degree are you sure about your own views? Have you signalled to readers more or less certainty than your support allows? What is the effect of a tone of certainty or of a degree of uncertainty on your readers' understanding and accepting of your refutation? Check to see that the tone does not change in a way you do not intend. Just as a writer's voice may be swept up into making unjust claims for a thesis, so the rebutter can become more extreme as the counterarguments progress. Often that progression is toward emotionalism and incivility. Is such a progress useful, really, no matter how good it feels?
- Consider how you close the refutation. There is probably no need to review points. And there is no use in a close that shouts "Gotcha!" or "Checkmate!" Try other options.

COMBINING ASSIGNMENT ELEMENTS

Teaching argument writing and writing actual arguments are two different activities. In teaching argument, a book like this must separate and define elements of argument. To be helpful to students, a writing teacher must simplify discussion of the writing process and simplify assigned tasks. However, to be effective as a writer of arguments, you must bring together and combine elements of argument, using the many resources of written language to achieve a subtle, complex product that no rhetorical theory or grammar can wholly account for. The book about argument and the teacher of argument analyze; you and other writers of argument synthesize.

Take advantage of connections, combinations, and composition, by which the elements of the task of writing argument are added together and by which their effect, finally, is greater than any or all of the parts. For writing argument, use what you know, learn more, read the argument situation with care, and bring to audiences both the challenge of change and the means that permit them to change.

You may return to any assignment you have completed and reconsider it in the light of all the other assignments. How might the assignment be improved with the addition of components from other assignments? How could you revise it so that it achieves its aims more surely, more interestingly? Think about argument tasks beyond the categories of the six assignments presented in this chapter. Pick up the entire kit of argument tools and consider how to use them in the next argument situation you find yourself in.

COPYRIGHTS AND ACKNOWLEDGMENTS

INDEX